Services Marketing: An Interactive Approach

Services Marketing: An Interactive Approach

FOURTH EDITION

Raymond P. Fisk
Texas State University

Stephen J. Grove
Clemson University

Joby John
University of Louisiana, Lafayette

SOUTH-WESTERN
CENGAGE Learning

Australia • Brazil • Japan • Korea • Mexico • Singapore • Spain • United Kingdom • United States

SOUTH-WESTERN
CENGAGE Learning·

Services Marketing: An Interactive Approach, Fourth Edition
Raymond P. Fisk, Stephen J. Grove and Joby John

Senior Vice President, LRS/Acquisitions & Solutions Planning: Jack W. Calhoun

Editorial Director, Business & Economics: Erin Joyner

Publisher: Mike Schenk

Executive Editor: Mike Roche

Developmental Editor: Ted Knight

Editorial Assistant: Megan Fischer

Senior Brand Manager: Robin LeFevre

Art and Cover Direction, Production Management, and Composition: PreMediaGlobal

Media Editor: John Rich

Rights Acquisition Director: Audrey Pettengill

Rights Acquisition Specialist, Text: Amber Hosea

Rights Acquisition Specialist, Image: Amber Hosea

Manufacturing Planner: Ron Montgomery

Cover Image(s): © iStockphoto/AlexSava; © iStockphoto/sjlocke

For product information and technology assistance, contact us at **Cengage Learning Customer & Sales Support, 1-800-354-9706.**

For permission to use material from this text or product, submit all requests online at **www.cengage.com/permissions**. Further permissions questions can be e-mailed to **permissionrequest@cengage.com**

Library of Congress Control Number: 2012948793

ISBN-13: 978-1-285-05713-2

ISBN-10: 1-285-05713-9

South-Western
5191 Natorp Boulevard
Mason, OH 45040
USA

Cengage Learning is a leading provider of customized learning solutions with office locations around the globe, including Singapore, the United Kingdom, Australia, Mexico, Brazil, and Japan. Locate your local office at: **www.cengage.com/global**.

Cengage Learning products are represented in Canada by Nelson Education, Ltd.

For your course and learning solutions, visit **www.cengage.com**

Purchase any of our products at your local college store or at our preferred online store **www.cengagebrain.com**.

Printed in the United States of America
1 2 3 4 5 6 7 17 16 15 14 13

This book is dedicated to

My dear, departed mother, Verleen Fisk

and

Fur Kids and U.T.

and

Denise and Jacob

Raymond P. Fisk is Professor of Marketing and Chair of the Department of Marketing at Texas State University. He earned his B.S., M.B.A., and Ph.D. from Arizona State University. Previously, he taught at the University of New Orleans, the University of Central Florida, and Oklahoma State University. Dr. Fisk was a Fulbright Scholar in Austria and has taught courses in Chile, Finland, Ireland, Jamaica, Mexico, and Portugal. Dr. Fisk's research interests are in service theater and service design. Dr. Fisk has published in the *Journal of Marketing, Journal of Retailing, Journal of the Academy of Marketing Science, Journal of Service Research, European Journal of Marketing, Services Industries Journal, Journal of Services Marketing, Journal of Service Management, Journal of Health Care Marketing*, and several other academic journals. Dr. Fisk published *Services Marketing Self-Portraits: Introspections, Reflections, and Glimpses from the Experts*. Dr. Fisk started and was the first Chair of the American Marketing Association's (AMA) Services Marketing Special Interest Group. Also, he is a past President of the AMA's New Orleans and Central Florida Chapters and a past President of the AMA Academic Council. Dr. Fisk serves as a member of the Distinguished Faculty for the Center for Services Leadership, Arizona State University. In 2005, he received the Career Contributions to the Services Discipline Award from the AMA Services Marketing Special Interest Group. In 2012, he received the Grönroos Service Research Award from the CERS Centre for Relationship Marketing and Service Management, Hanken School of Economics, Finland.

Stephen J. Grove is Professor of Marketing at Clemson University. He earned his B.A. and M.A. at Texas Christian University and his Ph.D. from Oklahoma State University. Previously, he taught at the University of Mississippi and Missouri Southern State College. Dr. Grove's research interests include impression management in service settings, the application of metaphors in marketing, and integrated marketing communications issues. Dr. Grove's research has appeared in the *Journal of Retailing, Journal of Advertising, Journal of Services Research, Journal of the Academy of Marketing Science, Journal of Advertising Research, Journal of Public Policy and Marketing, Journal of Macromarketing, Journal of Health Care Marketing, Journal of Business Research, Journal of Marketing Education, European Journal of Marketing, Journal of Services Marketing, Services Industries Journal, Managing Service Quality*, and several other academic journals. Dr. Grove published *Services Marketing Self-Portraits: Introspections, Reflections, and Glimpses from the Experts*. Dr. Grove is a past Chair of AMA's Services Marketing Special Interest Group and was a member of the AMA's Academic Council.

Joby John is Professor of Marketing and Dean of the B.I. Moody III College of Business Administration at the University of Louisiana, Lafayette. He earned his B.S. from Birla Institute of Technology and Science, India, his M.B.A. from Madras University, India, and his Ph.D. from Oklahoma State University. He is a former marketing officer at Pfizer (India) and ITC (BAT, India). He has taught or guest lectured in several countries, including Australia, Chile, Colombia, Estonia, Finland, India, Spain, and Sweden. Dr. John's primary teaching, research, and consulting are in the areas of services marketing, customer-focused management, and cross-cultural issues in marketing. Dr. John has published in the *European Journal of Marketing, Health Care Management Review, International Marketing Review, Journal of Consumer Marketing, Journal of Health Care Marketing, Journal of Services Marketing, Managing Service Quality, Psychological Reports, The Service Industries Journal* and several other academic journals. Dr. John published *Services Marketing Self-Portraits: Introspections, Reflections, and Glimpses from the Experts.* He is a past Chair of the AMA's Services Marketing Special Interest Group and a past President of the AMA's Boston Chapter. Dr. John has served on the Board of Directors of the Greater Lafayette Chamber of Commerce, and is currently serving on the Board of Trustees of the Lafayette General Medical Center.

BRIEF CONTENTS

Preface xix

PART ONE **Foundations of Services Marketing** **2**

Chapter 1 **Understanding Services Marketing** **6**
Chapter 2 **Frameworks for Managing the Customer's Experience** **20**
Chapter 3 **Plugging Into the Information Age** **34**

PART TWO **Creating the Interactive Experience** **46**

Chapter 4 **Planning and Producing the Service Performance** **48**
Chapter 5 **Designing the Service Setting** **64**
Chapter 6 **Leveraging the People Factor** **77**
Chapter 7 **Managing the Customer Mix** **95**

PART THREE **Promising the Interactive Service Experience** **110**

Chapter 8 **Setting a Price for the Service Rendered** **112**
Chapter 9 **Promoting the Interactive Service Experience** **126**

PART FOUR **Delivering and Ensuring a Successful Customer Experience** **144**

Chapter 10 **Building Customer Loyalty Through Service Quality** **146**
Chapter 11 **Regaining Customer Confidence Through Customer Service and Service Recovery** **160**
Chapter 12 **Researching Service Success and Failure** **174**

PART FIVE **Management Issues in Services Marketing** **190**

Chapter 13 **Developing Marketing Strategies for Services** **192**
Chapter 14 **Coping with Fluctuating Demand for Services** **212**
Chapter 15 **Thinking Globally: "It's a Small World After All"** **227**

APPENDIX **Careers in Services** **242**
GLOSSARY 250
NAME INDEX 253
ORGANIZATION INDEX 254
SUBJECT INDEX 256

CONTENTS

Preface xix

PART ONE **Foundations of Services Marketing** **2**

VIGNETTE: Apple Designs Elegant Service Experiences 3

Chapter 1 **Understanding Services Marketing** **6**

DEFINITION OF SERVICES 7

HOW DOES SERVICES MARKETING DIFFER FROM PHYSICAL GOODS MARKETING? 8

CHARACTERISTICS OF SERVICES 9

Intangibility 9
Inseparability 10
Variability 11
Perishability 11
Rental/Access 11

CLASSIFICATIONS OF SERVICES 12

Classifications Based on Services Fields 13
Classifications Based on Services Customers 13
Lovelock's Classification 14
The Services Marketing Triangle 15

OVERVIEW OF BOOK 16

Summary and Conclusion 17

Exercises 18

Internet Exercise 18

References 18

SPOTLIGHT 1.1 Service in Human History 7

SPOTLIGHT 1.2 Peace of Mind for You and Your Pets 12

SPOTLIGHT 1.3 Zappos: A Customer Service Champion 14

Chapter 2 **Frameworks for Managing the Customer's Experience** **20**

COMPONENTS OF THE SERVICE EXPERIENCE 21

FRAMING THE SERVICE EXPERIENCE 23

The Services Marketing Mix 23
The Servuction Framework 25

COMPARING SERVICE EXPERIENCE FRAMEWORKS 28

RAISING THE CURTAIN ON SERVICES THEATER 30

Summary and Conclusion 32

Exercises 32

Internet Exercise 32

References 32

SPOTLIGHT 2.1   It Used to Be Easier   22

SPOTLIGHT 2.2   Call-a-Bike: The Invisible System Makes This Service Possible   27

SPOTLIGHT 2.3   The Magic Castle: A Unique Service Experience   29

Chapter 3   **Plugging Into the Information Age   34**

SERVICES AND THE INFORMATION AGE   35

    Technology in the Core Service   36

    Technology as a Supplementary Service Support Tool   37

ENABLING THE INTERACTIVE EXPERIENCE   37

    Empowering Employees Through Technology   39

    Empowering the Customer   40

CURATING CUSTOMER INFORMATION   41

COPING WITH NEGATIVE IMPACTS OF SERVICES TECHNOLOGY   42

CHALLENGES OF USING TECHNOLOGY TO MANAGE CUSTOMER INTERFACES   42

    Weak Links in Technological Customer Interfaces   42

    Steps for Improving the Technology of Customer Interfaces   44

Summary and Conclusion   44

Exercises   45

Internet Exercise   45

References   45

SPOTLIGHT 3.1   TED: Ideas Worth Spreading   35

SPOTLIGHT 3.2   Facebook Becomes the Largest Social Gathering Place in the World   38

SPOTLIGHT 3.3   Privacy Is in Danger   41

PART TWO   **Creating the Interactive Experience   46**

VIGNETTE: Louvre Museum   47

Chapter 4   **Planning and Producing the Service Performance   48**

THE SERVICE PERFORMANCE   49

SUPPLEMENTING THE BASIC SERVICE PERFORMANCE   50

DIFFERENTIATING THE SERVICE PERFORMANCE   52

CUSTOMIZING THE SERVICE PERFORMANCE   54

SCRIPTING THE SERVICE PERFORMANCE   57

BLUEPRINTING THE SERVICE PERFORMANCE   59

THE INTERNET AND SERVICE PERFORMANCES   61

THE EMOTIONAL SIDE OF SERVICES   61

Summary and Conclusion   62

Exercises   62

Internet Exercise   63

References   63

SPOTLIGHT 4.1   Your Smartphone Is a Mobile Cash Register   52

SPOTLIGHT 4.2   The Self-Service Economy   53

SPOTLIGHT 4.3   Theater Training for Medical Doctors   56

Chapter 5   **Designing the Service Setting   64**

WHAT IS A SERVICE SETTING?   65

KEY CONSIDERATIONS IN DESIGNING THE SERVICE SETTING   66

The Duration of the Service Setting   66

Service Setting as an Operational Tool   66

Service Setting as a Service Identifier   66

Service Setting as an Orientation Tool   67

The Appeal of the Service Setting   69

Service Setting as the Workers' "Home Away from Home"   69

THE SERVICE SETTING AS A MARKETING TOOL   70

Managing Tangible Evidence   71

Frontstage Versus Backstage Decisions   73

Experimenting with the Service Setting   74

E-SERVICESCAPE AS A SERVICE SETTING   74

Summary and Conclusion   75

Exercises   76

Internet Exercise   76

References   76

SPOTLIGHT 5.1   Minimundus—Die Kleine Welt am Wörthersee
(The Little World on Lake Worth)   67

SPOTLIGHT 5.2   Blue Rock Studio: A Special Venue for Live Music   70

SPOTLIGHT 5.3   Rooms with Thrones Are Service Settings   72

Chapter 6   **Leveraging the People Factor   77**

SERVICE EMPLOYEES AND THEIR BEHAVIOR   78

Why Are Service Employees So Important?   78

Are All Service Employees Equally Important?   79

Which Are More Important: Technical Skills or Social Skills?   80

Ensuring Service Employee Excellence   81

Addressing Employee Poor Performance   83

EMPOWERING SERVICE EMPLOYEES   84

Benefits of Empowerment   84

Costs of Empowerment   85

THE NEED FOR SERVICE IMPROVISATION   87

THE EMOTIONAL SIDE OF SERVICES   88

COSTUMING SERVICE EMPLOYEES   88

MAXIMIZING SERVICE EMPLOYEE PRODUCTIVITY   90

Summary and Conclusion   93

Exercises   93

Internet Exercise   93

References   94

SPOTLIGHT 6.1   Soft Skills to the Rescue   82

SPOTLIGHT 6.2 Keeping the Workforce Energized at a Low Cost   83

SPOTLIGHT 6.3 What Service Organizations Can Learn from Stanislavsky   87

SPOTLIGHT 6.4 This Service Goes to the Dogs   92

Chapter 7 **Managing the Customer Mix   95**

SERVICE CUSTOMERS AND THEIR BEHAVIOR   95

CUSTOMER-TO-CUSTOMER INTERACTIONS   97

CUSTOMER-TO-EMPLOYEE INTERACTIONS   99

    Friendly Interactions   99

    Unfriendly Interactions   99

    Too Friendly Interactions   99

SELECTING AND TRAINING CUSTOMERS   100

    Customer Training Guidelines   100

    Customer Training Tools   102

MANAGING CUSTOMER RAGE   105

Summary and Conclusion   107

Exercises   108

Internet Exercise   108

References   108

SPOTLIGHT 7.1 Mardi Gras: New Orleans Knows How to *Laissez le Bon Temps Rouler*   97

SPOTLIGHT 7.2 Seatmates from Hell   98

SPOTLIGHT 7.3 Customers Behaving Badly   106

PART THREE **Promising the Interactive Service Experience   110**

VIGNETTE: The Broadmoor Hotel: Where Excellence and Value Meet   111

Chapter 8 **Setting a Price for the Service Rendered   112**

WHY DO SERVICE PRICES VARY?   113

YIELD MANAGEMENT IN SERVICES   114

PRICING OBJECTIVES AND APPROACHES   116

THE RELATIONSHIP BETWEEN SERVICE PRICE AND VALUE   117

CALCULATING SERVICE COSTS   118

PRICE BUNDLING   120

ADDITIONAL PRICING CONSIDERATIONS   123

Summary and Conclusion   124

Exercises   125

Internet Exercise   125

References   125

SPOTLIGHT 8.1 If Airlines Sold Paint   115

SPOTLIGHT 8.2 Price Unbundling: Creative but Annoying Airline Fees   119

SPOTLIGHT 8.3 What Is a Picture Worth?   124

Chapter 9   **Promoting the Interactive Service Experience   126**

SERVICES AND INTEGRATED MARKETING COMMUNICATIONS   126

MARKETING COMMUNICATIONS AND SERVICES   128

THE PROMOTIONAL MIX   130
   Advertising   130
   Sales Promotions   131
   Personal Selling   131
   Publicity and Public Relations   132

ADVERTISING THE SERVICE   132
   Advertising Objectives   132
   Guidelines for Advertising Services   133
   Enhancing the Vividness of Services Advertising   136

SALES PROMOTIONS AND SERVICES   137

PERSONAL SELLING AND SERVICES   139

PUBLICITY AND SERVICES   140

PROMOTING SERVICES ON THE INTERNET   141

Summary and Conclusion   142

Exercises   142

Internet Exercise   143

References   143

SPOTLIGHT 9.1   You Want Fries with That?   131

SPOTLIGHT 9.2   Sleepy Bear Redux   133

SPOTLIGHT 9.3   Humorous Service Organization Slogans   134

SPOTLIGHT 9.4   "… Would You Like to Supersize That?"   140

**PART FOUR   Delivering and Ensuring a Successful Customer
Experience   144**

VIGNETTE: "Shoppertainment": Creating and Delivering the Customer Experience   145

Chapter 10   **Building Customer Loyalty Through Service Quality   146**

WHAT IS SERVICE QUALITY?   148

HOW CUSTOMERS EVALUATE SERVICE QUALITY   151

WHY AND WHEN TO GUARANTEE A SERVICE   156

WHAT MAKES AN EXTRAORDINARY SERVICE GUARANTEE?   157

HOW TO DESIGN A SERVICE GUARANTEE   157

Summary and Conclusion   158

Exercises   158

Internet Exercise   159

References   159

SPOTLIGHT 10.1   Ritz-Carlton Hotels: Two-Time Malcolm Baldrige National
Quality Award Winner   150

SPOTLIGHT 10.2   Barcodes in Health Care Reduces Human Error
in Medications   154

SPOTLIGHT 10.3   Quality Improvement by Rating Child Care Services   155

Chapter 11   **Regaining Customer Confidence Through Customer Service
and Service Recovery   160**

CUSTOMER SERVICE   160

CUSTOMER SERVICE AS A STRATEGIC FUNCTION   161
Customer Service as an Information Resource   161
Customer Service as an Input for Service Design Improvements   162
Customer Service as an Opportunity to Enhance Customer Relationships   162

DEVELOPING A CUSTOMER SERVICE CULTURE   163

THE NEED FOR SERVICE RECOVERY   165
The High Cost of Lost Customers   165
When Is Service Recovery Needed?   167
Other Means of Identifying Recovery Needs   168

STEPS TO SERVICE RECOVERY   169
Apology   169
Urgent Reinstatement   170
Empathy   170
Symbolic Atonement   170
Follow-Up   171

HIDDEN BENEFITS OF SERVICE RECOVERY   171

Summary and Conclusion   172

Exercises   172

Internet Exercise   173

References   173

SPOTLIGHT 11.1   Planning for Customer Service: Improvisation Training
at Aer Arann   163

SPOTLIGHT 11.2   An Airline Passenger's Nightmare   166

SPOTLIGHT 11.3   The *Consumerist* Is "Where Shoppers Bite Back"   167

Chapter 12   **Researching Service Success and Failure   174**

WHY IS RESEARCHING SERVICE SUCCESS AND FAILURE NECESSARY?   174

WHY IS SERVICE SUCCESS SO DIFFICULT TO ACHIEVE?   175

RESEARCH METHODS FOR SERVICES   176
Observational Techniques   176
Mystery Shopping   179
Employee Reports   180
Survey Methods   180
Focus Groups   180
Experimental Field-Testing   180
The Critical Incident Technique   181
Moment of Truth Impact Analysis   184

CREATING A SERVICE QUALITY INFORMATION SYSTEM   185
What to Measure   186
What to Do with the Information   187
Summary and Conclusion   188
Exercises   188
Internet Exercise   188
References   189
SPOTLIGHT 12.1   The Internet and Your Privacy   178
SPOTLIGHT 12.2   Health Care Taps "Mystery Shoppers": To Improve Service,
Hospitals and Doctors Hire Spies to Pose as Patients and
Report Back   179
SPOTLIGHT 12.3   The Bizrate Smiley Scale   181
SPOTLIGHT 12.4   Survey Fatigue   185

PART FIVE   **Management Issues in Services Marketing   190**
VIGNETTE: IBM Wants You to Live on a "Smarter Planet"   191

Chapter 13   **Developing Marketing Strategies for Services   192**
OVERVIEW OF MARKETING STRATEGY IN SERVICE ORGANIZATIONS   192
SCANNING THE ENVIRONMENT   194
Economic and Competitive Environment   197
Ethical and Legal Environment   197
Social, Cultural, and Demographic Environment   199
Technology Environment   199
PLANNING THE SERVICES MARKETING STRATEGY   200
Planning the Strategy   200
Designing the Strategy   201
Implementing the Strategy   201
Controlling the Strategy   202
POSITIONING AND SERVICE SEGMENTATION   202
MARKETING MIX STRATEGY   204
STRATEGIC CHALLENGES FOR SERVICES   205
Leadership   205
Employees   205
Customers   206
Performance   207
Demand   207
Setting   207
Service Quality   207
SERVICE STRATEGIES FOR COMPETITIVE ADVANTAGE   208
Surpass Your Competition   208
Dramatize Your Performance   208
Build Relationships   209
Harness Technology   209
Jazz Your Delivery   209

Summary and Conclusion   210

Exercises   210

Internet Exercise   211

References   211

SPOTLIGHT 13.1   Green Marketing Issues in the Service Sector   198

SPOTLIGHT 13.2   Strategy Gaming for Cities: IBM's CityOne   200

SPOTLIGHT 13.3   Serving the Needs of Women Travelers   203

Chapter 14   **Coping with Fluctuating Demand for Services   212**

WHY IS SERVICES DEMAND A PROBLEM?   213

THE NATURE OF SERVICE DEMAND   213

CHASING DEMAND WITH SERVICE CAPACITY   216

SMOOTHING DEMAND TO FILL SERVICE CAPACITY   219

MAXIMUM VERSUS OPTIMUM CAPACITY   222

Summary and Conclusion   224

Exercises   225

Internet Exercise   226

References   226

SPOTLIGHT 14.1   Italians' Love for August Vacations Poses Challenges
to Visitors   214

SPOTLIGHT 14.2   The Peachtree Road Race: Atlanta Puts Its Best Foot
Forward   218

SPOTLIGHT 14.3   Funeral Homes Become Lively   220

Chapter 15   **Thinking Globally: "It's a Small World After All"   227**

SERVICES AND CULTURE   228

Cultural Orientation Toward Nature   229

Cultural Orientation Toward Activities   229

Cultural Orientation Toward Time   229

Cultural Orientation Toward Others   229

GLOBAL TRADE IN SERVICES   230

Outbound Service Export: Send the Service Provider to the Foreign
Market   231

Inbound Service Export: Bring the Foreign Customer to the Service
Provider   232

Teleservice Export: Deliver the Service to Foreign Markets Electronically   232

ENTRY STRATEGIES FOR GLOBAL SERVICE MARKETS   233

Foreign Direct Investment   233

Franchising   233

Joint Ventures   234

STANDARDIZATION VERSUS ADAPTATION OF GLOBAL SERVICES   234

Standardization   236

Adaptation   236

MULTILINGUAL SERVICE SYSTEMS   237

TECHNOLOGY AND GLOBAL SERVICES   238

Summary and Conclusion   239

Exercises   240

Internet Exercise   240

References   240

SPOTLIGHT 15.1   The Arab Spring Changes Government Services
in the Middle East   228

SPOTLIGHT 15.2   Globalism and Financial Services   230

SPOTLIGHT 15.3   Offshoring Services in India   233

SPOTLIGHT 15.4   Burger King Worldwide   236

SPOTLIGHT 15.5   The Olympics: The Most International Service   239

APPENDIX: CAREERS IN SERVICES   242

GLOSSARY   250

NAME INDEX   253

ORGANIZATION INDEX   254

SUBJECT INDEX   256

PREFACE

Services Marketing: An Interactive Perspective, fourth edition, focuses on the interactive nature of service experiences. Services are special kinds of experiences that occur when service organizations and their customers interact face-to-face or at long distances. This book explores the interactive aspects of services that create customer experiences.

Main Premise

Two recurring themes appear throughout this book: the theatrical nature of services and the role of technology in service delivery. Although we examine services interactions from various perspectives, the ancient art form of theater is its primary viewpoint. Theater has long provided a model for simulating human interaction. The *services as theater framework* facilitates analyzing service situations and designing services marketing activities. Several chapters expand on the concept of services as theater, which we pioneered and developed in our earlier writings. In addition, we stress the role that modern technology plays in forming, facilitating, and maintaining effective services interactions. Vast changes in information technology have enabled service organizations to reach and serve a much greater range of customers via person-to-machine and person-to-machine to person interfaces. With such technology, even small service organizations in remote locations can serve customers all over the world. *Services Marketing: An Interactive Approach,* fourth edition, explores many ways that technology can improve the performance of a service organization.

Content

As noted in the more detailed overview of the text at the end of Chapter 1, *Services Marketing: An Interactive Approach,* fourth edition, examines the foundations of services marketing and management issues specific to service organizations. We set the stage with chapters devoted to the special circumstances and environment facing the services marketer, the frameworks that provide insightful perspectives for the services marketer, and the significance of technology for exploiting the interactive nature of services. One distinctive aspect of the text is our coverage of four key activities that create the interactive experience for services customers: planning and producing the service performance, designing the service setting, leveraging the people (i.e., workers' roles), and managing the customer mix. In separate chapters, we also examine the dynamics of price and promotion for services, paying particular attention to how these marketing mix elements promise the interactive experience that service customers expect. Another feature of the text is its coverage of delivering and ensuring a successful customer experience. Here we examine service quality and guarantees, service recovery, and service measurement of success and failure. Finally, we offer some thoughts on management challenges in services marketing, such as developing strategies for success, coping with fluctuating demand, and thinking globally about services.

Features

Services Marketing: An Interactive Approach, fourth edition, maintains a strong global perspective through examples, graphics, and anecdotes related to services marketing in various countries, to multinational service firms, and to the international trade of services. To emphasize service industry growth in the global market, we include a separate chapter on global services. More importantly, as authors, we infused the book with a global perspective. One author was born in Germany and spent several years in Japan. Another was born in India and lived there for the first twenty-five years of his life, completing most of his education there before coming to the United States for his doctorate. All of us have traveled and lectured outside of the United States, and one of us has twice lived outside of the United States during sabbatical leaves. One of us conducted qualitative research on service encounters in Northern Europe, South Asia, and Australia during his sabbatical leave. Portions of the first edition of this text were written at the Instituto Superior de Estudos Empresariais, Universidade do Porto, and in a third-floor (fourth-floor to people in the United States and many other countries) apartment in Porto, Portugal. Portions of the fourth edition of this text were composed in Finland, India, and the United Kingdom. In short, we sought to avoid the tendency of U.S. authors to benignly neglect business activities that occur beyond the geographic boundaries of the United States.

Services Marketing: An Interactive Perspective, fourth edition, employs a broad perspective in its treatment of services marketing. It not only includes marketing of services as a core product, but also considers services that facilitate the marketing activities of manufacturing organizations. Services marketing is relevant to physical goods manufacturers as well as to the producers of services products. Because physical goods often become commodities over time as competitors match them, competitive advantage is achieved through service as a supplementary or facilitating feature. We offer insights into how many of the most successful manufacturing firms have differentiated their products by offering superior customer services. We also discuss firms like Apple and IBM, which have added many different layers of service to their manufactured products.

College textbooks are often encyclopedic. We chose a different approach. Across every edition, this textbook was designed to be a very concise treatment of services marketing. We hope readers find our book interesting and fun to read. In addition to being briefer, we have also sought to make it livelier and less technical than the typical college textbook and have avoided excessive detail in the interest of brevity. Wherever possible, we "spiced up" the book with interesting observations, illustrations, vignettes, and metaphors.

Each of the five parts in the text opens with a vignette that provides perspective by spelling out the objectives for each chapter. The fourth edition of *Services Marketing: An Interactive Approach* includes three new vignettes. Every chapter also has at least three "Spotlights" to illustrate key chapter concepts. Nearly two-thirds of these are new for this fourth edition. The end-of-chapter material includes "Internet Exercises," which point students to the Internet to research various concepts from the chapter.

Intended Audience

This book is intended for advanced undergraduate students and MBA students. We assume our readers are already familiar with marketing from other courses or personal experiences. Hence, we avoided repeating material that might appear in an introductory marketing text. Further, as noted earlier, we sought to make our book interesting to global audiences of students and faculty beyond the United States.

A brief textbook accommodates a wide range of teaching styles and preferences. Our textbook may be used as a standalone textbook or it may be augmented with cases, articles, or supplemental books. We did not include cases and articles in our book to provide those who adopt the text with the flexibility to customize their courses. We believe classroom service experiences are the result of the unique interactions between instructors and students. Teaching and learning styles are unique to each individual and to each instructor-student combination. The brevity of *Services Marketing: An Interactive Approach* provides the flexibility for individual adaptation by the instructor. As examples of this flexibility, the first three editions of our text were used in services marketing courses, both undergraduate and graduate, specialized executive education courses, and in related fields such as health care marketing and sports marketing.

Stylistic Considerations

Several stylistic decisions influenced this book. For instance, we prefer the more generic term "organization," to the more common "firm" or "company," because many service organizations are not corporations. In addition, we avoided the somewhat clumsy use of "he or she," which is often employed to be gender sensitive. Instead, we avoided pronouns altogether or we alternated the gender of specific examples from male to female.

This manuscript is composed according to the conventions of written English in the United States because it is the only written language in which the authors share formal training and years of experience. Nonetheless, we tried to avoid the use of American slang that might make the book more difficult to read for those more familiar with Australian, British, or Canadian English, or for those whom English is a second language.

Acknowledgments

Over the decades, we have had the great pleasure of working with and being friends with many leaders in the services field. Hence, it is not surprising that these talented people influenced our thinking and our writing. Among these services colleagues are Steve Baron, John Bateson, Len Berry, Mary Jo Bitner, Bernard Booms, David Bowen, Steve Brown, Kim Cassidy, Carole Congram, John Czepiel, Pratibha Dabholkar, Aidan Daly, Mike Dorsch, Bo Edvardsson, Mark Gabbott, Bill George, Liam Glynn, Cathy Goodwin, Christian Grönroos, Evert Gummesson, Dwayne Gremler, Lloyd Harris, Gillian Hogg, Christopher Lovelock, Robert Lusch, Parsu Parasuraman, Lia Patrício, Mark Rosenbaum, Ko de Ruyter, Ben Schneider, Lynn Shostack,

Jim Spohrer, Steve Vargo, and Valarie Zeithaml. Unfortunately, four of these pioneering services colleagues (Booms, Congram, Glynn, and Lovelock) are no longer living.

In addition, many people deserve our heartfelt thanks for their support and assistance in the creation of this textbook:

- At Texas State University, Christine Billingsley, marketing department administrative assistant, provided valuable assistance.

- At the University of New Orleans, Marilyn Schiro and Renée Kern, marketing department administrative assistants, provided valuable assistance.

- At Clemson University, marketing department staff members provided valuable assistance, as did Andy, Doug, Dave, George, Ken, Sylvija and Ted (the cats over the years who tiptoed over the computer keyboard on a regular basis), and the Islander Pub and Grill (where key ideas for the book were brewed).

- At Bentley College, several work study students helped with Internet searches for material and corporate Web sites.

- At the University of Central Florida, Professor Gordon Paul helped arrange the teaching opportunity in Portugal and provided valuable advice on the orientation of our book.

- At the Instituto Superior de Estudos Empresariais, Universidade do Porto, Professor Rui Guimãeres provided the opportunity to teach and write in Portugal. In addition, the staff of the Instituto (Isabel, Candido, and Antoinette) provided significant and very friendly assistance. *Muito obrigado!*

- At the many AMA conferences where BeerSIG sessions and parties were held, we send our thanks to our friends and colleagues and raise our glasses in celebration of the cognitive lubricants we shared.

Of course, we also owe a debt of gratitude to the reviewers of this and previous editions of our book for their many helpful suggestions:

David Andrus, Kansas State University
Daniel Butler, Auburn University
Deborah Cowles, Virginia Commonwealth University
Dawn Deeter-Schmelz, Ohio University
Bo Edvardsson, University of Karlstad
Susan Ellis, Melbourne Business School, Australia
Mark Gabbott, Macquarie University
Cathy Goodwin, http://www.relocationstrategy.com/
Audrey Guskey, Duquesne University
Michael Luthy, Bellarmine University
Rhonda Mack, College of Charleston
Anil Mathur, Hofstra University
Daniel Padgett, Auburn University
David P. Paul, Monmouth University

Maria A. Sannella, Boston College
Marla Royne-Stafford, University of Memphis
Stephen Tax, University of Victoria

We hope our readers find our efforts worthy of a thorough reading, and we welcome your comments and suggestions at our addresses below.

Raymond P. Fisk
ray.fisk@txstate.edu

Department of Marketing
McCoy College of Business
    Administration
Texas State University
601 University Drive
San Marcos, Texas 78666
USA

Stephen J. Grove
groves@clemson.edu

Department of Marketing
College of Business and
    Behavioral Science
Clemson University
Clemson, South Carolina 29634
USA

Joby John
jjohn@louisiana.edu

Moody College of Business
University of Louisiana at
    Lafayette
P.O. Box 40200
Lafayette, Louisiana 70504
USA

Services Marketing: An Interactive Approach

Foundations of Services Marketing

The chapters in Part One develop the foundations of services marketing. Chapter 1 covers the introductory aspects of marketing services and discusses a definition of services. Chapter 1 also considers how services marketing differs from physical goods marketing, characteristics of services, and classifications of services. Chapter 2 explains several frameworks for understanding the service experience. These frameworks include the services marketing mix, servuction, and services theater. Chapter 3 examines the impact of information technology on service experiences, including the implications of empowering employees and customers through technology. The chapter also considers technology issues such as ways to enhance the interactive experience, capture customer information, and manage customer interfaces.

Apple Designs Elegant Service Experiences

Apple is famous for designing elegant consumer electronics products, but it also deserves to be famous for designing elegant service experiences.

Steve Jobs and Steve Wozniak started Apple Computer, Inc. in 1976. Their first popular computer was the Apple II, but Apple rose to greater heights with a splashy marketing campaign for the Apple Macintosh computer in 1984 **(http://www.youtube.com/watch?v=OYecfV3ubP8)**. Since 1984, Apple has become legendary for its innovative design, but not without great challenges along the way.

The Macintosh was the most sophisticated personal computer in 1984, but Steve Jobs was ousted in 1985. Apple wandered through a bewildering number of mistakes after that ouster, which caused only modest improvements to the Macintosh. In ten years, Microsoft caught up with Apple's Macintosh software innovations (graphical user interfaces, or GUI) by introducing Windows 95.

Apple was nearly bankrupt when Steve Jobs returned to Apple in 1997. Michael Dell, founder of Dell Computers, was famously quoted then as saying about Apple, "What would I do? I'd shut it down and give the money back to the shareholders." Shortly after Steve Job returned to Apple in 1997, he was quoted as saying, "The cure for Apple is not cost-cutting. The cure for Apple is to innovate its way out of its current predicament." Jobs began talking about the idea of digital lifestyles. This was the first sign of a new approach at Apple. Apple had been known for iconic design before, but its decision to design for digital lifestyles enabled the company to expand and deepen this focus.

After Jobs's return, Apple launched the iconic iMac, iPod, iPhone, and iPad in an aggressive cycle of continuous innovation. Each new product received greater media attention than the previous one; however, few noticed how Apple was expanding its services to support its hardware and software. Apple's first major service was its Web site. Today, the Apple Web site offers extensive product information, a purchasing system, and support services.

Apple started its second major service with retail stores in 2001. As so often has happened for Apple, people laughed. The laughter was louder because other personal computer firms (such as Gateway) had failed with retail stores. However, Apple saw an opportunity to create unique retail stores that showcased its unique products. Today, Apple has more than 360 stores worldwide; they have a remarkably high sales per square foot ratio. Most importantly, the stores give customers and potential customers an opportunity to experience and play with Apple products. They also provide many additional customer services via their "Genius Bar."

So, by 2001, Apple had "bricks and clicks," like most technology companies. But then it began a cycle of product-service innovation, which caught its competition by surprise.

The first iPod was launched in 2001. It was a very simple device that played MP3 files. Several other companies made more sophisticated devices, but the iPod benefited from very simple, very intuitive design.

CHAPTER 1
Understanding Services Marketing
Definition of Services
How Does Services Marketing Differ
    from Physical Goods Marketing?
Characteristics of Services
Classifications of Services
Overview of Book

CHAPTER 2
**Frameworks for Managing the
Customer's Experience**
Components of the Service
    Experience
Framing the Service Experience
Comparing Service Experience
    Frameworks
Raising the Curtain on Services
    Theater

CHAPTER 3
Plugging into the Information Age
Services and the Information Age
Empowering Employees Through
    Technology
Empowering the Customer
Enabling the Interactive Experience
Capturing Customer Information
Coping with Negative Impacts of
    Services Technology
Challenges of Using Technology to
    Manage Customer Interfaces

Source: Apple (2011), "Let's Talk iPhone," Apple Special Event, October 4, 2011.

The iTunes music store, launched in 2003, was Apple's third major service. It provided a way for customers to purchase digital music and download it to their computer and/or iPod. At first, music could only be downloaded to an Apple Mac computer, for 99 cents a song. Shortly after, iTunes was broadened to make it available to Windows computer users, too.

The iPhone was announced in January 2007 to great fanfare. The essential innovation with the iPhone was the implementation of natural user interfaces such as touch interfaces. Apple was so convinced that the iPhone would be successful that it renamed the company Apple, Inc. on the same day that they announced the iPhone.

The App store was launched in 2008 as a service within iTunes. This was almost a year after the first iPhone was introduced. In short order, thousands of apps were being created for the iPhone by independent software developers. There are now more than 500,000 apps in the App store, which typically range in price from free to $10. Apple reported that 18 billion apps had been downloaded by October 2011. The download rate at that point was more than a billion per month. Apple collected a 30% fee on these apps but paid developers 70%, which totaled more than $3 billion dollars by October 2011 (Apple 2011).

The iPad was announced in January 2010 to even greater fanfare. New Apps designed specifically for iPads quickly appeared, but that was only the beginning. In the summer of 2011, Apple announced iCloud. Previously, Apple's MobileMe cloud-based service, which was created to support its many customers and products, suffered from numerous problems. Many customers perceived the MobileMe prices as too high, but there were serious problems with reliability and connectivity, too.

Apple's iCloud represents a rethinking of Apple's entire product–service ecosystem. Before iCloud, an Apple Mac or Windows PC was necessary to support and sync any Apple iOS devices. Now, iCloud is the service system that supports as many Apple products as a customer may own. As Steve Jobs stated when first introducing iCloud, now the Mac, iPod, iPhone, and iPad would just be devices served by the cloud. By making it free, Apple ensures that iCloud will become central to the Apple experience.

In business, it is common to talk about horizontal integration and vertical integration strategies. Apple, as usual, chose to "think different." Apple pursued an experience integration strategy by linking experience with Macs, iPods, iPhones, and iPads with the experience of using OSX software, iOS software, iTunes, the App store, and the Mac app store. Also, those experiences are further supported by additional experiences with the Apple Web store and the Apple retail stores. Apple's experience integration means the customer can navigate between these service systems in a nearly seamless fashion. Apple's approach is now being called an ecosystem strategy. To compete with Apple, its competitors must assemble its software, hardware, and services into a viable service ecosystem that serves its customers as well as Apple does.

Few companies have so profoundly transformed themselves as Apple did in slightly more than one decade. Starting in 2004, Steve Jobs battled pancreatic cancer. Cancer forced him to resign as CEO on August 24, 2011, and he died on October 5, 2011. In the hundreds of eulogies written about Steve Jobs, it was often noted that he was a creative innovator who changed the lifestyles of millions of people. President Obama noted, "…there may be no greater tribute to Steve's success than the fact that much of the world learned of his passing on a device he invented."

When Tim Cook, the new CEO of Apple, concluded Apple's announcement of the iPhone 4S (on the day before Steve Jobs died) he summarized the presentation with these words: "When you think about it, only Apple could make such amazing software, hardware and services. And bring them together into such a powerful, yet integrated experience" (Apple 2011).

Apple is now one of the largest and most technologically sophisticated consumer service companies. As of 2012, Apple was ranked by *Fortune* magazine as the world's most admired brand. It was also ranked as the number one firm in the world by market capitalization on several occasions in 2012. If Apple can maintain the creative spirit of Steve Jobs and sustain its ferocious innovation pace, it will continue to grow Apple's "insanely great" service ecosystem.

CHAPTER 1

Understanding Services Marketing

As the Apple example illustrates, services can be very complex, highly technical, tremendously challenging, and profoundly important. Apple provides its customers with numerous technology-based services. Imagine the challenges and opportunities that you would face if you were marketing a service for Apple. This chapter introduces the unique situations faced by services marketers, establishes the need for a different approach when marketing a service, and provides an outline for the entire book. The chapter has four specific objectives:

- **To examine the nature of services**
- **To differentiate the marketing of services from the marketing of physical goods and their facilitating services**
- **To explain the characteristics of all services**
- **To classify various services**

Services are now the dominant economic activity in developed countries around the world. Many countries—including the United States, Japan, Germany, the United Kingdom, and Australia—employ the majority of their labor forces in service occupations. In most countries, service activities have supplanted manufacturing as the driving force for economic growth and international trade (76.8% of GDP in the United States [The CIA World Factbook 2011]). (See Spotlight 1.1, which describes a historical perspective on the important role of service throughout human history.) In short, services are the lifeblood of all economies and a prime source of career opportunities for services marketing students. Figure 1.1 presents a humorous view of the service economy.

FIGURE 1.1 Service Economy

Frank and Ernest

====== **SPOTLIGHT 1.1** ======

Service in Human History

 Humans have walked the earth for approximately 250,000 years. Service activities of many types have been essential aspects of the evolution of human culture and civilization—certainly long before twentieth-century scholars directed attention to the service economy. Services are performed for people, which means that service activities are embedded in the five social institutions that sociologists describe as fundamental to human civilization: family, education, government, economy, and religion (Popenoe 1980). Most classifications of service entities would describe education, government, and religion as services (Fisk, Grove, and John 2008). Additionally, despite the fact that the economy includes agriculture and manufacturing, such instrumental services as finance, transportation, and communication were vital to the growth of human civilization. Finally, in addition to being the essential biological and social unit of human culture, the family is also the fundamental service unit. Services involve human relationships and interactions, the underpinnings of which are learned within the context of the family institution. In sum, the services performed within the five fundamental social institutions were essential to the evolution of human culture and civilization.

Source: Fisk, Raymond P. and Stephen J. Grove (2010), "The Evolution and Future of Service: Building and Broadening a Multidisciplinary Field," in *Handbook of Service Science*, Paul P. Maglio, Cheryl A. Kieliszewski and James C. Spohrer, eds., New York: Springer, 641–661, with kind permission from Springer Science+Business Media B.V.

DEFINITION OF SERVICES

A service can be almost any human activity. In this book we will use an old but versatile definition. A **service** is "a deed, a performance, an effort" (Rathmell 1966).

Note that services are not things, yet services often rely on things for their performance. A service is not a glass of cola, but a glass of cola can be served to you. A ride in a taxicab is a service, but the taxicab itself is not. An iPhone is not a service, but it provides access to a wide range of services. A service, you might say, cannot be dropped on your foot, stored in a box, or lost in a drawer.

> **Service** is "a deed, a performance, an effort" (Rathmell 1966).

Services range from ordinary activities to highly unusual ones. For example:

- The pushcart vendor selling hot dogs in front of an office building is providing a service. The person selling these hot dogs might be an independent entrepreneur who makes all the key marketing decisions about the services he offers, or she might be a college student working part-time on Pushcart Number 7 for a private company. In either case, the service provided is a part of everyday life.

- Services also include the high-risk oil field services pioneered by Red Adair **(http://redadair.com)**. When an oil field fire occurs anywhere in the world, crews of oil field firefighters like those at Boots and Coots **(http://www.bootsandcoots.com/)** rush to the scene and quickly assemble a firefighting solution that will extinguish the blaze. Depending on the severity of the blaze, the solution might take a few minutes or a few months. Very little is routine about the high-risk work of fighting oil field fires.

Like the pushcart vendor example, most services that individual consumers experience fall into the first category, known as consumer services. In fact, many services are such a common feature of our daily lives that we seldom stop to think about them unless they are poorly performed. High-risk oil field services, the second example, are one of the thousands of business-to-business services.

HOW DOES SERVICES MARKETING DIFFER FROM PHYSICAL GOODS MARKETING?

Before the development of the services marketing field, it was commonly believed that marketing concepts and strategies were universally applicable to all possible products and situations. Early services scholars challenged this assumption, however, provoking active debate during the 1980s (Berry and Parasuraman 1993; Fisk, Brown, and Bitner 1993). In the process of defining how services marketing differs from physical goods marketing, these early pioneers gave birth to the services marketing field. Lynn Shostack distinguished between physical goods and services along a continuum (see Figure 1.2) from *intangible dominant* services to *tangible dominant* physical goods (Shostack 1977).

FIGURE 1.2 Degree of Tangibility

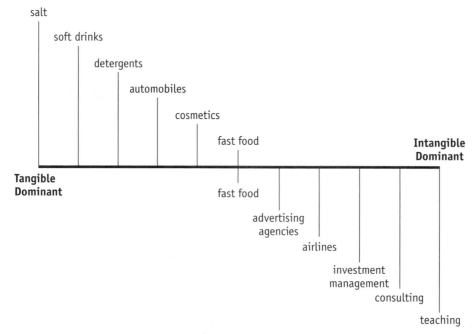

Source: G. Lynn Shostack (1977), "Breaking Free from Product Marketing," *Journal of Marketing,* 41 (April), 73–80. Reprinted by permission from the American Marketing Association.

Some services may have tangible aspects, and some physical goods may have intangible aspects. At one end of the continuum are pure services, at the other end pure goods. Although it is hard to argue that pure services or pure goods exist, counseling services and table salt would clearly fall at opposite ends of the continuum. According to Shostack, the proportion of tangibles to intangibles in a product determines whether a marketing offering is a good or a service.

The early debate over services marketing versus physical goods marketing tended to encourage people to think of services and physical goods as an either-or dichotomy. In truth, such a distinction is inaccurate. Manufactured goods such as lawn mowers and automobiles come with after-sales service, and other manufactured durable goods such as personal computers, copiers, and home appliances come with a warranty. Both the warranty and after-sales support represent *supplementary services* that augment the tangible good. Even nondurable and consumable products such as packaged foods often possess a customer service element. Indeed, most business-to-business goods include significant amounts of supplementary services. We will address supplementary services in more detail in Chapter 4.

More recently, the growth and success of the services marketing field has led to a new debate. Vargo and Lusch (2004a), in an award-winning article, proposed that a customer-centered service orientation is now dominant in marketing. To a great degree, this article represents a declaration of victory for the influence of services marketing thinking on the entire field of marketing. Hence, services marketing is relevant not only to services producers but to physical goods manufacturers as well. Many successful manufacturing firms have differentiated their products by offering superior customer service. This is the essence of Apple's success with retail stores, iTunes, and iCloud.

CHARACTERISTICS OF SERVICES

Services have typically been distinguished from physical goods by several general characteristics. The most easily recognizable of these is *intangibility*. The other characteristics are that services are *produced and consumed simultaneously*, are *variable*, and are *perishable*. We will use these four characteristics to describe common differences between the typical service and the typical physical good. Recently, these four characteristics received substantial criticism. Lovelock and Gummesson (2004) and Vargo and Lusch (2004b) argue that these four characteristics have numerous flaws, because they are not unique to all services. Nonetheless, these characteristics still have practical relevance. Lovelock and Gummesson (2004) propose a new services characteristic: rental/access, which we add to our discussion.

Intangibility

Services are often defined based on their most obvious feature of **intangibility**. Most services cannot be seen, touched, held, or put on a shelf, because they lack a physical existence or form. Yet, a service is not just an *intangible product*. Intangibility is not a modifier, but a state of being. The customer cannot purchase physical ownership of an "experience" (such as

Intangibility—Most services cannot be seen, touched, held, or put on a shelf.

entertainment), "time" (such as consulting), or a "process" (such as dry cleaning). This intangible nature prevents customers from examining services before their actual enactment.

One consequence is that service customers may feel a greater degree of risk when purchasing a service than when buying a physical good. Marketers often respond to this circumstance by adopting tactics that reduce the service customer's perceived risk. Professional service providers such as physicians, lawyers, accountants, and architects may accomplish this by displaying their degrees and certifications. Home contractors and hairstylists sometimes show pictures of previous work to their customers to help them visualize the tangible outcome of the intangible service process. Similarly, vacation resorts, hotels, entertainment venues, and amusement parks add tangibility by including photographs of their facilities in their marketing material. All of these tactics are designed to help the customer assess the intangible features of a service.

Inseparability

For most services, the production and consumption of the service performance occur simultaneously. The characteristic of **inseparability** is the primary source of the interactivity that is a central focus of this book. Inseparability suggests that interaction between the customer and the service provider must occur for the service to happen. Often, the customer is in the physical presence of the service provider; and in many instances (e.g., hotels, hospitals, airlines) the customer must also

> **Inseparability**—For most services, the production and consumption of the service occur simultaneously.

come to the site where the service is produced. Frequently, the service customer is an important *co-producer* of the service rendered. Through provision of information and performance of specific tasks, customers help create the very product they "consume." Consider the co-producer role of a patient visiting a physician's office or a client patronizing a hairstyling salon. In both instances, the nature and excellence of the service product are partially determined by the customer's cooperativeness and ability to direct or participate in the production process.

The fact that the *customer is in the service factory* as the service is being performed, and sometimes even co-produces the service, emphasizes the broad scope of marketing activities in service organizations. This simultaneity of production and consumption generates much closer contact with the customer than is commonly found in manufacturing. Services marketers must manage the customer's role in the interaction for the service to be delivered effectively and efficiently. For example, the syllabus you received for this course is a way for the professor to set expectations, rules of conduct, learning objectives, readings, course assignments, and the relevant due dates of class assignments. Your role as a co-producer of this service product is necessary for the service performance to succeed; the syllabus is one of several methods the professor uses in managing your role.

The simultaneity of production and consumption also makes it difficult to separate the service from the service provider. For example, it is not easy to comprehend the service product offered by a stage comedian, a college professor, a physician, or a lawyer (entertainment, education, medical diagnosis, and legal advice, respectively) independently of the providers themselves. In each of these cases, the people who fill the service roles are the service. In effect, the service customer is purchasing the skills of a particular individual.

Variability

Providing consistently excellent service is a difficult undertaking in the service sector. Unlike physical goods, services often rely on human performance, which can vary across workers and customers and from one time to the next. Further, because services are consumed as they are produced, little or no opportunity arises to correct a defective service before it reaches the customer. In other words, the **variability** of services makes it hard for service organizations to standardize the quality of service performance. The result of this characteristic is that service organizations inherently face many quality control problems. Service organizations need to devise their service delivery systems, hire and train personnel to facilitate positive customer interactions, and monitor and adapt their service performance to accommodate this feature. Even then, the opportunity always exists for something to go wrong with a service, which is a *live* performance. All professional service providers today (whether architects, law firms, or financial consultants) must recognize the importance of customer skills. In the past, the emphasis was on operations skills for workers in most service occupations, such as bank tellers, hospital registration nurses, and hotel front-desk staff. Progressive service organizations take customer skills into account in employee training, evaluation, and compensation.

> **Variability**—It is hard for a service organization to standardize the quality of its service performance.

Perishability

Most services are perishable, that is, they cannot be produced and stored before consumption; they exist only at the time of their production. The opportunity to generate revenue from a service performance disappears when some of the service provider's production capacity is not used during the service enactment. Empty airline seats or hotel beds are excellent examples of this phenomenon. This **perishability** characteristic is the major source of many supply and demand problems that services marketers face. Services marketers often focus their marketing on managing demand. Price promotions are used to shift demand for services such as golf courses, ski slopes, cinemas, bars, and restaurants. Another tactic is the reservation and appointment system for services such as hairdressing, dental treatment, real estate, and legal advice. Once services marketers learn to forecast how much production capacity (time, workers, physical space, etc.) is required to service the customers, they can use the reservation and appointment system to smooth fluctuations in customer arrivals and demand patterns.

> **Perishability**—Most services cannot be produced and stored before consumption. They exist only at the time of their production.

Rental/Access

Unlike physical goods, services do not involve transfer of ownership. Instead of ownership, services provide temporary possession or access. Services marketers rent a wide range of physical goods, which provide temporary possession of those goods. For the customer, it is often financially attractive to rent cars, dwellings, furniture, and other items. Service organizations offer customers access to the value their service provides for a wide ranges of fees. These fees are often based on the time of access. For example, hotels in New Orleans charge more for a hotel room during Mardi Gras than other times of the year, and the greens fees at a golf course are greater on a weekend than during the week.

Rental/Access—Services provide temporary possession or access instead of ownership.

Services possess these five characteristics—the traditional four plus **rental/access**—to varying degrees. Some services share a few characteristics but differ on other characteristics. Thus, it is possible to classify services into different categories. Services possessing similar characteristics can attempt similar marketing strategies and tactics. Which characteristics are present in the service depicted in Spotlight 1.2?

CLASSIFICATIONS OF SERVICES

The challenge of classifying services resembles the task of categorizing the multitude of life forms on our planet. In both cases, the almost infinite variety makes classification quite difficult. In particular, few classifications of services meet the scientific test of "mutually exclusive" categories. This section describes four classifications: classification based on services fields, classification based on services customers, Lovelock's classification, and the services marketing triangle.

SPOTLIGHT 1.2

Peace of Mind for You and Your Pets

 Veterinary Pet Insurance (VPI) **(http://www.petinsurance.com)** is America's oldest and largest medical insurer of pets. Jack L. Stephens, a doctor of veterinary medicine, founded the organization in 1980, and today VPI provides pet owners in all fifty states and the District of Columbia peace of mind. Nationwide Insurance, a large U.S. insurance company, purchased VPI in 2008. VPI's stated mission is "We empower pet owners to work with their veterinarian in making optimal healthcare decisions for their pets." To that end, it has issued more than a million policies protecting dogs, cats, birds, and other exotic pets. The policies cover more than 6,400 medical problems and conditions including accidents and illnesses. You can even purchase coverage for routine and preventive care. Pet owners with a VPI policy can visit any licensed veterinarian, veterinary specialist, or animal hospital in the world, and the insurance will help pay for the office calls, prescriptions, treatments, lab fees, X-rays, surgery, and hospitalization for covered medical problems. Whether one's pet experiences a minor problem or a life-threatening circumstance, VPI makes necessary care and high-tech treatment affordable and helps reduce the risk of people having to euthanize their pet because they can't afford the health care.

Source: Veterinary Pet Insurance (2011), **http://www.petinsurance.com/** (accessed September 7).

Classifications Based on Services Fields

Fisk and Tansuhaj (1985) classified services organizations into ten broad categories. We revised these categories and each is listed here with specific industry examples.

- **Health Care Services.** Hospitals, clinics, health maintenance organizations, and physicians.

- **Financial Services.** Banks, insurance companies, and brokerages.

- **Professional Services.** Accounting, law firms, real estate, advertising, architectural companies, engineering, construction, and consulting.

- **Knowledge Services.** (Educational) day care, tutoring, grade schools, vocational schools, colleges, universities, and employee training; (Research) management information services, research firms, information services, and libraries.

- **Travel and Hospitality Services.** Hotels, restaurants, airlines, and travel agencies.

- **Entertainment Services.** (Sports) automobile racing, cycling, baseball, basketball, football, hockey, and the Olympics; (Arts) ballet, opera, and theater; (Entertainment) rock concerts, circuses, and monster truck pulls.

- **Information Services.** Radio, television, cable, telephone, satellite, computer networking, and Internet services.

- **Supply Services.** (Channel) retailing, wholesaling, franchising, and agents (see Spotlight 1.3 for an example of how the online retailer Zappos offers shoes and great customer service); (Physical Distribution) shipping and transportation; (Rental and Leasing) costume rentals, automobile rentals, and construction equipment leases; (Utilities) power, gas, water, sewage, and other supply organizations.

- **Personal and Maintenance Services.** (Personal) employment, hairstyling, exercise clinics, morticians, and household services; (Maintenance) automobile repair, plumbing service, and lawn care service.

- **Governmental, Quasi-Governmental, and Nonprofit Services.** (Governmental) national, state, local, utility, and police services; (Quasi-Governmental) social marketing, political marketing, and also postal services because the U.S. Postal Service is a partially independent agency; (Nonprofit Services) religions, charities, museums, and clubs.*

Classifications Based on Services Customers

Services can be classified by the types of customers they serve. There are two major customer types. Consumer services are provided to customers who are

*The ten categories in this classification of services are nearly mutually exclusive. However, the government, quasi-governmental, and nonprofit services category can overlap with virtually any other category. Nonetheless, this category is included because these organizations operate quite differently from profit-seeking organizations.

SPOTLIGHT 1.3

Zappos: A Customer Service Champion

 In a little more than a decade, Zappos (**http://zappos.com**) has become a customer service champion. It was founded in 1999 as online shoe retailer, but rapidly grew beyond shoes. In 1999, it had revenue of $1.6 million, but by 2008, its revenue had grown to over $1 billion. Tony Hsieh, Zappos CEO, believes that Zappos is so successful because it focuses on customer happiness (Hieh's recent book is called *Delivering Happiness)*. According to Zappos, "Our unwavering focus on superior customer service has allowed us to expand our online offerings to include handbags, clothing and so much more!" This customer service philosophy includes free shipping and free returns for up to a year. Unlike many companies, customer service employees are not timed when they respond to customer calls. Rather, they are allowed to talk as long as the customer wants to talk.

Source: Shinn, Sharon (2010), "Entrepreneurial Sole," *BizEd*, 9 (5), 18–25; Whitby, Bob (2011), "Corporate Culture Shock," *American Way*, August 1, 40–44; Zappos (2011), **http://zappos.com/** (accessed September 8).

---

purchasing for their own personal needs and include a wide variety of activities that are prominently visible in any community: in banks, schools, churches, hospitals, grocery stores, restaurants, and such. Business-to-business services are provided to customers who are purchasing on behalf of their organizations. A wide variety of service organizations provide essential services to other businesses—including professional service, transportation, and telecommunications firms. Because of their nature, business-to-business services are rarely seen by the general public.

Lovelock's Classification

Christopher H. Lovelock (1983), in an award-winning article, proposed five different ways of classifying services such as nature of service act, relationships with customers, degree of customization, degree of demand fluctuation, and method of service delivery. Lovelock's first classification focuses on to what or whom the service is directed (a thing or a person) and the nature of the service act (tangible or intangible). The result is a four-category table of services (see Table 1.1). Tangible acts on a person's body include services such as health care, hotels, and airlines. Intangible acts on a person's mind include services such as education, advertising, and entertainment services. Tangible acts on physical possessions include services such as laundry/dry cleaning, appliance repair, and landscaping. Intangible acts on intangible assets include accounting, banking, and insurance services. Services in any specific category share similar problems and may provide possible solutions for other services in the category. For example, those services that fall in the category of tangible acts on a person usually involve face-to-face interaction with customers and often occur in an environment controlled by the service organization. To accommodate the special challenges this circumstance introduces, hotels might learn from hospitals, or hairstyling salons might learn from restaurants.

TABLE 1.1   Lovelock's Classification

What is the nature of the service act?	Who or what is the direct recipient of the service?	
	People	**Possessions**
Tangible actions	**Services directed at people's bodies:** ① Health care Hotels Airlines Beauty salons Fitness centers Restaurants/bars Haircutting Funeral services	**Services directed at physical possessions:** ② Laundry/dry cleaning Landscaping/lawn care Repair and maintenance Freight transportation Warehousing/storage Janitorial services Retail distribution Disposal/recycling
Intangible actions	**Services directed at people's minds:** ③ Education Advertising Arts and entertainment Broadcasting/cable Management consulting Information services Music concerts	**Services directed at intangible assets:** ④ Accounting Banking Insurance Legal services Programming Research Software consulting

Source: Lovelock, Christopher H. (1983), "Classifying Services to Gain Strategic Marketing Insights," *Journal of Marketing*, 47 (3), 9–20.

The Services Marketing Triangle

A triangular classification of services marketing was first developed by Grönroos (1990) and later elaborated by Kotler (1994) and Brown and Bitner (2006). See Figure 1.3 for the Brown and Bitner (2006) version. The services marketing triangle is based on three key components: organizations, providers, and customers. Linking these components are three forms of services marketing: internal marketing, external marketing, and interactive marketing. Internal marketing is the marketing effort by the organization directed at those who provide services. In a corporation, this effort might include a wide range of employees and midlevel managers. In a nonprofit organization, this effort might include employees, midlevel managers, and volunteers. External marketing is the marketing effort by the organization directed at the customers and includes many services marketing decisions: promotion, creative pricing, service product design and location and availability considerations. Interactive marketing is the marketing effort by the service providers directed at the organization's customers. It includes all the interactions between any service provider and any customer.

Brown and Bitner (2006) added the last aspect of the triangle, which is the role of promises in services marketing. Internal marketing *enables* promises. External marketing *makes* promises. Interactive marketing *keeps* promises. In short, interactive marketing is where the organization proves its commitment to serving customers. The importance of interactive marketing was the major reason we titled our book *Interactive Services Marketing*.

FIGURE 1.3 The Services Marketing Triangle

Source: From *The Service-Dominant Logic of Marketing: Dialog, Debate, and Directions*, ed.
Robert F. Lusch and Stephen L. Vargo (Armonk, NY: M.E. Sharpe, 2006): 397. Copyright © 2006
by M.E. Sharpe, Inc. Reprinted with permission. All Rights Reserved. Not for Reproduction.

OVERVIEW OF BOOK

As already noted, this book strongly emphasizes the interactive nature of services as the force behind contemporary service activities and their changing environment. Further, it discusses services both as core products and as facilitating services. The book comprises five major parts. Part One covers the foundations of services marketing, which includes understanding services marketing, an examination of frameworks for managing customer experiences, and a discussion of the role of technology in services. Part Two discusses creating the interactive experience and includes planning and producing the service performance, designing the service setting, leveraging the people factor, and managing the customer mix. Part Three examines promising the interactive experience, which includes pricing and promoting service performances. Part Four examines methods of delivering and ensuring positive customer experiences, which includes building customer loyalty, regaining customer confidence through customer service and recovery, and researching services success and failure. Part Five examines important management issues in services marketing. Such issues include developing marketing strategies for services, coping with fluctuating demand in services, and thinking globally. Figure 1.4 shows a simple model representing the different elements of services marketing discussed in this text.

FIGURE 1.4 Structure of the Book

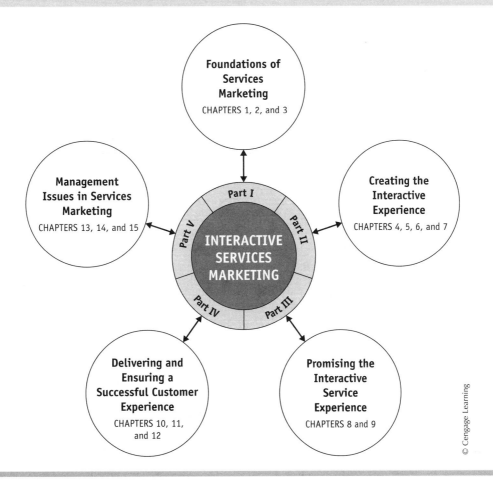

© Cengage Learning

Summary and Conclusion

In this chapter, we define a service as "a deed, a performance, an effort." The typical characteristics of many services are intangibility, simultaneity, heterogeneity, perishability, and rental/access. Services can be categorized based on the characteristics of the services fields, characteristics of service customers, by the nature of the service act, and with the services marketing triangle.

No one can avoid the service sector. The consumption of services plays a profoundly significant role in the daily lives of all human beings. Modern economies depend on the service economy for their well-being. Therefore, it is important to establish and sustain excellence in services marketing. Given the growing significance of service industries worldwide, students reading this book will be directly or indirectly involved in service industries in the future.

Exercises

1. Make a list of three service businesses that you have patronized today and answer the following:

   a. To what service industry classification do these service businesses belong? Use one of the classification schemes from the chapter.

   b. Describe how each of the fundamental characteristics of services influences the marketing of the service.

2. Think of an example of a service in each of the four categories in Lovelock's classification and answer the following:

   a. How do the marketer's challenges and opportunities differ across the four categories?

   b. How do the marketer's actions differ across the categories?

3. If your future career could be in any service industry, where would you prefer to work? Discuss your reasons.

Internet Exercise

 The Internet allows services organizations to reach the world. Google the keyword "Apple." There is a fruit by the same name, but Google won't find it first.

1. In how many other countries does Apple have operations?
2. What else can you learn about Apple from this search?
3. Pick any characteristic of services and relate it to how Apple does its marketing.

> **EXPLORE**
>
> Visit the companion site for this text at **www .cengagebrain.com** to explore key concepts in the service industry. You will find tools to help you expand your services marketing knowledge, including ACE self-tests, Web links to companies and organizations featured in this chapter, and much more!

References

Berry, Leonard L. and A. Parasuraman (1993), "Building a New Academic Field—The Case of Services Marketing," *Journal of Retailing*, 69 (Spring), 13–60.

Brown, Stephen W. and Mary Jo Bitner (2006), "Mandating a Services Revolution for Marketing," in *The Service-Dominant Logic of Marketing: Dialog, Debate and Directions*, Robert F. Lusch and Stephen L. Vargo, eds., Armonk, NY: M.E. Sharpe, Inc.

The CIA World Factbook, 2011, "United States," **https:// www.cia.gov/library/publications/the-world-factbook/geos/us.html** (accessed October 26).

Fisk, Raymond P. and Patriya Tansuhaj (1985), *Services Marketing: An Annotated Bibliography*, Chicago: American Marketing Association.

Fisk, Raymond P., Stephen W. Brown, and Mary Jo Bitner (1993), "The Evolution of the Services Marketing Literature," *Journal of Retailing*, 69 (Spring), 61–103.

Grönroos, Christian (1990), *Service Management and Marketing*, Lexington, MA: Lexington Books.

Kotler, Philip (1994), *Marketing Management: Analysis, Planning, Implementation and Control*, 8th ed., Englewood Cliffs, NJ: Prentice Hall.

Lovelock, Christopher H. (1983), "Classifying Services to Gain Strategic Marketing Insights," *Journal of Marketing*, 47 (Summer), 9–20.

Lovelock, Christopher H. and Evert Gummesson (2004), "Whither Services Marketing? In Search of a New

Paradigm and Fresh Perspectives," *Journal of Service Research,* 7 (1), 20–41.

Popenoe, David (1980), *Sociology,* 4th ed. Englewood Cliffs, NJ: Prentice-Hall, Inc.

Rathmell, John M. (1966), "What Is Meant by Services?" *Journal of Marketing,* 30 (October), 32–36.

Shostack, G. Lynn (1977), "Breaking Free from Product Marketing," *Journal of Marketing,* 41 (April), 73–80.

Vargo, Stephen L. and Robert F. Lusch (2004a), "Evolving to a New Dominant Logic for Marketing," *Journal of Marketing,* 68 (January), 1–17.

Vargo, Stephen L. and Robert F. Lusch (2004b), "The Four Service Marketing Myths: Remnants of a Goods-Based Manufacturing Model," *Journal of Service Research,* 6 (4), 324–335.

CHAPTER 2

Frameworks for Managing the Customer's Experience

The Part One opening vignette about the Apple organization **(http://www .apple.com)** describes a multifaceted company that serves customers around the globe with cutting-edge technology. The service experience it creates relies on various components that provide its users with the benefits they seek. Apple's service components include sales and support personnel, vast technological systems, bricks and mortar establishments as well as an online portal to its offerings, and the provision of a wide array of communication-related information. Supporting these components are the behind-the-scenes infrastructure that organizes and updates the assembly of products and services, the cadre of personnel that collectively produces the technological information that is communicated, and administrators who plan and coordinate all of Apple's activities. All these elements combine to deliver the overall service experience to Apple's customers. This chapter provides an understanding of the complexities of the service experience so that it can be managed efficiently and effectively. The chapter has four specific objectives:

- **To examine the key components of the service experience**
- **To describe three different frameworks that capture the customer's service experience:**
  - **Services marketing mix**
  - **Servuction framework**
  - **Services theater framework**
- **To provide an in-depth illustration of service as theater**
- **To discuss the emotional aspect of the service experience**

Think back to a recent experience you've had with a service organization. It may have been lunch with friends at a local restaurant, a dreaded appointment at the dentist's office, an airline flight to visit relatives over the holidays, or some other event. Now consider all the features of that service during your experience. For instance, during a recent trip to a restaurant, you may have appreciated the cleanliness of the silverware, the spotless tabletop, the waiter's smile and crisp uniform, the dining area décor, and the savory crab salad. On the other hand, you may also have been disappointed by the poor presentation of the meal, the menu's frayed edges, the wailing of a child at the next table, and many other elements that negatively affected your dining experience. In fact, you may have difficulty recalling all of the factors that might have influenced your service experience. Nevertheless, each factor contributes to your positive or negative feeling about the restaurant that you visited. Such information is invaluable to marketers as they strive to design and deliver a service that pleases customers.

The central aspect of any service experience is the service encounter. The **service encounter** is the period of time during which the customer directly interacts with some aspect of the service organization, often in a marketer-controlled environment. Service experiences may also occur remotely via automated technology, such as those fashioned by organizations that offer their services in cyberspace. Service encounters can vary from greatly satisfying to deeply disappointing, and can

Service encounter is the period of time during which the customer directly interacts with some aspect of the service organization, often in a marketer-controlled environment.

evoke a wide range of emotional and behavioral responses depending upon the service type, the service enactment, and the customers' perceptions.

Understanding service experiences begins with identifying those factors that contribute to customer responses to services. Some aspects of the service experience are more obvious than others (e.g., service provider courtesy versus an establishment's wall colors), and not all experiences involve the same aspects. Nevertheless, meaningful factors can be isolated that allow us to describe and analyze service experiences. By identifying the key components of a service experience, service marketers can create a useful service framework. Such frameworks can serve as a road map for analyzing factors that contribute to the customer's service experience.

Service frameworks may perform several important functions:

1. They help services marketers understand service experiences by breaking services down into their individual components.
2. They make communicating about diverse services much easier, because frameworks may include components applicable to all services.
3. They identify specific issues organizations should consider in designing their service delivery.
4. They specify relationships among various components that combine to produce the customer's service experience.

In many ways, a good framework gives the abstract phenomenon of the service experience a reality all of its own.

COMPONENTS OF THE SERVICE EXPERIENCE

Any service experience can be categorized into four components: (1) the service workers, (2) the service setting, (3) the service customers, and (4) the service process. Each service experience includes these four components to varying degrees. For instance, service workers play a less significant role in some service experiences than others. Consider, for example, the impact of workers in a movie theater versus the impact of a dental assistant cleaning your teeth. In addition, service experiences are often marked by emotional character. For instance, the helpfulness of the bank clerk or the ambience of the restaurant can influence customers' feelings positively or negatively. Spotlight 2.1 depicts how even a simple telephone conversation with a service worker can affect a customer's experience and create an emotional response.

Service workers include those who interact with the customer (e.g., waitstaff or bank tellers) and those who contribute to the service delivery out of the customer's sight (e.g., chefs or bank accountants). The *service setting* includes both the environment in which the service is provided to the customer (e.g., the dining room or the bank lobby) and areas of the organization to which the customer normally has little access (e.g., the restaurant kitchen or bank vault). The *service customers* are, of course, the persons receiving the service (e.g., the diner or the depositor) as well as others who share the service setting with them. Finally, the *service process* is the sequence of activities necessary to deliver

========== SPOTLIGHT 2.1 ==========

It Used to Be Easier

I got the hotel on the phone, but the minute I heard the voice on the other end of the line, I knew I was in trouble. I was in as much trouble as America itself. It was a young woman's voice. The voice of the New Age. The voice of an individual that modern education—no reading, no writing, no arithmetic, no discipline—has unleashed on the world. The voice of the person whose first question at a job interview is, "What is my career path?" The voice of the child that modern education has set loose on society to discover that, much to its horror and our inconvenience, it might someday have to deal with people who might require it to do something.

"Excuse me …?" the voice said.

"Puckett," I said. "I have a reservation for Suite 362, my usual. I won't be arriving till later tonight, but go ahead and check me in. You have my Amex on file."

Long pause.

"I don't find a reservation for a Duckett, sir."

Always a tester. Were you bigger than this? Were you known for your patience, your charity, your kindness toward people? Or did you want to reach into the phone and drag the poor child out so you could choke her to death?

"It's Puckett," I said. "*P-u-c-k-e-t-t.* Fort Worth's own."

"Fort Worth's what?"

"Could I have your name, dear?"

"I'm Janet Lawrence, sir, the assistant manager."

"Is the manager there?"

"He's at dinner right now."

"Can you switch me to the concierge?"

"She called in sick."

"Janet, can you see the bell stand from where you are?"

"Sir?"

"The bell stand. Can you see anybody over there? Maybe a blond guy, smiles a lot for no apparent reason. Looks like he's spent some time on a surfboard. See him anywhere?"

"You mean Sean?"

"That's him. He knows me."

"Sean is on duty, sir, but he's not around right now."

"Of course not. He's probably in the garage trying to help a guest find his Lexus that's been lost for two days."

"I'm sorry?"

"Janet, let me explain something to you. I don't know how long you've been at your job at the Sundance Palace, but I've been staying at your hotel in

==

the service (i.e., the various actions by both customers and the organization that comprise the dining or banking experience). We'll examine these four components of the service experience in detail in later chapters. For now, it is important to understand their broad impact and how they all combine to create a service experience. All four of the service experience components play a critical role in establishing the nature of a service experience. For instance, it is difficult to describe an airline flight without referring to pilots and attendants (workers), the seating area and the plane (setting), the passengers on the plane (customers), and the series of events during the flight (process). Further, each component may contribute essential details to the service. For example, the airplane setting may influence the experience through its noisiness, seating comfort, air circulation, lighting, age, decor, access to restroom facilities, reading material on board, and size of overhead compartments. However, not all service experience components are equally evident across all service interactions. For instance, when a service customer places a telephone order with U.S. catalog retailer L. L. Bean (http://www.llbean.com), the service setting is not a critical component of the service experience. To accommodate such circumstance, any service experience framework should allow the service components to vary in their relative importance.

the same suite—362—for more than ten years. I've spent maybe, oh, eighty or ninety million dollars in that hotel, and that doesn't include room service or the bar or the gift shop, or whether or not you can find my name on your computer, I assure you I do have a reservation. Just do me a favor and—"

"Here it is!"

"Good."

"Billy Clem Puckett. You're arriving tomorrow."

"It's Billy Clyde Puckett and I'm here now."

"You're in Fort Worth?"

"Yes, I am."

I think that sentence may have had a weary sound.

"Oh, I see. You're asking if you can have the room a day early?"

"Not the room, dear. The suite. The suite I always have when I stay with you. Or something similar. And I'm not a day early. I'm right on schedule. When Frank comes back from dinner, he'll explain it to you."

"Who's Frank?"

"Frank Simmons. You don't know the name of your manager, your own boss?"

"I know Sergio."

"Who's Sergio?"

"He's the manager."

"What happened to Frank?"

"If he was the previous manager, I believe I heard someone say he went to the Ritz-Carlton somewhere in Florida."

"Maybe I'll stay there tonight."

"I beg your pardon?"

"Nothing. Just hold me a room. Broom closet. Anything."

"Sir, I've punched it up. Three sixty-two is available."

"Fine."

"I should warn you that you will be on a smoking floor."

"I certainly hope so."

"I'm sorry?"

"Nothing. See you in a while."

I hung up, exhausted. I stared down at the floor. When I looked up, Kelly Sue was putting a fresh drink in front of me.

"It used to be easier," I said.

Source: Dan Jenkins (1998), *Rude Behavior*, New York: Doubleday, 50–52. © 1998 by D & J Ventures, Inc. Used by permission of Doubleday, a division of Random House, Inc.

FRAMING THE SERVICE EXPERIENCE

Several models have been developed over the years to provide an understanding of the service experience. The frameworks discussed here are just a few of those created by services marketing scholars. Each adds to our insight into the service experience in its own way.

The Services Marketing Mix

Much of traditional marketing thought is driven by the concept of the marketing mix, which identifies controllable marketing variables that organizations should use to target and satisfy customers. The most common version of the marketing mix, known as the "Four Ps" of marketing, emphasizes the key roles of product, price, promotion, and place in the development of a marketing strategy. However, Booms and Bitner (1981) suggested that service organizations need to

> **Services marketing mix** adds three new Ps—participants, physical evidence, and process of service assembly—to the four Ps of the traditional marketing mix.

augment these with three additional elements. The **services marketing mix** adds three new Ps—participants, physical evidence, and process of service assembly—to the four Ps of the traditional marketing mix. These three new elements capture the nature of services marketing and demonstrate the unique character of service products compared to physical goods. These three additional Ps also provide a framework for thinking about service experiences and highlight the critical components that characterize service exchanges.

According to Booms and Bitner (1981), *participants* refer to all people, whether customers or workers, who are involved in the service production. *Physical evidence* means the service environment and other tangible aspects of the service that facilitate or communicate the nature of the service, before, during or after its enactment. The *process of service assembly* refers to the procedures and flow of activities that contribute to the delivery of the service. In any given service experience, each of these additions to the traditional marketing mix may affect the responses of service customers. Hence, it is possible to target a specific customer segment by modifying one or more of these elements. For example, to appeal to a more discerning target market, a hotel can emphasize physical evidence to create an ambiance that distinguishes its service from that typically experienced by the business/overnight traveler (see Figure 2.1). Such efforts are visible in establishments such as the Marriott hotels **(http://www.marriott.com)** or Hyatt hotels **(http://www.hyatt.com)**, which stress lavish furnishings and spectacular lobbies.

F I G U R E 2 . 1 Emphasizing Physical Evidence

Similarly, an organization may separate itself from its competitors by focusing on service participants. For instance, the exceptional service reputations of Nordstrom's department stores **(http://www.shop.nordstrom.com)** and Ritz-Carlton hotels **(http://www.ritzcarlton.com)** are intimately tied to their methods of hiring, training, and motivating their sales associates. A service organization may also distinguish itself and target a specific market segment by altering its service process. For example, the Comfort Express Hotel in Oslo **(www.comforthotelxpress.no)** has a fully automated check-in and check-out system using Web and mobile phone technologies that allows guests to establish check-in times, set room preferences, and pay without ever having to deal with service personnel. When guests arrive, room numbers and access options that include using one's phone as a key or acquiring a keycard from a kiosk are communicated electronically (Hopkins 2011). Clearly, through these modifications to the traditional check-in process, the hotel offers a different customer experience.

Like the traditional four Ps, the additional three Ps are interrelated. Any effort to affect customer response by stressing aspects of one element may require or result in changes in the other elements. Redesigning the process of service assembly to emphasize more customer participation in the service production will require a change in participants' roles and the physical evidence. For example, adding a salad bar at a restaurant so that customers can select their own salad requires modifying the service environment and its layout. It also eliminates the need for the wait staff to bring a salad to the diner.

Overall, the services marketing mix framework identifies three categories of elements that are important when marketing a service. One of its strengths is that it builds on the marketing mix concept, which is well established in the marketing literature. This connection helps establish the legitimacy of the framework and accentuates the ways in which services marketing differs from the marketing of physical goods.

The Servuction Framework

Another framework for structuring the intricacies of the service experience is the servuction framework offered by Langeard, Bateson, Lovelock, and Eiglier (1981). The term *servuction* was coined to designate the service production system (i.e., *serv*ice prod*uction* = *servuction*). According to the servuction framework (see Figure 2.2), the elements of the service experience include the service's invisible organization and system (aspects contributing to the service production beyond the customers' view). The visible elements include the inanimate environment (the physical setting in which the service is performed), the contact personnel (the employees who directly interact with the customer to provide the service), and both customer A (the customer receiving the service) and customer B (others who may be present in the visible area). The bundle of service benefits a customer receives grows out of the interaction with the contact personnel (e.g., their courtesy and competence) and the inanimate service environment (e.g., its comfort and decor). However, that interaction is significantly influenced by what happens in the invisible organization and by other customers present at the service experience. For instance, actions that take place out of sight, such as handling the reservation, cleaning the room, and maintaining the heating/cooling systems, critically affect the quality of the ultimate service a hotel guest receives. Similarly, the number and character of

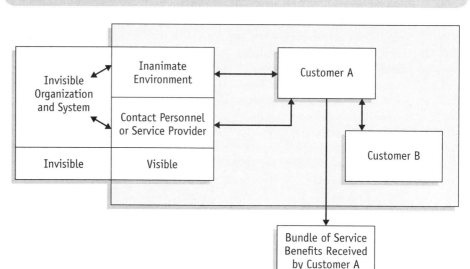

FIGURE 2.2 The Servuction Framework

Source: From Eric Langeard, John E. G. Bateson, Christopher H. Lovelock, and PierreEiglier (1981), *Services Marketing: New Insights from Consumers and Managers,* Cambridge, MA: Marketing Science Institute. © 1981 by Marketing Science Institute, Cambridge, Mass. Reprinted by permission.

other guests staying at the establishment may affect hotel experiences. Consider how important the many aspects of the invisible organization and system are for the service discussed in Spotlight 2.2.

Overall, the servuction framework suggests that a service is the culmination of many factors that contribute to its performance. Like the services marketing mix framework, it implicitly recognizes that any of these factors may be changed or altered to create a different service product. One strength of the servuction framework is that it is visual in nature. In a sense, it provides a snapshot of the elements that make up a service experience, making it easier to appreciate the intricacies associated with designing and producing a service.

Services theater framework involves the same theatrical elements as a stage production: actors, audience, setting, frontstage, backstage, and a performance.

The Services Theater Framework   Based on the metaphor of services as theater, the **services theater framework** (Grove and Fisk 1983; Grove, Fisk, and John 2000) involves the same theatrical elements as a stage production: actors, audience, setting, frontstage, backstage, and a performance (see Figure 2.3). The *actors* (service workers) are those who work together to create the service for the *audience* (customers). The *setting* (service environment) is where the action or service *performance* unfolds. The *frontstage* actions that service actors perform for the customers usually rely on significant support from the *backstage,* away from the audience's inspection, where much of the planning and execution of the service experience occurs. The setting's design and signage help define the service experience for both the actors and the audience. The setting can offer face-to-face or even long-distance interaction, by such means as mail, radio,

═══ **SPOTLIGHT 2.2** ═══

Call-a-Bike: The Invisible System Makes This Service Possible

To help commuters shave time off their daily train commute, Deutsche Bahn **(http://www.bahn.de/)**—Germany's rail operator—has deployed thousands of bicycles in cities such as Berlin and Munich as part of its Call-a-Bike program. Customers pick up the bikes at stations, random street corners, or wherever their previous user has left them. A blinking green light on the bike's lock lets would-be cyclists know the bike is available for use. Emblazoned with the railway's red "DB" logo, the bikes enable their users to pedal to destinations throughout the cities. To secure a bike, a customer must have a credit card and, preferably, a mobile phone. Riders must first register their credit card number with the railway and deposit 12 euros in their Deutsche Bahn Call-a-Bike account. Then, whenever they wish to use one of the bikes, they simply call a telephone number on the bicycle's lock to obtain a code that will release it. The cost of the service is 8 cents a minute and a maximum of 9 euros per 24-hour period, not to exceed 36 euros for any time beyond 4 days to a week. When finished, the user can simply leave the bike locked anywhere in the city and phone the railway at a number identified on the lock to stop the meter and indicate the location of the bike. Alternatively, Call-a-Bike offers customers the opportunity to acquire a cycle and complete the transaction via mobile phone apps. The bicycles are specially constructed, eight-speed units equipped with automatic headlights, shock absorbers, rust-proof frames, and specially designed screws that make stealing parts very difficult. The high-tech electronic pay and security system of the Call-a-Bike service reduces the likelihood of stolen bicycles.

Source: Call-a-Bike (2011), **http://www.callabike .de./i_english.html**, (accessed June 16).

---

television, telephone, or the Internet. The total performance is the dynamic result of the interaction of the actors, audience, and setting—a result that is often infused with emotional character. While other theatrical dimensions of the service experience such as costumes, props, scripts, and roles may be extrapolated from the theatrical metaphor, the ones noted here represent the most important and most obvious theatrical dimensions.

FIGURE 2.3 The Services Theater Model

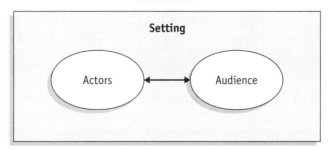

Source: Adapted from Stephen J. Grove, Raymond P. Fisk, and Mary Jo Bitner (1992), "Dramatizing the Service Experience: A Managerial Approach," in Advances in *Services Marketing and Management: Research and Practice*, Vol. 1, Teresa A. Swartz, David E. Bowen, and Stephen W. Brown, eds., Greenwich, CT: JAI Press, 91–121.

The services theater framework points the way to several important observations. For example, in addition to their skill level, service actors (hotel clerks, hairstylists, ticket agents, etc.) may influence an audience's perception of the service performance through their appearance and behavior. Their dress, grooming, demeanor, and ability to perform necessary tasks will affect customers' emotional response and evaluation of the service they receive, much as actors' costumes and roles influence an audience's appreciation of a theatrical production. Similarly, the setting's scenery, props (i.e., equipment), and various atmospheric aspects (e.g., lighting, decor) define the character and facilitate the experience for the audience in terms of service expectations and quality.

Due to the intimate interplay between backstage and frontstage elements in most service productions, backstage human and operational support make a strong contribution to a successful frontstage service performance. Without adequate backstage effort, the actors' timing and delivery of their parts may be disrupted, the setting's communication and functional capabilities may be compromised, and the overall service performance may be undermined. Further, keeping the two regions separate is critical. Audience entry to the backstage might prove disastrous. In many service operations, the nature of the physical environment and the actors' behavior backstage are quite different from those encountered frontstage. One need only consider the stark contrast between the appearances and activities associated with the kitchen and dining area of most restaurants to confirm the importance of keeping these regions apart.

Sometimes an organization may decide to allow customers access to some backstage activity to differentiate itself. For example, well-known service organizations such as Benihana's **(http://www.benihana.com/)** and Jiffy Lube **(http://www.jiffylube.com)** perform several activities commonly associated with the backstage in full view of the audience (meal preparation and automobile oil changes, respectively). In such cases, the organization must attend to the same theatrical considerations in designing and performing these activities as it does for other frontstage service aspects.

In sum, the service theater framework recognizes that organizations providing service as their core product offer a theatrical production framed and staged using various stage elements that can evoke emotional and behavioral responses from their customers. A major strength of this approach is that it describes the service experience in the familiar terms of theater. In addition, like a theatrical production, service performances are a gestalt fashioned by the direct or indirect effects of interrelated stage elements. Each element may be designed to create a different performance and customer experience. Consider how the venue discussed in Spotlight 2.3 has utilized the various theater elements to fashion a unique experience for its customers.

COMPARING SERVICE EXPERIENCE FRAMEWORKS

As noted earlier, the three frameworks of the service experience presented in this chapter do not exhaust the long list of those offered as a guide to services marketers. Scholars have posited many other frameworks. These three frameworks focus on service experiences that bring together the service customer and the

━━━━ **SPOTLIGHT 2.3** ━━━━

The Magic Castle: A Unique Service Experience

 In an authentic Victorian mansion nestled in the Hollywood hills of California exists the private clubhouse for the Academy of Magical Arts. The fraternal organization is devoted to the advancement and appreciation of the ancient art of magic and is particularly committed to preserving magic as an art form, entertainment medium, and hobby. From an initial membership of 150, the Academy has grown to nearly 5,000 members, and its focal point, the Magic Castle, has become a popular venue for those fortunate folks and their guests. The Magic Castle is a private club that offers first-class dining with three seatings nightly in the 1908 surroundings, magic entertainment in three different showrooms, an opportunity to explore the unique and sprawling setting for secrets and surprises (including the Castle's resident ghost), and even a nearby hotel. All visitors, members and their guests alike, must be twenty-one (except for Sunday brunch), and a strict dress code is enforced (no casual attire is allowed). Special offerings at the Magic Castle include classic Victorian séances that celebrate the life of Harry Houdini, magic classes, and an amazing gift shop. All these aspects combine to create a unique service experience.

Source: Magic Castle (2011), **http://www.magiccastle.com** (accessed June 16).

service provider in a physically defined service setting. Not all services are delivered in such a manner. For instance, radio and television broadcasts, utilities, and the Internet involve no face-to-face interaction between service workers and customers, nor do they require that the customer be present at the point of the service production. The frameworks presented in this chapter may seem to offer service dimensions that do not apply in all circumstances. In fact, the breadth of their scope simply identifies more dimensions than are necessary to understand some types of services.

Overall, the three frameworks share several characteristics (see Table 2.1). First, each identifies components present at any service encounter. Second, they

TABLE 2.1 Comparison of Different Frameworks of the Service Encounter

Framework Components	Services Marketing Mix Framework	Servuction Framework	Theatrical Framework
Setting	Physical evidence	Invisible area Visible area	Backstage Frontstage
Workers	Participants	Contact personnel	Actors
Customers	Participants	Customer A (focal customers) Customer B (other customers)	Audience
Process	Process of service assembly	Bundle of benefits	Performance
	Booms and Bitner (1981)	Langeard et al. (1981)	Grove and Fisk (1983)

© Cengage Learning

all capture the interactive nature of the service experience by communicating the interrelated aspect of their various elements. Finally, each framework demonstrates that services are rendered across diverse types of service experiences. In other words, each framework is broad enough to describe a variety of service organizations, from hospitals to automobile repair shops and from airlines to catalog retailers.

Which framework is best? The answer depends on the individual doing the judging. Clearly, we believe the service theater framework works well. From our perspective, it offers an easily grasped structure for comprehending service experiences and does the best job of capturing the elusive emotional nature of service encounters. However, as the reader, you are left to your own assessment. The framework you prefer will likely affect how you think about services overall.

RAISING THE CURTAIN ON SERVICES THEATER

We will emphasize the service theater framework throughout most of the text. Why? Well, for one reason it is easy to use. Services theater is a framework that most people intuitively understand—after all, everyone knows something about theater! Also, the service theater framework comes complete with a set of common concepts that are simple and rather fun to apply. Conceiving various services as theatrical productions can be both enjoyable and productive. In addition, in recent years considerable argument supports the emergence of a new "experience economy" as the new millennium unfolds—an economy where products are "staged" events that "engage" buyers in a "personal" way to create value (Pine and Gilmore 2011). A conceptual framework that depicts service products in theatrical terms seems a natural fit with the foundations of an experience economy and may offer better understanding of services as that economy takes hold.

As we delve deeper into what the services theater framework has to offer, let's apply the framework to a common service—one familiar to most readers—a fast-food restaurant such as Subway **(http://www.subway.com).** Subway operates nearly 35,000 eateries in ninety-eight countries around the globe and offers a dining experience that brings together each of the components of a service encounter in a theatrical fashion. The *actors* in Subway's service theater are, of course, the establishments' workers who are visible to the customer. Their personal front, that is, their appearance and manner, may have a significant impact on the diner's experience. Hence, the Subway actors are well groomed and costumed in uniforms that contribute to a standard image of quality through a consistent color scheme; green, a color associated with freshness, is emphasized in the workers' uniforms (and in other visible dimensions of Subway's service, such as their table tops and signage). The actors build sandwiches in an efficient and timely manner in clear view of customers who queue up and pass before the assembly line of workers and direct them in creating the sandwich of choice. Further, the Subway actors, like their theatrical counterparts, must know their specific parts and be committed to creating an enjoyable experience for their customers. The interaction between the customer and the workers is cordial, but tightly scripted to expedite the sandwich construction. Yet, if a Subway actor falters by working too slowly or making a mistake, his or her fellow cast members are expected to help out and provide assistance—after all, "the show must go on!"

The Subway customers are, indeed, an *audience* to the teamwork and coordination among the Subway actors, and the patrons are expected to contribute to the process or action by knowing and adhering to certain expectations. For example, the Subway audience must behave properly in line, provide quick and accurate information to the workers regarding their sandwich desires, and have appropriate payment ready at the cash register. Just as the Subway actors have an obligation to carry out their *roles* without disruption, the audience has an obligation to contribute to Subway's performance by cooperating with the workers and other customers and by subscribing to the protective practice of overlooking minor mishap—for example, incorrectly counted change—in the interest of the overall service experience. Theater audiences can be expected to ignore a stage performer's missed cue or bungled line, and their counterparts at Subway usually behave similarly.

The *setting* of the typical Subway establishment offers the audience a *front-stage* marked by the visible food assembly area and an area with tables and benches for in-store dining. Various *props* in the form of equipment (e.g., ovens, drink dispensers, bread storage units) and signage that includes menu choices and decorative wall coverings imprinted with subway routes may also be present. The lighting, décor, background music, and other atmospherics support the notion that Subway is designed as a comfortable, open, and bright dining alternative. Of course, each Subway location has a *backstage* region—away from the audience's view—where supplies are kept and where the service operation management does much of its planning, organizing, staffing, directing, and controlling. The Subway audience is not allowed in the backstage, nor should it be. The backstage is where actors get out of character, regroup, and/or relax away from the peering eyes of customers; it's also where operational support of Subway's frontstage activity occurs. Customers are not privy to those activities that might undermine their overall impression of the Subway's service or unnecessarily disrupt the work performed in the back region.

Subway's service *performance*, then, is created and delivered through the interplay among the Subway's actors, audience, and setting. Your dining experience when visiting a Subway outlet is affected by each of these theatrical elements separately and in combination. To ensure a pleasant experience, the elements and their influence must be considered in advance and carefully controlled during the service enactment. Just as a theatrical production requires planning and coordination for a stellar performance—one that creates a positive experience for the audience—a production of service theater such as the one performed by Subway requires a similar effort. Significant departures from optimal actors' roles, setting impact, or audience participation can result in a performance that leaves the customer with a poor or dissatisfying experience. Managing a successful service performance, then, requires a vigilant effort to direct the production from its conception to its "curtain call." Subway seems to be doing this quite well; after all, it now has more stores worldwide than McDonald's (www .msnbc.msn.com 2011)!

Summary and Conclusion

The customer's evaluation of a service depends on his or her experience. For a successful service experience to take place, the services marketer must understand how all of the various parts of the organization involved in the production and delivery of the service work together. Based upon the frameworks presented here, readers are likely to conceive of the service experience in one of three ways: as a set of variables added to the marketing mix, as a servuction system, or as a theatrical performance. Understanding service experiences requires analyzing workers, customers, the setting, and the process. Each service framework dissects the service experience into its component parts to help services marketers analyze the components and determine the combination that will enable their organization to create a service reality that meets the needs of their customers.

Exercises

1. Based on the different functions offered by service frameworks, describe how a service experience framework might be of use to the manager of an auto rental business such as Enterprise Rent-A-Car **(http://www.enterprise.com).**
2. Consider the typical airline company such as Delta **(delta.com),** SAS **(http://www.scandinavian.net),** or JAL **(http://www.jal.com).** Using the theatrical model of the service experience, identify and analyze the theatrical elements of an airline service in flight.
3. Compare and contrast the service experience a hairstyling salon provides for its customers using each of the service frameworks presented in the chapter. Which framework provides the most effective means of understanding the service experience? Why?
4. Using Figure 2.2 as a guide, develop a servuction framework rendition of the service offered by an oil-change shop such as Jiffy Lube **(http://www.jiffylube.com).** Be sure to include all components just as they appear in the model.

Internet Exercise

Use the service theater framework to analyze online retailer, Lands' End **(http://www.landsend.com).** As you do so, identify the following:

1. Frontstage aspects of the service
2. Backstage aspects of the service
3. Possible problems in the service performance if the backstage activities are poorly devised or performed
4. Roles of the parties involved

EXPLORE

Visit the companion site for this text at **www.cengagebrain.com** to explore key concepts in the service industry. You will find tools to help you expand your services marketing knowledge, including ACE self-tests, Web links to companies and organizations featured in this chapter, and much more!

References

Booms, Bernard H. and Mary Jo Bitner (1981), "Marketing Strategies and Organizational Structures for Service Firms," in *Marketing of Services*, James H. Donnelly and William R. George, eds., Chicago: American Marketing Association, 47–51.

Grove, Stephen J. and Raymond P. Fisk (1983), "The Dramaturgy of Service Exchange: An Analytical Framework for Services Marketing," in *Emerging Perspectives on Services Marketing*, Leonard L. Berry, Lynn G. Shostack, and

Gregory D. Upah, eds., Chicago: American Marketing Association, 45–49.

Grove, Stephen J., Raymond P. Fisk, and Joby John (2000), "Services as Theater: Guidelines and Implications," in *Handbook of Services Marketing and Management*, Teresa A. Swartz and Dawn Iacobucci, eds., Thousand Oaks, CA: Sage Publications, 21–35.

Hopkins, Curt (2011), "First All-Automated Hotel Opens in Norway," **www.readwriteweb.com,** January 21.

Langeard, Eric, John E. G. Bateson, Christopher H. Lovelock, and Pierre Eiglier (1981), *Services Marketing: New Insights from Consumers and Managers*, Cambridge, MA: Marketing Science Institute.

Pine, B. Joseph II and James H. Gilmore (2011), *The Experience Economy, Updated Edition* (Kindle edition), Boston, MA: Harvard Business School Press.

CHAPTER 3

Plugging Into the Information Age

The **(http://www.apple.com)** vignette at the beginning of Part One described the many Apple technologies that have become common information tools. Consider how iPhone and iPad users have changed their daily information usage habits. Walk into any public space, such as a park or a coffee shop, and watch how people are using their iPhones and iPads. They are finding and sharing information from any number of apps: logging into Facebook from an iPhone app instead of a laptop or desktop computer, listening to the morning news from a radio app instead of the radio, and watching a sporting event from an app instead of the television. They are reading a newspaper, magazine, or book from an app instead of a physical newspaper, magazine or book and checking on the weather forecast from an app instead of the television. As Apple says, "There's an app for that." Information is becoming very portable and instantaneously served via apps.

This chapter focuses primarily on information technology. Even though many other forms of technological progress affect the services field, we believe that information technology has the most profound influence on all service organizations. This chapter explores the many opportunities and challenges information technology presents to the field of services marketing and the many ways it can be harnessed to meet the needs of services marketers. The chapter has seven specific objectives:

- To explore the service economy and the information age
- To show how services marketers can use information technology as an employee tool for improving customer service and increasing productivity
- To demonstrate how services marketers can enlist information technology to empower their customers
- To explain how information technology can help bridge the physical distance between organization and customer and enable the interactive experience
- To illustrate the various ways in which services marketers can employ information technology to learn more about their customers and respond to them more effectively
- To caution service organizations about the negative impact of technology
- To convey the many challenges of using technology to manage customer interfaces in service industries

Try to imagine living in a world without smartphones, televisions, and personal computers. There's no way to call home. No way to watch the world's news tonight. No software for creating presentations or proposals. In historical terms, we have only recently left such a world, but how far away it seems!

S E R V I C E S   A N D   T H E   I N F O R M A T I O N   A G E

Human society in the twenty-first century is in the midst of a revolution comparable in scale and consequence to the industrial revolution of the mid-nineteenth century. The most significant force in this current revolution is information technology—the merging of computer and communication technologies. A dizzying array of information technology is available at our fingertips. The information age is causing other simultaneous revolutions, such as globalization of markets and the reorganization of business hierarchies. Information business models such as Amazon **(http://www.amazon.com)**, eBay **(http://www.ebay.com)**, Google **(http://www.google.com)**, and Facebook **(http://www.facebook.com)** emerged in the Internet era. As Spotlight 3.1 shows, TED.com has quickly become a globally influential nonprofit service organization.

The twentieth century was indelibly altered by information technology. Entire service industries emerged that created, delivered, or managed information. From credit rating to polling services to marketing research, such industries offered intangible core products. Further, virtually no corner of the service economy has remained untouched by information technology. Hence, the world entered the twenty-first century in the throes of the information revolution.

Not since the industrial revolution has the world experienced such profound changes. The industrial revolution altered human society in ways that endured until the arrival of the information revolution. For example, the notions of a nine-to-five workday and a five-day workweek owe their prominence to the industrial revolution's need for workers to perform their labor in a regimented fashion in a factory. Today, thanks to the widespread adoption of computer technology and vast improvements in telecommunications, millions of people all over the world perform all or part of their jobs at home and at least partially set their own work hours. In the modern economy, it is possible (and frequently necessary) for service organizations to be open for business twenty-four hours a day, seven days a week, and 365 days a year.

SPOTLIGHT 3.1

TED: Ideas Worth Spreading

Short video files have become quite popular in recent years. YouTube **(http://www.youtube.com)** has probably become the best-known source of such videos. Humorous videos featuring cats, dogs, and babies are often memorable, but rarely educational. Meanwhile, the nonprofit organization TED (http://www.ted.com) has become the king of educational videos. Richard Saul Wurman started TED in 1984 as a conference dedicated to technology, entertainment, and design (the source of the name TED). The conference featured cutting-edge presentations, but operated as an expensive, invitation-only event.

In 2001, Chris Anderson bought TED and sought to broaden the reach of the conference and the range of topics it presented. The conference is still very expensive

and sells out a year in advance. A major development was the creation of TEDTalks, which are conference presentations released as free videos. Typically no longer than eighteen minutes, these brief educational videos quickly became viral successes. For example, Sir Ken Robinson's 2006 talk on schools killing creativity became the most frequently watched video on TED, with more than 9 million viewings.

Today, TEDTalks reach a vast global audience with an amazing array of topics. The slogan "Ideas Worth Spreading" has become TEDTalks's claim to fame. The TED Open Translation Project is a recent effort to recruit volunteers to translate TEDTalks into a wide range of languages.

Source: **http://www.ted.com**.

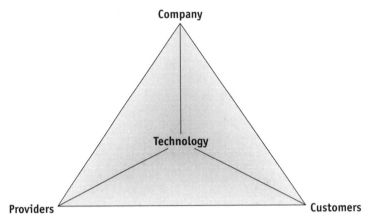

FIGURE 3.1 The Services Marketing Pyramid

Source: Adapted from A. Parasuraman and Dhruv Grewal (2000), "The Impact of Technology on the Quality-Value-Loyalty Chain: A Research Agenda," *Journal of the Academy of Marketing Science,* 28 (1), 168–174.

How does information technology affect a company, its employees, and its customers? With the pervasive use of technology, Parasuraman and Grewal (2000) ask that we add technology to the services marketing triangle model discussed in Chapter 1 to create what they call the "Services Marketing Pyramid Model" (see Figure 3.1). The pyramid model emphasizes the need to effectively manage three technology linkages to enhance service delivery: technology–company, technology–employee, and technology–customer. Technology should not be seen as the top of the pyramid, but as the back of the pyramid. Done correctly, technology is in the background supporting all of the organization activities. Technology can also be used to integrate services offerings across multiple delivery channels (Patrício, Fisk, and Cunha 2008). For example, Apple has made it possible for consumers to order products online **(http://www.apple.com/)** and pick them up in a local Apple retail store.

Technology in the Core Service

All service industries rely on essential technologies to provide their core service. Hence, we can refer to medical, transportation, communication, financial, educational, and entertainment technologies. Some of these industries use low levels of technology; others use sophisticated technology. Nonetheless, every service organization can benefit from technological strategies that improve the excellence of the service it provides.

A service organization can pursue a carefully cultivated strategy of improving its core technology as a means of improving service quality. For example, among health care services, improvements in technology can significantly increase the reliability of medical diagnosis and treatment. Consider the impact of the electrocardiogram and laser surgery. Because reliability is one cornerstone of service quality, technology can be a formidable tool for increasing service quality. Technology may have the advantage of being hard for competitors to match quickly. Hence, the organization that establishes a technological lead in serving its customers can profit accordingly.

Technology as a Supplementary Service Support Tool

More and more, service organizations are using technology as a tool to supplement their core service. Service organizations are now heavy users of telecommunications and computer technology. Home-based service organizations now serve the needs of clients around the world with a combination of computers, smartphones, e-mail, and Web sites.

ENABLING THE INTERACTIVE EXPERIENCE

In the twentieth century, telecommunications technology enabled *three stages of communications interactivity* between the marketer and the customer (see Figure 3.2). In Phase 1, in the early part of the twentieth century, information was broadcast to the public in a one-way flow via radio and, later, television. Phase 2, in the later part of twentieth century, introduced partial interactivity. One early example of this stage was the use of toll-free telephone numbers in radio and television commercials inviting customers to call the company after hearing or watching an advertisement. The end of the twentieth century saw the arrival of Phase 3, a fully interactive stage in which customers can interact directly with the marketer. The Internet provides the best example of this interaction. An example of Phase 3 is the many technology-based services that the *Wall Street Journal* has added to its repertoire. The newspaper's interactive edition **(http://www.wsj.com)** offers news briefings, discussion groups, and a free and comprehensive careers resource **(http://careerjournal.com).** Also featured are toll-free telephone numbers for ordering such items as special reprints, the *Wall Street Journal* classroom edition, and the *Wall Street Journal* directory assistance service for more information on any of its services.

Perhaps the most unusual aspect of Phase 3 in Figure 3.2 is that customers can achieve a high-bandwidth communications connection with one another.

FIGURE 3.2 **Three Phases of Communications Interactivity**

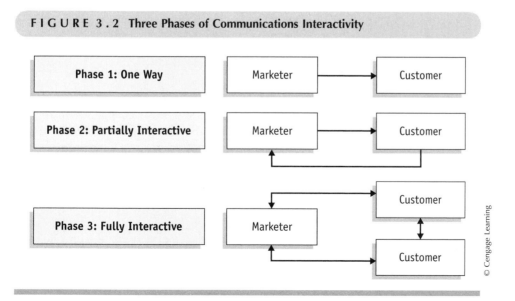

© Cengage Learning

This phenomenon has significantly altered the nature of word-of-mouth communications and rapidly become a powerful influence on modern communications. It includes customer user groups, chat rooms, blogs, and social networks such as Facebook (**http://www.facebook.com**) or **LinkedIn** (**http:www.linkedin.com**).

The latest telecommunications allow the rapid transmission of, and immediate response to, vast quantities of information via high-quality audio, video, and text over great distances at low cost. E-mail messages often are received in nearly the same instant they are sent. Telecommunications make it easy to update vast amounts of information and include last-minute details that would have been impossible with printed forms. Perhaps more important, as information has become one of the most fundamental of economic values, the cost of disseminating it electronically has correspondingly begun to vanish. In short, information is a product with virtually no marginal cost of distribution. After setup costs (equipment and labor), the costs of digital dissemination to the reader (or viewer) rapidly diminish, until at some point the cost per person is virtually zero. These cost advantages make remote services delivery appealing to many service organizations.

The World Wide Web is a stunning example of the tremendous growth of global communications on the Internet. The Web is an Internet service whereby organizations and individuals can provide text, pictures, sound, and even video to information seekers. The Web allows a wide range of entrepreneurs to offer an amazing variety of commercial services on the Internet. These services include electronic directories, such as Yahoo!; electronic shopping malls, such as Amazon; direct company-to-customer sites such as AT&T (**http://www.att.com**)**;** advertising agency services, such as Ogilvy and Mather (**http://www.ogilvy.com**)**;** online publishing sites, such as Hotwired (**http://www.hotwired.com**)**;** and software services, such as Siebel Systems (**http://www.siebel.com/**)**.** See Spotlight 3.2 for an example of how people interact with each other on Facebook.

SPOTLIGHT 3.2

Facebook Becomes the Largest Social Gathering Place in the World

There are hundreds of social networking sites. MySpace (**http://www.myspace.com**) was once the dominant social media site but floundered after being purchased by Rupert Murdoch's News Corp (**http://www.newscorp.com**). News Corp learned the painful lesson that interactive media are vastly different than traditional media. For traditional media, the value of the medium is created primarily by the content creators (reporters, producers, writers, editors, etc.). For interactive media, the users of interactive media create the value.

Facebook (**http://www.facebook.com**) was not the first social media site, but quickly became the dominant social networking site. As of this writing, Facebook is rapidly approaching a billion registered users. Why did it become so successful? Many people think it was the much simpler Web interface that

Facebook offered versus MySpace. Ease of use is important, but the heart of the story is that Facebook made it very easy for people to do two essential interactions. In normal face-to-face human interactions, people interact with their friends and tell their friends what they like and don't like. Facebook created easy-to-use electronic simulations of those two interactions.

Facebook has become so influential today that many people spend their days in the regular electronic embrace of their friends on Facebook. You are probably one of them. You regularly check your friends' posts. You tag some of those posts with a "Like." You comment on some of the posts, too. You might chat live with a friend on Facebook at the same time. You might play a game such as Farmville with some of your friends. Your friends are always just a click away on Facebook.

Empowering Employees Through Technology

During the early history of computers, powerful bureaucracies of data managers created and managed corporate computer systems and thereby controlled the flow of information. Such arrangements were logical in the days of massive computers, but eventually the miniaturization of information technology resulted in devices such as laptop computers and smartphones that could be operated by one person. Service organizations are rapidly putting these devices in the hands of their employees and networking the employees with other workers and the world at large.

Technology Devices   Few service organizations could survive today without the heavy use of telephones and computers. In addition, the use of video recorders, bar code readers, and laptop or handheld computers is rapidly increasing. These technologies have enabled service organizations and their employees to meet customers' needs in ways that were unthinkable a few years ago. For example, field service workers now videotape key aspects of service calls, monitor parts inventories with bar code readers, and carry a vast array of service manuals compactly stored on CDs. They can also stay in close contact with their head office via smartphones and upload service data to corporate computers via their smartphone and laptop computer. Another way in which technology can improve service is through *service robots*. Medical robots today enable surgeons to perform heart surgery without opening the chest and to undertake brain surgery too delicate for the human hand, thus revolutionizing critical and life-saving surgical procedures.

Computers are now ubiquitous in service industries. A bank employee checks customer balances on a computer. An insurance agent inputs information for a new policyholder into a computer database and produces premium and benefit schedules in the blink of an eye. A retail clerk rings up a purchase on a computerized cash register that accurately and quickly completes the transaction with the customer. Doctors are using computers to identify and order the appropriate drugs and treatments for patients.

Handheld computer devices have become a particularly important tool in service industries. Examples of these devices abound: the bar code reader of a FedEx agent, the handheld ordering device of a restaurant waiter, and the inventory bar code readers of the grocery store clerk. Recently, smartphones like the iPhone and tablet computers like the iPad have made inroads into work practices. All of these devices allow service workers to perform their tasks more efficiently and effectively than they could using paper records or bulkier computer systems.

Networking   Networking is the act of establishing a communication link among two or more individuals, organizations, or other entities not in the same physical location. Telephone and computer-based audio and video conferencing allow service organizations to improve the speed, quality, and volume of communications among customers, intermediaries, and suppliers. Most organizations are accelerating their networking of such information technology devices to enable ever-faster information flow among employees as well as to and from the home office. An example of this trend is Dropbox (**http://www.dropbox.com**), which allows employees easy electronic file sharing across the globe. Computer networking can allow service workers to respond to customer inquiries, validate information, submit reservations or orders, and access information pertinent to service delivery. Networking is also essential for home-based service organizations. Many such enterprises now serve the needs of widely dispersed clients via computers, telephones, and e-mail. It is even possible for groups of home-based service organizations to form flexible networks or virtual corporations that quickly adapt to customer needs.

Empowering the Customer

One of the earliest technological alternatives to the human performance of a service was the self-service machine, such as the vending machine. Whether selling colas, candy, condoms, or combs, the vending machine is the equivalent of a mechanical service retailer. Automated teller machines (ATMs) are an elaborate and sophisticated extension of the vending machine concept. Such devices offer low-cost service in places and at times where it would be prohibitively expensive to serve customers with human help.

As self-service technologies have become more commonplace, numerous studies have advanced understanding of what customers want from self-service technologies (Barnes, Dunne, and Glynn 2000; Dabholkar 2000; Meuter et al. 2000). Parasuraman (2000) has shown that customers vary in their degree of technology readiness. Barnes, Dunne, and Glynn (2000) argue that introducing self-service technologies necessitates a segmentation approach. The evidence suggests that consumer markets and business-to-business markets are seeing growing numbers of customers who seek and embrace self-service technology.

Numerous technologies offer an automated alternative to human service. For example, in many cities, a newspaper subscriber whose paper fails to arrive one morning can request redelivery via an automated telephone system without talking to another human. A credit card customer can go to the credit card company's Web site to check an account balance. Many retailers offer self-service checkout instead of having to check out with a cashier. In many countries, it is even possible to use your mobile phone as a wireless payment device.

Computer systems are increasingly used in delivery services. For instance, FedEx, the world's largest express delivery company, created a sophisticated package-tracking system that shows where each of the 3.1 million packages it handles each day is during every moment of its journey. Previously, the customer had to call FedEx to have a package traced. Then, the company provided its largest customers with a computer terminal to track their many shipments on their own. Today, any customer (large or small) can use the FedEx Web site **(http://www.fedex.com)** to track a package. American Airlines **(http://www.aa.com)** has followed a similar pattern of technology-supported service development. Initially, American created its computer-based SABRE reservation system to expand its own ability to serve customers, but the system subsequently became a major revenue source for the airline. At first, SABRE was available only via a travel agent or American Airlines representative, but any consumer can now access an Internet version called Travelocity **(http://www.travelocity.com).**

Developments in technology have allowed the creation of *intelligent agents* as a new services tool. Customers use software agents to perform tasks previously performed by service representatives. For example, a software agent can perform the work of a travel agent by searching computerized airline schedules and establishing a tentative flight booking, which the customer can approve. PC-based home banking is an example of an agent-based self-service whereby a customer, using software from the bank, can check account activity and perform transactions such as transferring money and paying bills. Conceivably, we may someday routinely "have your agent get with my agent" for any service.

CURATING CUSTOMER INFORMATION

Advances in information technology have allowed organizations to collect large quantities of information about customers and to create and deliver customer services hitherto unimaginable. Organizations can move from mass marketing to targeting individuals. To be successful, customer databases must be designed with the goal of delivering specific levels of customer service.

Creating customer databases requires several steps. The first step in this process is to group customers into categories: current customers, prospective customers, and lapsed customers. Second, the database should contain data on the recency and frequency of each customer's purchases. Third, an effective database should contain specific details on each customer's purchases over a period of about twelve months. Fourth, the database should include any other relevant customer information that will improve the company's ability to serve customer needs (preferred sizes, birthdays, credit card numbers, etc.). Some of the simplest and most effective uses of customer databases are to track customers' purchase patterns. The data generated allow organizations to control distribution and recognize tiny changes in customer demands.

The most effective use of customer databases is to make them easily accessible to the frontline service provider. For example, a retail salesclerk at a men's clothing store can quickly access a specific customer's file and provide customized clothing advice. Such performances require customer databases for frontline service providers in an easy-to-use format. The information must also be available where the customer is being served. The astute services marketer will make every service encounter an opportunity to build the customer database by creating a system that collects and stores information from each transaction.

Services marketers must be cautious about privacy issues as they create and use customer databases. Although customers may not mind being known to a company with whom they do business regularly, they may fear the potential invasion of privacy that results when an organization knows all the details of their purchasing patterns. Today, any direct marketer can store large quantities of information about its customers' purchasing habits. For instance, Dell Computers **(http://www.dell.com)** sells its computers via the Internet to customers worldwide. When customers connect to Dell.com via their Dell account, they can review,

---

==== **SPOTLIGHT 3.3** ====

Privacy Is in Danger

 Privacy issues related to consumer technology have been controversial for a long time. Easy access to customer information makes it possible to misuse that information. Major Internet service providers like Google and Facebook have succumbed to the temptation to sell the personal information they have on customers to their advertisers. Each time such actions have been publicized, their users have responded with outrage.

Arguably, there is a simple and ethically correct way for service organizations to handle issues of customer privacy. It starts by respecting the customer's right to control his or her personal information and carefully getting permission to share it. Service organizations should never assume they automatically have permission for new uses of personal information without explicitly asking for permission.

configure, and price Dell's computer systems; order a system online; and track orders from manufacturing through shipping. The online customer accounts allow Dell to be more responsive to customer needs, yet it comes at the cost of the customer's sense of anonymity. The importance of the privacy issue is likely to vary by individual and also by culture. As you can see in Spotlight 3.3, service organizations should vigilantly guard against invading customer privacy.

COPING WITH NEGATIVE IMPACTS OF SERVICES TECHNOLOGY

To improve service quality, technology must continue to play a critical role in establishing the competitive position of service organizations in the twenty-first century. Nevertheless, we offer this caveat: even though much popular media attention focuses on high technology (electronics, aerospace, genetic engineering, robotics, etc.), this focus can be misleading. Service organizations often find that while implementing the latest and greatest technology systems, they have made no provisions for the absence of the technology during a power failure. For example, one author recently visited a restaurant whose cash registers were shut down because of a sudden power loss. No one in the restaurant was capable of processing the patrons' payments manually. Service organizations seeking a competitive edge by being the first to bring a new technology-assisted service delivery to market may also find that the pursuit can be expensive and embarrassing when it fails. Often, customers need a manual solution instead of a technological solution. Bitner (2001, p. 10) writes, "While technology has drastically altered the relationship between customers and firms, customers still want what they have always wanted: dependable outcomes, easy access, responsive systems, and compensation when things go wrong."

Employment levels are another potentially negative effect of technology. In many service industries, employment levels may fall in absolute terms as technology replaces workers or reduces the need for them. For example, the widespread use of ATMs in the banking industry has reduced employment opportunities for bank tellers. In general, service workers in low-skilled jobs may find that automated technology can replace them. However, highly skilled service workers are much less likely to lose jobs because of technology. Further, technology will create many new services jobs requiring high skill levels. For example, banks may require fewer tellers today, but they have increased their use of computer programming and computer security staff.

CHALLENGES OF USING TECHNOLOGY TO MANAGE CUSTOMER INTERFACES

Service organizations that add more technology to their operations often face many challenges arising from the many weak links in the technological customer interfaces of services. However, several steps can be taken to overcome these weak links.

Weak Links in Technological Customer Interfaces

A variety of weak links in technological customer interfaces cause many service organizations to provide frustrating service experiences.

Automated Idiocy   The rush to automate service functions often leads to systems that automatically do stupid things. As an example, one of the authors registered with travel service Expedia **(http://www.expedia.com)** in its early days. Expedia offered to send a free notice of low fares via e-mail as part of the registration. After requesting this free service, an e-mail message arrived announcing low airfares to Dublin, Ireland. However, the airfares had expired. The author complained, and received a reply that Expedia was experiencing technical difficulties with the service. The next week, he received another e-mail message from Expedia announcing the same expired airfares again. At that point, the author had his name removed from the list.

Time Sink   New services technology can be a "time sink" that steals precious time from the user. For example, waiting times increase when a new technology operates more slowly than the prior technology (Internet versus telephone). A time sink can also occur as the user struggles to learn and master the new technology. Remember the last time you bought a software upgrade only to discover that you had to relearn the software?

Law of the Hammer   This law is based on the idea that a small child with a hammer sees every other object as a nail. The creators of technology are similar in their obsessions. They are prone to design for the maximum degree of technological sophistication. However, complicated design features that excite a technologist often leave a customer frustrated. Consider the case of many Web sites you may have visited that are confusing or cumbersome due to unnecessary technological "bells and whistles."

Technology Lock   One of the biggest problems in customer interface design occurs because technological designs persist long after their functional value is gone. For example, the QWERTY keyboard (named for the sequence of letters on the top left of the keyboard) dates back to the first manual typewriters. At the time, because a typist could easily type faster than the manual keys could move, the keys would jam constantly. To solve this problem, the keys were rearranged to slow down the typist. It was a terrific solution at the time; however, you may wonder why we are still using the same slow keyboard many decades after the disappearance of manual typewriters.

Last Inch   Many customer interface design problems occur at the point of contact between the customer and the technology. Current customer interfaces are rather primitive and require significant training to operate successfully. As noted in the previous paragraph, computer keyboards follow a rather primitive design. The mouse and trackball are limited tools, too. Indeed, these computer interface tools are so primitive that repetitive stress injuries are relatively common. Voice recognition is considered a better alternative, but the challenges of converting human speech to computer code have proven formidable.

Hi-Tech Versus Hi-Touch   How many times have you called a company and encountered a confusing set of automated telephone instructions? After weaving through a maze of menu choices, did you still find that your query did not really fit any of the options or that you were unsure which choice was correct? You really needed to speak to a person, not a machine! Phone mail can become phone jail. Fortunately, a Web site has emerged **(http://gethuman.com/us/)** that informs customers how to escape from such automation and get hold of a human being at hundreds of U.S. companies and government agencies.

Steps for Improving the Technology of Customer Interfaces

The following four steps can significantly improve the technology of customer interfaces:

- ▪ **Provide Marketer Input into the Technology of Customer Interface Design.** Marketers are rarely included in the early stages of customer interface design. The marketer can help prevent the hazards of automated idiocy, time sink, law of the hammer, technology lock, and last inch.

- ▪ **Stay Customer-Focused, Not Machine-Focused.** Staying focused on the customer rather than the machine is essential to successful customer interface design. In particular, the design should address how customers use the service and make it as easy as possible for them to do so. Customer-focused technology adapts to customer needs.

- ▪ **Make Services Technology Invisible to the Customer.** Too often, the underlying technology of a customer interface is obtrusive. Customers are not necessarily interested in technology, and it should be placed in the background. Ideally, the technology should be virtually invisible to the customer.

- ▪ **Insist on Flexible Design.** Services marketers should insist on technological designs that offer employees and customers maximum flexibility. Too many companies replace flexible employees with inflexible technology. Technology with limited flexibility is hard for employees and customers to use effectively. Technology that is truly flexible will be fun for employees and customers to use.

Summary and Conclusion

Information technology underlies most of the significant twentieth-century improvements and will play a significant role in the twenty-first century. Using technology to deliver services requires training service employees and often training the service customer as well. Without such training, a new technology can actually undermine an organization's service quality. A retail clerk poorly trained on a new scanner-based cash register will perform much worse than one well trained to read prices by hand. On the customer side, patrons must be trained to use many technological advances such as ATMs, smartphones, and computer software before realizing their value. The service quality we receive can be damaged by the previous customer's lack of training.

Information technology is a key aspect of rising consumer expectations all over the world and has played a major role in the social upheaval experienced by many countries. Today, millions of people worldwide watch major news events in real time. The world is in the midst of a vast information revolution that is remaking human society in ways as pervasive as the changes wrought by the industrial revolution. As this happens, the range, sophistication, and quality of services delivered via technology to the customer of the future may far exceed anyone's current expectations.

Exercises

1. Count and list the number of electronic communication devices you used during the past twenty-four hours. How many of these were (a) one-way devices (radio, television, and satellite), and (b) two-way devices (smartphones, iPads and laptops)? From your list, select an example of your use of a service offering with one of these devices and discuss how the technology enhanced the service delivery.

2. Pick a service organization in your community and develop a plan showing how it could improve its service through the use of information technology tools:

   a. for its employees.

   b. to allow customers more or easier contact with the service organization.

3. Identify a service experience you had that was made more difficult by ineffective service technology. Describe the service encounter in detail to highlight the role of technology. What could the service organization do to improve the service technology?

Internet Exercise

EXPLORE

Visit the companion site for this text at **www.cengagebrain.com** to explore key concepts in the service industry. You will find tools to help you expand your services marketing knowledge, including ACE self-tests, Web links to companies and organizations featured in this chapter, and much more!

Visit the Apple iTunes Web site (**http://www.apple.com/itunes/whats-on/**) and explore the online music services that Apple introduced to the world. Study how the iTunes software and iPods, iPhones, and iPads are designed to work together to give music lovers a personal, portable music library. Also explore the many additional forms of digital content available from iTunes (the App Store, television shows, movies, music videos, books, podcasts, and iTunes U).

References

Barnes, James G., Peter A. Dunne, and William J. Glynn (2000), "Self-Service and Technology: Unanticipated and Unintended Effects on Customer Relationships," in *Handbook of Services Marketing and Management*, Teresa A. Swartz and Dawn Iacobucci, eds., Thousand Oaks, CA: Sage Publications, 89–102.

Bitner, Mary Jo (2001), "Self-Service Technologies: What Do Customers Expect,?" *Marketing Management*, 10 (Spring), 10–11.

Dabholkar, Pratibha A. (2000), "Technology in Service Delivery: Implications for Self-Service and Service Support," in *Handbook of Services Marketing and Management*, Teresa A. Swartz and Dawn Iacobucci, eds., Thousand Oaks, CA: Sage Publications, 103–110.

Meuter, Matthew L., Amy L. Ostrom, Robert I. Roundtree, and Mary Jo Bitner (2000), "Self-Service Technologies: Understanding Customer Satisfaction With Technology-Based Service Encounters," *Journal of Marketing*, 64 (July), 50–64.

Parasuraman, A. (2000), "Technology Readiness Index (TRI): A Multiple-Item Scale to Measure Readiness to Embrace New Technologies," *Journal of Service Research*, 2 (4), 307–320.

Parasuraman, A. and Dhruv Grewal (2000), "The Impact of Technology on the Quality-Value-Loyalty Chain: A Research Agenda," *Journal of the Academy of Marketing Science*, 28 (1), 168–174.

Patrício, Lia, Raymond P. Fisk, and João Falcão e Cunha (2008), "Designing Multi-Interface Service Experiences: the Service Experience Blueprint," *Journal of Service Research*, 10 (May), 318–334.

Creating the Interactive Experience

Chapters in this section are based in part on the services theater perspective. Chapter 4 discusses the many considerations that influence planning and delivering a service performance. A positive customer experience requires coordination of the various components of the service encounter. Chapter 5 examines the role of the services setting in communicating and delivering the service. In particular, we examine the service setting as the stage for enactment of service performances. Chapter 6 considers the issue of managing the service performers, that is, the employees. We call it "leveraging the people factor" because of the tremendous capacity of employees to affect customers' perceptions of service quality in a service organization. Finally, Chapter 7 contemplates the role of the customers—the audience in the service process. Service customers can influence service performance success.

Foundations of Services Marketing
CHAPTERS 1, 2, and 3

PART TWO
Creating the Interactive Experience

CHAPTER 4   Planning and Producing the Service Performance
CHAPTER 5   Designing the Service Setting
CHAPTER 6   Leveraging the People Factor
CHAPTER 7   Managing the Customer Mix

Management Issues in Services Marketing
CHAPTERS 13, 14, and 15

Part I

Part V

Part IV

Part III

INTERACTIVE SERVICES MARKETING

Delivering and Ensuring a Successful Customer Experience
CHAPTERS 10, 11, and 12

Promising the Interactive Service Experience
CHAPTERS 8 and 9

Louvre Museum

People visit the famous Louvre Museum **(http://www.louvre.fr)** from all over the world. Housed in a former medieval fortress that was subsequently the palace of the kings of France, the building itself is of great significance and contributes to the ambience of this historic museum.

With four floors of exhibits, each visitor has the opportunity to spend as much or as little time at the museum as desired. However, it seems that all visitors want to see the famous *Mona Lisa* painting by Leonardo da Vinci; most go see it first even though it is not close to the museum entrance. The painting's popularity creates traffic jams in front of it every day. The worldwide popularity of the book *The Da Vinci Code* has only increased the painting's fame.

To improve the Louvre Museum experience, the room that houses the *Mona Lisa* was renovated in 2005 to handle more than 1,500 visitors an hour. The new room design features improved lighting, better crowd circulation, and special antireflection glass to protect her from the constant flash of cameras. So complicated was this renovation, that the *Mona Lisa* was to be taken off display for one day while it was reinstalled. Because the *Mona Lisa* is so popular, the Louvre administration contacted 6,000 travel companies to let them know when the *Mona Lisa* would be moved.

Other changes to the Louvre include a 1989 modern glass and steel pyramid designed by I. M. Pei that now serves as the entrance to the museum. This project included numerous modern features to better accommodate visitors: an underground parking area for buses and cars, a shopping area, and an amphitheater.

Source: © Zoran Karapancev/Shutterstock.com; Daniel Michael and Anne-Michele Morice (2005), "Job One at the Louvre: Don't Stand in Front of Smiling Woman; Curator, Guides Work Around Mona Lisa's Celebrity; A Rare Day Off—to Move," *Wall Street Journal* (Eastern Edition) (March 23), A1. Reprinted by permission.

CHAPTER 4
Planning and Producing the Service Performance
The Service Performance
Supplementing the Basic Service Performance
Differentiating the Service Performance
Customizing the Service Performance
Scripting the Service Performance
Blueprinting the Service Performance
The Internet and Service Performances
The Emotional Side of Services

CHAPTER 5
Designing the Service Setting
What Is a Service Setting?
Key Considerations in Designing the Service Setting
The Service Setting as a Marketing Tool
Cyberspace as a Service Setting

CHAPTER 6
Leveraging the People Factor
Service Employees and Their Behavior
Empowering Service Employees
The Need for Service Improvisation
The Emotional Side of Services
Costuming Service Employees
Maximizing Service Employee Productivity

CHAPTER 7
Managing the Customer Mix
Service Customers and Their Behavior
Customer-to-Customer Interactions
Customer-to-Employee Interactions
Selecting and Training Customers
Managing Customer Rage

CHAPTER 4

Planning and Producing the Service Performance

The Louvre Museum (**http://www.louvre.fr**) carefully plans its service operations and designs the needed behind-the-scenes infrastructure for its customer. If done well, you might not notice the organization's efforts that enable you to find what you are seeking in a museum or other service organization. Customers are often oblivious to what really goes on behind the scenes to render a service. Yet, processes that take place away from the customer's view can significantly affect the customer experience. The nature of the museum experience comes from specific processes that the customer encounters in the museum. Consider the sequence of multiple steps that must occur at the Louvre Museum to stage its service performance. This chapter presents a conceptual and technical examination of planning and producing a service performance. The chapter has four specific objectives:

- **To examine the role of service performance as core or supplementary elements of the product**
- **To demonstrate techniques that might be used to differentiate the service offering**
- **To describe the key elements that come into play when customizing the service performance**
- **To explain the techniques of scripting and blueprinting that are used to plan service performances more precisely**

Retired baseball star and accidental philosopher Yogi Berra once proclaimed, "You can observe a lot just by watching!" This simple comment is a truism because everyday activities and physical surroundings often go unnoticed. A customer who simply takes the time to observe a service closely is likely to notice such elements as employees working at various tasks, the colors and comfort of the service setting, and other customers sharing the service's environment. The casual observer may even suspect that these features are part of some grand design to affect customers' service evaluation. Customers who watch more carefully, however, may discover other dimensions of the organization's service. For instance, they may discover that the hues and decor of the service setting are coordinated to evoke a sense of tranquility, or that the employees' activities seem to follow some unknown yet detectable pattern. Ultimately, the perceptive onlooker is likely to surmise that when it comes to services, Yogi Berra was right. You really can observe a lot just by watching!

With physical goods, the description "what you see is what you get" is frequently accurate, but services often have imperceptible features. As discussed in Chapter 2, frameworks that describe service experiences recognize that a significant portion of a service occurs out of the customer's sight. Much of the preparation, coordination, execution, and support of the service in the visible area or interactive part of the service delivery system is concealed. The customer may not comprehend all of the aspects of the service system surrounding the frontstage. However, a customer is likely to have even less knowledge of the backstage activities necessary to create a successful service encounter. With services, "what you get" is a lot more than "what you see"!

As with stage productions, many details must come together to create a service performance (Grove and Fisk 1983; Grove, Fisk, and Bitner 1992; Grove, Fisk, and John 2000). Like their theatrical counterparts, many of these elements often go unnoticed by customers because they occur backstage or are obscured by the action unfolding on stage for the audience. Even when these service particulars are in open view, they may be overlooked because they are indistinguishable from the setting and staging of the performance. Often, the customer becomes aware of these elements only when they fail to contribute to a performance as planned. The dirty spoon in the restaurant and the inaccurate billing statement at the automobile repair shop are similar to the missing stage prop and the poorly timed sound effect in a theatrical production. Their unexpected and unsatisfactory state brings attention to their role in the service enactment. In short, when a service is performed as planned, most customers are unlikely to appreciate the character and importance of the elements that contribute to its excellence.

Any organization creates value by delivering products as solutions to customer needs. As we have seen in the service theater framework, services as products are performances staged by people—employees and customers as actors and audiences in a setting. Thus, in planning a product and producing the service performance, managers are scripting a process, designing a service setting, leveraging its workers, and managing its customers. Put together, these aspects are essential product decisions in a service firm.

THE SERVICE PERFORMANCE

Viewing services as performances makes sense for many reasons. Whether the service is a physician's care, a taxi ride, a football game, or a freight delivery, the service the customer receives is an activity rendered for consumption. The care, the ride, the game, and the transportation activities have no physical character by themselves. Instead, like theater productions, they are performances often fashioned and delivered through the efforts of people (the physician, cab driver, football player, or truck driver) and equipment and facilities (the x-ray machine, taxi, football stadium, or delivery truck). In addition, many other concerns visible and invisible to the service customer (the physician's waiting room atmosphere, the care and maintenance of the taxicab or football field, the freight dispatcher's personal skills) have theatrical aspects. As with their theatrical counterparts, service performances rely on a good deal of planning and design. However, to plan a service performance successfully, we must understand its characteristics.

First, service performances are multifaceted phenomena. The organization's core service is often enhanced by a host of supplementary service elements to provide the complete service performance. Take, for instance, the case of a typical hotel. A traveler secures a hotel room as a place to rest and sleep until the following day. Overall, the basic service that the hotel is expected to provide is a night's stay in a clean, comfortable, and quiet abode. However, most hotels offer many other elements to accommodate guest wants and needs. Restaurants, lounges, telephone service, fitness centers, and billing and reservation systems supplement the hotel's provision of a room. Supplementary service elements can also be a source of competitive service differentiation.

Second, as a performance, a service exists only during its enactment. Although this feature presents challenges for the services marketer (e.g., quality control), it also offers the opportunity for services to be customized to fit an individual patron's needs or desires. The fact that a service offering does not take shape until it is performed allows the provider to adapt to customers' special requests or unusual circumstances. Many services can be built to the customer's specifications. Hairstyling, financial planning, physical therapy, and advertising are examples of services that are adapted to individual customers' needs or desires. However, profitability or cost control concerns may limit service performance customization, even when it seems to be needed.

Third, a service performance occurs over time and involves a sequence of events. Consider the mail delivery service provided by the U.S. Postal Service **(http://www.usps.com).** Many steps involving customers, postal workers, equipment, and facilities combine to transfer a letter from origin to destination. Various acts may be identified and chronologically arranged to give a clear picture of the mail delivery service. Efforts to do so can aid management's comprehension and design of service delivery.

SUPPLEMENTING THE BASIC SERVICE PERFORMANCE

Products, whether goods or services, consist of a core and supplementary elements. The core of a hotel's product is the use of a room, but the supplementary elements include numerous ancillary services. The core is the basic need-satisfying ability of the product, while the supplementary elements enhance the core.

Service products can be classified like physical goods into categories, such as convenience, shopping, or specialty services. *Convenience services* are perceived to be low risk. Customers want to exert little effort and select the most accessible provider of that service. Examples include a taxi, a shoeshine, grocery stores, drug stores, and of course, convenience stores. *Shopping services* are those for which the customer needs to develop a preference or choice and will make comparisons of prices and quality, which requires a search activity. Examples include insurance, air travel, travel agency, and college. *Specialty services* are those for which the customer has a preference in brands and in service provider characteristics, indicating an extra willingness to look for a specific service provider. Examples include legal services, museums, and religious services.

Any service organization may supplement its core products in many ways. Using the metaphor of a flower, Lovelock (1994) identified eight types of supplementary service *petals* that might surround an organization's basic service performance at the flower's center (see Figure 4.1). These elements are service procedures or elements that pertain to information, consultation, order taking, hospitality, caretaking, processing exceptions, billing, and payment. Even though it may be unreasonable to expect some of these petals to grow from the core of certain services—hospitality is unlikely to be necessary for utility companies—other services might eventually become flowers in full bloom. For example, supplementary services from each petal described by Lovelock are likely to accompany the core service performance of an airline, a hotel, or a hospital. The petals

FIGURE 4.1 Lovelock's Service Petals

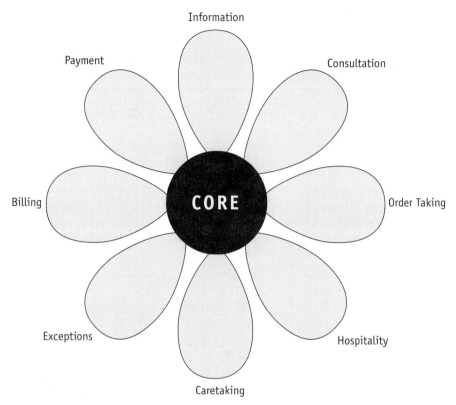

Information

Payment   Consultation

Billing   **CORE**   Order Taking

Exceptions   Hospitality

Caretaking

Source: Christopher H. Lovelock (1994), *Product Plus: How Product + Service = Competitive Advantage*, New York: McGraw-Hill, 179. Reprinted with the permission of The McGraw-Hill Companies.

that Lovelock describes provide an excellent starting point for organizations to explore ways to augment their service.

Features that enhance the efficiency and effectiveness of service performance can augment an organization's frontstage activity (e.g., providing a kiosk that offers airline travelers an automated ticketing option) or its backstage support, such as Ritz-Carlton's **(http://www.ritzcarlton.com)** database of customer preferences. Supplementary elements sometimes allow organizations better opportunities to customize their service. Ultimately, the addition of any service supplements should increase customer satisfaction. *Supplementing a service performance* sometimes involves increasing its complexity. The dry cleaning store that adds pickup and delivery to its basic service and the travel agency that augments its service by offering flight insurance are examples of adding complexity. Barnes & Noble **(http://www.barnesandnoble.com)** provides an excellent illustration of supplementing a service performance. Beyond its core service of retailing a wide selection of books, tapes, and magazines, the stores offer patrons a broad array of computer software, food service, and a comfortable place to enjoy their merchandise. Similarly, Home Depot **(http://www.homedepot.com)**, a large U.S. retailer of building and home maintenance supplies, supplements its basic service by offering customers "how to" classes on popular home improvement projects and arranging contacts with individuals who can meet customers' contracting

---

SPOTLIGHT 4.1

Your Smartphone Is a Mobile Cash Register

Many services are delivered "on the go." Consider services that come to your home, such as pizza delivery, appliance repair services, landscaping services, or home health services. At least three of the eight supplementary services in Figure 4.1—order taking, billing, and payment—can be burdensome activities for such service providers as well as for the customer. Plug-in credit card readers and "apps" for your smartphone have changed the way these services conduct business and deliver these supplementary services. Service providers can now simply swipe the customer's credit card or type in the credit card number, and voilà! The transaction is processed and receipts automatically e-mailed or sent via text message to the customer.

Technology—such as "Square" designed for the iPhone and the iPad, the MerchantWARE Mobile designed for the BlackBerry, and the GoPayment designed for phones running on Google's Android operating system—makes such activities possible. Compared to the cost of the traditional cash register with a card-processing terminal, even stores are finding a switch to these mobile cash registers more efficient and effective. In the future, look for more service petals to be included in these apps—which started as credit card payment systems for smartphones.

Sources: David Rocks and Nick Leiber (2011), "Turning Smartphones into Cash Registers," *Bloomberg Business-Week* (February 14–20), 44–46; and, **http://www.practica-lecommerce/artciles/2497-11-Credit-Card-Apps-Swipers-for-iphones.**

---

needs. By adding such aspects to its core service, an organization can respond to customers' wants more effectively and maintain or enhance its competitive stature. See Spotlight 4.1 for an illustration of how supplementary elements for services delivered at the customer's location can be streamlined with mobile technology.

Sometimes, supplementing an organization's basic service occurs as a natural response to competitive forces. Shortly after one provider offers a supplementary service and its utility is confirmed, other competitors are compelled to introduce their own version of the element. From the followers' standpoint, failure to copy the competitors' success could result in losing more ground in the marketplace. Consider the case of the upscale hotel and the express check-in option. Soon after its introduction, virtually every major hotel had developed a similar system. In the hotel industry, this pattern is common. Once, the provision of complimentary toiletries or a chocolate on the pillow was distinctive, but these supplementary service innovations quickly became commonplace. Organizations occasionally attempt to make up the ground they lost while following the leader by offering minor improvements to the original innovation. For example, the inconspicuous chocolate on the pillow grew in size and in number as the idea made its way among hotel operators across the globe. One hotel chain even decided to replace the innocent chocolate with a cookie the size of a small automobile to ingratiate itself with the customer in a much grander way. This particular phenomenon has probably almost run its course. Before it does, however, we fully expect to see weary travelers return to their room some evening to find a pepperoni pizza propped on the pillow.

DIFFERENTIATING THE SERVICE PERFORMANCE

The decision to supplement the service performance does not always stem from another organization's innovation. Sometimes organizations may take calculated risks to differentiate their service performances. Such a pioneer might achieve a competitive advantage over other service organizations in its industry if it were able to offer greater convenience (Berry, Seiders, and Grewal 2002), much like the hotel that first introduced express registration. When supplementing service performance with innovative elements, the organization must remain alert to whether it enhances the customer's service experience. Supplementing service without evaluating the innovation's efficacy can be disastrous. Even well-considered and closely studied changes to a service performance can fail. Burger King **(http://www.burgerking.com)** attempted to alter the nature of its fast-food operation by offering table service at certain hours of the day. Customers didn't like the change, however, and the venture failed.

Planning a service performance involves both striving to keep up with competition and carefully studying opportunities to distinguish the organization by supplementing its core service. Service innovations are often easy to copy, neutralizing the competitive advantage. According to Levitt (1981), the *augmented product* an organization develops today can easily become tomorrow's *expected product* from the customer's point of view. (See Spotlight 4.2 for a discussion of how self-service technology is becoming commonplace in service performance.) Hence, organizations should keep a vigilant eye on ways to develop the *potential product*. In services marketing terms, the potential product can incorporate any means of attracting customers in the future by supplementing the already augmented service performance. Hotels currently experimenting with self-service check-in procedures represent service organizations pursuing a potential service product. There is no turning back. Deleting supplementary service elements from the offering would be inconsistent with the quest to develop newer and better products. In reality, however, a service organization can also distinguish itself by offering a simpler service performance. Now that some popular fast-food establishments such as McDonald's **(http://www.mcdonalds .com)** offer increasingly complex services, others have achieved success by

---

══ SPOTLIGHT 4.2 ══

The Self-Service Economy

 It seems that everywhere one looks these days there is more and more evidence that self-service technology is gaining widespread acceptance. Airports, theaters, the post office, and large-scale retailers have adopted technology that allows customers to check in, check out, process information and the like—all without having to deal directly with a service employee. Many service organizations allow customers to "manage their accounts" online. It all began with the automated teller machines at banks and the automated gas pumps at service stations, and has grown steadily. Researchers at the Information Technology and Innovation Foundation estimated in 2010 that "if self-service technology were more widely deployed, the U.S. economy would be approximately $130 billion larger annually."

Self-service can increase customer service without increasing labor costs. It provides great convenience for customers, saves customers' time, and makes it possible for service personnel to abandon registers to perform other tasks that convert to customer service. If you are flying out of Amsterdam's Schiphol Airport, for example, you can self-tag your check-in bags. Schiphol experiments with an increasing number of off-airport procedures and rolls out self-service innovations for the Netherlands's KLM Airlines on a regular basis and urges other airlines using its airports to follow suit.

Sources: **http://www.itif.org/publications/embracing-self-service-economy** (accessed June 15, 2011); and, **http://www.futuretravelexperience.com/2011/04/schiphols-self-service-self-tagging-innovation/** (accessed June 15, 2011).

limiting the number of menu options, removing inside dining, and reducing their hours. Although new entrants into the competitive arena may adopt this approach, an organization that has already supplemented its service performance can hardly delete those service elements without sacrificing customer patronage.

The decision to supplement the service performance requires careful consideration. Apart from the caveats previously noted, organizations must be sensitive to the cost-effectiveness of developing and implementing supplementary service elements. Altering the service performance by adding complexity may increase material costs (e.g., technology and physical structures) or labor costs (e.g., hiring and training additional workers). Therefore, the supplementary element should be carefully scrutinized in terms of both service effectiveness (increasing the level of customer delight) and efficiency (ability to process customers more quickly). One way to make such cost–benefit decisions is through trials of new performances. Much as theatrical productions try out new material by performing at out-of-town venues, large service organizations can explore new supplemental service performances by testing them at a few outlets or for a short time. Any assessment of a supplemental service should include appraising its fit with the organization's service strategy. This evaluation is particularly crucial if the supplementary service represents a significant departure from the service's existing performance. Failure to consider strategic fit can result in a service performance that leaves the customer confused and bewildered about the service organization. The Italian restaurant that alters its menu to offer a few popular non-Italian dishes or the automobile repair shop that adds a dry cleaning service may find that customers become confused about the nature of these organizations.

Supplementing the service performance can range from minor changes that enhance customer experiences to major changes that significantly alter the nature of the performance. The complexity of planning such changes naturally depends on the nature of the supplement. A decision to offer a complimentary chocolate on the hotel guest's pillow will have a different effect than a decision to supplement the hotel's service by allocating hotel space for large suite-style rooms with large work desks. The latter decision requires more careful analysis and evaluation. In both cases, however, a supplemented service performance is a means to compete in a crowded marketplace.

CUSTOMIZING THE SERVICE PERFORMANCE

Product differentiation in services can come in the form of customization, which requires special consideration. Customization plays a key role in providing a competitive advantage for the organization. Many service performances may be characterized by specific steps or an entire process to accommodate the particular needs, wants, or desires of individual customers. Because many services are produced and consumed simultaneously and often involve interaction between a service provider and the patron, *customization* is an attractive option for both the customer and marketer. For the customer, it amounts to personalizing the product; for the marketer, it is a way of differentiating the product from other

> **F I G U R E 4 . 2 What Sarge Wants**

providers. Sometimes customization is a necessity, such as in the delivery of a medical diagnosis where the physician has little choice but to treat each patient individually. Occasionally, as in the case of an aerobics instructor who decides to offer the service of a personal fitness trainer, customization may be discretionary. In either case, customization introduces special considerations to the planning of the service performance.

The notion of planning a service performance that satisfies each customer's wants may be quite attractive (see Figure 4.2). Each customer has slightly different preferences for any service, and accommodating those preferences may seem desirable. However, significant trade-offs occur between the service *effectiveness* of customizing each service to the customer's individual desires and the service *efficiency* of producing a standardized service for all customers. Consider the case of public transportation. Developing a public transit system that carried every customer from door to door might be theoretically possible, but such a system is not likely to be financially or logistically feasible. Its inefficiency would immediately far outweigh its ability to satisfy customers' individual needs. Thus, service customization does have drawbacks. In fact, some have argued that instead of customizing the service performance, service organizations should industrialize their delivery processes in the interest of speed, consistency, and economy. As Lovelock and Wirtz (2007) suggest, such features may be more important to many customers than a customized service.

To plan a service performance that incorporates customization, an organization must have a good understanding of each customer's needs or wants. The service organization must also possess workers and technology that can adapt to customers' wants. Customization involves a lot more than the "Hi Bob!" tactic (a weak attempt to personalize the service performance by greeting patrons by their first names). Customizing a service requires considerable skill and effort to uncover and respond to each customer's preferences. Customers usually make their wishes known regarding the service performance, but not always. Sometimes the organization and its personnel must work hard to discern what each customer wants. Some insurance companies, for example, train their representatives to identify client preferences by developing excellent listening skills. Service organizations must educate their customers to reveal their desires. For example, hotels often use signs and oral communications to urge guests to ask for anything that the hotel can do to make their stay more pleasant. Complicating the challenge of discerning customer needs and wants is the fact that in many services (e.g., a four-star restaurant, a medical exam, or legal advice) customer desires must be discovered as the service is being performed.

Knowledge of a customer's preferences or needs is only half of the customization issue. An organization's ability to respond to many different customer desires by modifying the service performance requires superior employee skills and technological support, which may be hard to develop or to fund. Technology can be expensive, and skilled labor may be scarce and costly to train and compensate. Organizations whose service is based on meeting a full range of individual customers' preferences (e.g., real estate agencies or health clinics) have few options. The success of the enterprise depends on serving each customer as an individual. These organizations must therefore plan for and invest in those service components that help personalize the service for their customers. However, organizations choosing customization should carefully weigh the costs and benefits of altering even a single step in the service performance. The efficiency sacrificed to meet divergent customer wants, combined with the costs that accompany the more skilled labor and advanced technology required, might outstrip the revenue benefits to the organization.

On the positive side, customizing the service performance can greatly enhance a service experience and the perception of service quality. One way to customize service experiences is through the use of theatrical tools. (See Spotlight 4.3 for a discussion of how customizing health care performances by teaching doctors acting skills might improve the health care.)

As Daly (2004) argues, teaching services workers the acting skill of improvisation can significantly improve a service organization's ability to customize the service performance.

By identifying and responding to a customer's individual preferences, an organization shows that it is serious about delivering excellent service. Planning a customized service performance may not always be desirable or

---

SPOTLIGHT 4.3

Theater Training for Medical Doctors

What do theater courses have to do with medical doctors? A study at the Virginia Commonwealth University found that the bedside manner scores of internal medicine students improved after the students took a course offered by theater professors. Trained observers rated students' overall empathetic communication to be 6.88 on a 10-point scale before the class, and 8.56 four months later. Meanwhile, the control group's rating slipped from 6.38 to 5.82. Together the Mayo Medical School and the Mayo Clinic Center for Humanities in Medicine partnered with the Guthrie Theater to teach storytelling skills to medical students through improvisation, writing, movement, and acting exercises.

Sources: Rachel R. Hammer, Johanna D. Rian, Jeremy K. Gregory, J. Michael Bostwick, Candace Barrett Birk, Louise Chalfant, Paul D. Scanlon, and Daniel K. Hall-Flavin, (2011), "Telling the Patient's Story: using theater training to improve case presentation skills," *Medical Humanities*, 37, 3-4; and, Alan W. Dow, David Leong, Aaron Anderson, Richard P. Wenzel, and VCU Theater-Medicine Team, (2007), "Using Theater to Teach Clinical Empathy: A Pilot Study," *Journal of General Internal Medicine*, 22 (8), 1114-1118.

feasible—think of fast-food operations or public transportation. Nonetheless, developing and maintaining the capacity to accommodate a wide range of customer preferences can distinguish organizations in many service industries. Ritz-Carlton hotels are known worldwide for their ability to accommodate customers' preferences successfully. In an industry where standardization of quality is a lofty goal, Ritz-Carlton set its sights on striving to meet every customer's individual needs. That commitment enabled the hotel chain to win the United States's coveted Malcolm Baldrige National Quality Award twice. It accomplished this through the efforts of its highly skilled and motivated workforce as well as through investment in technology that tracks guests' preferences in a computer database.

Planning a service performance that embodies such customization is a huge commitment, but can pay big dividends in customer satisfaction and perceptions of service quality. Producing a superior service experience through customization enhances an organization's image, creates greater loyalty among customers, and builds stronger preferences for the service supplier.

SCRIPTING THE SERVICE PERFORMANCE

A careful observer is likely to recognize that service performances follow a sequence of events. Even the casual onlooker will note that a service delivery—whether it is hairstyling, automobile repair, or a musical broadcast—has a beginning, middle, and end. In many cases, the service performance involves several different acts, although they may not be obvious to the customer. Experts may help customers understand what is involved in performing a particular service by developing a behavioral script of its enactment and creating a blueprint of its design (Shostack 1984, 1987).

A **service script** is a chronologically ordered representation of the steps that make up the service performance from the customer's point of view. Scripts can be quite *simple* or *elaborate*, depending on the service. For instance, the script for an ATM transaction at a bank involves significantly fewer events than the script for a journey on an air carrier. Service scripts may also be described as either *weak* or *strong*, depending upon the degree of specificity in the script. Services with significant customization have weaker scripts than standardized services produced for masses of people.

> A **service script** is a chronologically ordered representation of the steps that make up the service performance from the customer's point of view.

Regardless of a script's complexity, it is easy to underestimate the number of frontstage events in a service unless you carefully study its enactment from the customer's perspective. Consider the last time you had your hair cut. That event involved a significant number of steps, probably beginning with a telephone call for an appointment and concluding when you left the shop. In between, a sequence of events occurred that included announcing your arrival to the receptionist, finding a seat, waiting your turn, reading magazines in the waiting area, engaging in small talk with other customers, being seated in the styling chair, greeting the stylist or barber, providing directions regarding your styling

FIGURE 4.3 Example of a Service Script: The Case of Legal Consulting Services

1. Call the attorney's office for an appointment.
2. Drive to the office at the appointed time.
3. Find a parking place and park your car.
4. Enter the building and try to orient yourself.
5. Read the signs to find out where to go.
6. Ask for directions.
7. Take the elevator and walk through various corridors.
8. Check at the receptionist of the front office of the the legal firm.
9. Sit in the waiting area until your turn comes.
10. Go with the assistant to the attorney's office.
11. Discuss your situation in an interview.
12. Respond to a series of questions to complete the information for the attorney.
13. Arrange for follow-up visit or action.
14. Check out at the front desk and pay your bill.
15. Find your way out of the office and the building and back to your car.
16. Drive out of the parking lot.
17. Wait for attorney to call.
18. Receive instructions or make decision for next action if necessary.
19. Call attorney's office for follow-up visit if necessary.

© Cengage Learning

preferences, and so on. Numerous steps are evident in most services when they are scrutinized closely. The script comprising the steps can be used as a planning tool for service organizations.

When carefully developed, a script can provide a detailed account of the process of frontstage service delivery. As noted before, a service script captures the many discrete acts involving customers during a service encounter. A service script may also be a normative tool that provides an account of what *should* happen during a service's enactment from the customer's point of view. To illustrate the difference, see the service script example in Figure 4.3. On one hand, the example script describes what a client is likely to encounter during a legal consulting service performance. On the other hand, the script identifies specific aspects of the frontstage service delivery the legal firm must address because they affect the client's service experience. For example, the availability and ease of parking (step 3) and the waiting time for the attorney's call (step 17) are two important aspects if client satisfaction is a goal.

By describing the events that occur in the typical performance of any specific service from the customer's perspective, an organization can learn how to ensure that customers perceive the performance as successful. Expectations associated with each event or step in the script may be studied to help the organization plan a performance that meets or exceeds customers' standards.

BLUEPRINTING THE SERVICE PERFORMANCE

A **service blueprint** is a graphic representation of the essential components of the service performance, both frontstage and backstage.* It identifies the customers, the service personnel, the points of interaction between customers and workers, the contact points between workers and other workers, and the frontstage evidence and backstage processes or activities. Most important, the blueprint shows how these combine to create the service performance. Much of what occurs on the frontstage is the result of a service organization's backstage activities. In other words, the blueprint provides a tool that defines both the frontstage enactment of a service performance and its backstage support.

> A **service blueprint** is a graphic representation of the essential components of the service performance, both frontstage and backstage.

Most people recognize a blueprint's use for the design and construction of buildings: it is a technical drawing that lays out the details of the prospective structure. In other words, a blueprint depicts a future reality. A service blueprint functions in much the same way. It is a design and communication tool enabling marketers to envision and plan exactly how the service performance will be carried out.

Although no rigid rules specify how a service blueprint should be developed, services marketers must make certain that it represents all steps, both visible and invisible, to the service customer. This process requires those in charge to become familiar with the operational aspects of the service. Often, workers from different departments or positions in the organization must come together to develop an accurate blueprint of the total service. This step is required because no individual is likely to have a complete understanding of the many dimensions of the organization's service. It is doubtful, for instance, that the window clerk, mail sorter, or postal carrier could give as accurate a description of the mail delivery service individually as they could by combining their knowledge.

Devising a service blueprint may sometimes be complicated, particularly if the service performance comprises many components. Figure 4.4 presents a possible blueprint for a simple service transaction, a visit to the local pub.

Developed after hours of careful scrutiny and firsthand observation, the blueprint depicted in the figure points to several features of the service performance. First, it identifies the frontstage activity that constitutes the service encounter from the customer's point of view. It relates the steps or acts that combine to create the customer's pub experience. In doing so, it identifies the points of interaction between the customer and the service provider (steps 5, 6, 8, and 9) and between the customer and the pub's physical environment (steps 1, 2, and 7). The blueprint also shows the backstage processes undertaken in delivering the service and indicates where these steps affect the frontstage service performance.

*For an in-depth discussion of "blueprinting," the reader is directed to G. Lynn Shostack's works, "Designing Services That Deliver," Harvard Business Review, 62 (January–February), 1984, 133–139; and "Service Positioning Through Structural Change," Journal of Marketing, 51 (January), 34–43. Also see G. Lynn Shostack and Jane Kingman-Brundage (1991), "How to Design a Service" in The AMA Handbook for Marketing for the Service Industries, C. A. Congram and M. L. Friedman, eds., AMACOM, 243–252; and Evert Gummesson and Jane Kingman-Brundage (1991), Quality Management in Services, Paul Kunst and Jos Lemmink, eds., Van Gorcum.

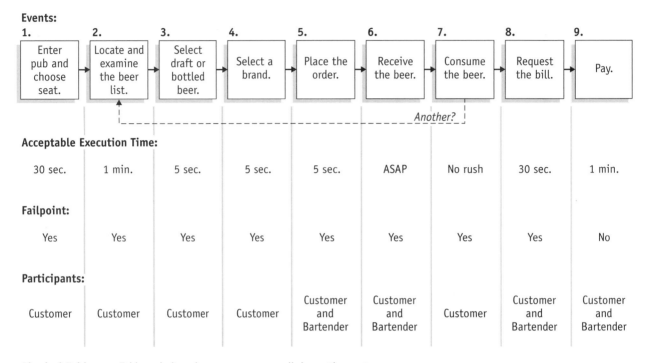

FIGURE 4.4 Example of a Service Blueprint: Visit to a Local Pub

Events:

1.	2.	3.	4.	5.	6.	7.	8.	9.
Enter pub and choose seat.	Locate and examine the beer list.	Select draft or bottled beer.	Select a brand.	Place the order.	Receive the beer.	Consume the beer.	Request the bill.	Pay.

Another?

Acceptable Execution Time:

30 sec.	1 min.	5 sec.	5 sec.	5 sec.	ASAP	No rush	30 sec.	1 min.

Failpoint:

Yes	Yes	Yes	Yes	Yes	Yes	Yes	Yes	No

Participants:

Customer	Customer	Customer	Customer	Customer and Bartender	Customer and Bartender	Customer	Customer and Bartender	Customer and Bartender

Physical Evidence: Tables, chairs, glassware, menus, wall decorations, etc.

Line of Visibility to Customers:　　　　　　　　　FRONTSTAGE

　　　　　　　　　　　　　　　　　　　　　　　　BACKSTAGE

Physical Evidence: Storage areas, refrigerators, kegs, kitchen equipment, trash cans.

Key Activities: Selecting, stocking, and repurchasing materials; scheduling employees; etc.

© Cengage Learning

The greater the **complexity** of the service, the greater the number of steps in its service blueprint.

The greater the **divergence** of the service, the greater the amount of flexibility or variability involved in any particular step in the service blueprint.

Further examination of the blueprint shows that the pub service involves a low level of complexity. **Complexity** refers to the number of steps involved in the service performance and subsequently depicted in the service blueprint. The figure also demonstrates some divergence in the pub's service delivery. **Divergence** refers to the amount of flexibility or variability involved in any particular step of the service performance. Any service process may be described in these two terms (Shostack 1987). Our pub example possesses few steps and only a small measure of variability (steps 3 and 4). In contrast, consider what a blueprint of the service provided by an upscale hotel such as the Ritz-Carlton might look like!

The visual and holistic representations of service performance contained in a blueprint assist services marketers in several ways. Besides performing a function similar to a service script, a service blueprint gives employees a clear picture of the overall service and in doing so may help define the importance of workers' roles in the overall service performance. Further, a blueprint may help an organization improve its service by directing attention to steps that should be altered, added, or deleted. As an example, Lia Patrício (2006) developed blueprinting techniques for analyzing and prototyping financial services for a Portuguese bank. Service blueprints are thus indispensable tools for planning an organization's service performance.

THE INTERNET AND SERVICE PERFORMANCES

The Internet revolutionized the service industry with the introduction of new services, online versions of existing services, and Internet-based services to organizations whose core product is not a service. Ranging from retailing to information services, entirely new services have cropped up. Consider the "apps" industry spawned by the introduction of Apple's iPhone. Want to discover or learn more about your family genealogy? Visit Ancestry.com **(http://www.ancestry.com)** or OneGreatFamily.com **(http://www.onegreatfamily.com).** Just about any service that involves information processing has an online version. Organizations such as Amazon.com and eBay **(http://www.ebay.com)** are examples of organizations that perform their services via the Internet only. Other service organizations have felt the need to add to their brick-and-mortar presence with online services. For retailers such as L.L. Bean **(http://www.llbean.com)** or Lands' End **(http://www.landsend.com),** online services provide a powerful way to present their electronic catalogs to people. They still mail catalogs and deliver products via a packaged goods delivery organization such as UPS **(http://www.ups.com)** or FedEx **(http://www.fedex.com).** For other organizations, such as Barnes & Noble, online services provide a necessary addition to their retail outlet. When the core product is physical, organizations can use the Internet to add services to supplement their offering in the form of product information, customer service, billing and payment, and so on. Just as brick-and-mortar service providers can be scripted and blueprinted, Internet services can be scripted and blueprinted in planning and producing the service performance.

THE EMOTIONAL SIDE OF SERVICES

The various frameworks discussed in chapter 2 bring attention to the components of the service encounter in different ways, yet implicit in each is the realization that services involve people—people as customers or employees, people who interact with each other, and people who are affected by their surroundings. It is not surprising, then, that organizations must consider the emotional aspects of behavior in their design and implementation of service. Customers' and workers' service experiences can be positive or negative depending upon the emotions that are displayed or evoked during an encounter. Cordial employees, pleasant surroundings, and congenial fellow customers may all contribute to a patron's good feelings about a service and to a worker's job satisfaction. Consider your last visit to the mall or grocery store and how those various elements left you feeling. In Chapter 5, we explore the emotional impact of the service setting. In Chapter 6, we examine the role that service workers play in fashioning customer feelings. In Chapter 7, we delve into the emotional consequences of customer-to-customer interaction.

Summary and Conclusion

Service performances involve many details and activities that are difficult for the casual observer to detect. Even careful scrutiny of a service performance is unlikely to uncover its complicated nature entirely because many aspects of service performances occur backstage and away from the customer's view. Given this fact and other characteristics of services, we can view services as similar to a theatrical performance. In order for an organization to deliver excellent service performance, it must understand the concept of performances in general. For instance, performances can be scripted in terms of their frontstage enactment and blueprinted in terms of their overall production.

Sometimes performances may be customized to meet the particular needs, wants, or preferences of the audience. To produce a superior service experience, organizations often find it necessary to supplement their basic service performance with new and different elements. When planning a service performance, organizations should consider scripting/blueprinting, customization, and supplementary service elements. Scripting and blueprinting provide direction regarding essential service aspects. Customization can increase customer satisfaction with the performance. Supplementary service elements can keep an organization competitive by enhancing and differentiating the core product.

Exercises

1. a. Carefully think about your service experience in the services marketing classroom. Take 10 minutes to list as many factors as you can that affect that experience. Compare your list with the lists of other class members. Create a list that accurately identifies factors affecting students' services marketing classroom experience. Determine which of those factors are (i) most obvious, (ii) least obvious, and (iii) most likely to be the result of backstage activities.

   b. Consider the service encounter that occurs when you visit a bank to cash a check. Based on your knowledge of that encounter, develop a service script, simple blueprint, and a list of the three most important steps in terms of customer satisfaction.

2. Using some of the costs and benefits of customizing a service as broadly presented in this chapter together with your own observations, develop a list and short explanation of three benefits and three potential costs associated with customizing home delivery of your local newspaper by delivering it at a time specified by the customer. Would such a modification be reasonable? Why or why not?

3. Think of a hotel where you have recently stayed or a hotel in your area. Develop a list of the supplementary services it offers. Rank these services in terms of importance. Which of them if not provided might affect your decision to stay there? Which do you consider unnecessary extras?

Internet Exercise

Pick two competing online service companies such as priceline.com and expedia.com.

1. Draw blueprints of both service performances.
2. How are the two competitors differentiated as reflected in your blueprint?
3. What opportunities might you consider to further differentiate the two services if you were one of them?
4. What backstage operations must be in place to make your suggested changes work?

References

Berry, Leonard L., Kathleen Seiders, and Dhruv Grewal (2002), "Understanding Service Convenience," *Journal of Marketing*, 66 (3), 1–17.

Daly, Aidan (2004), "Let's Improvise!" in *QUIS9—Service Excellence in Management: Interdisciplinary Contributions*, Bo Edvardsson, Anders Gustafsson, Stephen W. Brown, and Robert Johnston, eds., Karlstad, Sweden: Karlstad University Press, 7–15.

Grove, Stephen J. and Raymond P. Fisk (1983), "The Dramaturgy of Service Exchange: An Analytical Framework for Services Marketing," in *Emerging Perspectives on Services Marketing*, Leonard L. Berry, G. Lynn Shostack, and Gregory D. Upah, eds., Chicago: American Marketing Association, 45–49.

Grove, Stephen J., Raymond P. Fisk, and Mary Jo Bitner (1992), "Dramatizing the Service Experience: A Managerial Approach," in *Advances in Services Marketing, and Management: Research and Practice*, vol. 1, Teresa A. Swartz, David E. Bowen, and Stephen W. Brown, eds., Greenwich, CT: JAI Press, 91–121.

Grove, Stephen J., Raymond P. Fisk, and Joby John (2000), "Services as Theater: Guidelines and Implications," in *Handbook of Services Marketing and Management*, Teresa A. Swartz and Dawn Iacobucci, eds., Thousand Oaks, CA: Sage Publications, 21–36.

Gummesson, Evert and Jane Kingman-Brundage (1991), *Quality Management in Services*, Paul Kunst and

Jos Lemmink, eds., Assen/Maastricht, Netherlands: Van Gorcum.

Levitt, Theodore (1981), "Marketing Intangible Products and Product Intangibles," *Harvard Business Review*, 59 (May–June), 94–102.

Lovelock, Christopher H. (1994), *Product Plus: How Product 1 Service 5 Competitive Advantage*, New York: McGraw-Hill.

Lovelock, Christopher H. and Jochen Wirtz (2007), *Services Marketing: People, Technology, Strategy*, 6th ed., Upper Saddle River, NJ: Prentice Hall.

Patrício, Lia Raquel (2006), "Enhancing Service Delivery Systems Through Technology," doctoral dissertation, Universidade do Porto, Porto, Portugal.

Shostack, G. Lynn (1984), "Designing Services That Deliver," *Harvard Business Review*, 62 (January–February), 133–139.

Shostack, G. Lynn (1987), "Service Positioning Through Structural Change," *Journal of Marketing*, 51 (January), 34–43.

Shostack, G. Lynn and Jane Kingman-Brundage (1991), "How to Design a Service," in *The AMA Handbook for Marketing for the Service Industries*, C. A. Congram and M. L. Friedman, eds., New York: AMACOM, 243–252.

CHAPTER 5
Designing the Service Setting

You have probably noticed the interior decor and ambiance of service establishments you have visited. Consider the atmosphere created at the Louvre (**http://www.louvre.fr**). What does the architecture of a former medieval fortress, the palace of the kings of France, contribute to the ambiance of this two-century-old museum? What do the ultramodern glass pyramids designed by I. M. Pei do for the 800-year-old Louvre building? These various aspects of the Louvre's physical setting probably received careful consideration before they were chosen. The meanings they convey had to be consistent with the mission of the museum and attractive to visitors to this world-famous museum. This chapter presents several important observations and ideas regarding the design of a service setting. The chapter has four specific objectives:

- **To examine the various features of a service setting**
- **To discuss the key considerations involved in designing the service setting**
- **To explain the role of the service setting as an aspect of marketing a service**
- **To discuss e-servicescapes as a service setting**

Perhaps the world's most famous and most successful service setting is America's Disney World (**http://www.disney.com**) in Orlando, Florida. Every morning, thousands of people spill out of cars and buses and scurry into the carefully maintained premises of Disney World. Founder Walt Disney created Disney World as an expansion of his first theme park, Disneyland, in California. The grander size of the Disney World property offered the opportunity to control the visitors' experience from the moment they leave the highway and enter the Disney grounds. Every aspect of the Disney World service setting is carefully designed and maintained to maximize the customer experience.

From the beginning, the Walt Disney Company viewed its theme parks as entertainment to be staged in much the same way as its cartoons and movies. An important aspect of this perspective is the company's careful attention to the frontstage impact of everything its customers experience. Although the backstage activities that support the frontstage performance are also stressed, Disney ensures that all backstage activities remain out of sight to enhance the effectiveness of the frontstage performance. It would not be good, after all, for a small child to see Mickey Mouse carrying his head. The company applies its entertainment philosophy to everything it does—even Disney stores are designed to entertain people who come to shop. The stores address such details as planning sight lines to accommodate the height of a typical three-year-old. In addition, the stores have a purpose beyond simply selling Disney merchandise: they are designed to create favorable impressions of the Walt Disney Company, which executives believe will translate into greater numbers of patrons at its movies and theme parks.

WHAT IS A SERVICE SETTING?

A **service setting**, sometimes called a **servicescape**, includes all aspects of the physical environment in which the service provider and customer interact (Bitner 1992). The service setting has a significant impact on the process of service delivery and customers' perceptions of the service. In many ways, a service setting is like the packaging for a physical good. It can facilitate or hinder the use of the product and can serve an important communication function. Specifically, the service setting design can affect the movement and interaction between customers and workers. In addition, the scenery, equipment, decor, and other physical cues may help customers form an impression of an organization and its service offering. In the words of Shostack (1977, p. 78), the "setting can play an enormous role in influencing the 'reality' of a service in the consumer's mind."

> A **service setting**, sometimes called a **servicescape**, includes all aspects of the physical environment in which the service provider and customer interact.

Marketers have long recognized the potential importance of the physical environment for defining and facilitating the service exchange. Among the setting's features that influence the character of a service are the colors or brightness of the surroundings, the volume and pitch of sounds, the scents or aromas, freshness and temperature of the air, the use of space, the style and comfort of the furnishings, the environment's design and cleanliness, and a host of other *atmospherics* (Kotler 1973). All of these represent tangible cues that help determine a service's reality. Consider the various elements that constitute such service settings as a movie theater, an opera hall, a gambling casino, a hospital, a hotel, an airport, a shopping mall, or a university.

Service settings create the all-important first impression for customers. They set the tone for the entire service experience. In the absence of previous knowledge concerning a service establishment, a servicescape can help customers determine what to expect from the service organization. Consider walking into a new or unfamiliar restaurant for the first time. Its decor and other atmospheric features may help you to surmise the type of food served, the possible price range, the potential level of staff attentiveness, and so on. Further, the openness of the design, the arrangement of the tables, the placement of the decorative items, and even the choice of the various types of restaurant equipment may influence the process of service delivery.

So far, we have referred to service settings as physical surroundings where customers and employees engage in various service-related activities. This discussion suggests that customers are in the *service factory*. We can extend the same concept to include other types of settings: (1) *postalspace*—for mail-order services; (2) *telespace*—for long-distance telephone service; or (3) *cyberspace*—for online services. Although the interaction between customer and provider in these service environments occurs at arm's length, the settings themselves are controlled by the service organization and may be designed with the customer in mind.

KEY CONSIDERATIONS IN DESIGNING THE SERVICE SETTING

From a marketing perspective, numerous considerations affect the design of a successful service environment. The following is a discussion of some of the more important issues to be considered when designing a service setting.

The Duration of the Service Setting

A service organization's physical setting becomes more significant when the customer spends substantial time in the environment, as during hospitalization, vacation stays at hotels, or airline flights. Longer contact with the service environment amplifies the potential effect of the setting's features. The customer has a greater opportunity to be impressed by the setting's attractiveness and ambiance or upset by its shortcomings and discomfort. The feeling and function of the hotel, hospital room, airline seat, or physician's waiting area (all places in which the customer may spend an extended amount of time) receive more use and more evaluation when the experience lasts longer. In fact, environmental aspects that might normally be overlooked (e.g., an unpleasant aroma in the air, constant faucet drips, a tear in the seat fabric) may take on much greater importance when the customer confronts them over a long period. The air may become stifling, the drip may become torturously annoying, or the tear may become a gaping cavern of discomfort. Further, customers are likely to be exposed to a larger array of setting elements the longer they remain in the service environment. Organizations must pay particular attention to the service setting's communicative and operational aspects when contact with the service environment is prolonged.

Service Setting as an Operational Tool

The service setting design also plays an important role in determining service efficiency. If the service setting is properly designed, it lowers operational costs and expedites the process of service delivery. The layout of the servicescape and its equipment can enhance or hinder service delivery. A cluttered setting or one that relies on outdated equipment can prevent workers from moving about with ease and can impede their task performance. In contrast, a well-equipped setting designed with the workers' roles in mind can greatly improve an organization's service productivity.

Service Setting as a Service Identifier

The setting design also increases in importance when it helps differentiate a service. For example, although they represent the same generic services, Novotel (**http://www.novotel.com**) and Sheraton Hotels (**http://www.starwoodhotels .com/sheraton**) or McDonald's (**http://www.mcdonalds.com**) and Hard Rock Cafe (**http://www.hardrockcafe.com**) each generate widely differing perceptions, partly by their distinctive setting characteristics. The design of each servicescape creates markedly different offerings for these service organizations. In some instances, a service's setting represents its chief means of distinguishing itself and becomes the most important element in the organization's services marketing mix.

Consider the case of the Hard Rock Cafe or the Planet Hollywood restaurants **(http://www.planethollywood.com).** Although each establishment pays close attention to other aspects of its marketing effort, their respective physical environments (resplendent with artifacts and exhibits from the rock-and-roll and motion picture industries) are key features of the establishments. The significance of service settings increases when targeting an intended market segment, as is often the case for retail stores, restaurants, or hotels. In such cases, the setting provides cues designed to attract and appeal to a specific type of audience. The Hard Rock Cafe's environment is designed to target a specific segment of the casual dining market, one quite different, for instance, from New York's Harley-Davidson Café **(http://www.harley-davidsoncafe.com).** The latter is a popular restaurant that showcases more than ninety years of the motorcycle manufacturer's history in this service setting. In short, the design of a service organization's physical setting can be an effective positioning tool. Spotlight 5.1 illustrates how the setting can be a service identifier.

Service Setting as an Orientation Tool

The design of service settings can facilitate or hinder the customer's understanding of the service process. If the service delivery system is a novel one, an open design emphasis will allow customers to observe the process of service delivery as they move through the system. Fuddruckers **(http://www.fuddruckers.com)**, a chain of hamburger restaurants throughout the United States and other countries, is a good example. The service script at Fuddruckers incorporates several distinctive aspects, such as allowing customers to participate in the service production process by "dressing" their own sandwiches at a well-stocked condiment bar. First-time visitors to Fuddruckers might be confused about the proper sequence of service events if not for the spacious and open design of the restaurants' physical environment. New customers can observe and learn the service process while in line.

=== **SPOTLIGHT 5.1** ===

Minimundus—Die Kleine Welt am Wörthersee (The Little World on Lake Worth)

Minimundus (**http://www.minimundus.at/en/**) is a tourist park of miniature buildings from around the world. It was built in 1958 in Klagenfurt, Austria, near Lake Worth. The park covers six acres (26,000 square meters) that is landscaped to be compatible with the many clusters of building exhibits. Parts of the park resemble a tropical rain forest, a desert, mountains, a lake, a river, a canal, and an ocean. Such a shrunken world creates a rather surreal service landscape. Adult tourists and even children stroll like giants around the park.

Each Minimundus building is reproduced in 1:25 scale. To make the models look more realistic, Minimundus staff use original materials (marble, sandstone, basalt, etc.). Building a new model can take

months of painstaking work. More than 150 building models are exhibited. They include the Eiffel Tower from France, the Taj Mahal from India, the Tower of London, the Sagrada Familia from Spain, the Statue of Liberty from the United States, the Neuschwanstein Castle from Germany, Vatican City, and the Sydney Opera.

The Minimundus park also features working models of ships, trains, and even a space shuttle that blasts off every hour. A new children's exploration trail was opened in 2009. It includes an "adventure playground," where children can sail on a play boat, ride elephants, or build sand castles.

Source: Minimundus.at (2012), **http://www.minimundus.at/en/** (accessed September 10, 2012).

FIGURE 5.1 A Typical Grocery Store Layout

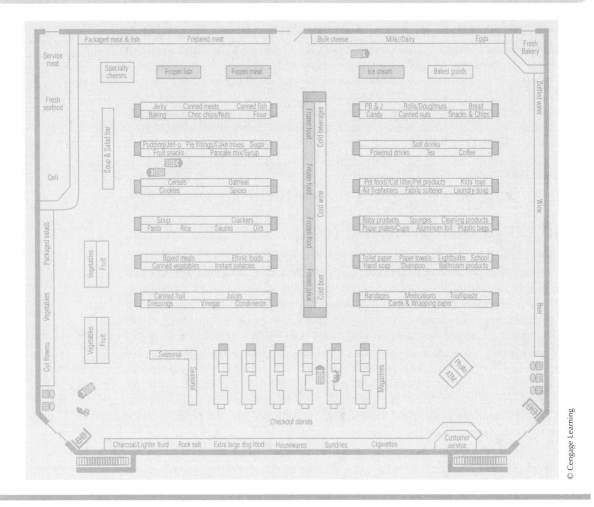

© Cengage Learning

Organizations that market new service concepts are wise to rely upon various physical cues to communicate information about their service offerings (see Figure 5.1). Effective signage is critical in such circumstances. When the service setting is complex, sprawling, or confusing, well-placed signs or maps providing clear directions prevent customer frustration or disorientation. Mass transit systems such as the London Underground **(http://www.tfl.gov.uk/)** or the cruise ship of Carnival Cruise Line **(http://www.carnival.com)** require effective orientation signage. In some cases, it may also help to augment signage with audio or visual aids, such as announcements over public loudspeakers and brochures. For instance, beyond the many signs and directional devices placed throughout the physical environment of Amsterdam's Schiphol Airport **(http://www.schiphol.nl/index_en.html)**, the establishment provides visitors with a mini-brochure in many languages that clearly depicts its servicescape (see Figure 5.1). The map becomes a handy reference tool to help the airline passenger navigate the airport's complex service setting.

The Appeal of the Service Setting

Most service organizations whose customers spend significant time in their physical setting must plan a functionally and aesthetically appealing environment. However, service organizations must remember that the setting characteristics that attract one type of customer may repel another. An **approach environment** is a setting in which the customer feels comfortable and wants to spend time, whereas an **avoidance environment** is a setting that the customer finds undesirable and uninviting (Mehrabian and Russell 1974). For instance, customers seeking excitement and stimulation in a vacation destination would find a sedate and tranquil servicescape unappealing. Such customers are more likely to consider a Club Med **(http://www.clubmed.com)** destination as an approach environment. Interestingly, any particular customer may find the same service setting to be an approach environment in one circumstance and an avoidance environment in another. For example, an exciting nightclub might be an attractive environment for a couple who want to party with friends but a noisy nuisance when the same two people want to spend private time with each other. Spotlight 5.2 describes a music performance venue with a very appealing service setting for musicians and their fans.

An **approach environment** is a setting in which the customer feels comfortable and wants to spend time, whereas an **avoidance environment** is a setting that the customer finds undesirable and uninviting.

Service organizations cannot design their settings to be all things to all people. They can, however, identify and study a desirable market segment for their particular service offering, as well as develop an array of environmental features to transform their physical setting into an approach environment for that targeted group. Paradoxical as it seems, an organization may want to incorporate some aspects of an avoidance environment (or ignore certain approach characteristics) even as it attempts to attract customers to its place of business. For example, services that rely upon a relatively high rate of customer traffic to generate revenue may not want customers to become too comfortable in their servicescapes. Fast-food restaurants, for instance, often adorn their establishments with hard plastic seating, bright lights, and loud colors, which are likely to discourage patrons from lingering too long. The trick is to balance features that bring customers into the service establishment and make them feel at ease, while at the same time prompting them to spend only as much time there as necessary.

Service Setting as the Workers' "Home Away from Home"

A design consideration often overlooked is that the service setting is also the workers' *home away from home*. Delta Air Lines **(http://www.delta.com)** actually uses this metaphor when training its flight crews by urging staff to think of the airplane as their home when entertaining guests. The amount of time customers spend in a service environment may vary depending upon the service delivered, but the service workers normally spend much more time in that same environment. Consequently, background music, lighting, décor, and other aspects of the servicescape that may appeal to the occasional customer may eventually become annoying features that seriously hinder workers' performance. For instance, the dim lights that customers find romantic in a restaurant can make it difficult for the wait staff to perform its tasks. Similarly, song selections that may please patrons when heard once can overwhelm workers who must listen to the same songs day after day. Many retail employees develop an unbridled disdain for Christmas carols played incessantly during the holiday season.

=== **SPOTLIGHT 5.2** ===

Blue Rock Studio: A Special Venue for Live Music

 In the Texas Hill Country, high atop a ridge overlooking the Blanco River and a very large flat rock in the river known as Blue Rock, sits the Blue Rock Studio (**http://www.bluerocktexas.com).** It is a recording studio and the home of Billy and Dodee Crockett. Once a month, the Crocketts open their home to provide a live music performance venue as a benefit to a singer/songwriter they love. To understand what is different about the physical environment of Blue Rock Studio requires comparing it to more typical music performance spaces.

Live music venues around the world are often quite large or rather small. Sports arenas are often places where the most famous music bands perform, like U2 or the Rolling Stones. Such massive arenas are popular, but often have poor sound quality, and audiences only have a distant relationship with performers. A Jumbotron display helps but is little better than a big screen TV at home. At the other extreme are the honkytonks and dive bars where aspiring musicians sing while the audience talks and drinks. Blue Rock Studio offers a special music venue that is very different from the extremes of massive or dismal venues.

The Crocketts built their house and recording studio with the intent of staging live performances in it, too. Their large home is the centerpiece of nineteen acres of land that includes guesthouses, a swimming pool, and walking trails. The middle of the house contains a performance hall, which holds a little more than a hundred people. During the performance, there is no talking and no drinking alcohol, just undivided attention on the performer. The monthly concert series is announced on the Blue Rock Web site, and tickets are reserved two months in advance. Most events sell out quickly; in less than an hour for extremely popular performers. Regular attendees know that the Blue Rock looks and feels like going to a good friend's house to hear a live music performance.

Singer/songwriters are the focus of the monthly concert series. Texas has many successful singer/songwriters. Many of them have performed at Blue Rock, such as Sam Baker, Shawn Colvin, Joe Ely, Ruthie Foster, Eliza Gilkyson, Butch Hancock, and

---

Organizations should pay careful attention to creating a service environment that balances the needs of the customer with the needs of the worker. In short, the service setting should be comfortable for the workers and facilitate their ability to perform their appointed tasks as well as appeal to the service customers.

THE SERVICE SETTING AS A MARKETING TOOL

Any service organization can use its physical environment as a marketing tool. Despite the service setting's potential impact on audience perceptions of an organization, few organizations base their service design decisions on significant customer input. This oversight is unfortunate; the service setting may be the services marketing mix variable that best creates the organization's image. Many organizations that have researched customers' preferences have successfully distinguished themselves through their physical setting. For example, Westin Hotels (**http://www.starwoodhotels.com/westin)** introduced its Heavenly Bed (a pillow-top mattress, down blanket, five pillows, and three sheets) as a way of appealing to today's more sophisticated travelers (McCann 2000).

Overall, service settings can accomplish a variety of marketing goals, such as communicating a new concept, repositioning an organization in the eyes of its target market, or attracting new market segments. Some movie theaters, for example, have begun to offer a distinctive service by developing specially designed settings that attract specific market segments. Likewise, many airlines have set themselves

Jimmy La Fave. Many legendary singer/songwriters have performed, too, including Christopher Cross, Jimmy Webb, and Jesse Winchester. Most of these musicians perform acoustically with only minor accompaniment. Every performance is audio and video recorded for the musicians. Musicians rave about the audience, the acoustics, the comfortable setting, and the wonderful hospitality they receive from the Blue Rock staff.

Here's what visitors to Blue Rock Studios experience. The studio is in a remote part of the Texas Hill Country, not too far from Austin, Texas. Attendees have to wend their way along several country roads as they twist and turn deeper into the hills. Upon arrival, they park among the cypress trees and walk down the hill to the house.

A line forms in the front, regular attendees greet each other, and at 7 P.M., the audience is invited inside to claim their seats. There is no assigned seating, so attendees place their tickets on the chairs they select. All the chairs face the small stage, which is positioned in front of a large stone fireplace. Each month, Dodee Crockett decorates the stage with

different visual props inspired by the theme of each performance. Guests are invited to wander about the house and outdoor areas before the concert begins.

Attendees might have coffee, tea, or a dessert served in the kitchen by very friendly volunteer staff. They might enjoy these snacks sitting on the large outdoor patio and enjoying the scenic views of the blue rock below and the surrounding hills as twilight approaches. Guests might visit the recording studio and watch a video from prior presentations. They can buy CDs by that night's performer, a Blue Rock T-shirt, coffee mug, or the annual *Blue Rock Review*.

The music starts at 7:30. The lights are dimmed and the Crocketts approach the stage to introduce the performer. A hush falls over the audience in anticipation of the show. At the Blue Rock, the carefully planned venue allows the performers and the audience to focus on enjoying the music in an intimate setting.

Source: As experienced by the first author.

apart by developing clubrooms exclusively for members who pay an annual fee to use them. In pursuing marketing goals that rely on the service setting, organizations commonly focus their attention upon three broad issues related to a setting's design: (1) managing tangible evidence, (2) frontstage versus backstage decisions, and (3) experimenting with the service setting.

Managing Tangible Evidence

A service's physical environment can be its most important tangible aspect. Organizations should therefore strive to ensure that every aspect of the setting makes the desired impression on their customers. They should carefully consider the potential impact of even the smallest physical element. A dirty utensil, burned-out light bulb, or littered parking lot may each seem unimportant when compared to the service performance as a whole, yet each may project a poor image of the overall organization to customers. In contrast, the restroom that is cleaned hourly, the cheerily decorated customer waiting area, and the uncluttered service representative's desk may help a service provider exude an aura of excellence. Spotlight 5.3 describes how many service organizations manage the tangible evidence of their restrooms.

In the quest to manage tangible evidence, service organizations should first determine the specific image desired (e.g., modern or traditional, upbeat or serene) and then select the appropriate equipment and furnishings to reflect that impression. It may help to think of these elements as props in the staging of

════════ **SPOTLIGHT 5.3** ════════

Rooms with Thrones Are Service Settings

It is time to plunge into the difficult topic of public toilets as service settings. The patrons of service organizations often need to use public facilities for their bodily functions. However, public toilets are rarely pleasant experiences. They often look and smell bad. Nonetheless, not all public toilets are unpleasant experiences.

Cintas Corporation (**http://www.cintas.com**) sponsors an annual "America's Best Restrooms" Contest (**http://www.bestrestroom.com/us/sponsor .asp**). Cintas provides a wide range of specialized services to businesses, which includes restroom supplies. The company's contest Web site lists winners since 2002, including the 2011 winner, The Field Museum in Chicago. In 2012, there were ten finalists, including three restaurants, two arenas, an art center, a nightclub, a hotel, a grocery store, and a gas station. The Buc-ee's (**http://www.bucees.com**) in New Braunfels, Texas, was one of the nominees. Billed as the world's largest convenience store, it has 68,000 square feet of space and sixty gas pumps. Its restrooms feature eighty-three toilet stalls and artwork. At Buc-ee's, you can sit on your own throne.

Sources: **http://www.bestrestroom.com/us/sponsor.asp**; **http://www.bucees.com**.

a service performance. In addition to its functional or task-related role in the process of service delivery, each element contributes to the audience's overall perception of the service organization. Whether it is an airline seat, a restaurant booth, or a hotel elevator, the impact of a physical setting feature extends beyond its obvious purpose to include an important communicative aspect that helps customers form an impression of the service.

Any service setting includes many elements that serve as tangible evidence for the customer. Therefore, the elements must work together to create a consistent and focused impression. Selection and maintenance of the different props create a broad picture of the service that can be undermined by a single, inconsistent cue. For instance, a hotel's attempt to position itself as upscale and sophisticated through tasteful décor, meticulous landscape, and carefully selected furnishings could be ruined if customers detect evidence of cutting corners with inferior bedding, cheap lobby fixtures, or frayed carpeting.

By carefully managing its tangible evidence, a bowling alley can be transformed into a cosmic environment through the addition of dimmed lighting, glow-in-the-dark balls and pins, rock music, fog machines, and a disco ball. An outpatient medical facility can become a temporary drive-through flu shot clinic if some of the setting features of fast-food restaurants are added. An aging hotel can be returned to its original grandeur through a complete refurbishment of its physical features. The key is for services marketers to recognize and harness the significant power of the servicescape.

The service worker's appearance, dress, and demeanor are also tangible evidence and merit equally careful consideration. As discussed in the next chapter, these tangible cues may also influence customers' perceptions of the service. Thus, it makes sense for organizations to ponder these aspects of the workers' role when making hiring, training, and professional development decisions. Further, as with other environmental cues, an organization should attempt to ensure that the image generated by its workers matches its overall desired effect or message. Consider the excellent job that the various Disney properties do in this regard and how well their "cast members" contribute to their guests' general perception of the organization.

Frontstage Versus Backstage Decisions

Another broad issue regarding the physical setting involves decisions about the setting's frontstage and backstage. As noted in earlier chapters, the frontstage area of a service setting is always on display to customers, while the backstage is concealed from view. The customer can see all the aspects of a service delivery that occur frontstage, such as the décor, furnishings, and contact personnel. Hence, organizations should place special emphasis on selecting and controlling these elements. If an organization doubts its ability to project a consistent impression with a frontstage feature, it should consider moving that feature backstage away from the customer's view.

The backstage of a service operation is a region separated from the frontstage physically or temporally and is seldom subject to direct customer scrutiny. Much of the planning, organizing, and implementing of the service's delivery occurs here. The apparatus supporting the frontstage performance are found backstage, such as important pieces of equipment, key personnel, and the critical activities necessary for a successful customer experience. Because customers do not see this area, its outward appearance requires less attention. Problems that occur backstage can be corrected without customers knowing that they ever occurred. The backstage is also a refuge for frontstage personnel. The backstage is where workers come to relax, let their hair down, loosen their ties, and recuperate from the demands of being *onstage.* For this reason and the inherently delicate nature of customers' service impressions, it is imperative for organizations to be vigilant in maintaining the boundaries between the two regions. The customer who unwittingly stumbles into the backstage (or is carelessly allowed access to it) runs the risk of destroying the tenuous impression of service excellence. The ability of customers to *suspend disbelief* regarding many aspects of how the service is assembled can be seriously compromised by the sight of an unkempt storage room, dirty kitchen, foul-mouthed manager, or archaic workstations.

In some instances, it may serve an organization well to move some of its backstage activities and equipment frontstage. This approach can be an effective marketing maneuver when some aspects of the service generate considerable customer-perceived risk. For instance, allowing customers to view the mechanics working on their cars might be a good decision, because customers are often unsure of just what they are paying for in automobile repairs or maintenance. In addition to reducing a source of risk, moving a backstage activity to the service's frontstage may add an entertainment feature to the service delivery that becomes an indispensable part of the customers' experience. Benihana **(http://www.benihana.com)** and other Japanese-style steakhouses have forged a special type of restaurant experience by preparing meals in full view of their patrons. Similarly, many automatic car washes occupy the customer's attention and reduce their perception of waiting time by allowing them to view the service through huge picture windows.

A service organization can differentiate itself from its competition by either increasing or decreasing the frontstage of its service delivery system. If attempting the former, it must pay careful attention to the image-generating capacity of those elements not commonly found in the frontstage. The backstage employees, equipment, and activities that are moved into the customer's line of vision are subject to the same type of concerns that normally apply to the frontstage setting. This attention adds a measure of difficulty to managing any service organization that opts for this approach. An organization that wishes to reduce its susceptibility to service delivery problems may be well advised to shrink the frontstage by moving some of the service assembly, service personnel, or setting features to the back region. By doing so, the organization may be better able to control customers' impressions of service excellence.

Experimenting with the Service Setting

Experimenting with the service setting allows managers to try out new setting features on a limited basis before embracing them. Before reengineering the interior design of an airplane, adding or removing physical features of the hospital room, or redecorating the automobile dealership showroom, it is a good idea first to determine the impact that such a change may have upon the service customers, workers, and processes. This evaluation can be accomplished by experimenting with the setting.

One approach to experimenting with the service setting is to introduce the change for a short time (assuming that the alteration does not require a significant restructuring of the physical setting). Asking customers and employees for their opinions can help determine the desirability of the changes. If a service organization maintains several establishments with similar setting configurations, it can choose to explore a change in its servicescape in one location and compare its impact with other baseline service settings. This method also applies to generating makeovers on a grander scale. In essence, organizations that test an environment in this manner before full-scale adoption are creating prototypes of service settings.

The feedback generated from experimenting with a service setting can yield valuable insights regarding possible changes. In some cases, it may even reveal that an alternative that seems desirable isn't worth the cost of instituting changes on a wider scale. Hotel chains such as La Quinta **(http://www.lq.com)** and Marriott **(http://www. marriott.com)** have showcased prototypes of their rooms on large trucks that travel from location to location. Alternatively, they may design laboratory rooms in warehouses where would-be guests can test and evaluate setting innovations.

From a managerial standpoint, experimenting with the service setting is a good idea when the benefits (better customer response, facilitation of workers' efforts, etc.) exceed the costs (e.g., time, money, and effort) of conducting the experiment. It is also important to consider the losses that may be associated with making a poor decision by changing the servicescape unnecessarily or inappropriately. Experimentation is particularly advisable when a significant aspect of service delivery moves from frontstage to backstage, or vice versa. In addition, the greater the change to a service setting, the more an organization gains from experimenting.

E-SERVICESCAPE AS A SERVICE SETTING

An **e-servicescape setting** is any Web site on the Internet. E-servicescape settings are subject to the same concepts that apply to managing the tangible evidence of a conventional service environment.

As we saw in Chapter 3, the Internet spawned numerous online electronic services. For many of these organizations, their Web site is their primary means of interaction with customers. Customers can access such Web sites from any country and at any hour of the day. For example, Amazon.com **(http://www.amazon.com)** has expanded from books to a wide variety of other items. Customers anywhere in the world may *enter* Amazon.com by logging on to the company's Web site and can find their way to various *sections* of the emporium via the menu on its home page. This service organization has an e-servicescape setting.

An **e-servicescape setting** is any Web site on the Internet. E-servicescape settings are subject to the same concepts that apply to managing the tangible evidence of a conventional service environment (Hopkins et al. 2009). The atmospherics of a Web site should be functional and aesthetically appealing. The site should also incorporate the appropriate approach-avoidance features that encourage customers to spend more time shopping at the site. Further, the e-servicescape setting should be designed so that the mechanics of moving through its various pages never cause visitors to become disoriented. Fundamentally, what the customer sees at any Web site is the service's frontstage, and the technology being used should never hinder the customers' service experience. All elements of the backstage, such as the computer program in HTML code, should remain hidden from customer view. In addition, just as customers sometimes windowshop at a bookstore in a mall, e-shoppers may browse a Web site for entertainment and curiosity purposes. To aid e-shoppers, a Web site should have interactive features and response mechanisms that mirror the communications encountered when visiting a store in physical space. Therefore, the type, depth, and presentation of graphics and text must be carefully choreographed and continually tested for effectiveness. After all, the goal is to make e-shoppers feel comfortable, provide them with the necessary facts concerning the array of products, and respond to their needs—exactly the same concerns that a neighborhood grocer or mall merchant might have when dealing with its customers.

E-servicescape Web sites can be measured for their ambient conditions (atmospherics, entertainment value, context, etc.); their spatial layout and functionality (navigability and reliability); and their signs, symbols, and artifacts (content information, text, and graphics). These factors affect a visitor's attitude toward the Web site and his or her purchase intentions (Hopkins et al. 2009). Zeithaml, Parasuraman, and Malhotra (2002) developed e-SQ, a measure of online service quality, which includes such setting-like characteristics as information availability and content, ease of use, and graphic style, among other criteria important to the customer. Clearly, designing e-servicescape service setting is becoming more and more sophisticated.

Summary and Conclusion

A service organization's physical setting is the most controllable of all the elements contributing to the customer's experience. It is therefore important for a service organization to ensure that the setting performs well operationally and symbolically. In this quest, it is also important for the organization to recognize that any decisions regarding the physical environment may impact the service workers as well. By carefully attending to the various considerations and prescriptions offered in this chapter, an organization may discover ways to establish a competitive advantage, facilitate the process of service delivery, or appeal to new or different target audiences. The service setting is an important marketing tool that can attract and delight customers. An organization has a great many ways to achieve this goal through decisions about the physical setting.

Exercises

1. Pick an example of the most impressive service setting that you have experienced.

   a. Describe the service setting features that most impressed you.

   b. Do you think other service organizations could develop similar features for their settings? Why or why not?

2. Think of a restaurant that you like to patronize.

   a. What are your favorite aspects of its service setting?

   b. How could the service setting be improved? (Be specific and realistic in your suggestions, but also creative.)

3. Describe the setting in a service experience where you think the frontstage was poorly designed, maintained, or managed. What were your specific impressions? What improvements would you recommend?

4. Consider the service setting of a hospital, hotel, or retail bank. What features are commonly found in its frontstage? What features are likely to be found backstage? Could some of its frontstage aspects be moved backstage, or vice versa? If so, under what conditions would such a move be desirable?

Internet Exercise

 Pick a Web site that sells goods or services online.

1. Explain the key features of the cyberspace setting.
2. Assess the key features as an operational tool, service identifier, orientation tool, or in terms of their appeal.
3. Describe how the Web page layouts facilitate or hinder the ordering process.
4. What is your overall assessment of the cyberspace setting?

EXPLORE

Visit the companion site for this text at **www .cengagebrain.com** to explore key concepts in the service industry. You will find tools to help you expand your services marketing knowledge, including ACE self-tests, Web links to companies and organizations featured in this chapter, and much more!

References

Bitner, Mary Jo (1992), "Servicescapes: The Impact of Physical Surroundings on Customers and Employees," *Journal of Marketing*, 56 (April), 57–71.

Hopkins, Christopher D., Stephen J. Grove, Mary La Forge, & Mary Anne Raymond (2009), "Designing the E-Servicescape: Implications for Online Retailers," *Journal of Internet Commerce*, 8 (1), 23–43.

Kotler, Philip (1973), "Atmospherics as a Marketing Tool," *Journal of Retailing*, 49 (4), 48–64.

McCann, Jen (2000), "Beds Take Center Stage in Room Design," *Hotel and Motel Management*, 215(19), (November 6), 160–162.

Mehrabian, Albert and James A. Russell (1974), *An Approach to Environmental Psychology*, Cambridge, MA: Massachusetts Institute of Technology.

Shostack, G. Lynn (1977), "Breaking Free from Product Marketing," *Journal of Marketing*, 41 (April), 73–80.

Zeithaml, Valarie A., A. Parasuraman, & Arvind Malhotra (2002), "Service Quality Delivery through Websites: A Critical Review of Extant Knowledge," *Journal of the Academy of Marketing Science*, 30(4), 362–375.

The Louvre Museum (**http://www.louvre.fr**) values its employees, and its employees have played an important role in the attractiveness of the museum. Their presence and manner enhance the visitors' experience at the popular venue and complement the museum's image and status. How many service organizations have you visited where the employees seem bored and unhappy with their work? Why do frontline employees seem disinterested or even rude while serving customers? On the other hand, surely you have been served by pleasant, courteous, and professional frontline employees. What makes the difference? At the Louvre, the employees' behavior seems well coordinated and professional. What Louvre management practices enable the employees to work in this fashion? These issues are covered in this chapter. The chapter has six specific objectives:

- **To analyze why employees are key success factors in service organizations**
- **To demonstrate how and when to empower employees**
- **To consider the need for improvisation**
- **To examine the emotional side of services**
- **To explain the messages companies convey by costuming their employees**
- **To provide an understanding of how to maximize employee productivity**

Greg thought he had planned his trip well by allowing 2 hours to reach the train station from the airport—more than enough time for the thirty-minute shuttle van ride to meet his train. Even if the plane was moderately late, he would have time to spare. Unfortunately for Greg, his flight landed nearly an hour after its scheduled arrival time. Scurrying frantically, Greg made his way to the Jolly Trolly—only to discover that he had narrowly missed the van and the next wouldn't be leaving for twenty minutes! However, as Greg explained the situation to the shuttle dispatcher with desperation in his voice, the unexpected occurred. Noting that he had been in similar binds, the dispatcher summoned a backup van and instructed its driver to take Greg directly to the train station. Thanks to the dispatcher's empathy and quick response, Greg arrived with five minutes to spare. Greg made a mental note to remember the name of the shuttle company, Jolly Trolly, and vowed to tell others of the experience and the great service that was provided.

Contrast Greg's travel experience with that of Cindy's financial planning experience. Cindy entered her financial planner's office ten minutes before her scheduled appointment. The planner's secretary was engrossed in a telephone conversation and glared at Cindy with annoyance when she approached to announce her arrival. The secretary coldly muttered, "Mr. Portfolio will be with you shortly" and returned to her telephone conversation. Cindy pushed aside scattered magazines and newspapers and found a seat on the waiting area couch. Ten minutes turned to twenty, and twenty minutes stretched into thirty. Occasionally, Cindy would attempt to make eye contact with the secretary, hoping that she might help move things along or at least explain and apologize for the delay. When the secretary rose to get herself a cup of coffee, she neglected to offer a cup to Cindy. Although she tried not to eavesdrop, Cindy could not help overhearing the secretary's telephone commentary, which involved sharp criticism of Mr. Portfolio, punctuated with occasional profanity. Finally, weary of the wait and uncomfortable with the conversation she was hearing, Cindy approached the secretary once more to inquire about the delay. The secretary, making no attempt to hide her disdain for yet another interruption, barked at Cindy, "He'll be with you as soon as he can!" and returned to her diversion. Pushed to the edge, Cindy implored, "Do you have any idea when that might be?" Without looking up, the disagreeable secretary sarcastically responded, "How should I know? I only work here." Cindy turned around, left, and never returned.

Both Greg's and Cindy's experiences vividly illustrate the huge impact service personnel have on how customers perceive and respond to a service organization. Greg's encounter with the shuttle company was positive because an employee made the extra effort to solve his problem. Cindy's encounter was extremely negative because an employee failed to treat her with respect. Greg is likely to use the shuttle service in the future and may generate additional business for it by praising its service in conversations with colleagues and friends. Cindy took her business elsewhere and may actively dissuade her friends from consulting Mr. Portfolio, though he may never know why she and other clients have abandoned him.

Although service organizations may attribute long-term success to many elements, often the quality of their service personnel has the greatest impact. The challenge for service organizations is to discover ways to leverage "the people factor", that is using employees to differentiate one's service from the competition (Berry 1988). Understanding the critical role service personnel play in determining an organization's success is a starting point.

SERVICE EMPLOYEES AND THEIR BEHAVIOR

This section discusses why service employees are important, why some employees are more important than others, the differences between employees' technical and social skills, and methods for achieving employee excellence.

Why Are Service Employees So Important?

In earlier chapters, we established that services are often characterized by the inseparability of the service provider from the customer. In the delivery of services such as health care, hospitality, and legal advice, the customer and the service provider must interact in order for the service to occur. For example, it is impossible for a patient to receive medical treatment without interacting with a health care worker or for a customer to receive a haircut without interacting with a hairstylist. In short, many services are processes of interaction between the customer and the service workers.

What makes the personnel aspect of services so noteworthy is that the behaviors and appearance of service workers are open to customer scrutiny. This same concern isn't true for manufactured goods. Customers have no reason to care about the appearance or behavior of the workers who assemble their smartphones. In contrast, the service workers with whom customers interact are integral parts of the service and are significant to their evaluation of it. In much the same way those actors on stage shape the theatrical performance, the service workers' appearance (i.e., their dress, grooming, attractiveness.) and behaviors (i.e., their helpfulness, expertise, courtesy.) affect customers' perception of the service received. Further, because the core of a service can't be seen and the service outcome is sometimes indiscernible, customers often rely on service workers as quality cues. Not surprisingly, organizations that realize this—such as hardware giant Home Depot **(http://www.homedepot.com),** Nordstrom department stores **(http://www.shopnordstrom.com),** and Ritz-Carlton Hotels **(http://www.ritzcarlton.com)**—have differentiated themselves from their competitors by stressing the people factor.

Are All Service Employees Equally Important?

From the customer's point of view, it would be naive to suggest that all service organization employees are equally important. Workers who interact directly with the customer typically have the greatest influence on perceptions of the service. However, service performances are also dependent on the actions of those who labor behind the scenes out of the customers' sight. The airline baggage handler, the restaurant cook, and the hospital pharmacist all enact their roles in the backstage area of their respective service settings. The misrouted suitcase, the undercooked meal, or the incorrectly filled prescription will upset the frontstage performance of their fellow workers and undermine a customer's service experience. The skill with which backstage personnel perform their tasks affects customers' assessment of service excellence, particularly if the staff fails to perform adequately. However, as is the case with those who labor in a conventional factory, the backstage employees' appearance and behaviors are probably of little concern to the customer. While these personal aspects may affect other employees with whom the backstage worker interacts, they are far less significant than they are for the frontstage personnel.

Frontstage employees who link an organization with its customers (Bowen and Schneider 1985) are **boundary spanners;** they represent the service in the customers' eyes. The flight attendant, teacher, nurse, bank teller, waiter, and other frontline employees *are* the service to the customer. Service workers provide human evidence of service quality through both their technical and social skills. **Technical skills** are the proficiency with which service employees perform the tasks associated with their position, for example, how well the hairstylist cuts your hair or how accurately the clerk processes your order; **social skills** are the manner in which service employees interact with customers and fellow workers, for example the level of friendliness, caring and communication the hairstylist or clerk demonstrates. As boundary spanners, service employees' technical and social skills affect

Boundary spanners are the frontstage employees who link an organization with its customers; they represent the service in the customers' eyes.

Technical skills are the proficiency with which service employees perform the tasks associated with their position.

Social skills are the manner in which service employees interact with customers and fellow workers.

customer perceptions of service quality. The inaccurate teller or the grumpy waiter creates negative impressions of the service organization. Conversely, the well-prepared teacher or the congenial flight attendant may evoke positive evaluations.

Which Are More Important: Technical Skills or Social Skills?

From the customer's point of view, *how* a service is performed is often as important as *what* its enactment entails. The perception of service excellence is quite fragile and influenced by many elements. Some aspects of service delivery, such as the worker's social skills, may seem insignificant at first glance yet play a major role in customers' decisions to patronize a service provider again.

Customers cannot always evaluate the technical skills of service personnel, because they lack an adequate understanding of the service's technical complexities. Further, because the technical skills required to perform the service often vary little from one service organization to the next, frontstage personnel's social skills become even more important. A customer might receive the same ticket information, fare quotation, and billing options from two different travel agents—one pleasant and well groomed, the other brusque and disheveled. The customer's service experience and subsequent evaluation are likely to differ based on the social skills of the two agents.

Great social skills by no means compensate for poor technical skills, though. For example, no amount of conviviality on the part of the travel agent is going to offset the customer's ire over an incompetently arranged itinerary. To remind personnel of their role in the organization's service performance, many organizations provide their workers with performance guidelines. These provide direction to workers regarding the technical and social skills they should exhibit. Figure 6.1 displays the guidelines Ritz-Carlton Hotels expects its employees to follow. The guidelines are printed on a laminated card to be carried in an employee's pocket at all times.

Louis Armstrong, the world famous jazz musician, provides an excellent example of the importance of both technical and social skills for fashioning a superior service performance. Armstrong was a trumpet player of great technical skill who is credited with developing many innovations in jazz music. However, Armstrong was equally well known for his exuberant stage personality, which helped popularize jazz music throughout the

---

FIGURE 6.1 Southwest Airlines Mission Statement

The Mission of Southwest Airlines
    is dedication to the highest of Customer Service delivered with a
    sense of warmth, fiendliness, indivdual pride, and Company Spirit.

Southwest Airlines, Co.

world. In short, Armstrong's legendary success and influence on jazz music reflect his combination of great technical and social skills. In a health care application, consider how technical and social skills mingle to create a physician's "bedside manner"—a reflection of empathy, responsiveness, and competency.

Ensuring Service Employee Excellence

Axioms abound extolling the critical role of a service organization's employees ("We're only as good as our workers allow us to be," "Our people are our product"), but these axioms must be backed by action. Finding, training, and motivating personnel who can do an outstanding job of performing the service and representing the organization are a major undertaking. To increase the likelihood that service employees will be excellent performers, organizations should consider four key directives: hire intelligently, train intensively, monitor incessantly, and reward inspirationally.

Hire Intelligently   Personnel are the backbone of most service organizations' success. Successful organizations such as Southwest Airlines **(http://www.southwest.com)** and Nordstrom department stores set high standards for their employees and may screen dozens of applicants before selecting one for a position vacancy. They use multiple interviews and screening devices to determine whether an applicant has what it takes to flourish in their operation. Particular care is given to ascertaining how well an applicant fits into the organization's service culture. Because service delivery is often a team effort, it's important that every team member is committed to the organization's goals. Although applicants for both front-stage *and* backstage positions should be scrutinized, it is imperative to recognize the special conditions surrounding employees who interact with customers. The appearance and demeanor of frontstage employees have an impact on customers' assessment of the service organization just as employees' technical proficiency does. Only those people who can meet the demands of being onstage should be hired for frontstage roles. Moreover, to leverage the people factor, organizations must offer appropriate inducements to attract the best applicants.

Train Intensively   Service organizations should take the time to prepare their workers for the roles they perform. *Double-barreled training* (Davidow and Uttal 1989) that focuses on employees' technical *and* social skills development is necessary. Hotels typically use this approach to train frontline personnel and even medical schools recognize the value of such education (see Spotlight 4.3). Service organizations can make skill development an ongoing process by offering incentives and opportunities for workers to learn and grow in the organization. They can *cross-train* personnel to perform multiple tasks within the organization. Such employee knowledge provides organizations with more flexibility during unexpected worker shortages, and it helps employees appreciate the diversity of roles necessary to stage a successful service performance. More important, as noted earlier, organizations must avoid putting underprepared personnel in

===== **SPOTLIGHT 6.1** =====

Soft Skills to the Rescue

 In many positions within the service sector, particularly those positions that put the employee in contact with the customers, something more than job-specific technical skills are needed. What service organizations desire are a set of **soft skills** from their workers that lead to strong interaction with customers and relationship building. While any job-seeker is likely to have many desirable soft skills to some degree, the good news is that anyone with weaknesses in the area of soft skills can improve them with effective training. What soft skills do service organizations desire? Likely to be found among are such attributes as communication capability (listening, written, verbal), a strong work ethic and positive attitude, flexibility/adaptability, interpersonal and team player abilities, time management skills, problem solving capability, self-confidence, the capacity to accept and learn from criticism and multicultural sensitivity. When an organization's employees possess competencies such as these, the likelihood of interaction that results in a superior customer experience increases greatly!

Source: Randall S. Hansen and Katharine Hansen (2011), "What Do Employers *Really* Want? Top Skills and Values Employers Seek from Job-Seekers," **http://www.quintcareers.com** (accessed August 8, 2011); Lorenz, Kate (2009), "The Top 10 Soft Skills for Job Hunters," **http://jobs.aol.com/2009/01/26** (accessed August 8, 2011).

the field to interact with customers. A service worker who displays a sullen or surly side can destroy the service performance. Training that involves nurturing workers' soft skills (see Spotlight 6.1) helps organizations prevent such occurrences and equips employees with methods of meeting the public in a positive manner.

Monitor Incessantly   Continual assessment of service workers' performance should be conducted using both formal and informal means of gathering information regarding their behavior. Customer comment cards and "management by wandering around" provide a good start. However, superior organizations augment these methods with other approaches such as *mystery shopping* (using researchers posing as customers to assess the quality of the service the employee delivers), surveys of customers regarding specific transactions, and even peer evaluations. Utilizing information technology to provide customers an easy and simple means to provide feedback via e-mail, Web sites, and various social media could also be valuable. The key is to use multiple sources of information to evaluate the workers' social and technical skills. Such information can identify employees who need to sharpen their abilities or those employees whose performances deserve special recognition for excellence.

Reward Inspirationally   It is important to provide positive feedback to frontstage and backstage service employees who turn in excellent performances. Rewarding desirable behaviors motivates workers and increases the likelihood that those behaviors will occur again. The opportunity for rewards also serves as a powerful insulator against worker defection. Rewards may be monetary (e.g., pay increases or bonuses) or nonmonetary (e.g., special recognition or career advancement opportunities), or some combination of both. Spotlight 6.2 discusses some means that are used to motivate employees in the service sector that do not require great sums of money. To be truly motivating, the rewards

---

SPOTLIGHT 6.2

Keeping the Workforce Energized at a Low Cost

Many organizations in the service sector face the constant difficulty of keeping their workforce energized, particularly those is many high-contact positions such as waitstaff, clerks, and the like. Low pay and challenging work conditions, coupled with ample employment opportunities in competing organizations when the economy is doing well, provide fertile ground for increased worker disenchantment. Workers' efforts can suffer or worse—they can seek employment elsewhere; the grass is always greener over the hill, right? Each time a worker leaves, it costs the service firm money to recruit, hire, and train a replacement, and a reduction in efficiency comes with an inexperienced new worker. Meanwhile, deteriorating worker performance can have deleterious effects on customer satisfaction. What can organizations do to demonstrate appreciation to their workers as a means of keeping them around and motivating them to excel? There are various ways to appreciate workers that are not directly linked to financial costs absorbed by the firm in the form of monetary bonuses, salary raises, and the like. Methods include providing praise and recognition for outstanding work (it's simple, cost-free, and effective), allowing top performers to occasionally set their own work schedules, rewarding excellent performance with a bonus day off, providing employees a discount on the service you provide, offering training and advancement opportunities, and—if feasible—access to desired parking spaces. In difficult economic times or whenever a firm is strapped financially, implementing efforts such as these have the potential to increase employee satisfaction and motivation.

Source: Elizabeth Murray and Robyn Rusignuolo (2010), "Rewarding Outstanding Performance: Don't Break the Bank—Some of the Most Effective Methods of Rewarding Outstanding Performers Involve Little or No Money," *Franchising World*, (January 1), **http://www.thefreelibrary .com** (accessed August 23, 2011).

---

must be meaningful from the worker's point of view. Insignificant rewards have no motivational value. Service firms should offer the types of rewards that inspire positive behavior. Various prominent service organizations, such as Ritz-Carlton Hotels and the Scandinavian airline SAS **(http://www.flysas.com),** have successfully implemented reward systems that connect with their employees.

Addressing Employee Poor Performance

Of course, it is also important to provide feedback to workers when their performance has failed to live up to desired standards as identified through the monitoring activity discussed earlier. If monitoring employee performance uncovers repeated poor performance, the service organization faces an uncomfortable situation. Whether the employee's tasks are carried out frontstage or backstage, a poor performance is never acceptable. When a poor performance occurs in full view of the customer frontstage, it is intolerable. Workers who fail to exhibit good technical or social skills in their roles should be given the opportunity to "reinvent" themselves through further training or development. Different motivational tools might be considered as well. If they are frontstage employees, they should be removed from contact with customers, if possible, until the problem is corrected; after all, their poor performance is likely to create a negative impression of the service organization. In the same vein, the frontstage worker who can't or won't be retrained should probably be reassigned to a back region service position or, as harsh as it may sound, be dismissed to avoid destroying the customers' perception of service excellence.

EMPOWERING SERVICE EMPLOYEES

To leverage the people factor, many service organizations have empowered their employees by giving them the authority to respond immediately to customer needs. Organizations such as FedEx **(http://www.fedex.com)**, Ritz-Carlton Hotels, and Nordstrom department stores are well known for having cheerful, energetic, and motivated employees. Their success is often attributed to the fact that their workers have the *responsibility* and the *authority* to satisfy customers. In a sense, their workers are given a stake in the organization's success.

> **Empowerment** is the management practice of sharing information, rewards, knowledge, and power with frontline service employees so that they can better respond to customers' needs and expectations.

Empowerment is the management practice of sharing information, rewards, knowledge, and power with frontline service employees so that they can better respond to customers' needs and expectations (Bowen and Lawler 1992, 1995). Employees with access to these critical elements can customize their interactions with customers to better meet their needs or wants. However, as Bowen and Lawler (1992) have argued, not every organization profits from empowering employees. The benefits and costs of empowerment must be carefully weighed (Chan and Lam 2011).

Benefits of Empowerment

Empowerment can offer several important positive outcomes to the service organization and its customers (Bowen and Lawler 1992). Among them are quicker responses to customer needs, quicker responses to dissatisfied customers, greater employee satisfaction, greater employee enthusiasm, more creative employee input, and increased employee and customer loyalty.

Quicker Responses to Customer Needs During Service Delivery   Empowered service employees need not ask management for permission to help customers. Upon identifying a customer's need, an employee can quickly take the action that serves the customer best. Such a response helps to improve customers' perception of service excellence. An empowered response is precisely what the shuttle dispatcher did for Greg in the example discussed at the beginning of this chapter.

Quicker Responses to Dissatisfied Customers During Service Recovery
When mistakes are made, empowered service employees can take rapid action to remedy the problem. A speedy response may be particularly helpful in reducing a customer's frustration and anger over service failure. Rather than making the customer wait to receive satisfaction—perhaps fueling further disdain—the customer's ire can be addressed immediately. A quick response may even communicate how important the customer is to the service organization.

Employees Are More Satisfied with Their Jobs and Themselves   Granting service employees more control over their job performance can improve their level of job satisfaction and enhance their self-esteem. The decision latitude that comes with empowerment can make employees feel they have a greater stake in the organization's well-being. Instead of simply having a minor part in the service production, the empowered employee is conscious of playing a significant role in the overall service performance.

Employees Will Act More Warmly and Enthusiastically with Customers
Satisfied and empowered service employees are likely to provide more attentive customer care. Further, their improved attitudes lead to improved quality in their customer interactions. Empowered employees are more approachable and more willing to field special requests. They no longer tolerate customers as necessary nuisances, but truly welcome them as clients or guests.

Empowered Employees Are a Great Source of Ideas   Empowered service employees are often quick to suggest new ideas for service improvement to management because they have a greater sense of ownership in the organization. They often occupy a boundary-spanning position, which makes them a particularly good source of ideas regarding customer treatment or ways of addressing service delivery more effectively or efficiently.

Great Word-of-Mouth Communication and Retention   The superior service made possible by empowering employees can also create superior customer word-of-mouth communication as well as increase the likelihood that customers will remain loyal to the organization. The customer who receives excellent service from an empowered employee often shares that experience with others and is likely to form a stronger bond to the service organization in response to the great service he or she received. After all, when empowerment is exercised, the organization has treated that customer as a special guest!

Costs of Empowerment

The benefits of empowerment are certainly attractive, but turning frontline service employees loose has several potential drawbacks. Among the various costs of empowerment (Bowen and Lawler 1992) are greater monetary investment in selection and training, higher labor costs, slower or less consistent service delivery, possible violations of fair play, and giveaways and bad decisions.

Greater Monetary Investment in Selection and Training   The demands placed on empowered service employees are significantly greater than those placed on employees who follow a rigid script. Hence, it takes more effort to select and train empowered workers. Such effort translates into higher costs for employee recruitment and training. It is more expensive to locate and develop empowered employees, because they must be capable of a much wider range of behaviors. On the other hand, placing workers in positions where they meet the public without adequate knowledge of how to exercise their new problem-solving authority could be disastrous.

Higher Labor Costs   The higher cost of training service employees to make the correct decisions when empowered may prevent an organization from using part-time workers who may also be with an organization for only a short term. Instead, organizations may need to recruit more full-time employees, who are generally paid more as well as provided with better benefit packages. In addition, empowered workers probably command higher wages, because they are generally better qualified and better trained than their non-empowered counterparts.

Slower or Less Consistent Service Delivery   Employees who exercise their empowerment are likely to spend more time with each customer and/or may be inconsistent in the way they serve some patrons. Customers not requiring special attention sometimes wait while the empowered employee satisfies another patron's request. Worse yet, empowered employees may manifest their authority in widely differing ways. Hence, service delivery efficiency may be compromised and uneven responses to customer problems may ensue.

Possible Violations of Fair Play   Customers who observe an empowered service employee giving other customers special treatment may perceive such treatment as unfair if they are not accorded the same attention. The result can be dissension among customers and dissatisfaction with the organization that has treated them poorly by comparison. Ironically, what is done to please one customer may displease another.

Giveaways and Bad Decisions   Finally, empowered service employees may make ill-advised decisions or go beyond reasonable standards to satisfy customers. In extreme cases, incidents of "service sweethearting" that involve frontline employees giving unauthorized free or discounted services or goods can occur (Brady, Voorhees, and Brusc 2012). Careful training, monitoring, and experience can reduce the risk of giveaways and bad decisions, but they cannot eliminate the possibility of it altogether. Keeping records of occasions when empowered decisions result in customer accommodation may help reduce the likelihood of bad decisions. Nevertheless, some costs associated with unnecessary or excessive acts of empowerment are inevitable.

The question of whether to empower service employees is a function of several contingencies (Bowen and Lawler 1992). In general, empowerment makes sense for service organizations that adopt customized service as a business strategy and stress the development of long-term relationships with customers as a goal. Empowerment is also well suited to organizations supported by complex technology and operating in a complicated business environment—conditions that make empowering workers attractive. Empowerment is also more feasible if an organization is populated by managers and employees with strong interpersonal skills and high growth needs. Service organizations that do not meet these criteria are probably best served by retaining a production-line approach to service delivery, one that tends to treat all customers alike and does not require employees to have much problem-solving expertise. Four-star hotels, accounting firms, and investment banks are examples of service organizations that should opt for employee empowerment; fast-food operators and dry cleaners are likely to be better off with a production-line approach.

As an aside, the decision to empower frontline service employees requires midlevel managers to learn to share some of their authority with those beneath them on the organizational chart. Much of the typical managerial decision making transfers to the rank-and-file worker in an empowered organization. This circumstance is not always agreeable to those surrendering some of their authority. Hence, the effort to make workers comfortable and adept at empowerment must also address the concerns of those who will manage the empowered employees. Moreover, some employees may not be good candidates for empowerment (Cattaneo and Chapman 2010) or may not wish to be empowered due to a perceived increase in their workload (Chan and Lam 2011). Having the responsibility and the authority to satisfy customers may be a frightening proposition to some people!

THE NEED FOR SERVICE IMPROVISATION

Improvisation is closely related to the concept of empowerment. Empowered service workers are often encouraged to improvise in their service tasks; in other words, they are given the freedom to creatively adapt to various service situations in the effort to provide a superior experience to the customer. Improvisation is likely to be more important in some service circumstances than others. For instance, services such as financial advice, education, the performing arts, and repair services require workers who can adapt to the different situations that arise in the process of service delivery. Many restaurants and even chains such as Denny's **(http://www.dennys.com)** and Romano's Macaroni Grill **(www.macaronigrill.com)** attempt to provide a better customer experience by training staff to read and adapt to diners' body language, eye contact and offhand remarks (Nassauer 2012). To help understand the nature of improvisation, organizations might consider looking to theater or jazz music for guidance on how to prepare for and implement improvisation successfully. Techniques imparted by theatrical improvisation provide service workers with skills in reading and responding to customers' cues (Daly 2010), while lessons from jazz improvisation provide valuable guidance on coordinating a team effort among a service's ensemble (John, Grove, and Fisk 2007). Spotlight 6.3 discusses an application of the Stanislavsky method of training actors as a means of developing service workers' improvisation abilities.

SPOTLIGHT 6.3

What Service Organizations Can Learn from Stanislavsky

 Konstantin Stanislavsky (1863–1938) is generally considered the founder of the modern, realistic approach to acting, and it has been argued that many of the tenets underlying his method of training actors are applicable for developing service employees' frontstage skills. Critical to the Stanislavsky method is the actor's ability to live a particular part on stage, not unlike the requisite of service organizations for workers who are dedicated to the role of serving the customer. With a focus upon mental and physical relaxation that helps actors concentrate on their creative state, Stanislavsky's approach seems particularly helpful in honing service workers' improvisation abilities. By emphasizing the importance of and imparting skills regarding accepting one's role in the overall performance, relaxation techniques, concentration and observation abilities, voice and body expression, emotional recall, ensemble playing and the like, the Stanislavsky method has the potential to develop service employee's capacity to read and respond to customers' needs in an empathetic and genuine manner. Although time and energy are needed to fully develop an actor's or service employee's ability via the Stanislavsky approach, the payoff in terms of a proficient and credible performance is achieved. The method seems particularly relevant for services that require personalization and customization, are high priced, often unpredictable, and frequented by discerning customers. Corporate banking, exclusive hotels or restaurants, and various forms of professional services are likely candidates.

Source: Stephen J. Grove, Raymond P. Fisk, and Mary C. La Forge (2004), "Developing the Impression Management Skills of the Service Worker," *The Services Industries Journal,* 24 (2), 1–14. Reproduced by permission of Taylor & Francis LLC.

THE EMOTIONAL SIDE OF SERVICES

Services often rely heavily on their workers to help fashion perceptions of service quality. Often, it is an organization's frontline workers who are responsible for creating a positive response for its service and, ultimately, a superior customer experience (c.f., Schneider et al. 2002), particularly in those services that require improvisation and customization to accommodate customers' needs or wants. Ideally, customers in those circumstances will be impressed with the workers' friendliness, concern and manner and their general affective character. It is a significant role that service personnel play in service delivery and requires that workers display a cheerful disposition, genuine concern, and unrelenting care toward the customer—even when their true feelings may be quite the opposite. Essentially, service employee emotions—positive and negative—have a contagion effect that influences customers' emotional responses (Du, Fan, and Feng 2011). The demands of manifesting positive "emotional labor" (Hochschild 1983) can be stressful and mentally challenging. Anyone who has dealt with customers for very long has probably found it difficult to feign a smile in response to an annoying patron or refrain from a "wisecrack" to an unreasonable request. While the payoff of customer satisfaction is certainly a desirable outcome of emotional labor (Hennig-Thurau et al. 2006), organizations should ensure that their employees are not overburdened or under supported in that quest. Some have suggested that service management should strive to create a service climate that is conducive to a positive customer experience via employees' emotional labor; that is, organizations should develop "emotional intelligence (EI)" (Kidwell et al. 2011) by hiring, training, and managing workers whose interaction with customers creates a favorable emotional response. Such responsibility can take a toll on frontline service workers. Organizations should manage their people policies accordingly.

COSTUMING SERVICE EMPLOYEES

An essential decision for many service businesses is whether to costume their employees. Costumes, or rather uniforms, are the equivalent of packaging the service employee. According to Solomon (1985), costuming employees offers the following four advantages: providing evidence, sending a message, reducing risk, and ensuring consistency.

- **Providing evidence.** The customers of service organizations have fewer tangible cues of a product's excellence to evaluate than do the consumers of physical goods. Uniforms offer an organization the opportunity to add a measure of tangibility to their service. The style, colors, and various accessories associated with a uniform can become an important form of physical evidence. Consider the evidence provided by the uniforms adorning the frontline personnel of McDonald's **(http://www.mcdonalds.com)**, UPS **(http://www.ups.com)**, and Singapore Airlines **(http://www.singaporeair.com)**.

- **Sending a message.** Uniforms can send a message to service customers by projecting a desired image based on their design. Employee dress can communicate that the organization and its services are formal or informal, traditional or modern, upbeat or sedate, novel or predictable. As such, service workers' uniforms may be an important positioning tool for service organizations.

- **Reducing risk.** Uniforms may also help the service delivery process for an organization by making its employees more identifiable to customers. When a customer needs to locate an employee in the service setting, the task is easier if the employee is wearing a uniform. In addition, the uniforms help reduce customers' perceived risk by implying a cohesive group structure among the employees and sense of organizational purpose.

- **Ensuring consistency.** Another function of uniforms is to make the appearance of service employees more consistent. Donning similar styles, colors, or patterns helps to evoke a perception of stability and reliability. A common style of dress among workers may even facilitate a perception of more consistent employee performance.

At first glance, it would appear that the many advantages of using uniforms make it easy to decide to costume the service workforce. However, some potential drawbacks can emerge. One is that uniforms may undermine workers' individuality or sense of self. In addition, some workers may find wearing a uniform day after day too restrictive and resent not being able to use their dress as a means of self-expression. Further, regardless of the style of uniform, such organizational mandates may appear rigid. Organizations must assess the psychological and financial costs associated with using uniforms versus the benefits uniforms might provide. Finally, the uniform must be congruent with the overall image that the organization is attempting to portray through its other forms of physical evidence, such as physical setting and marketing communications.

Employee dress codes are a related decision. Service organizations that don't require employee uniforms are sometimes confronted with problems when employees dress in ways that their managers consider unsuitable. No organization can afford to take an "anything goes" approach. However, two contrasting positions have been taken by different service organizations.

The Walt Disney Company is well known for its detailed dress code. Both men and women employees are given precise instructions on acceptable dress. The dress code specifies hair length and acceptable cosmetics and jewelry. The code also prohibits facial hair for men (although Walt himself wore a mustache). The company's purpose in creating this dress code was to ensure that employees convey an "all-American" look. Predictably, this dress code caused some problems for Disneyland Paris **(http://www.disneylandparis.com).** The style of dress and grooming that seemed reasonable in the United States (and even in Japan) was unpopular with employees from European cultural backgrounds. Ultimately, Disney found it necessary to accommodate its European employees by modifying the dress code for Europe.

At the other end of the spectrum is the dress code of Carl Sewell of Sewell Cadillac in Dallas, Texas. Sewell believes in keeping his dress code simple. His only rule is "Be tasteful." He also urges his employees to ask themselves, "Would I want my picture to appear in tomorrow's paper, given what I am wearing now?" (Sewell and Brown 2009). Sewell has used this simple dress code successfully for many years.

MAXIMIZING SERVICE EMPLOYEE PRODUCTIVITY

Among the critical decisions made about service employees, none is more important than spurring them to perform their tasks with excellence. This complex matter often occurs in many service organizations where many employee positions can be unappealing, poorly compensated, and mostly unappreciated. Against this backdrop, service employees can easily fall short of giving their tasks the amount of attention that management would like. All workers have an opportunity to exercise discretionary effort (Berry 1988) in fulfilling any assignment, and they often fail to give it their all. **Discretionary effort** is the difference between the maximum effort one can bring to a task and the minimum effort needed simply to get by (see Figure 6.2). The challenge for service organizations is to motivate their employees to operate at the maximum end of the discretionary effort scale.

> **Discretionary effort** is the difference between the maximum effort one can bring to a task and the minimum effort needed simply to get by.

As services marketing scholar Len Berry (1988) points out, performing at the maximum end of the discretionary effort scale requires employees both *willing* and *able* to discharge their responsibilities. Falling short on either count will create problems for the service organization (see Figure 6.3). Workers who are able but unwilling run the risk of alienating customers or being viewed as malcontents. Those willing but unable will be condemned as incompetent. If an employee is both unwilling and unable to perform required duties, the organization faces a serious predicament. In contrast, when an organization's workers labor at the maximum end of the

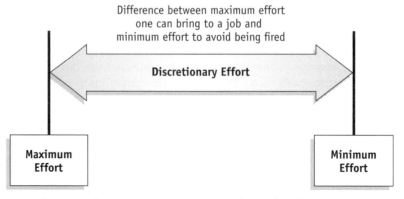

F I G U R E   6 . 2   Discretionary Effort

Difference between maximum effort
one can bring to a job and
minimum effort to avoid being fired

Discretionary Effort

| Maximum Effort | Minimum Effort |

Source: Based on Leonard Berry (1988), "How to Improve the Quality of Service" (audiotape presentation), Chicago: Teach 'Em, Inc.

FIGURE 6.3 Service Worker Profile

Willingness

	High	Low
Ability High	Ideal Worker	Needs Motivation
Ability Low	Needs Training	Major Problem

Source: Based on Leonard Berry (1988), "How to Improve the Quality of Service" (audiotape presentation), Chicago: Teach 'Em, Inc.

---

discretionary effort scale, its customers will seldom hear employees muttering, "I don't know," "I only work here," or "That's not my department!" Instead, they are likely to provide customer attention that is destined to delight.

The concept of discretionary effort has obvious implications. To leverage the potential advantage that employees represent, the service organization must pay great attention to ensuring and sustaining employee excellence. It is not enough simply to recruit and develop good workers; their excellence must be continually encouraged. Unfortunately, the front-desk clerk, flight attendant, or hospital orderly that starts out by giving the job maximum effort may ultimately slip in performance over time. The day-to-day grind associated with the demands of many service positions can have that effect. Luckily, addressing issues discussed earlier in this chapter that deal with hiring, training, monitoring, and rewarding service employees can help promote and maintain the maximum effort so desired by service organizations.

Workers' productivity can be improved in other ways, too. For instance, service organizations can benefit greatly from instituting a program of internal marketing (Berry 1981; Grönroos 1981, 2007; Stauss 1995). **Internal marketing** is the policy of treating employees as internal customers of the service organization, responding to employees' needs or wants, and promoting the organization and its policies to the employee. This approach recognizes that employees are internal customers who can be attracted to or alienated from their job and their company depending upon how well the organization markets to them. Successful internal marketing means discovering employee needs, designing jobs with their preferences in mind, and promoting the organization to them. Happy employees are more productive, less likely to quit, go above and beyond when performing their tasks and attract others who are just as committed to the job (Spreitzer and Porath 2012). A first step in marketing to an organization' internal customers is to consider what

> **Internal marketing** is the policy of treating employees as internal customers of the service organization, responding to employees' needs or wants, and promoting the organization and its policies to the employee.

makes a job attractive to the employee. Beyond a high salary, other job characteristics such as a pleasant work environment, gain-sharing programs, flexibility in work times or benefit packages, good colleagues, respectful treatment from management, empowerment, and a host of other factors may be important. To attract and maintain a workforce that provides excellent service, an organization should consider creating an employment experience that attends to several of these characteristics. Inherent in any internal marketing effort is the realization that, like external customers, an organization's internal customers are a diverse group and are likely to have diverse wants or preferences that should be considered if possible. Well-implemented internal marketing can create a bond between the employee and the service organization that will encourage workers to perform their tasks at the maximum end of the discretionary effort scale. Hence, internal marketing is a potentially effective means of motivating service personnel. Spotlight 6.4 underscores the notion that not all workers in an organization have the same needs (woof).

To maximize employee productivity further, service organizations should consider ways to harness technology to facilitate workers' performance of their appointed tasks. Developing better ways of doing repetitive or unchallenging tasks, or simplifying complex ones through new equipment or procedures, can make the workers' jobs easier. At the same time, supporting service personnel with the appropriate technology can ensure a more satisfying experience for the customer. Consider the important role that touch-screen software on cash registers and computer terminals has played in expediting the process of service delivery, the accuracy of ordering and billing, and the attractiveness of the clerk's position across a variety of service applications (e.g., hotels, restaurants, catalog retailing). The ease of using such technology makes service employees more likely to perform their tasks well and, ultimately, apply maximum discretionary effort. It also increases the likelihood that customers will be served quickly and with few hassles.

SPOTLIGHT 6.4

This Service Goes to the Dogs

The Charleston, South Carolina, and Dover, Delaware, Air Force Bases are among many airfields that have resorted to a new tactic to solve a difficult problem. Plagued by throngs of herons, egrets, and gulls at Charleston and snow geese at Dover, which were causing costly damage to military planes, the installations secured the services of Flyaway Farm and Kennels (**http://www.flyawaybash .com**)—an organization dedicated to the humane handling of such nuisances. Flyaway Farm and Kennels provide trained border collies to patrol the premises and scare off the birds that have found refuge from the expanding suburbs in the drainage ditches and tall grass of the air fields. The specially trained border collies, with their black and white coloring, resemble predators that are a natural threat to the birds, such as wolves and coyotes. Their mere appearance sends a message to the winged troublemakers that the airbase is unsafe and a strong motivation to nest elsewhere. The result is a drastic reduction of the bird population on the air fields' grounds and fewer collisions between the birds and the airplanes. Flyaway Farm and Kennels has successfully provided similar services to public airports, golf courses, and other venues. Clearly, not all service "workers" are people!

Source: **http://www.flyawaybash.com** (accessed September 8, 2011).

Summary and Conclusion

Across many service industries, different organizations offer essentially the same core product. One significant way service organizations can differentiate themselves from their competitors is through their personnel. Because customers equate the workers who serve them with the service itself, the performances of frontstage personnel (supported by the efforts of their backstage counterparts) are critical to customers' perceptions of excellence. Hence, service organizations should devote significant efforts to hiring the best people, training them well, monitoring their behaviors, and rewarding them nicely. In that effort, specific attention goes to decisions regarding such diverse issues as empowering workers, creating a dress code, and practicing internal marketing. The need for improvisation and the ramifications of emotional labor should also be considered. Ultimately, to employ the people factor effectively, service organizations must understand that the additional costs associated with motivating employees to operate at the maximum end of the discretionary effort scale are worth the payoff: customer delight.

Exercises

1. Identify a local service organization known for empowered employees. Investigate how its training program allows employee empowerment.
2. Analyze the training you or a friend received in a current service job.
   a. What were its strengths?
   b. What were its weaknesses?
3. During the next week, pick a two-day period and count the number of service workers you encounter who are wearing a costume or uniform. List the organizations they represent and briefly describe the uniform.
   a. Did managers in these organizations wear observable uniforms as well?

b. Do you think it is a good idea for managers to wear uniforms? Why or why not?
4. Describe a recent service encounter in which the service personnel exhibited maximum discretionary effort. Now describe an encounter that reflected a minimum effort. What was your feeling toward the organization and its employee(s) in each circumstance?
5. Find an organization in your community that you believe is practicing internal marketing. How do its internal marketing activities benefit the customer? Specifically, which of its marketing practices target its internal customers?

Internet Exercise

 Using the Internet, investigate the practice of employee empowerment.

1. Why are employees a key factor in service organizations?
2. What skills should service employees possess?
3. When should employees be empowered?
4. Should empowered employees wear costumes?

References

Berry, Leonard L. (1988), "How to Improve the Quality of Service" (audiotape presentation), Chicago: Teach 'Em, Inc.

Berry, Leonard L. (1981), "The Employee as Customer," *Journal of Retail Banking*, 3 (1), 33–40.

Bowen, David E. and Edward E. Lawler (1992), "The Empowerment of Service Workers: What, Why, How, and When," *Sloan Management Review*, 33 (Spring), 31–39.

Bowen, David E. and Edward E. Lawler (1995), "Empowering Service Employees," *Sloan Management Review*, 36 (Summer), 73–84.

Bowen, David E. and Benjamin Schneider (1985), " Boundary-Spanning-Role Employees and the Service Encounter: Some Guidelines for Management and Research," in *The Service Encounter: Managing Employee/ Customer Interaction in Service Businesses*, John A. Czepiel, Michael R. Solomon, and Carol F. Surprenant, eds., Lexington, MA: Lexington Books, 127–148.

Brady, Michael K., Clay M. Voorhees, and Michael J. Brusco (2012), "Service Sweethearting: Its Antecedents and Customer Consequences," *Journal of Marketing*, 76 (2), 81–98.

Cattaneo, Lauren Bennett and Aliya Chapman (2010), "The Process of Empowerment: A Model for Use in Research and Practice," *American Psychologist*, 65 (7), 645–659.

Chan, Kimmy Wa and Wing Lam (2011), "The Trade-Off of Servicing Empowerment on Employees' Service Performance: Examining the Underlying Motivation and Workload Mechanisms," *Journal of the Academy of Marketing Science*, 39 (4), 609–628.

Daly, Aidan (2010), "The Efficacy of Improvisation Training for Businesses to Business Services," presentation at AMA Frontiers in Services Conference, Karlstad, Sweden.

Davidow, William H. and Bro Uttal (1989), *Total Customer Service*, New York: Harper & Row.

Du Jiangang, Xiucheng Fan, and Tianjun Feng (2011), "Multiple Emotional Contagions in Service Encounters," *Journal of the Academy of Marketing Science*, 39 (3), 449–466.

Grönroos, Christian (1981), "Internal Marketing—An Integral Part of Marketing Theory," in *Marketing of Services*, James H. Donnelly and William R. George, eds., Chicago: American Marketing Association, 236–238.

Grönroos, Christian (2007), *Service Management and Marketing: Customer Management in Service Competition*, 3rd ed., Chichester, England: John Wiley & Sons, Ltd.

Hennig-Thurau, Thorsten, Markus Groth, Michael Paul, and Dwayne D. Gremler (2006), "Are All Smiles Created Equal? How Emotional Contagion and Emotional Labor Affect Service Relationships," *Journal of Marketing*, 70 (3), 58–73.

Hochschild, Arlie (1983), *The Managed Heart*, Berkeley, CA: University of California Press.

John, Joby, Stephen J. Grove, and Raymond P. Fisk (2007), "Improvisations and Service Performances: Lessons from Jazz," *Managing Service Quality*, 16 (3), 247–268.

Kidwell, Blair, David M. Hardesty, Brian R. Muthra, and Shibin Sheng (2011), "Emotional Intelligence in Marketing Exchanges," *Journal of Marketing*, 75 (1), 78–95.

Nassauer, Sarah (2012), "How Waiters Read Your Table," *Wall Street Journal*, (February 22), D1.

Ritzcarlton.com (2007), http://corporate.ritzcarlton.com/en/About/GoldStandards.htm (accessed on February 23, 2007).

Schneider, Benjamin, David E. Bowen, Mark G. Ehrhart, and Karen M. Holcombe (2002), "The Climate for Service: Evolution of a Construct," in *Handbook of Organizational Culture and Climate*, N. M. Ashkanasy, C. P. M. Wilderom, and M. F. Peterson, eds., Thousand Oaks, CA: Sage Publications, 21–36.

Sewell, Carl and Paul B. Brown (2009), *Customers for Life* (Kindle Edition), New York: Random House Digital.

Solomon, Michael R. (1985), "Packaging the Service Provider," *Service Industries Journal*, 5 (March), 64–72.

Spreitzer, Gretchen and Christine Porath (2012), "Creating Sustainable Performance," *Harvard Business Review*, 91 (January/February), 92–99.

Stauss, Bernd (1995), "Internal Services: Classification and Quality Management," *International Journal of Service Industry Management*, 6 (2), 62–78.

The Louvre (**http://www.louvre.fr**) attracts museum patrons from all over the world. Managing these visitors requires careful attention to the customer mix, especially because of the different cultures, languages, and customs that they bring with them when they come to the venue. This chapter is about managing the customers' role in a service interaction. The chapter has five specific objectives:

- To examine the role of customers and their behavior in the service delivery process
- To study the impact of customer-to-customer interactions in service settings
- To identify the nature of customer-to-employee interactions in service settings
- To present strategies for selecting and training customers to reduce customer problems and to improve the service experience
- To examine the difficult circumstances that can lead to customer rage

Ron and Jon are "customers from hell." Maybe you know them. The two friends delight in tormenting the staff at the service establishments they patronize. Ron likes to pretend he cannot hear them. He gives them blank stares when they ask questions. Then, when he does respond, Ron makes outrageous requests. Jon prefers to torment the staff with inane questions or pester them with comments about how they could be doing their jobs better. Together, the two friends make life miserable for any unfortunate service worker they encounter. What would you do if you were a fellow customer witnessing such abusive behavior? Would you ignore it or would you complain to management? Moreover, how would you handle the situation if you were an employee serving such rude customers? Would you politely tolerate such torment or would you tell Ron and Jon off? Finally, what course of action would you take if you owned a service establishment that Ron and Jon were plaguing? Would you tell your service workers to just keep smiling or would you ask Ron and Jon to leave? The answers to these questions are not easily determined and points to the dilemma that employees and management sometimes face when serving customers.

SERVICE CUSTOMERS AND THEIR BEHAVIOR

Anyone who has worked in the frontstage of a service organization has heard the adage "The customer is always right" and knows the adage is not always true. A customer may lack the ability to use the service correctly or have difficulty getting along with other customers. Sometimes a patron enters a service establishment expecting quite different service from what the organization actually delivers. Invariably, that customer will be disappointed. Consider the case of a passenger who expects full-service treatment on a discount airline such as Southwest Airlines **(http://www.southwest.com).** At other times, customers may be unable to participate in the co-production of the service because they don't understand their role in the process. Disorganized or unprepared patrons often undermine the efforts of tax advisers, wilderness guides, financial consultants, and other service providers. And some customers have difficulty getting along with the service staff or other customers, perhaps because too many customers are present or because the mix of customers is not right. And some customers are just downright belligerent or disagreeable—the proverbial *customers from hell.*

To ensure satisfying service experiences for all their patrons, service organizations must address several issues related to customers. Organizations must take care to attract those customers for whom the service design is intended. Careful targeting through promotions, pricing, and other marketing tools can lure the correct segment to a service and reduce the likelihood of disappointment on the part of customers who should never have entered the service system. Service organizations should educate the customer regarding how he or she can best enjoy the service. Marketing communications, such as advertisements, brochures, and signage, must provide customers with the information they need to partici-

> The **customer mix** refers to the array of people of differing ages, genders, socioeconomic backgrounds, knowledge or experience, ethnicity, and so on, who patronize a service organization.

pate in the service correctly. Finally, service organizations need to develop a plan for managing their customer mix in the service setting. The **customer mix** refers to the array of people of differing ages, genders, socioeconomic backgrounds, knowledge or experience, ethnicity, and so on, who patronize a service organization. Service organizations need to develop policies and response repertoires for handling the occasional difficulties that occur when serving numerous types of customers simultaneously.

Few human problems are more significant than the problem of *getting along* with other people. Social conflict manifests itself in many ways—as political disagreement, marital discord, human rights violations, wars among nations, and various other types of divisive strife. The interests of the individual, the social unit, and society are at stake when people fail to get along; few social situations are free from that risk. Those marketing a service are not exempt from this circumstance. Beyond the necessary cooperation between service provider and patron, the service experience often involves multiple customers whose presence may influence one another. Ultimately, fellow customers may affect a person's service experience, positively or negatively. As described in Spotlight 7.1, mastering the delicate balance between too few and too many controls is an essential aspect of excellent customer management.

Our discussion so far has focused on the potentially negative influences of disruptive service customers. Customers can produce a variety of positive influences on other patrons, too. In general, friendly and helpful customers can contribute greatly to their fellow patrons' service experience. They can make visiting or using the service establishment a pleasant event. Nonetheless, it is possible for customers to be *too* friendly or *too* helpful. Perhaps you have had the experience of waiting in the checkout line at a grocery store and being delayed while an excessively friendly customer holds up the line by chatting with the cashier. One of the authors has a relative with the seemingly magical ability to make new friends everywhere he goes. Fellow store patrons unfortunate enough to become his prey often are hard-pressed to escape his conversational stranglehold.

SPOTLIGHT 7.1

Mardi Gras: New Orleans Knows How to *Laissez le Bon Temps Rouler*

 The city of New Orleans, Louisiana, is famous for its annual Mardi Gras celebrations that bring millions of tourists from all over the world to the "world's greatest free party." In many ways, the Cajun slogan *"Laissez le bon temps rouler"* (meaning "Let the good times roll") summarizes the city's approach to coping with rowdy Mardi Gras crowds. The task of managing the potentially volatile mix of revelers falls to the New Orleans Police Department. The New Orleans police have earned an enviable reputation for managing the throngs of people with minimal difficulties. Police carefully monitor each of the fifty-plus major parades that accompany the several weeks of Mardi Gras festivities. This process involves police on foot, on horseback, and in cars that follow along the parade route. Plainclothes police officers are also used. Part of the police force's success is due to careful training to ensure that minor problems don't escalate into dangerous conflicts.

As each parade "rolls" through the streets of New Orleans, masked riders throw tons of free baubles to the screaming crowds. Public drinking of alcohol occurs during the parades. In addition, some maskers are known to encourage women to expose their breasts in exchange for beads. Despite these potentially explosive sidelights, the parades roll year after year with virtually no problems. At the end of each parade, an army of maintenance crews and equipment sweeps, scoops, and flushes the streets of the city in preparation for yet another Carnival celebration on the next night.

Helpless grocery clerks ensnared in conversation with him soon find a line of irate customers forming. Even normal customer behaviors can be perceived negatively by some people or in some contexts. As we see in the next section, human behavior is so complex that different customers ascribe different meanings to the same experience.

CUSTOMER-TO-CUSTOMER INTERACTIONS

Other customers who are present at a service encounter can positively or negatively affect a customer's evaluation of the service. That notion is visually depicted in the Servuction Framework that appears in Chapter 2. The presence and behavior of other customers influences the organization's service quality and may have a more profound impact on customers' experience than contact with service personnel. Spotlight 7.2 shows the results of a survey on what airline travelers dread about their fellow passengers who may be seatmates. Sometimes those sharing the service environment have different needs or preferences. Consider a shared service setting such as a railroad car where one passenger wishes to open the window and another wants to keep it closed. Such a situation can cause dissatisfaction with the organization's efforts to manage conflicts between customers because a conflict is likely to occur. As another example, tourists from countries where smoking in public is heavily restricted may find it difficult to adjust to the norms of nations that allow smoking in public places. The reverse is true, too. Those who are used to smoking in public may find rules prohibiting smoking bothersome and difficult to understand and obey.

Regardless of their behaviors, the sheer number of customers sharing a setting may affect service experiences. A crowded servicescape may result in

SPOTLIGHT 7.2

Seatmates from Hell

 Have you ever booked an airline reservation, motored to the airport, stood in line at the security check-in, boarded the aircraft, and finally plopped down into your seat, only to find a seatmate from hell parked next to you? The challenge of enduring a flight lasting hours while sitting next to some folks can be daunting. What type of fellow passenger do fliers hate to sit next to the most? A survey of passengers revealed, by percentage, the following lineup as the most dreaded seatmates:

- People with bad breath and body odor (19%)
- Wailing babies (15%)

- Hyperactive children (13%)
- "Big-bodied" people (12%)
- Sneezers and sniffers (10%)
- "Rowdy stag/hen" parties (10%)
- "Armrest occupiers" (8%)

Also mentioned were shoeless passengers, drunkards, and loud talkers. Flying these days can be difficult enough without encountering a seatmate from hell!

Source: Gallagher, Noel (2009), "Fellow Passengers with Bad Breath and BO Have Been Voted the Worst People to Sit Next to in Skyscanner's Most Recent Poll," **http://www .skyscanner.net.**

short tempers and insensitivity to others, or in services such as comedy shows or spectator sports, the presence of a large crowd may enhance the service experience by creating excitement and stimulating audience participation (Lovelock and Wirtz 2011).

Despite the practical importance of customer-to-customer interactions, few studies have explored the effect of other customers on an individual's service experience and perception of the service organization. Researchers have largely ignored the potential influence of such interactions on how customers assess an organization's service quality. Several scientifically developed surveys of service quality, such as SERVQUAL (Parasuraman, Berry, and Zeithaml 1991, 1993; Parasuraman, Zeithaml, and Berry 1988) and SERVPERF (Cronin and Taylor 1992) fail to explicitly address the interaction among customers as a factor affecting quality evaluation. Among the scant research findings on this topic is the discovery that customer density and perceived crowding in a service setting have a significant impact on customers' emotional and behavioral responses toward the service (Hui and Bateson 1991). In addition, research has determined that for a customer who encounters other customers who are unruly or potentially disruptive, the manner in which the service employees react to that situation affects the initial customer's evaluation of the service organization (Bitner, Booms, and Tetreault 1990).

In another study that investigated the impact of Florida tourists on other visitors to tourist attractions, it was discovered that customers could sometimes enhance or detract from one another's satisfaction with a service organization (Grove and Fisk 1997). The tourists' comments indicated that fellow customers had a broad impact on one's service experience with both positive and negative effects. In sum, (1) customers often influenced one another, (2) other patrons were just as likely to enrich a service experience as to diminish it, and (3) the impact others had could be attributed to their sociability or responses to group norms. In particular, others' expressions of concern or hostility and verbal or physical behaviors while sharing the service setting led to satisfying or dissatisfying customer-to-customer relationships.

CUSTOMER-TO-EMPLOYEE INTERACTIONS

Interactions between service customers and employees can be equally delicate. Chapter 6 examined the employee side of these interactions. This section explores the customer's side of customer-to-employee interactions. In particular, we address three categories of customer interactions with employees: (1) friendly, (2) unfriendly, and (3) too friendly.

Friendly Interactions

Friendly interactions between the customer and the employee result in the optimal service organization situation. Positive interplay between service patron and provider is most likely to lead to a successful interaction. For example, when an exchange between patient and physician is cordial, both patient and doctor are apt to be more satisfied with a service encounter in the practitioner's office. Open communication and cooperation between the two will probably follow, increasing the likelihood of mutual satisfaction with the service provided. In services where the customer is an important co-producer of the service received, friendliness toward the personnel can help fashion a better service experience for all of those involved.

Unfriendly Interactions

Unfriendly interactions have negative effects on service experiences. Often they arise from misunderstandings about the customer's role versus that of the employees. Sometimes discord occurs because one customer has inadvertently hit the other's "hot button" with an inappropriate comment, misguided gesture, or some other offensive behavior. A customer's sour or grumpy mood may also even trigger unfriendly interactions. In short, any incidence of unfriendly interactions can jeopardize the effectiveness of a service organization. Since customers don't work for the service organization, it's not possible to force them to behave in a benevolent manner. An unfortunate consequence is the service job quickly becomes less attractive for a worker who must regularly accommodate unfriendly or belligerent customers. Given the difficulty of finding and retaining employees to fill some frontstage service roles, unfriendly interactions that become commonplace may undermine an organization's future. At what point should an organization stop tolerating the unfriendly customer?

Too Friendly Interactions

Excessively friendly customer-to-employee interactions may also mar service delivery and the service experience. As mentioned before, such behavior can be a major distraction to the service employee and may delay service to subsequent customers. You may have seen examples of the customer who is too friendly with service personnel: the chatty and bothersome airline passenger, the solicitous diner who befriends a waiter, or the lonely bank patron who adopts a teller as a surrogate relative.

Managing aggressively friendly customers can be particularly difficult if not awkward, because they usually mean no harm. Finding a comfortable way to escape the excessive interaction is often daunting. Some workers have a substantial response repertoire for rude or unfriendly customers but a limited one for the too friendly nuisances and their overly familiar banter. Service organizations should consider including means of deflecting customers who are too friendly as part of their employee training.

SELECTING AND TRAINING CUSTOMERS

Selecting the right customers and training them to participate in the service encounter are both crucial steps. Just as the audience of a theatrical production has a responsibility to participate in staging the show by adhering to certain norms, customers must also follow basic rules of conduct. As members of the service audience, customers not only must refrain from undermining other customers' service experience, they must strive to enable the service actors to perform at their best. The organization should inform customers regarding the expectations of a service participant (e.g., the proper protocol and procedures to evoke a satisfying service), and customers are obliged to cooperate. Whether it's learning how to use an airline ticket kiosk correctly, to give a physician an accurate account of illness symptoms, or to accommodate the rights of others sharing the service setting, the audience plays an active role in service production. While customers are essentially co-producers of their service experience across all service types, in some cases—such as education, psychological counseling, and landscape design—they play a more active role. Through it all, the service customer (like the theater patron) is expected to accept the dramaturgical rule "The show must go on" by tolerating or overlooking minor imperfections in aspects of the service performance in the interest of the overall production.

The customer becomes an important strategic component of the service in several situations. Besides playing a central part in situations where they have extensive direct contact with the service organization and its personnel, customers have an even more significant role when the service has self-service features (e.g., ATMs or fast-food restaurants). In such cases, the patron is instrumental in determining the service's outcome. Customer importance is also evident for those services requiring a high degree of personalization (e.g., insurance or legal services). Patrons of these services must provide the proper inputs (e.g., by communicating special needs or wants) to enable the service personnel to give a satisfying performance. Finally, as addressed earlier in this chapter, customer issues take on added significance for those services that cater to many patrons simultaneously. Whether sharing the same service setting or attempting to use the same service at the same time (e.g., attempting to acquire concert tickets over the telephone), other patrons deeply affect the customer's satisfaction with the service provider by their presence and behavior. It bears noting that some patrons' decision to visit or avoid a particular service establishment may be influenced by the number and/or the profile of the customers typically found there.

Customer Training Guidelines

When it comes to training the customer to ensure a better service experience for all involved, service organizations should consider several factors.

First, satisfying all customers with the same service delivery is virtually impossible, particularly because many patrons have different ideas regarding what is appropriate and reasonable in any situation. As the old adage states, "One man's ceiling is another man's floor." For example, one group of customers may be enjoying themselves in exuberant conversation, while those around them are miserable because the conversation is too loud. One solution to this problem is for organizations to educate customers about the types of behavior expected of them when visiting their particular servicescape. Signage, recorded messages, instructions from the organization's personnel, or information provided by helpful fellow patrons can help establish a common understanding of appropriate conduct among a service organization's customers.

Second, as documented by research cited earlier in the chapter (Grove and Fisk 1997), significant differences in individuals' evaluations of other customers' behaviors are often rooted in easily observable characteristics. Respondents often link dissatisfying events to other patrons whom they perceive to be of a different age group, nationality, or other visible characteristic. Older customers may note how noisy or rude younger ones are; younger customers may be sensitive to the aggressive queuing behavior of some older people. Other customers may be distressed by fellow patrons who dress differently or speak a different language. Knowing that some people may respond negatively to easily recognized customer characteristics allows service managers and employees to anticipate and prevent problems. Various strategies and tactics can address those visible demographic or physical characteristics that seem to create discord among differing groups of service customers. Targeting specific groups with special promotions, maintaining separate areas for guests with children, and striving to seat customers in homogeneous groups are examples of some possible solutions that might be considered.

Third, service organizations should be alert for a tendency among some customers to be less inhibited when they are out of town or among strangers. Indeed, some people may intentionally travel great distances on vacation or visit service establishments where they are unknown. Distance affords them the opportunity to behave freely with less worry about the consequences of their actions (Eiser and Ford 1995). Such customers may engage in disruptive or discourteous behaviors that they would not dream of adopting at home. Managers of service organizations that cater to an ever-changing customer base should be prepared to cope with and reduce possible problems caused by an *out-of-towner effect* that can lead to rowdiness.

Fourth, those service organizations that attract a diverse customer base should be wary of some customers' tendency to criticize foreigners. Many dissatisfying incidents reported in the tourist study discussed earlier involved the behavior of persons from other countries (Grove and Fisk 1997). Occasions when foreigners disrupted others' enjoyment by speaking out of turn, talking too loudly, cutting in line, or not attending to their personal grooming were common. Many of these problems occur because some patrons may not understand that other customers sometimes possess different culturally defined protocols. For example, queuing behavior may be orderly and *proper* among the British, yet anything but orderly among Italians. Even when customers are aware of such differences, they may find it difficult to tolerate behavior that rubs against their personal beliefs concerning appropriate conduct. The same type of cultural sensitivity that is routinely imparted to an organization's work force should also be directed to its customers. Signage, verbal proclamations, and observable efforts by the service personnel to accommodate behavioral differences due to cultural backgrounds can help solve this dilemma through gentle reminders advocating consideration of others.

Fifth, beyond attempting to control potential problems arising from a diverse customer mix in their physical setting, service organizations should attempt to encourage *random acts of kindness* among customers. Communicating the importance and benefits of helping others at various points during a service's delivery can increase the incidence of positive behavior. Announcements, comments, or even written communication praising patrons for adhering to appropriate comportment or performing extraordinary gestures of goodwill can prompt similar future actions and send a message to others of their desirability. Organizations might even consider systematic efforts to identify good Samaritans among their customers to recognize and reward their exemplary behavior.

Finally, service organizations must develop more ways of improving customer-to-customer relationships. One suggestion might be to adopt approaches used in theater and entertainment (Grove and Fisk 1992). For example, in the performing arts a warm-up act often helps put an audience in the right frame of mind for a feature performance. In addition, theater ushers, programs, and signs inform patrons regarding appropriate behavior. In the same vein, line managers might provide information to prevent problems among patrons from occurring. To reduce the stress of long waits, many tourist attractions use automated video displays to entertain people in line. Where lengthy delays are common, organizations should consider similar approaches. Unfortunately, these devices do not eliminate the hazards of disruptive behavior during those waits. Hence, service personnel must be prepared to occasionally act as *police officers* in managing customer-to-customer relationships (Lovelock and Wirtz 2011).

Customer Training Tools

Skillfully managing customer participation and customer-to-customer interactions helps organizations improve the service's value from the customer's point of view. Three different tools are available for this purpose: customer scripts, customer education, and customer compatibility management.

Customer Scripts   When the service requires a high degree of customer participation, organizations can enhance performance by educating customers regarding their role in the service script. As discussed in Chapter 4, a service script represents the likely sequence of events involving customers and employees during the service delivery process. When customers have a clear understanding of the service script and their part in it, their perceptions of control increase because they can predict and influence the flow of action. Ultimately, an increased sense of control results in more satisfied customers.

Many successful service organizations have recognized the importance of training their customers to ensure that they follow the script correctly. An obvious example includes self-service restaurants, where signs and directions from employees help move customers through the steps required to create their meals. Signs on tables and doors help ensure that customers will clean up after themselves. Another example of script training is the extensive effort to train airline passengers regarding the proper use of ticket kiosks. When the kiosks were first introduced, airlines promoted their adoption by familiarizing customers with the practical aspects of the new technology and helped them psychologically overcome the depersonalization of a formerly personal service.

If all customers understand the script and perform their parts properly, few conflicts should arise among participants. A good example is the Benihana (**http://www.benihana.com/**) restaurant chain, where interaction among customers is part of the service concept. Customers sit around a central cooking area in groups of eight to ten while a Japanese chef prepares each meal. Often, customers are seated next to complete strangers, which might cause social distress in other situations. Yet this arrangement is the accepted script at Benihana; indeed, it is a distinguishing characteristic of the restaurant's success.

Many service organizations, however, attract customers in a variety of market segments that may each be enacting slightly different scripts at the same time. Recreational and hospitality services such as ski resorts, ocean cruises, and large hotels fall into this category. A hotel, for instance, may simultaneously serve a large trade show convention, a group of businesswomen, families on vacation, and honeymoon couples. Each of these customer segments among the customer mix has different purposes for staying at the hotel and has different needs during the visit; in other words they possess contrasting customer scripts. To minimize potential clashes among such different customer groups, some hotels try to separate them physically or encourage them to use the hotel at different times. Educating the customers about the various scripts in operation may also help. For example, letting hotel guests know what time of day the trade show conventioneers will check out and offering an alternative checkout time may avoid frustrating delays and complaints.

Customer Education   Also, as discussed throughout this chapter, customer education minimizes service customer problems. Theme parks provide numerous safety instructions for their attractions and ensure that they are strictly followed. College professors provide students with course syllabi to delineate the requirements and expectations related to their classes. In each case, clear communication contributes to both the customer's and the organization's service performance. Consider the example of the surgery services provided by a hospital. Many hospitals carefully educate patients who are about to undergo surgical procedures. They impart a vast array of details related to the patient's preparation, operation and postsurgery events, including the nature of the procedure and how the patient is likely to feel following surgery.

Customer Compatibility Management.   Martin and Pranter suggested that service organizations should engage in compatibility management (1989). **Customer compatibility management** is the practice of selecting and targeting the appropriate customer mix to encourage satisfying customer-to-customer relationships when customers interact, yet have different reasons for using the service or different backgrounds. If successful, the effort to manage customer compatibility can attract new patrons and retain existing ones by creating a better service experience. At a time when keeping customers is so important, compatibility management is critical to an organization's broader endeavors at relationship marketing (Clark and Martin 1994).

> **Customer compatibility management** is the practice of selecting the appropriate customer mix to encourage satisfying customer-to-customer relationships when customers interact, yet have different backgrounds or different reasons for using the service.

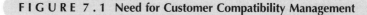

FIGURE 7.1 Need for Customer Compatibility Management

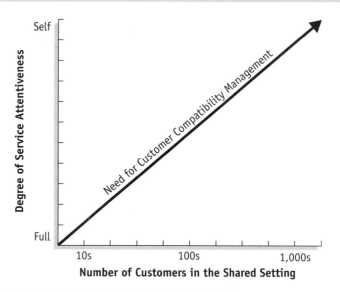

© Cengage Learning

Most service organizations must pay careful attention to their customers' behaviors. For example, airlines, restaurants, hotels, and hospitals often deliver services to customers who share the service setting and therefore may influence one another's service experience. As illustrated in Figure 7.1, service organizations that serve large numbers of customers simultaneously must take extra precautions to prevent problems. For example, many professional sports teams around the world have encountered serious problems when unruly fans have not only disrupted the games but also in some cases caused injury or death to other spectators (Grove et al. 2012). Wembley Stadium in England became known for its security at soccer games after some serious incidents resulted in deaths during the late 1980s, while San Francisco's Candlestick Park beefs up it security for major sporting events by 25% in a effort to minimize episodes of fan rage (Carlton 2012). Crowding, unruly behavior, or the wrong mix of patrons can upset or destroy the fan experience or the enjoyment of any service performance.

A service establishment's attentiveness may affect its customers' actions. Figure 7.1 suggests that full-service organizations serving small groups of people may require lower levels of customer-to-customer management than self-service organizations serving hundreds or even thousands of people at a time. The former include services such as four-star restaurants and guided tours that cater to customers who hold similar expectations regarding proper customer behavior during the service experience. On the other hand, services such as concerts, sporting events, and tourist attractions create significant compatibility management challenges. The problem is that these services attract a heterogeneous mix of patrons with different backgrounds, different reasons for using the service and divergent expectations regarding appropriate service-related behavior. In these cases, attentiveness is minimal and problems ensue. Even modestly staffed service environments such as retail stores and airlines often require careful management of customer-to-customer relations.

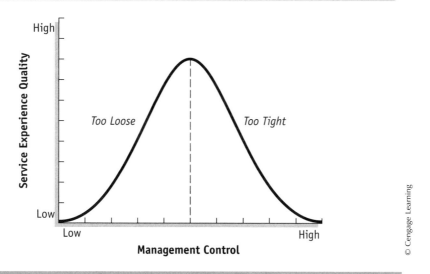

FIGURE 7.2 **Optimizing Service Experience Quality**

Too Loose

Too Tight

Service Experience Quality

High

Low

Management Control

Low

High

© Cengage Learning

Related to the degree of attentiveness are efforts to manage customer behavior. Many customers link the quality of service experiences to the degree of management control over customers (see Figure 7.2). However, a service organization that exerts too much control over its customers may be perceived as repressive and may lose customers.

MANAGING CUSTOMER RAGE

News reports from around the world chronicle a growing number of customer rage incidents. **Customer rage** is the expression of mild to extreme anger about some aspect of the service experience. These customer rage incidents create serious problems for managers of the service organizations they affect. Evidence suggests that incidents of customer rage are increasing (McColl-Kennedy et al. 2009). Consider, for instance, the rage described in the following incidents:

> **Customer rage** is the expression of mild to extreme anger about some aspect of the service experience.

- **Parking rage.** As a result of a near collision in a Phoenix parking lot, a taxi driver and his passenger beat and stomped the other motorist to death as the victim's wife watched in horror (Stern 2011).

- **Fan rage.** A melee and stampede in Egypt involving soccer fans of a victorious home team, Al-Masry, and supporters of a heavily favored visiting side, Al-Ahly, resulted in seventy four deaths (*USA Today* 2012).

- **Air rage.** A fight broke out between two men on a flight from Washington, D.C., to Ghana when one of the combatants reclined his seat into the lap of the other. F-16 fighter jets were called upon to escort the plane back to Dulles Airport (Topping 2011).

These incidents only hint at the full breadth and severity of customer rage incidents and the damage, ranging from verbal indignation to vandalism, physical injury, and even death. Petulant exhibitions of anger that lead to curse words, fisticuffs, damage to personal property, or damage to the immediate surroundings are common manifestations of customer rage. Fellow patrons and workers have both been the unsuspecting targets of rage. Clearly, such disruptive customer behaviors pose severe problems for service organizations afflicted by rage incidents that go beyond the incidents' immediate harm. These problems might include bad publicity that keeps customers at bay, legal actions that carry financial costs, and the untold ramifications of traumatized customers and employees.

SPOTLIGHT 7.3

Customers Behaving Badly

 Anyone who has worked for a service organization—which is just about everybody—knows that the adage "The customer is always right" is simply not true. While it is a noble effort to approach customer service with that frame of mind, sometimes customers exhibit behaviors that are far from "right" (Fisk et al. 2010). Patrons who are initially welcome as part of an organization's desired customer mix occasionally engage in actions that makes them a liability. Some time ago, a marketing scholar labeled such patrons as *jaycustomers* (Lovelock 1994). Six different types of jaycustomers were originally identified and later augmented with a seventh. Included among them are rule-breakers, thieves, cheats, belligerents, family feuders, vandals, and deadbeats. *Rule breakers* are those who violate the directives established by an organization to protect customers and/or workers or to facilitate the smooth operation of the service. *Thieves* are customers who fail to pay for the service they receive from an organization—not unlike shoplifters who plague retail establishments. *Cheats* are customers that exploit organizations' goodwill or guarantees by feigning dissatisfaction in order to avoid payment or other desirable outcomes; examples include insurance fraud and returning products after use. *Belligerents* are patrons who become loud, confrontational, or worse when some aspect of service delivery is not to their liking; in other words, they exhibit customer rage. *Family feuders* are a subset of the belligerents; they are customers who become argumentative with other customers and often start heated exchanges among folks who are related or acquaintances. *Vandals* are those who mar or physically abuse the service setting, undermining its aesthetic appeal, operational excellence, and/or safety. *Deadbeats* represent customers who become delinquent in their payment for services rendered—a circumstance that may or may not be a temporary.

What can an organization do when it is plagued by jaycustomers? Each type of jaycustomer may require a different approach. Clearly, greater security and monitoring may reduce the incidence of rule breaking, thievery, cheating, and vandalism, and may even help expunge occasions of belligerence and family feuding. Yet, efforts such as carefully considering the number and clarity of rules and determining the reasons behind one's inability to pay can provide information that can lead to the reduction of rule breaking and deadbeat behavior, respectively. Training workers to isolate and address expressions of customer rage—whether the rage is manifested as belligerence or family feuding—can minimize the behavior's impact on others. Quick responses to repair or remove vandalized equipment or facilities may reduce the likelihood that others will take the lead from the first perpetuators and continue to vandalize. Approaches that involve creative ways to help a deadbeat meet his or her obligations may keep such originally desirable customers around for the long run.

Obviously, organizations would prefer that jaycustomer behavior did not occur, but identifying and addressing it can limit its deleterious effects. Spotlight 7.3 describes customer rage as belligerent customers.

Source: Lovelock, Christopher H. and Jochen Wirtz (2011), *Services Marketing: People, Technology, Strategy*, Upper Saddle River, NJ: Prentice-Hall; Lovelock, Christopher H. (1994), *Product Plus*, New York, NY: McGraw Hill.

Service organizations often find themselves bedeviled by customer rage incidents (Grove, Fisk, and John 2004). Unruly customer acts are increasingly common. These episodes include theme park rage, restaurant rage, help desk rage, parking lot rage, cash register rage, jury rage, and even e-rage. It seems that whenever one picks up the newspaper today, stories emerge of amusement park patrons fighting in line, angry restaurant patrons pitching a fit, befuddled computer users lashing out at help-desk attendants, customers skirmishing over parking spaces, shoppers acting out their frustrations over slow checkout lines, and faceless Internet users angrily flaming their e-commerce retailers. It appears that no service setting is a safe haven from customer rage.

It is the service sector that is most frequently afflicted with customer rage incidents at all levels of severity. Service organizations require interaction between customers and employees, often in the presence of multiple consumers who share a common service setting. In addition, the "real time" character of service delivery and the many uncontrollable elements that combine to create a service experience make service quality notoriously variable. It is not surprising then that service encounters are a veritable petri dish for customer rage. In addition, service organizations often are capacity constrained; that is, they regularly experience insufficiencies of workers, space, or equipment to handle customers effectively (think of the 7 p.m. crush of diners at popular restaurants on any given Friday evening in the United States). In short, most cases of customer rage are intimately linked to the service employees, service setting, fellow customers, and service process.

Will service encounters in the future contain even more hostility than today? We believe such a distasteful and dangerous possibility may occur unless service managers (1) address the need to reduce common targets of customer rage in service encounters, (2) manage customer temperaments, (3) take extra steps to avoid the triggers of rage, and (4) actively pursue treatments for preventing or managing customer rage. Smart services managers will do everything possible to make sure that their service encounters with customers are characterized by civility rather than marred by rage.

Summary and Conclusion

The concept of managing customers is relatively new to the services field. Smart customers seek out the best services. Similarly, smart service organizations seek out the best customers. Therefore, organizations should decide on the optimal behaviors they desire from customers in terms of their participation in the process of service delivery, interaction with other customers, and treatment of the service personnel. Once they determine optimal behaviors, organizations can work to develop a clientele that fulfills this vision. Producing a satisfying customer experience begins with locating the right customers, educating them to reap the greatest rewards from the service, and ensuring their compatibility with other customers.

Other customers can either increase a customer's sense of satisfaction with a service organization or undermine it. Unfortunately, many retailers of consumer services have largely ignored this truth. When it comes to educating the customer, managing customer-to-customer relationships, and supervising customer-to-employee relationships, organizations may find it difficult to come up with creative measures that both ensure positive experiences and prevent negative ones. Nevertheless, in service encounters a single failure can persuade a customer to take her or his business elsewhere. Enlightened organizations must see to it that their customers understand their role in the process of service delivery and get along with their fellow patrons and the service employees.

Exercises

1. During the next few days, monitor the number of occasions when the behavior of other customers influences your service experience.

   a. Which customer behaviors *improved* your service experience?

   b. Which customer behaviors *detracted* from your service experience?

   c. Describe any examples of customers helping each other.

   d. Describe any examples of customers annoying each other.

2. On your next visit to a service establishment or online service entity:

   a. Try to be particularly friendly to the service provider. How did the service provider respond to your friendliness?

   b. Did you perceive any messages (written or oral) that *educated* you about how to participate in the service delivery?

3. Select a service and examine its specific guidelines and rules for customer behavior and participation. Why are the instructions given, and what might the consequences be without these instructions?

Internet Exercise

Examine how students at your school use the Internet to communicate with other students and with their professors.

1. Are students discussing their student experiences in chat rooms, discussion forums, and blogs?
2. Does your school encourage or discourage such customer-to-customer interaction?
3. Are students interacting with their professors by using blogs, discussion forums, or via instructional software such as Blackboard or WebCT?
4. Does your school encourage or discourage such customer-to-employee interaction?

EXPLORE

Visit the companion site for this text at **www.cengagebrain .com** to explore key concepts in the service industry. You will find tools to help you expand your services marketing knowledge, including ACE self-tests, Web links to companies and organizations featured in this chapter, and much more!

References

Bitner, Mary Jo, Bernard H. Booms, and Mary Stanfield Tetreault (1990), "The Service Encounter: Diagnosing Favorable and Unfavorable Incidents," *Journal of Marketing*, 54 (January), 71–84.

Carlton, Jim (2012), "Curbing Hooliganism at Candlestick," *Wall Street Journal*, January 21–22, Sec. A, 2.

Clark, Terry and Charles L. Martin (1994), "Customer-to-Customer: The Forgotten Relationship in Relationship Marketing," in *Relationship Marketing: Theory, Methods and Applications*, Jagdish N. Sheth and Atul Parvatiyar, eds., Atlanta, GA: Emory University, 1–10.

Cronin Jr., Joseph J. and Steven A. Taylor (1992), "Measuring Service Quality: A Reexamination and Extension," *Journal of Marketing*, 56 (July), 55–68.

Eiser, Richard J. and Nicholas Ford (1995), "Sexual Relations on Holiday: A Case of Situational Disinhibition?" *Journal of Social and Personal Relationships*, 12 (3), 323–340.

Grove, Stephen J. and Raymond P. Fisk (1992), "The Service Experience as Theater," in *Advances in Consumer Research*, vol. 19, John Sherry and Brian Sternthal, eds., Provo, UT: Association for Consumer Research, 455–461.

Fisk, Ray, Stephen Grove, Lloyd C. Harris, Dominique A, Keefe, Kate L. Daunt, Rebekah Russell-Bennett, and Jochen Wirtz (2010), "Customers Behaving Badly: A State of the Art Review, Research Agenda, and Implications for Practitioners," *Journal of Services Marketing*, 24 (6), 417–429.

Gallagher Noel (2009), "Fellow Passengers with Bad Breath and BO Have Been Voted the Worst People to Sit Next to in Skyscanner's Most Recent Poll," **http://www.skyscanner.net/news/articles/2009/07/002674-bad-breath-and-bo-get-up-travellers-noses-most-annoying-passengers-revealed-by-skyscanner.htm** (accessed February 9, 2012).

Grove, Stephen J. and Raymond P. Fisk (1997), "The Impact of Other Customers upon Service Experiences: A Critical Incident Examination of 'Getting Along,'" *Journal of Retailing*, 73 (1), 63–85.

Grove, Stephen J., Raymond P. Fisk, and Joby John (2004), "Surviving in the Age of Rage," *Marketing Management* (March/April), 41–46.

Grove, Stephen J., Gregory M. Pickett, Scott A. Jones, and Michael J. Dorsch (2012), "Spectator Rage as the Dark Side of Engaging Sport Fans: Implications for Services Marketers," *Journal of Service Research*, 15 (1), 1–18.

Hui, Michael K. and John E. G. Bateson (1991), "Perceived Control and the Effects of Crowding and Consumer Choice on the Service Experience," *Journal of Consumer Research*, 18 (2), 174–184.

Lee, Louise (2006), "Kick Out the Kids, Bring in the Sales," *Business Week* (April 17), 42.

Lovelock, Christopher (1994), *Product Plus: How Product + Service = Competitive Advantage*, New York: McGraw-Hill, Inc.

Lovelock, Christopher H. and Jochen Wirtz (2011), *Services Marketing*, 7th ed., Upper Saddle River, NJ: Prentice Hall.

Martin, Charles L. and Charles A. Pranter (1989), "Compatibility Management: Customer-to-Customer Relationships in Service Environments," *Journal of Services Marketing*, 3 (Summer), 6–15.

McColl-Kennedy, Janet R., Paul G. Patterson, Amy K. Smith, and Michael K. Brady (2009), "Customer Rage Episodes: Emotions, Expressions and Behaviors," *Journal of Retailing*, 85 (2), 222–237.

Parasuraman, A., Leonard L. Barry, and Valarie A. Zeithaml (1991), "Refinement and Reassessment of the SERVQUAL Scale," *Journal of Retailing*, 67 (Winter), 420–450.

Parasuraman, A., Leonard L. Berry, and Valarie A. Zeithaml (1993), "Research Note: More on Improving Service Quality Measurement," *Journal of Retailing*, 69 (Spring), 140–147.

Parasuraman, A., Valarie A. Zeithaml, and Leonard L. Berry (1988), "SERVQUAL: A Multiple-Item Scale for Measuring Consumer Perceptions of Service Quality," *Journal of Retailing*, 64 (Spring), 12–37.

Stern, Ray (2011), "Taxi Driver and Passenger Beat Man to Death During Parking Lot Squabble, Avondale Cops Say," **http://blogs.phoenixnewtimes.com/valleyfever/2011/08/taxi_driver_and_passenger_beat.** (accessed February 7, 2012).

Topping, Alexandra (2011), "Air-Rage Fight over Reclining Seat Forces United Airlines Flight to Return Home," **http://www.guardian.co.uk/world/2011/jun/01/united-airlines-flight-seat-fight** (accessed February 7, 2012).

USA Today (2005), March 17, International Edition, 8B. "Egypt soccer fans rush field after game, 74 dead" (2012), *USA Today*, **http://www.usatoday.com/sports/soccer/2012-02-01-2351436719** (accessed February 8, 2012).

Promising the Interactive Service Experience

Part Three examines the complexities of making promises to current and prospective customers about the interactive service experience. Organizations convey such promises through prices charged for services and through promotional messages. Chapter 8 develops an analysis of service pricing that includes pricing objectives, the relationship between service price and value, ways to calculate service costs, and price bundling. Chapter 9 explores the many ways of promoting services and discusses the promotional mix of advertising, personal selling, publicity/ public relations, and sales promotion for services.

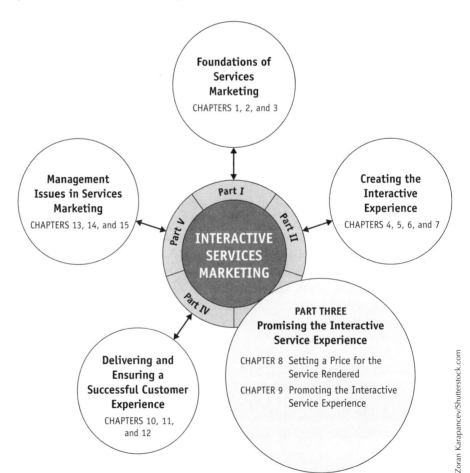

Foundations of Services Marketing
CHAPTERS 1, 2, and 3

Management Issues in Services Marketing
CHAPTERS 13, 14, and 15

Creating the Interactive Experience
CHAPTERS 4, 5, 6, and 7

Part I

Part V

Part II

INTERACTIVE SERVICES MARKETING

Part IV

Delivering and Ensuring a Successful Customer Experience
CHAPTERS 10, 11, and 12

PART THREE
Promising the Interactive Service Experience

CHAPTER 8 Setting a Price for the Service Rendered

CHAPTER 9 Promoting the Interactive Service Experience

The Broadmoor Hotel: Where Excellence and Value Meet

The Broadmoor Hotel (http://www.broadmoor.com/) in Colorado Springs, Colorado has a strong heritage of excellence. It received a Forbes (http://www.forbes.com/) Five-Star rating 52 times and an AAA (http//:www.AAA.com/) Five Diamond rating 36 times, making them the longest running consecutive winner in both cases. The hotel first opened in 1918 and has enjoyed remarkable ratings by other travel industry experts such as Travel+Leisure Magazine (http://www.trave-landleisure.com/), Zagat (http://www.zagat.com/) and Fodor's (http://www.fodors.com/). But the Broadmoor is much more than simply a hotel: it is a resort, and various other aspects of its sprawling grounds have enjoyed accolades as well, including its restaurants, golf course, spa, tennis facilities and meeting areas. To make that all happen, the Broadmoor has practiced many principles of success. These principles include continually improving upon its servicescape and technology, hiring and training employees to be service enthusiasts and making certain enough staff are available to deliver the level of service excellence its customers expect. It employs over 1,800 staff members from twenty three countries and offers them more than forty training courses that focus on the basics of hospitality and beyond. New hires receive more than 175 hours of training in their first year. Clearly, the Broadmoor is committed to an outstanding service culture. Of course, its pricing and promotional decisions contribute to its success as well.

While approximately 70% of its bookings involve business functions, the Broadmoor does not neglect the recreational traveler and that can be seen in it pricing efforts and promotional activities. Rooms that may run from $300 to $550 or more a night on a regular basis are sometimes reduced significantly during slow periods. In addition, the Broadmoor offers an array of attractive price packages that price bundle a room in its award-winning hotel with golf, tennis or spa activities and meal and merchandise discounts. Other packages are offered for various holidays, family gatherings, romantic getaways or special events such as jazz or 'sommelier boot camp' weekends.

Upscale hotels and resorts such as the Broadmoor employ a specialized approach to promoting their properties. Essentially, the promotional strategy must be as exclusive as the clientele. If the Broadmoor was "popularly priced," like Holiday Inn (http://www.sixcontinentsho-tels.com) or Motel 6 (http://motel6.com), it would invest heavily in mass advertising. But lower-profile publicity and public relations are more effective tools for reaching an exclusive hotel clientele. For example, the Broadmoor Hotel strives to be ranked by all the groups that grade and evaluate the hospitality industry such as those organizations mentioned earlier. The publicity its high ratings generate greatly augments the relatively limited emphasis the resort places on mass advertising. An even more important source of promotion is the word-of-mouth publicity that delighted guests provide. To supplement these approaches, the hotel employs a small conference sales staff and uses sales promotions for the seasonal hotel rates and special packages mentioned earlier.

CHAPTER 8
Setting a Price for the Service Rendered
Why do Service Prices Vary?
Yield Management in Services
Pricing Objectives and Approaches
The Relationship Between Service Price and Value
Calculating Service Costs
Price Bundling
Additional Pricing Considerations

CHAPTER 9
Promoting the Interactive Service Experience
Services and Integrated Marketing Communications
Marketing Communications and Services
The Promotional Mix
Advertising the Service
Sales Promotions and Services
Personal Selling and Services
Publicity and Services
Promoting Services on the Internet

Sources: **http://www.broadmoor.com** (accessed August 3, 2012); and Czaplewski, Andrew J., Eric M. Olson and Stanley F. Slater (2002), "Applying the RATER Model for Service Success," *Marketing Management*, Vol. 11 (January/February), 14-17.

CHAPTER 8

Setting a Price for the Service Rendered

In the Broadmoor Hotel vignette, the hotel's pricing of guest rooms and suites helps create the perception of a highly valuable service. Beyond its regular pricing plans, the Broadmoor **(http://www.broadmoor.com)** also offers seasonal rates and special packages. In addition to the hotel suite provided, these rates include extra services and amenities, such as private tours of world-class art galleries, chamber music, and special gourmet meals.

Service prices can vary by the time of purchase or use of the service. To understand why one organization must offer widely varying prices requires us to analyze the service organization's productive assets and their productivity. Asset-utilization efficiency issues and other challenges make pricing a difficult decision for the services marketer. Price bundling and other pricing strategies are a logical response to such complexity.

This chapter explores the challenges and opportunities service organizations face regarding pricing decisions. The chapter has seven specific objectives:

- To examine why service prices vary so much
- To explore yield management in services
- To explain the role of pricing objectives in service organizations
- To analyze the challenge of establishing value for a service offering
- To show how service costs may be calculated
- To explore price bundling strategies for services
- To examine additional pricing considerations

Pricing service offerings is often a confusing issue for both the service organization and its customers. Organizations often struggle to determine the costs of providing an intangible offering, which makes it hard to set an accurate price. Service organizations must account for the cost of serving the customer by attributing detailed costs of activities in the frontstage and backstage that are tied to the specific service purchased. For example, how precise is the cost calculation needed to price the dry-cleaning of a shirt versus a jacket? Understandably, customers face similar uncertainty determining whether the price they pay for a service is, in fact, reasonable. Service valuation involves a great deal more subjectivity than in the case of packaged goods, where material and labor cost is easily attributable to a unit produced.

Pricing services can be complex. Table 8.1 illustrates cellular telephone service pricing for the basic service from four major providers in the United States. Customers sign on to one of several plans from the service provider, each with different monthly rates, equipment fees, per-minute costs, and a contract carrying the penalty of an extra fee for early termination. When selecting a plan, customers must determine which options best meet their particular calling habits. It appears that cellular prices have now converged to the mean, reflecting the commoditization of mobile phone services and deserving the label of "dumb pipe" given to the cellular (mobile) phone lines.

TABLE 8.1   Nationwide Basic Individual Wireless Plans: $39.99 monthly

Plan Elements	AT&T	Sprint	T-Mobile	Verizon
Included minutes	450	450	500	450
Additional minutes	.45/min.	.45/min.	.45/min.	.45/min.
Nights and weekends	5,000 min.	Unlimited	Unlimited	Unlimited
Data services	$2 per MB	$15	200 MB available with next level plan priced $5 more per month	1.99 per MB; personal email: $5
Domestic messaging	.20 per text/ instant message and .30 per picture/video message	300 messages at $5	Unlimited	.20 per text/ instant message, .25 per picture/ video message

© Cengage Learning

The fact that price is designated by different labels in different service industries only adds to this confusion. For instance, you pay a *commission* to a stockbroker, a *membership fee* to a fitness club, a *finance charge* to a credit card company, a *premium* to an insurance firm, a *fare* for transportation, *rent* for housing, and a *rate* for telephone services. Deregulation of major service sectors and changes in the external environment for services have increased the strategic role of service pricing. For all of these reasons and more, service organizations find pricing difficult.

WHY DO SERVICE PRICES VARY?

The following examples reflect some of the complexities in pricing service offerings:

■ Two airline passengers with identical schedules sitting in adjacent seats on the same flight may have paid different prices.

■ A long-distance telephone call to the same telephone number from the same location may be priced differently depending on the time of day or day of the week.

■ The price of a movie ticket may vary according to the screening time, with matinees typically costing less than evening performances of the same movie at the same theater.

Why do prices differ so much for the same service? The answer involves the inseparability and perishability characteristics of services discussed in Chapter 1.

In each of the preceding pricing examples, the price paid differs based on *when* the customer either makes the purchase or uses the service. Airlines may vary ticket prices depending on how many days ahead of departure a reservation is made. These *advance fare* tickets may have different prices at Twenty One days, Fourteen days, and Seven days. Tickets purchased on the day of departure can be very expensive. Some *walk-up fares* are astronomical. Paradoxically, some airlines also offer low-priced *standby* fares for any vacant seats (i.e., excess capacity) at the time of departure. If you have used Priceline **(http://www.priceline.com)** for travel arrangements, you probably would have noticed the complexity and fluidity of prices. The price structure for telephone services reflects a similar response to demand variation. Telephone companies calculate traffic on their lines and identify different load levels (the number of calls across different times of the day and days of the week). To accommodate fluctuations in customer usage, most phone companies offer day, evening, night, and weekend discount rates.

Similarly, movie theaters experience peak attendance for their evening shows and much lower attendance during the afternoons. Thus, they often set matinee prices significantly lower to generate traffic at that time of day. Fluctuating service demand, when coupled with capacity constraints in services, underscores the importance of pricing as a marketing tool. For example, consider how restaurants use *early-bird* prices to encourage customers to dine early or how hotels may charge a lower rate for guests who reserve well in advance. The hospital that is only half full of patients is worrisome because hospital services have high fixed costs in proportion to their total costs. The *fixed costs* of providing the service are fairly constant regardless of the number of patients served. For example, the hospital must pay the fixed costs of its hospital building and equipment whether it is serving 1,500 patients or only 15 patients. The *variable costs* (i.e., the costs of serving one additional patient) are minimal compared to the fixed costs of maintaining and operating the hospital. Service organizations must find creative ways to maximize revenues and reduce costs per customer served.

YIELD MANAGEMENT IN SERVICES

Sophisticated, computer-based *yield management systems* are widely used in some service industries (e.g., airlines and hotels) to set prices that generate or shift demand to create greater efficiency and profitability (Desiraju and Shugan 1999). For example, hotels with empty rooms lose the potential revenue of those rooms forever. For that reason, service organizations must achieve maximum usage of their assets. Services that face great variation in demand may employ yield management systems to offer prices adjusted when the reservation is made or when the service will be used. Offering a different price at different time periods, depending upon a service's cycle of demand (e.g., hour of day, day of week, week of month, month of year), is one of the services marketer's most effective responses to the challenge of maximizing asset usage.

In essence, the objective of yield management is to maximize profits from the fixed operating assets—labor, equipment, and facilities. As with any business, profits are maximized by increasing revenues and decreasing costs. To maximize a service's revenues, the assets should be used for the highest paying customer at any given time. The service organization can accomplish this goal by focusing on

---

SPOTLIGHT 8.1

If Airlines Sold Paint

Buying paint from a hardware store

CUSTOMER: Hi, how much is your paint?

CLERK: We have regular quality for $12 a gallon and premium for $18. How many gallons would you like?

CUSTOMER: Five gallons of regular quality, please.

CLERK: Great. That will be $60 plus tax.

Buying paint from an airline . . .

CUSTOMER: Hi, how much is your paint?

CLERK: Well, sir, that all depends.

CUSTOMER: Depends on what?

CLERK: Actually, a lot of things.

CUSTOMER: How about giving me an average price?

CLERK: Wow, that's too hard a question. The lowest price is $9 a gallon, and we have 150 different prices up to $200 a gallon.

CUSTOMER: What's the difference in the paint?

CLERK: Oh, there isn't any difference, it's all the same paint.

CUSTOMER: Well, then, I'd like some of that $9 paint.

CLERK: Well, first I need to ask you a few questions. When do you intend to use it?

CUSTOMER: I want to paint tomorrow, on my day off.

CLERK: Sir, the paint for tomorrow is $200 paint.

CUSTOMER: What? When would I have to paint in order to get the $9 paint?

CLERK: That would be in three weeks, but you will also have to agree to start painting before Friday of that week and continue until at least Sunday

CUSTOMER: You've got to be kidding!

CLERK: Sir, we don't kid around here. Of course, I'll have to check to see if we have any of that paint available before I can sell it to you.

CUSTOMER: What do you mean check to see if you can sell it to me? You have shelves full of that stuff; I can see it right there.

CLERK: Just because you can see it doesn't mean that we have it. It may be the same paint, but we sell only a certain number of gallons on any given weekend. Oh, and by the way, the price just went up to $12.

CUSTOMER: You mean the price went up while we were talking?

CLERK: Yes sir. You see, we change prices and rules thousands of times a day, and since you haven't actually walked out of the store with your paint yet, we just decided to change. Unless you want the same thing to happen again, I would suggest you get on with your purchase. How many gallons do you want?

CUSTOMER: I don't know exactly. Maybe five gallons. Maybe I should buy six gallons just to make sure I have enough.

CLERK: Oh no, sir, you can't do that. If you buy the paint and then don't use it, you will be liable for penalties and possible confiscation of the paint you already have.

CUSTOMER: What?

CLERK: That's right. We can sell you enough paint to do your kitchen, bathroom, hall, and north bedroom, but if you stop painting before you do the other bedroom, you will be in violation of our tariffs.

CUSTOMER: But what does it matter to you whether I use all of the paint? I already paid you for it!

CLERK: Sir, there's no point in getting upset; that's just the way it is. We make plans based upon the idea that you will use all of the paint, and when you don't, it just causes us all sorts of problems.

CUSTOMER: This is crazy! I suppose something terrible will happen if I don't keep painting until Sunday night?

CLERK: Yes sir, it will.

CUSTOMER: Well, that does it! I am going somewhere else to buy paint!

CLERK: That won't do you any good, sir. We all have the same rules. You might as well just buy it here, while the price is now $13.50. Thanks for flying—I mean painting—with our airline.

Source: Anonymous.

---

increasing the number of people using the service while charging the maximum price possible. Most capacity-constrained services closely monitor their yield. Airlines call it the *load factor*; hotels refer to it as *revpar*.

The inherent trade-off between price and demand makes yield management a difficult strategy for the services marketer (See Spotlight 8.1). All other factors being equal, if an organization raises the price of its service, usage drops. Conversely, if it lowers its prices, service usage increases. Greater usage does not necessarily mean higher profits, however, unless the price charged is sufficiently high. It should be clear that yield management requires an intimate understanding of customers' purchase patterns and price sensitivities. Establishing service value is critical for effective yield management. The other component of yield management involves cost management. Because profits equal revenues minus costs, it is important to control the costs of producing and delivering the service.

PRICING OBJECTIVES AND APPROACHES

Pricing strategies, driven by pricing objectives, are linked to the service organization's overall marketing strategy. All service organizations (except nonprofits and government agencies) focus pricing strategies on covering costs and making a profit. The two types of pricing objectives are profit-oriented objectives and volume-oriented objectives. **Profit-oriented** objectives stress generating high returns on the service's investments in resources and labor; **volume-oriented** objectives stress processing large numbers of customers or their possessions. Organizations can develop strategies to accomplish these objectives by approaching price determination in three ways (see Figure 8.1).

> **Profit-oriented** objectives stress generating high returns on the service's investments in resources and labor; **volume-oriented** objectives stress processing large numbers of customers or their possessions.

An operations perspective focuses on the price floor, that is, the minimum price that covers all costs of producing the service. It is sometimes referred to as a *cost-based approach* because the service organization begins by carefully calculating all costs and then sets its price accordingly after adding a profit margin to the total. A revenue perspective is a *customer-based approach* that focuses on the price ceiling, or the maximum price

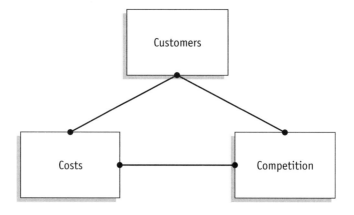

FIGURE 8.1 Three Approaches to Price Determination

© Cengage Learning

customers are likely to pay. In this case, the marketer begins with a range of prices acceptable to the customer and sets a price that reflects customers' perception of the service's value while taking into account the desired profits. Finally, a *competition-based approach* establishes the service's price in relation to the competition. Depending on how an organization wants to be perceived, prices are set above, below, or equal to competitors' prices. Ideally, all three approaches combine to address the three critical factors that affect price: customers, costs, and competition. Collectively, these factors are often referred to as the *three Cs of pricing*. The sweet spot is where a service provider is able to charge a price higher than the competition because of higher perceived value. The sour spot is where the service provider has to charge a lower price because of lower perceived value.

THE RELATIONSHIP BETWEEN SERVICE PRICE AND VALUE

Establishing the value of intangible service offerings is difficult because value lies in the eye of the beholder. **Value** is an assessment of the benefits of a service versus the costs associated with it. If a customer *perceives* that the benefits she receives from the service (i.e., need satisfaction) exceed her costs (i.e., the price), she is likely to believe the service offers her good value. All types of benefits and costs can be

> **Value** is an assessment of the benefits of a service versus the costs associated with it.

weighed in the determination of value, but two particularly important elements are *need satisfaction* and *price.* The problem services marketers face is the real-time nature of services, which makes it hard for customers to evaluate them in advance. Some services, such as restaurants or resorts, may allow customers to evaluate physical cues associated with the intangible service performance (e.g., the servicescape). Other services, such as insurance or investment counseling, may conspicuously lack such cues. In general, the benefits of most services (e.g., vacations and hairstyling) can be ascertained only during or after the service has been experienced. In some instances (e.g., medical advice, automobile repair), the benefits may be hard to determine even after the service has been rendered (Zeithaml 1981). Paradoxically, given the difficulty of evaluating the benefits of a service, customers often use price as a surrogate indicator of service excellence. Some organizations employ the competition-based approach to service pricing and set prices higher than those of their competitors to evoke a perception of greater value.

Customers often use a cost–benefit analysis to determine the value of a service offering. For example, a customer might decide that it is worth the extra time and effort to travel to a favorite restaurant simply because the food or the ambiance is much better than at lower-priced restaurants nearby. In other words, the customer perceives greater value at the favorite restaurant because the benefits it offers exceed the costs of choosing it. Generally, the longer the customer has been loyal to a service provider, the greater the perceived value of the service. Such a cost–benefit comparison suggests that perceived value can be raised either by increasing customer perceptions of benefits, lowering perceptions of costs, or both. Improved service features could enhance perceived benefits. Demonstrating the impact of the perishable nature of services, customers are also willing to pay more to get a service done immediately. The cliché should be—"Time is more valuable than money." Making the service more convenient to purchase and easier to use could reduce perceived costs.

The perceived value of a service is reflected in the *price/demand elasticity* for the offering. A highly *elastic* service is one for which price changes greatly affect customer demand. Conversely, an *inelastic* service is one for which price changes have little effect on customer demand. Elastic services tend to be discretionary (e.g., skiing vacations). Inelastic services tend to be necessities (e.g., telephone service). Different customer segments display different sensitivities to price changes. Understanding price sensitivity is integral to the success of the yield management systems discussed earlier.

CALCULATING SERVICE COSTS

As we noted earlier, the inherent characteristics of services make cost calculations for service offerings much more difficult and complicated than for physical goods. The cost of producing a service is determined by the costs of labor, physical facilities and equipment, raw materials, and supplies. In general, the total cost of producing each unit of a service involves both the fixed and variable costs of using these assets. Some of these costs are *direct costs* associated with each unit of sale; others are the *indirect costs* shared by several services and not directly linked to each unit of sale. An example of a direct cost for a motel room is the price of laundry and bathroom supplies for the room. An example of an indirect cost for that room is the *allocated overhead cost* of maintaining and staffing the front desk. *Fixed costs* such as motel property mortgage payments or debt financing occur regardless of the number of customers served, whereas *variable costs,* such as the cost of bath soaps and electricity, depend on the number of rooms sold. Spotlight 8.2 illustrates the passing of variable costs to the customer by charging for meals on short flights in the airline industry.

A significant difference between goods and services is that services often share indirect costs with other services that use the same resources. These indirect costs are sometimes referred to as *shared costs.* If the customers of different services share space, equipment, and other facilities, their fixed costs (based on the amount of time for which the resources are contracted) are called *shared fixed costs.* If the costs of these shared resources also vary by the number of customers, they are called *shared variable* costs. In general, most costs shared among services are fixed costs. Figure 8.2 illustrates how these costs are factored in when calculating the price of a service. When the per unit fixed costs (FC), shared costs (SC), and variable costs (VC) are added to produce the per unit total cost (TC), the organization determines the price (P) by adding the desired net profit per unit (NP) to this per unit total cost. Thus, $P = TC + NP$, where $TC = FC + SC + VC$.

Take the hypothetical example of Pontchartrain Manor, a ten-room motel that must calculate costs and set the price for a room for one night. If the mortgage payment for the entire facility is $10,000 per month, the daily allocation for a

---

Price Unbundling: Creative but Annoying Airline Fees

The U.S. Department of Transportation reported that passengers of U.S. airlines paid a whopping $5.7 billion in fees in 2010. Baggage fees brought in $3.4 billion, with Delta alone raking in almost $1 billion in 2010. If you paid for a change in your reservation, you contributed to the $2.3 billion fees airlines made in cancellation revenues, which average at $250 for a change you made in your itinerary. Southwest Airlines promotes itself as a no-frills, no-fee airline, with great success. In addition to these fees, passengers have become used to paying for meals on flights. Most U.S. airlines charge $8 to $10 for a snack box or a meal on flights, and about $6 for an alcoholic beverage. Other examples of prevailing and forthcoming fees include frequent-flier award ticket fees, premium seating fees, early boarding fees, pillow and blanket fees, Wi-Fi fees, lavatory fees, and, infant-in-your-lap fees. With these annoying hidden fees, airline passengers may be unpleasantly surprised with the final cost of flying compared to what they paid for airfare.

Source: **http://www.foxnews.com/us/2011/06/14/us-fliers-shelled-out-sky-high-57-billion-in-airline-fees/** (accessed August 22, 2011); and **http://www.airfarewatchdog.com/blog/3800552/top-ten-most-obnoxious-hidden-airline-fees** (accessed August 22, 2011).

---

single room is $33. If the motel has one full-time front-desk manager, one daily housekeeper, and one weekly groundskeeper, and the total staff pay comes to $3,000 per month, the shared fixed cost is $100 per day for the whole motel, or $10 per room per day. Suppose now that the variable cost of laundry and room supplies for Pontchartrain Manor is estimated at $7 per room per day. The total cost, which is the sum of the fixed cost ($33), shared cost ($10), and variable cost ($7), is $50. If we add a profit margin of $10 per day to each room, the room rate at Pontchartrain Manor will be $60 per night.

The difference between the price charged to the service customer and the variable costs attributable to each unit of sale is the *contribution margin*. Contribution margin is the amount allocated to covering the fixed (and shared) costs. The remainder of the contribution margin after this allocation is subtracted becomes the service's *net profit*. In the example of Pontchartrain Manor, the contribution

FIGURE 8.2 Calculating Service Price

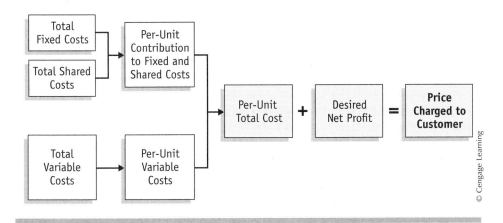

margin is $53 (room rate of $60 minus variable cost of $7), and because the fixed cost is $43 (a per-room mortgage of $33 plus shared cost of $10), the net profit is $10.

Each service organization needs a certain number of customers to recover all of its costs and make a profit. Just as with physical goods, the price charged for the offering and the costs of producing it determine the number of customers needed to make a specific amount of profit. A *breakeven analysis* shows the number of goods that must be sold to cover costs at a given price. Similarly, a service's *breakeven point* is the number of units of a service that must be sold or the number of customers that must be served to cover costs. The breakeven point is calculated by dividing the sum of the total fixed costs and total shared costs by the difference between the price and the unit variable cost. To calculate the breakeven point for the Pontchartrain Manor, we divide the total fixed and shared costs per month ($13,000) by the difference between the $60 room rate and the $7 variable cost ($53). The Pontchartrain Manor thus needs to sell 245 nights' accommodation per month (out of a possible 300), averaging about 80% occupancy per day, to break even.

Most services provide a variety of offerings, which can make the breakeven analysis quite complicated. The breakeven point changes with price and varies according to the demand fluctuations that are so prevalent in services. Because variable costs are usually much lower than fixed costs (note that in the motel example the fixed costs were $43, whereas the variable costs were $7), the service provider can leverage the fixed assets into providing more services at a low incremental cost. Services marketers can take advantage of this opportunity by offering a combination of offerings in a price bundle. The next section explores creative price bundling opportunities.

PRICE BUNDLING

> **Price bundling** links several service offerings or features into one attractive price to give different customer segments a packaged service offering.

Price bundling links several service offerings or features into one attractive price to give customers from different segments a packaged service offering. The bundle includes features perhaps not as desirable when priced individually (Guiltinan 1987). The varying needs of service customers offer possibilities for flexible pricing. For instance, in the absence of tangible cues for a service offering, some customers associate a high price with high quality when assessing a service against the range of competing offerings. In contrast, other customers constitute a market segment that considers a low price the most important factor and is willing to seek it out. This segment finds organizations with self-service delivery systems particularly attractive. Higher-paying customer segments respond best to tailored versions of service offerings or customized service bundles. As a result, organizations can adjust prices to reflect service variations for different segments. As with the marketing of physical goods, segments should be carefully selected based on their size and potential profitability so that an organization's total portfolio of customers provides the maximum return on its assets.

Service organization assets can be leveraged to produce and deliver multiple offerings, either separately or in bundles, to attract the maximum number of the highest-paying customers to the organization. Thus, price bundling allows the service provider to meet a wider range of customers' needs. The more closely aligned a service bundle is with the customer's desires, the more loyal the customer is likely to remain. Loyal customers guarantee service usage and make it easier to schedule service capacity. Therefore, organizations should consider offering price bundles to help prevent switching behavior and realize the advantages of customer loyalty.

For a service organization with multiple products, price bundling is an effective way to cross-sell service offerings or to present patrons with a customized package at a price much lower than the sum of the parts. Figure 8.3 depicts how price bundling increases total revenues. In the second graph, an organization generates total revenues of $320 (derived from 100 customers of product A, priced at $1, and 110 customers of product B, priced at $2). Note that some customers buy both offerings A and B. Now, if the organization offers a product bundle, AB (product A and product B together), for a combined price of $2.50—a figure that reflects a $.50 savings—and thereby attracts 120 customers to the bundle, its total revenues will be much higher than the previous $320.

Of course, the number of service customers selecting offering A and those selecting offering B will be fewer than before the AB product bundle was made available. If only 80 customers of A and 70 customers of B are left, then the combined revenues from offerings A, B, and AB will be $520, as seen in the third graph in Figure 8.4. Customers who purchase the offering AB will include some who previously bought offerings A and B (these customers were earlier paying full price for both); customers who purchased product B but did not buy product A, and vice versa; and new customers who had not previously bought either product. Price bundling is prevalent in services such as retail banking, vacation packages, cable television, fitness centers, clubs, and car washes. It is a particularly attractive pricing option for capacity-constrained services and services that share resources. Service customers see the interdependence or complementary nature of the bundled services as a logical and desirable choice. Service providers consider them attractive because a larger group of customers share the high fixed costs relative to variable costs and the price charged for a bundle covers more of those fixed costs. Because the variable costs associated with price bundling are minimal, most of the revenues derived from the additional customers go straight to the service's contribution margin.

Some additional distinctions regarding service price bundling are important to note. For instance, *pure* price bundling means that only the specified bundle of offerings is available to the customer. In contrast, *mixed* price bundling means that both the product bundle and the separate offerings in the bundle are available. As noted, the price of a bundle is lower than the sum of the separate offerings it includes. Because customers differ in price sensitivity and in their time of purchase preferences, customizing the service price to attract different segments is likely to maximize profits and profitability. With multiple levels of pricing based on conditions of purchase or use, more customer segments are likely to purchase the service than if a single price were offered (Dolan and Simon 1996). An organization can identify segments based on the nature of the service offering and bundles of products they desire, buyer characteristics pertaining to volume, user status (new versus old), timing of purchase and use, and any pertinent characteristic related to the perceived value that each segment places on the service. In the airline industry, for example, higher-paying customers receive benefits

FIGURE 8.3 Customer Segmentation with Price Bundling

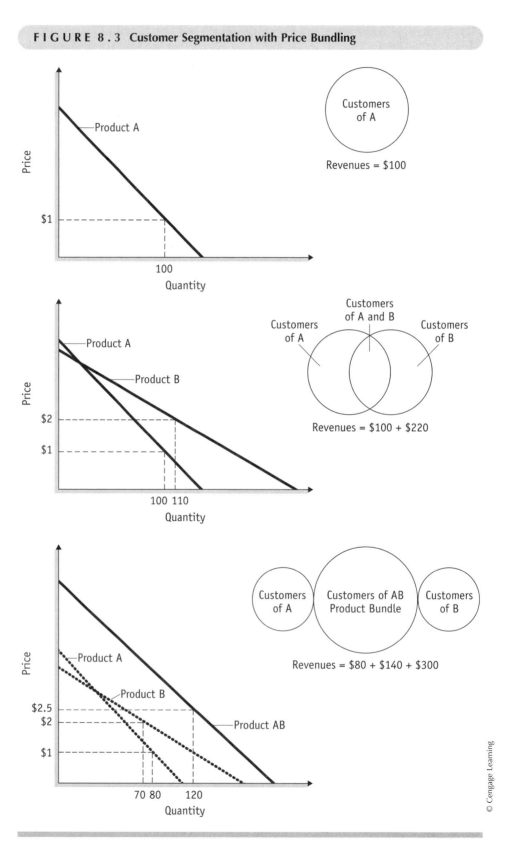

such as advance purchase waivers and cancellation privileges. The pricing of cellular phone service described in Table 8.1 illustrates how different combinations of service features can be bundled for different price packages. To set the features in the bundle and price all of the bundles developed, the services marketer must understand the value of each feature to the customer.

Most services rely on direct interaction with customers; therefore, production must wait for interaction to begin, which makes that interaction an excellent opportunity to customize both the service offering and its price. The idea of cross-selling service offerings is a direct outcome of offering multiple services through shared resources or through customers' purchase, use, or consumption behavior.

ADDITIONAL PRICING CONSIDERATIONS

Several additional pricing considerations must be taken into account when formulating pricing strategies for services. Table 8.2 lists some of these considerations. Services provide a wide range of opportunities for creative pricing. Long-term profitability and maximization of revenues from assets should always be the driving force behind services' pricing decisions. When a specific service provider prices its products higher than the competition, an implied positioning of the service versus the competing services takes place. For example, Marriott **(http://www.marriott.com/)** prices its various hotels according to the position of each class of its hotel chains in that particular segment of the hospitality market. The timing of service purchase can be used to differentiate pricing for different segments. Consider air travel, for instance. The business traveler with little flexibility in travel plans is willing to pay a higher price for a specific date and time of travel. Short notice travel decisions drive the ticket price even higher. Contrast that with the family vacation planned in advance and the customer willing to be somewhat flexible to secure better ticket prices. Service providers also attempt to establish membership relationships with customers by providing special value (price versus amount of service) benefits for their

TABLE 8.2 Pricing Considerations for Services

Factors to Consider in Pricing	Implications for the Services Marketer
Positioning	Price–quality relationship among the range of competing products
Time of demand	Segments differ in price sensitivity with differences in time of purchase or use
Membership	Discount and affinity benefits retain customer loyalty and increase switching costs
Customization	Tailored versions of products or customized bundling of products attract more customers
Participation	Lower price for customer effort, such as in self-service

© Cengage Learning

============ SPOTLIGHT 8.3 ============

What Is a Picture Worth?

 Snapfish (**http://www.snapfish.com**) or Shutterfly (**http://www.shutterfly.com**) have nothing to do with fishing! These and other photo and video storage and sharing Web sites offer a number of services. Not only can you store, organize, and print your photos, but you can also add tags and network with others on the site. You can request an e-mail alert when a tag is added to any of your photos. Picasa, owned by Google (**http://www.picasa.google.com**), is compatible with TiVo, and allows you to view photos on your television and share with other TiVo users. Flickr (**http://www.flickr.com**), which Yahoo! bought in 2005, claims to host over 3 billion digital images, and Photobucket (**http://www.photobucket.com**)

claims more than 7 billion uploaded images. The free service on Flickr allows 200 free-to-upload photos, while Photobucket offers completely free, unlimited space for your photo files and uploads. Or, for a mere $25 a year with Flickr, you can get unlimited storage. Fotolog lets you upload one photo a day for free—or ten a day for $5.50 a month. Smugmug (**http://www.smugmug.com**) charges $40 a year for its standard service, which includes unlimited storage and uploading of photos and videos can be uploaded on its Power and Pro accounts.

Source: Adapted from Lynch, Larry M (2011), "A Comparison of the Top 5 Photo Sharing Websites," **http://www.brighthub.com/multimedia/photography/articles/29672.aspx** (accessed on August 05, 2011).

---

patronage that effectively increase switching costs. Spotlight 8.3 captures several of these notions in its discussion of price as it applies to online services, such as photo storage services.

Prices of services are also differentiated by the extent of customization of service provided to the customer. When a service is tailored to the specific customer, providers can charge a higher price. Similarly, the service price decreases when the customer participates in the production, as in self-service situations.

For a more detailed discussion of pricing objectives and other possible considerations in the pricing of services, see Indounas and Avlonitis (2009).

Summary and Conclusion

The nature of services makes pricing a more complex process than pricing physical goods. Intangibility and perishability can make it difficult for customers to know what is a reasonable price for a service. Likewise, organizations have a difficult time determining the actual costs of providing a service. Further, the costs that do exist are often shared across service offerings, increasing the difficulty of setting accurate prices. The variable costs of producing a service are much smaller in proportion to the total costs of the offering than is typical of packaged goods. One of the most important tasks in pricing services is shifting customer demand to times and product bundles that increase profitability. For that reason, price customization and price bundling are common in services. The interactive nature of the production and consumption of services provides many opportunities for price bundles targeted to different customers and segments. Service organizations should recognize that price represents more than the cost customers must pay. Price is a vehicle for building relationships, conveying quality, and contributing to the long-term profitability of the service organization.

Exercises

1. Examine the price variations at a service organization and plot the different price points over the demand cycle (e.g., different times of the day, week, month). Why are the prices different, and what would the demand levels be without the price variations?
2. Find an example of an organization that uses price bundling and construct the various combinations of service features by which prices vary. What are the price advantages in the bundle? What market segments are attracted to the bundle rather than to the individual service features? How are the total sales in the organization affected by the price bundling?
3. Interview a service marketer to identify the various costs of the service provided. Then, using the information on costs and the price charged for the service, find out the marketer's break-even number in terms of either customers or sales needed.

Internet Exercise

EXPLORE

Visit the companion site for this text at **www .cengagebrain.com** to explore key concepts in the service industry. You will find tools to help you expand your services marketing knowledge, including ACE self-tests, Web links to companies and organizations featured in this chapter, and much more!

Visit the Web sites of your personal bank and one of its competitors. Record prices of various checking accounts available to the individual customer.

1. What is the fee structure for the checking accounts? What are the features that define each account and its price to the customer?
2. What are the key aspects of differentiation among the prices of these accounts within each bank?
3. How do the two banks differentiate themselves based on the pricing of financial services?

References

Desiraju, Ramarao and Steven M. Shugan (1999), "Strategic Service Pricing and Yield Management," *Journal of Marketing*, 63 (1), 44–56.

Dolan, Robert and Hermann Simon (1996), *Power Pricing*, New York: Free Press.

Guiltinan, Joseph (1987), "The Price Bundling of Services: A Normative Framework," *Journal of Marketing*, 51 (2), 74–85.

Indounas, Kostis and George J. Avlonitis (2009), "Pricing Objectives and Their Antecedents in the Services Sector," *Journal of Service Management*, 20 (3), 342–374.

Zeithaml, Valarie (1981), "How Consumer Evaluation Processes Differ Between Goods and Services," *in Marketing of Services*, J. H. Donnelly and W. R. George, eds., Chicago: American Marketing Association, 186–190.

CHAPTER 9
Promoting the Interactive Service Experience

As shown in the Broadmoor Hotel **(http://www.broadmoor.com/colorado-springs-resort/)** vignette, the Broadmoor Hotel promotes its services with the same care it devotes to every other aspect of its operations. Publicity and public relations are especially important, because the hotel seeks affluent customers who are "in the know."

This chapter explores the challenges of promoting services and examines ways of adapting promotional and marketing communication efforts to the characteristics of services. The chapter has eight specific objectives:

- **To emphasize the need for an integrated approach to marketing communications for services**
- **To examine the role of the marketing mix in communicating with customers of a service**
- **To discuss the role of the promotional mix in marketing communications for services**
- **To examine the growing use of the Internet in promoting services**
- **To examine the advertising of services**
- **To explore sales promotions for services**
- **To present the role of personal selling in services**
- **To discuss the role of publicity for services**

Close your eyes and try to picture the service an insurance company delivers. What does it look like? What shape does it have? Is it colorful? What about its size? You can't answer these questions because the insurance the company provides—like many services—lacks a physical presence. It is impossible to form a precise picture of something inherently formless. The intangibility of service products at their core constitutes a major obstacle to their successful promotion. The difficulty you had mentally picturing insurance corresponds to the problem confronting organizations attempting to promote their services. How do service organizations effectively communicate something that can't be seen or, for that matter, doesn't even exist yet? Remember, services are delivered in real time! Fortunately, the interactive nature of most services allows many opportunities to address this problem.

SERVICES AND INTEGRATED MARKETING COMMUNICATIONS

Integrated marketing communications (IMC) refers to the pursuit of a single positioning concept for an organization or its products, which is achieved by planning, coordinating, and unifying all the communication tools at an organization's disposal, including advertising, packaging, public relations, personal selling, online links, and more (Schultz, Tannenbaum, and Lauterborn 1996). Whether by design or by default, many service organizations have been integrating their marketing communications to some degree for years. Unfortunately, some research suggests that services marketers could be doing a better job of harnessing the potential of IMC (Grove, Carlson, and Dorsch 2007).

The challenge of marketing intangible products that exist in real time forces service organizations to consider ways to overcome the "fuzziness" of their offerings, and IMC is one solution. It may be helpful to reflect again on the theatrical model of services as a guide for creating consistent impressions. When we picture services as performances for an audience, we see the need to carefully coordinate actors and setting, frontstage and backstage activity, and actor–audience interaction. In a theatrical production, everything contributes to the audience's experience, and so it is with services. Olive Garden restaurants **(http://www.olivegarden.com),** Ritz-Carlton Hotels **(http://ritzcarlton.com),** Scandinavian airline SAS **(http://www.sas.se),** and many other service organizations have established consistent images for their respective businesses by attending to how communication affects their service delivery systems. Other service organizations should follow their lead and present a clear, well-defined position for their service with every communication device at their disposal. Workers' appearance and manner, the servicescape, the frontstage aspects of the service performance, the service name, and all the traditional promotional tools should reflect that same position.

One key aspect of IMC in today's marketing environment is the opportunity that integrated marketing communication offers an organization to build customer relationships by prompting customers to connect with the organization through though various communication vehicles (Duncan 2005; Grove, Dorsch, and Carlson 2011). Whether it's an engaging broadcast advertisement that motivates a consumer to seek more information from the advertiser's Web site or providing direct response doorways, such as toll free numbers, e-mail addresses and Web site locations via ads, packaging, handbills or other communication devices, the possibility to provide additional product or organization information, create customer databases, and forge a link with the customer exists if the endeavor is well executed. This opportunity to build relationships with customers is especially powerful when the new media channels such as Facebook, YouTube, and Twitter are embraced by organizations (Hennig-Thurau et al. 2010). The payoff of such an undertaking is potentially great, particularly for service organizations that can take advantage of the link to help customers better appreciate their offerings, reduce perceived risk, and compile profile information that allows the organization to better target customers with desired service products and features. Beyond simply including the doorway, the various communication tools in an IMC effort must encourage customers to take advantage of the direct response opportunities and, once contacted, the organization needs to have the back-end design and support to establish and nurture the link to the customer in a timely and meaningful manner. Service organizations that do so can create a dialogue with their customer that provides rewards for both parties. Unfortunately, there appears to be room for improvement in that regard (Grove, Dorsch, and Carlson 2011).

MARKETING COMMUNICATIONS AND SERVICES

The intangibility of services creates challenges for services marketers. A customer often has difficulty comprehending just what she is purchasing before, during, and even after a service is delivered. For that reason, service organizations need to tangibilize their offerings (see Figure 9.1). **Tangibilizing the service** means making the service more concrete, thus enabling customers to understand it better (Shostack 1977). Numerous tools can help services marketers do this. In fact, every element of the services marketing mix (the "seven Ps") discussed in Chapter 2 may be used for this purpose.

> **Tangibilizing the service** means making the service more concrete, thus enabling customers to understand it better.

Promotion is the one element among the seven Ps that explicitly communicates with customers. Hence, organizations rely on promotion to help customers understand their services. Yet, with a little thought, each of the other services marketing mix elements can contribute to that end, too. Communicating with the customer may not be the primary concern when an organization sets a price, designs a physical setting, or establishes a distribution plan. However, decisions regarding these and the other service marketing Ps implicitly help customers gain a clearer picture of the service they can't see.

Price can help establish the quality of the service. For instance, as noted in Chapter 8, a higher price communicates higher quality, whereas a lower price suggests less exacting standards. If you buy a first-class seat on an airline, you expect a greater level of attentiveness than if you purchase a seat in the coach section. *Place,* the location of the service establishment, may convey something about the service's nature. Customer expectations regarding a dry-cleaning business located in an upscale section of town are likely to be quite different from those related to a similar operation in a less affluent neighborhood. Knowing where the service is located may give customers an idea about its physical appearance, its size, the type of customers who patronize it, and even those who work there. *Product* characteristics may communicate to the customer: The number of versions of the basic service available, whether it comes with a guarantee, and the name the organization chooses all influence customers' perception of a service. Restaurants that offer a guarantee of lunch in fifteen minutes are establishing definite expectations regarding promptness of service and implicitly conveying quite different expectations regarding ambiance and comfort. Think of how effectively the brand name Think of how effectively the brand name Sin City Brewing **(http://sincitybeer.com)** conveys the business's focus in a memorable and distinctive way.

Participants in the service delivery (workers and customers) potentially generate a lot of information about the service. The number of customers and their demographic profile communicate something about the popularity of the service and its ideal target market. Similarly, employee dress, appearance, and actions may convey the service's degree of formality and the feeling the organization has for its customers. Compare, for example, a retailer such as Burberry **(http://www.burberry.com)** with Big Lots **(http://www.biglots.com/).** *Physical evidence* can communicate a desired service

---

F I G U R E 9 . 1 Tangibilizing the Service

---

image in several ways. As suggested in Chapter 5, the choice of décor, furnishings, and equipment can establish the service as traditional or modern, classify it as upbeat or sedate, and communicate whether it is self-service or full service. Consider how the physical evidence of an Irish pub sends a message about the nature of the service, which is quite different from that of a night club.

The process of service assembly conveys valuable messages regarding the level of attentiveness, the degree of customization possible, and even the desired role of customers as co-producers of the service. By observing and participating in its enactment, the customer receives important information regarding these and other features of the service offering. Many automobile maintenance shops (particularly those performing oil changes and lubrication services) allow customers to view the work that is being performed on their vehicle. Many high-contact services (such as medical care or hairstyling) encourage the customer to actively participate in the service delivery. In each case, the way in which the service is assembled is informative to customers.

In sum, service organizations have many opportunities to tangibilize their services by using any or all of the services marketing mix elements at their disposal. To help their customers better understand the service in question, service organizations should pay careful attention to the potential communication role of their marketing decisions with respect to each of the services marketing mix elements.

THE PROMOTIONAL MIX

Although all of the services marketing mix elements may communicate important information to the customer, promotion is the method of choice for this purpose since it is the one element that is designed specifically to communicate with audiences. The promotion element of the marketing mix informs, persuades, reminds, and adds value. *Informing* is a critical way of helping the customer comprehend the nature of the intangible service. Conveying a variety of details regarding service delivery in an organization's communication can accomplish this task. An organization may succeed in *persuading* the customer to respond positively to the service by portraying the product in a favorable and attractive light or by providing incentives to customers to patronize the service. Organizations whose services are purchased infrequently, such as some types of home maintenance (e.g., chimney sweeping or radon testing) or preventive medicine (e.g., dental checkups or veterinary services), must make a concerted effort to maintain customers' awareness of the service. Various promotional activities, particularly advertising, can effectively *remind* customers that such services are available to satisfy needs or wants the customer may have overlooked. The overall promotional effort can also *add value* to an organization's service offering. All elements of the services marketing mix can be coordinated to infuse a service offering with an extra measure of attractiveness, appeal, or stature. For example, consider the added value to its overall service that the Walt Disney Company **(http://disney.go.com/)** generates through its many promotional activities. In addition to informing, persuading, and reminding its customers, Disney's promotions augment the service experience by casting the organization in an alluring light.

> The **promotional mix** consists of advertising, sales promotions, personal selling, publicity, and public relations.

To promote one's service, organizations can rely on a number of communication tools that are commonly referred to as the promotional mix. The **promotional mix** consists of advertising, sales promotions, personal selling, publicity, and public relations. A service organization's promotional effort might include *any* or *all* of these elements in various combinations, depending upon its objectives, resources, and other factors. Each element has attributes that make it more or less appealing as a promotional device in different circumstances. As a service organization's goals change, its promotional mix will change, too. For example, a new hotel will most likely emphasize advertising to quickly spread the word about the new property. Later, the hotel may shift its focus to sales promotions to increase occupancy during periods of slack demand.

Advertising

Depending upon the media used and the nature of the message, advertising can reach large audiences quickly and provide them with valuable information, persuasive arguments, forceful reminders, and an enhanced service image. As with marketing physical goods, advertising is the primary means of communicating with service customers and is often the cornerstone of an organization's promotional effort. Consider the many advertisements that you encounter in any given day for services ranging from fast food to health care and more.

SPOTLIGHT 9.1

You Want Fries with That?

 Recognizing that its customers were ordering their fries less often—despite the fact that they were rated number one in 2011 according to a Zagat's fast-food survey—and facing stiff competition from key rivals like Wendy's and Burger King, McDonald's decided it needed to rekindle interest in its mainstay offering. To accomplish that, it ran a promotional campaign on a limited budget (less than $250,000) that prompted customers to associate its fries with something other than simply burgers and beverage—with favorite moments of their life. In essence, it changed the question, "You want fries with that?" to a statement that evoked personal scenes in which McDonald's fries were a welcomed addition. The phrase appeared in online, in-store, and out-of-store media as well as signage, Facebook, and Twitter communications and even packaging. Customers were encouraged to reflect on their supreme McDonald's fries experience and fill in the blank (You Want McDonald's Fries with _____) and

register it online or via their mobile devices. Customers were also encouraged to share their responses via Facebook and Twitter, creating more entries from the social media The incentive? Twenty-five thousand dollars awarded to some lucky winner to make their vision happen.

To maintain interest over the duration of the campaign, hundreds of Arch Card awards valued at $50 were distributed weekly. The results were indeed excellent. The contest had 270,000 entries, in excess of 120,000 online searches for McDonald's fries (nearly 40% higher than a year earlier) and over 17,000 tweets with an overwhelmingly high (95% positive/neutral) hashtag. Overall, the sales of fries increased 4% compared to the year before.

Source: "2012 PRO Award Finalist: Arc Worldwide/Leo Burnett for McDonald's," **http://chiefmarketer.com /promotional-marketing/2012-pro-award-finalist-arc-worldwideleo-burnett-mcdonalds** (accessed August 14, 2012).

Sales Promotions

Sales promotions create excitement and generate business for a service organization in the short run. Sales promotions such as contests, sweepstakes, premiums, sales, coupons, and free samples provide a means for the service organization to stand out from the competition and attract customers. Consider the sales promotion discussed in Spotlight 9.1 as a means for McDonald's (http://www.mcdonalds.com/) to create excitement and newfound interest in its fries with only a limited budget. Sales promotions are particularly well suited to stimulating demand for a service with excess capacity to fill, as will be discussed in Chapter 14.

Personal Selling

Personal selling is an attractive tool for informing or persuading customers about complex or expensive services such as maintenance on computer systems or advertising and promotion contracts for corporations. The face-to-face nature of personal selling allows the salesperson to respond to customers' questions, fully explaining and sometimes demonstrating via technology critical aspects of the service offering. Personal selling is a key element in the promotion of professional services (e.g., legal advice, architectural consulting), financial services (e.g., financial planners, insurance agents), and business-to-business services (e.g., advertising agencies, research firms).

Publicity and Public Relations

Publicity and public relations are excellent means of promoting services, particularly new or high-risk offerings. Effective public relations can foster an admirable image and cast an innovative or risky offering in a positive light. For example, publicity in the form of media reviews is critical to the success of theater, dance, opera productions, and other entertainment offerings. Publicity serves a similar role in the early acceptance of new services across a wide range of service industries. Public relations can overcome negative publicity about service events ranging from airplane crashes to restaurant food poisonings. It can also generate product appeal by linking a service to a popular event (e.g., music festival or sports event) or social cause (e.g., environmentalism or elimination of world hunger).

A D V E R T I S I N G   T H E   S E R V I C E

This section examines advertising objectives, guidelines for advertising, and methods for enhancing the vividness of services advertising.

Advertising Objectives

The goals of services advertising are similar to those of advertising in general, yet how service organizations achieve those goals is likely to be different. Advertising goals (and the goals of promotion in general) are sometimes encapsulated in the acronym AIDA, which represents the four goals of attracting customers' *attention, interest, desire,* and *action.* These objectives are ordered in a hierarchical sequence leading to the ultimate goal of product purchase. First, an advertisement must gain the customer's attention to a service and make him or her aware of the service organization. Next, it should pique the customer's interest; in other words, motivate the customer to process information that the ad may possess. The advertisement may then stimulate a desire for the service that ultimately leads to action, perhaps by underscoring a unique or desirable feature that the service possesses. As with physical goods, a service advertisement can be directed toward any or several of the AIDA objectives. The goals chosen reflect the communication needs of the service provider (e.g., making customers aware of a new service offering or creating a positive attitude toward it) and influence its decisions regarding advertising strategy (i.e., media choice, message development, etc.). For example, law school graduates or newly minted physicians probably want to announce their newly opened practice with advertisements that generate awareness and provide details of their expertise. In contrast, an airline locked in a competitive battle over a route between two cities may find it advantageous to use comparative advertising to develop desire and action from would-be fliers.

Beyond the objectives captured by the AIDA acronym, it is important to recognize the key role that advertising plays in supporting other promotional efforts. A strong advertising campaign can make the personal selling task of an insurance agent much easier, generate publicity/help manage public relations about the newest offering by a telecommunications company, and pave the way for effective sales promotions for fast-food restaurants or hotels. Think of the importance that advertising likely carried for the sales promotion discussed in Spotlight 9.2.

===== **SPOTLIGHT 9.2** =====

Sleepy Bear Redux

 The Wyndham Hotel Group began a new campaign in the summer of 2012 designed to generate newfound interest in its Travelodge brand. It focused on its longtime mascot, Sleepy Bear, and new sponsors, National Geographic and the Association of Zoos and Aquariums. The "Stay Close to Adventure" campaign posed Travelodge's 440 properties in North America as the perfect hotel choice for travelers seeking out-of-town adventure on a budget. As part of the campaign, Sleepy Bear—now over fifty years old—was revamped and modernized with new attire; computer animation; and big, friendly eyes. Utilizing TV, print, online, and at-property advertising, travelers were introduced to the updated mascot and Travelodge's "Zoocation" promotion, which allowed guests who booked a room directly with the hotel to receive a free child's ticket to any of 115 zoos across the United States when an adult ticket was purchased. Also part of the promotion were five Travelodge-branded family events at zoos throughout the United States, "Zoo to You" activity books handed out at the hotels, and a donation to the American Zoo Association to benefit black bear conservation on behalf of Travelodge.

Source: wyndhamworldwide.com/ (2012), "Freshly Animated Sleepy Bear Stars in Travelodge Marketing Campaign," **http://www.wyndhamworldwide.com /media/press-releases/press-release?wwprdid=1191** (accessed August 16).

Guidelines for Advertising Services

George and Berry (1981) proposed several guidelines for advertising a service. These guidelines address the challenge that services marketers face when they must communicate with their customers about a product that is essentially a performance. Among the guidelines that service advertisers should embrace are:

- Provide tangible cues.

- Capitalize on word-of-mouth communication.

- Make the service understood.

- Establish advertising continuity.

- Advertise to employees.

- Promise what is possible.

Service organizations can overcome the service's lack of physical presence and the accompanying high degree of perceived risk by *providing tangible cues.* For example, they can use spokespersons—William Shatner, best known for his role as Captain Kirk of the *Star Trek* TV series and motion pictures, has been a spokesperson for priceline.com **(http://www.priceline.com/)** for a number of years. Some service organizations' advertisements show the service equipment or facilities—United Parcel Service **(http://www.ups.com)** shows its trucks and airplanes. Others provide numbers and facts—British Airways **(http://www .BritishAirways.com)** proclaims its on-time performance over a specified period. Each technique adds concreteness to the service and helps enhance the perception of service quality.

Service organizations can address the variability of services by *capitalizing on word-of-mouth communication.* Word-of-mouth communication is generally considered more credible than commercial advertising because it comes from personal and impartial sources. To reduce the likelihood of choosing the wrong dentist, accountant, college professor, or hairstylist, customers often rely on the opinions of others. Service organizations' advertisements can include testimonials from satisfied customers or encourage patrons to speak to their peers about the service to simulate or stimulate word of mouth communication.

Some organizations may need to develop advertisements that *make the service understood* because many services are complex and abstract. Insurance companies and other intangible services (e.g., consulting or education) often employ symbols, logos, or slogans that convey key aspects of their offering. Examples are Prudential Insurance's **(http://www.prudential.com)** use of the Rock of Gibraltar, Travelers Insurance's **(http://www.travelers.com)** umbrella, or Merrill Lynch's **(http://www.ml.com)** bull. In some instances, organizations may even "walk the customer through" the process of service delivery by showing or explaining the process in the advertisements. When FedEx **(http://www.fedex.com)** introduces an innovation designed to expedite its core service of overnight package delivery, it goes to great lengths to inform customers of the innovation's operation, often relying on humorous television spots to convey the new feature. Such advertising efforts help customers mentally grasp the nature of the service. See Spotlight 9.3 for some humorous slogans that help make the service understood.

SPOTLIGHT 9.3

Humorous Service Organization Slogans

On a septic tank truck sign:
   "We're #1 in the #2 business."
Sign over a gynecologist's office:
   "Dr. Jones, at your cervix."
At a proctologist's door:
   "To expedite your visit, please back in."
On a plumber's truck:
   "We repair what your husband fixed."
On a plumber's truck:
   "Don't sleep with a drip. Call your plumber."
Pizza shop slogan:
   "7 days without pizza makes one weak."
At a tire shop in Milwaukee:
   "Invite us to your next blowout."
On a plastic surgeon's office door:
   "Hello. Can we pick your nose?"
At a towing company:
   "We don't charge an arm and a leg.
We want tows."
On an electrician's truck:
   "Let us remove your shorts."
On a maternity room door:
   "Push. Push. Push."
At an optometrist's office:
   "If you don't see what you're looking for, you've
come to the right place."

On a taxidermist's window:
   "We really know our stuff."
In a podiatrist's office:
   "Time wounds all heels."
At a car dealership:
   "The best way to get back on your feet—miss a
car payment."
Outside a muffler shop:
   "No appointment necessary. We hear you
coming."
In a veterinarian's waiting room:
   "Be back in 5 minutes. Sit! Stay!"
At the electric company:
   "We would be delighted if you send in your
payment. However, if you don't, you will be."
In a restaurant window:
   "Don't stand there and be hungry. Come on in
and get fed up."
In the front yard of a funeral home:
   "Drive carefully. We'll wait."
At a propane filling station:
   "Tank heaven for little grills."
And don't forget the sign at a Chicago radiator shop:
   "Best place in town to take a leak."

Source: Anonymous.

George and Berry (1981) suggest recurrently using themes, symbols, and other cues to *establish advertising continuity* in the service customer's mind. Advertising efforts emblazon the organization's logo across all types of physical evidence, such as items carrying the golden arches symbol of McDonald's. Advertising campaigns may also stress similar service attributes over time, like the low-cost, no-frills, and dependable character of Southwest Airlines **(http://www.southwest.com)**. Such actions create recognition for a service and reinforce its desired image.

Advertising to employees should be a consideration when developing service advertisements. Service employees represent a secondary audience for an organization's advertisements because they see the same ads that customers see; hence, it makes sense to design advertising communications with employees in mind to motivate and/or educate them. Advertising that portrays employees in a positive light can boost morale. Depicting employees engaged in desired activities associated with the service can be a reinforcing educational device. The former sends a subtle but powerful message of how the organization perceives its employees, while the latter communicates expectations regarding their performance. Over the years, Delta Air Lines' **(http://www.delta.com)** advertising campaigns have positioned it as a people-oriented carrier through narratives starring actual workers. Research substantiates the notion that employees' pride, customer focus, and effectiveness will increase when an organization portrays its workers accurately and positively (Celsi and Gilly 2010).

Finally, the advice to *promise what is possible* alerts service advertisers to the potential pitfall of overpromising and underdelivering. An old adage suggests that you can sell anything to anyone once. Advertisements can be designed to make a service so appealing that it is almost impossible for anyone to resist. Low costs, terrific experiences, and wonderful results are easily promised, particularly because services are intangible, variable, and perishable. As we know, a service cannot be seen, is subject to great variation in excellence, and doesn't exist until the customer purchases it. Such circumstances make it tempting to oversell what an organization can actually deliver. In the rush to generate patronage, advertisements may set customer expectations so high that they are impossible to meet. When expectations are greater than the service can deliver, customer dissatisfaction is predestined, and the organization is doomed to disappoint. Overpromising and underdelivering can spawn significant negative word-of-mouth communication, which is difficult to overcome and further undermines an organization's well-being. The lesson for service advertisers is simple. Be appealing, but realistic.

Not all of these guidelines apply to every service advertisement. Some of George and Berry's (1981) prescriptions fit certain circumstances more than others. For example, an advertisement promoting an abstract or complex service such as financial advice that is largely produced through workers' skills and abilities may need to make the service understood and appeal to an organization's employees as well as its customers. In contrast, an advertisement for airline travel and other services whose quality may vary widely should probably stress tangible cues and promise what is possible. Figure 9.2 displays a print advertisement for [need an airline ad here]. How many of George and Berry's guidelines does it appear to reflect?

FIGURE 9.2 Singapore Airlines Ad

Singapore Airlines

Enhancing the Vividness of Services Advertising

A **vividness strategy** is an advertising approach that uses concrete language, tangible objects, and dramatization techniques to tangibilize the intangible.

Legg and Baker (1987) offer further suggestions for creating service advertisements that help customers process service information more effectively. One is a **vividness strategy;** that is, an advertising approach that uses *concrete language* (specific information rather than abstract terms), *tangible objects* (physical and well-known representations of the service), and *dramatization techniques* (stories about the service that demonstrate its performance) to add tangibility to the intangible service that is being promoted. How well these tactics work depends on considerations such as the newness or uniqueness of the service. Attempts at vividness seem particularly important when customers know little about the service organization or its offering. Choices in advertising media and the type of service provided dictate the feasibility of a vividness strategy. For instance, dramatization is easier on television or streaming video on the Internet than in newspaper advertising, while an advertisement for a highly intangible service such as insurance may require greater attention to concrete language than an advertisement for a restaurant.

Legg and Baker also suggest developing an advertising effort that establishes a strong link between an organization's name and its service offering through **interactive imagery strategy**. This goal can be accomplished with advertisements that contain *pictorial representations* combining the two. For example, the logo for Domino's Pizza (**http://www.dominos.com**) is a pizza box with domino markings. Image-laden *verbal associations* in a service' name such as Jiffy Lube (**http://www.jiffylube.com**) or Meals-on-Wheels (**http://www.meals-on-wheels.com**) can also accomplish this goal. Another way to employ an interactive imagery strategy is to use *letter accentuation*, which involves conveying some aspect of the service through visually transforming letters in the organization's name. Efforts such as these are particularly effective at improving customers' recall of the service name and its nature.

> **Interactive imagery** uses pictorial representations, verbal associations, and letter accentuations that combine an organization's name and its service to establish a strong link between service name and performance in customer minds.

Finally, Legg and Baker argue, advertisers should create messages that teach customers about a service's backstage operations and what to expect as part of the service delivery script. The former can provide additional information about the quality of a service; the latter can help ensure satisfaction by creating realistic expectations. For example, an advertisement may display the care that a mechanic devotes to an automobile or set an expectation about the time needed for the repair. Both provide valuable information that can influence customers' choice of a service provider and their evaluation of the service they ultimately receive. In a sense, it is similar to the advertising guidelines, make the service understood, discussed earlier.

George and Berry's guidelines and Legg and Baker's prescriptions provide a starting point for devising effective service advertisements. Although each framework offers its own unique insights, both stress the importance of displaying concrete information (e.g., physical evidence, numbers, or facts) to add tangibility to the service. A basic proposition is that service advertisers need to convey such information more prominently than do advertisers of physical goods (Shostack 1977). Some evidence suggests that they do exactly that. Grove, Pickett, and Laband (1995) studied more than 17,000 newspaper advertisements and nearly 10,000 television advertisements and found that the incidence of concrete information was greater among service ads than those for physical goods. The greater the advertised product's intangibility, the more factual information the advertisements provided. Although these recommendations apply to organizations that advertise consumer services, it is likely they apply to business-to-business services, too. Similarly, the soundness of these and various other services advertising frameworks remains to be established in the international arena, and there is much room for continued examination of effective service advertising (Stafford 2005; Stafford et al. 2011).

SALES PROMOTIONS AND SERVICES

The use of sales promotions to generate interest and patronage for service organizations is not new. Merchants and retailers discovered long ago the powerful impact of simple devices such as discounted prices, free samples, and contests. Sales promotions come in many shapes and forms, yet all are designed to draw

FIGURE 9.3 Example of An Internet Coupon for a Service

customers based on some type of special attraction beyond the product. Behind an organization's push to use sales promotions may be a desire to win new customers or to hold the interest of existing ones. Either way, the airline that drops its fares for a limited period of time, the hotel that introduces a special weekend package or bundle of services, the restaurant that offers an early-bird discount, or the satellite network promoting an introductory package are all attempting to increase patronage in the short run and familiarize the customer with the service organization. Most of the time, however, they hope that customers who were attracted to the service by a sales promotion will return after it is over.

Organizations select many service sales promotions to cope with the cyclical demand that service businesses often experience. To encourage trial, some services provide coupons, sometimes distributed through the Internet (see Figure 9.3). Sales promotions are sometimes used as a defensive measure as well. For example, it is common to find competing organizations simultaneously employing similar promotional devices. When one airline drops its fares to win customers, competitors soon follow. Likewise, when McDonald's runs a sweepstakes in the important summer months, competitors such as Burger King (http://www.BK.com), Wendy's (http://www.wendys.com), and others often institute sweepstakes or other sales promotions of their own. The risk of not joining in the sales promotion frenzy could be potentially disastrous to an organization's flow of customers.

Beyond being a powerful tool to manage swings in demand, a sales promotion can become a feature that the customer comes to associate with the service. When carefully selected, a sales promotion device can be used by an organization to infuse a service offering with a desired characteristic. The excitement of a sweepstakes or contest, the goodwill of a premium, the thrill of a special sales event can enhance customers' perceptions of the service as a whole.

A particularly effective tool in some cases is event sponsorship, which allows a service organization to target customers by lending its support to an activity they find appealing. One such example is Chick-fil-A restaurants' **(http://www .chickfila.com)** sponsorship of a college football bowl game, the Chick-fil-A Bowl, held in Atlanta every year. If the sales promotion attracts new customers or builds loyalty among existing ones, it may actually add to a service's tangibility by exposing the customer to the service. After all, what could be more tangible than experiencing the service? Thus, sales promotions for services can attract customers, accommodate cyclical demand, enhance customers' perception of the service, and add tangibility. When supported with a strong advertising effort, sales promotions can create a measure of customer excitement that pays big dividends. However, organizations that rely heavily on sales promotions to generate sales run the risk of creating a circumstance in which some customers may seldom patronize the service unless a sales promotion is offered, thus producing a continuous cycle of coupons, sweepstakes, premiums, and so on.

PERSONAL SELLING AND SERVICES

As with advertising a service, selling a service is difficult because the offering cannot be shown. The customer can't tap on a service or kick its tires. He can't gaze at its attractive lines, turn it over to view its underside, or open it up to see what makes it tick. Likewise, the person who sells a service cannot display what it looks like because it doesn't exist yet. Instead, the salesperson must convince the buyer of the service's attributes and quality in some other manner. Evidence of its likely excellence must be tempered with caution to protect against overselling what can be performed. The salesperson may cite testimonials from satisfied customers or a list of the organization's noteworthy clients. Who wouldn't be encouraged to use a service that has satisfied high-profile customers or has many loyal patrons? The salesperson may use visual aids, such as videos and computer applications, to explain the service in detail. In addition, the service organization must recognize that the salesperson's appearance and demeanor during the selling process act as potential cues regarding the actual service and the service organization. Some specific concerns regarding the selling of services are summarized in the following list (George, Kelly, and Marshall 1983).

■ Orchestrate the service purchase.

■ Facilitate quality assessment.

■ Tangibilize the service.

■ Emphasize organizational image.

■ Use references external to the organization.

■ Recognize the importance of all public contact personnel.

■ Recognize customer involvement during the service design process.

Any service organization must make an effort to establish a strong relationship with the buyer that stands the test of time and insulates the service from its competition. Only successfully delivering on promises made during the selling

---

SPOTLIGHT 9.4

"… Would You Like to Supersize That?"

Most of us at one time or another has probably become annoyed by a service worker asking us a question such as, "Would you like to upgrade to Plan B?" or "Do you want the extended warranty for your purchase?" Actually, such *suggestive selling* and/or *up-selling* can be quite a boon to an organization's revenue flow, even if it is only occasionally successful. Consider the following: a restaurant employs five servers per shift and runs two shifts each day of the week. If each server is able to secure a sale of just one more dessert or appetizer, priced at $5, through suggestive selling, over a year's time that would create $18,200 (5 servers × 2 shifts × 7 days × $5 × 52 weeks) of additional revenue! Clearly,

suggestive selling can lead to significant increased sales. Of course, the trick is to do it well, and that requires a skill that can be imparted during the training of frontstage service personnel. For instance, the up-selling suggestion cannot be too tightly scripted or programmed. If it is, the effort becomes robotic and cold, and it is likely to be a turn-off to the customer. To ensure it is done properly, organizations should monitor the performance of the service workers on this activity, possibly with mystery shoppers. Before instituting a program of suggestive selling, it behooves an organization to consider the ethicality and social ramifications of encouraging customers to possibly spend more and/or consume more than originally intended.

---

process and maintaining contact with the customer over time can achieve such a relationship. Clearly, the Internet, e-mail, and social media networks provide organizations with myriad new means of connecting to and maintaining a relationship with customers.

Oftentimes in the context of providing the service to customers, the opportunity exists to engage in *suggestive selling*—the act of offering additional or complementary service-related options—both in person or via electronic media. Although it may seem that such selling is seldom successful, it's important to recognize that it can generate significant results even if a sale is only occasionally made. Spotlight 9.4 demonstrates the potential benefits that suggestive selling can generate and points to the need to incorporate it as part of employee training.

PUBLICITY AND SERVICES

It is much simpler to sell familiar services to customers than those they have never heard of. For this reason, service organizations gain tremendously from good publicity. The best publicity an organization can receive comes from delighted customers. To attract customers, service organizations often strive to link their service name with something positive. Being newsworthy in a positive way (e.g., donating to charities or supporting popular social causes) casts a service in an attractive light. Also, being a technology leader or customer service champion can put an organization in the news and attract customers. Consider the positive exposure gained by Malcolm Baldrige National Quality Award winners Ritz-Carlton, FedEx, or AT&T **(http://www.att.com).**

Conversely, service organizations must have plans in place to overcome or control negative publicity when it occurs. Remember, services *are* variable! The ability to address negative publicity successfully is one of the reasons airlines like ValuJet, now called AirTran **(http://www.airtran.com),** has been able to continue flying despite a past disaster. Consider the negative publicity faced by organizations that have their computer systems hacked, putting their customers' or clients' identities at risk, and the efforts at damage control that must be made to keep the goodwill of the organization's current and potential customers. The Internet has created a different publicity environment for service organizations because both positive and negative publicity can be spread more rapidly, particularly among the ever-growing social media channels. As of 2010, user-generated content at sites such as Facebook, Twitter, MySpace, and YouTube accounted for more than 11% of the global Internet traffic (Alexa 2010), and a good portion of that pertained to shared comments or insights regarding products on the market. Moreover, conscientious Internet users can track news stories that come across traditional news media Web sites and popular blogs. A RSS feed from such sites allows users to passively receive new content as a story summary with a link to the content. This capability requires news reader software, which is provided free by many popular Web sites, such as AOL, Yahoo!, and Google. In short, RSS feeds nearly automate the tracking of news, which only accelerates the impact of positive or negative publicity.

PROMOTING SERVICES ON THE INTERNET

The Internet has profoundly influenced the nature and process of promoting services. The Internet enables service organizations to qualify and target narrow segments of customers in novel and interactive ways. Search engine optimization tools can be used to make sure that the service organization is being found by customers when they search on Google or Yahoo!. Internet advertisements can be designed to attract and link customers to online sources of information regarding service organizations and, in the case of retailing, even link them to shopping locations and a wide array of information. Internet advertisements are often coupled with various types of sales promotions. Some organizations offer online coupons that can be downloaded and printed (see Figure 9.3). Customers can enter contests on the Internet, such as Pizza Hut's **(http://www.pizzahut.com)** annual NCAA **(http://www.ncaa.com)** college basketball "Pick 'Em Challenge."

Internet advertising has become so successful that service organizations are shifting their promotion strategies and budgets toward more online advertising (Vollmer, Frelinghuysen, and Rothenberg 2006). One of the most important features of Internet advertising is the ability to carefully track the effectiveness of each ad based on how customers respond to it. A second key feature is the ability to create interactive multimedia ads that exceed the typical fifteen- or thirty-second broadcast advertising limits. Such ads can link back to many parts of the organization's Web site for additional information. Nevertheless, there appears to be a need for effectively integrating an organization's Web site with marketing communication tools (Grove, Dorsch, and Carlson 2011).

Service organizations can also combine e-mail or social media sales messages with Internet advertising to create a powerful combination of advertising and selling. For instance, airlines such as Delta **(http://www.Delta.com),**

American **(http://www.AAcom),** and US Airways **(http://www.usairways.com)** e-mail information about special fares to travelers who request this service. If a fare advertised in the e-mail is of interest, the traveler can click on the airline's Web site address and purchase a ticket. Visitors to the airline's Web site find all sorts of informational and promotional materials. Similarly, many organizations are taking advantage of social networking sites like Facebook by posting notes pertaining to their offerings in the hope of building business and generating traffic to their bricks-and-mortar and/or Internet location (Graham 2011). In summary, the Internet provides powerful promotional tools for services marketers.

Summary and Conclusion

Promoting a service organization and its services is a challenge that requires careful planning and implementation. Every contact point with a service organization carries potentially strong promotional significance. Hence, services marketers need to consider ways to use all seven Ps of the marketing mix to create a desired message. If left to chance, it is unlikely that a consistent service image will develop. An organization needs to use the same foresight it devotes to determining a traditional promotional mix when it considers the communication abilities of the various components of its service delivery system. Such an integrated approach pays big dividends in positioning and establishing the service in customers' minds. Through it all, the need to accommodate the intangible aspects of services should drive any promotional decision. Ultimately, the goal of any service's promotional effort should be to attract and win customer support.

Exercises

1. Locate and make a copy of an advertisement for a service in a magazine, newspaper, or direct mail communication. Identify the various ways in which it reflects George and Berry's guidelines for services advertising. Do you consider the advertisement good or bad? Why?

2. Search Facebook for service advertisements that reflect each of Legg and Baker's forms of interactive imagery: pictorial representations, verbal associations, and letter accentuation. Save copies of them and explain how they fit each category.

3. Surf the Internet to locate examples of an online coupon and a contest offered by a service organization. Print a copy of each and be prepared to discuss whether you think each sales promotional device is a good one.

4. Choose a service organization's marketing communications activities and analyze what it communicates to its customers through each of the various services marketing mix variables. From your point of view, does it do a good job of integrating its marketing communications? Why or why not?

5. Pick a service organization and investigate how it uses the Internet to promote its services:

   a. What e-mail messages does it send to customers?

   b. Where does it place its Internet advertising?

   c. How does it use the organizational Web site for promotion?

Internet Exercise

Locate an online advertisement of a nationally known service organization, preferably one not mentioned in this chapter. Study it carefully.

1. Describe it in terms of the guidelines for services advertising by George and Berry presented in the chapter.
2. Does it do anything to increase the vividness of the service?
3. How could the advertisement be improved?

References

Alexa (2010), "The Top 500 Sites on the Web," **http:// www.alexa.com/topsites/global** (accessed September 6, 2012).

Celsi, Mary Wolfinbarger and Mary C. Gilly (2010), "Employees as Internal Audience: How Advertising affects Employees' Customer Focus," *Journal of the Academy of Marketing Science*, 38 (4), 528–539.

Duncan, Thomas R. (2005), "IMC in Industry: More Talk Than Walk," *Journal of Advertising*, 54 (4), 5–9.

George, William R., J. Patrick Kelly, and Claudia E. Marshall (1983), "Personal Selling of Services," in *Emerging Perspectives on Services Marketing*, L. L. Berry, G. L. Shostack, and G. D. Upah (eds.), Chicago: American Marketing Association, 65–67.

George, William R. and Leonard L. Berry (1981), "Guidelines for Advertising of Services," *Business Horizons*, 24 (July/August), 52–56.

Graham, Jefferson (2011, August 10), "Car Dealers Use Social Media to Drive Traffic," *USA Today*, B3.

Grove, Stephen, Michael Dorsch, and Les Carlson (2011), "Integrating the Website into Marketing Communications: An Empirical Examination of Magazine Ad Emphasis of Website Direct Response Opportunities over Time," in *The Sustainable Global Marketplace: Proceedings of the Annual Conference of the Academy of Marketing Science*, Vol. 40, M. Conway (ed.), 448–451.

Grove, Stephen J., Les Carlson, and Michael J. Dorsch (2007), "Comparing the Application of Integrated Marketing Communication (IMC) in Magazine Ads Across Product Type and Time," *Journal of Advertising*, 36 (Spring), 37–55.

Grove, Stephen J., Gregory M. Pickett, and David N. Laband (1995), "An Empirical Examination of Factual Information Content Among Service Advertisements," *The Service Industries Journal*, 15 (2), 216–233.

Hennig-Thurau, Thorsten, Edward C. Malthouse, Christian Friege, Sonja Gensler, Lara Lobschat, Arvind Rnagaswamy, and Bernd Skiera (2010), "The Impact of New Media on Customer Relationships," *Journal of Service Research*, 13 (3), 311–330.

Legg, Donna and Julie Baker (1987), "Advertising Strategies for Service Firms," in *Add Value to Your Service*, C. Surprenant, ed., Chicago: American Marketing Association, 163–168.

Schultz, Don E., Stanley I. Tannenbaum, and Robert F. Lauterborn (1996), *The New Marketing Paradigm: Integrated Marketing Communications*, Chicago: NTC Business Books.

Shostack, G. Lynn (1977), "Breaking Free from Product Marketing," *Journal of Marketing*, 41 (April), 73–80.

Stafford, Marla Royne (2005), "International Services Advertising (ISA)," *Journal of Advertising*, 34 (Spring), 65–86.

Stafford, Marla Royne, Tim Reilly, Stephen J. Grove, and Les Carlson (2011), "The Evolution of Services Advertising in a Services-Driven National Economy," *Journal of Advertising Research*, 51 (1), 136–152.

Vollmer, Christopher, John Frelinghuysen, and Randall Rothenberg (2006), "The Future of Advertising Is Now," *Strategy + Business*, 43 (Summer), 38–51.

Delivering and Ensuring a Successful Customer Experience

Part Four examines means of ensuring customers a successful experience. Chapter 10 explores methods of delivering service quality and guaranteeing services. Chapter 11 investigates methods of regaining customer confidence through customer service and service recovery. Chapter 12 examines service success and failure, explaining why studying service success and failure is necessary, analyzing why service success is difficult to achieve, describing research methods for services, and managerial uses of service measurement.

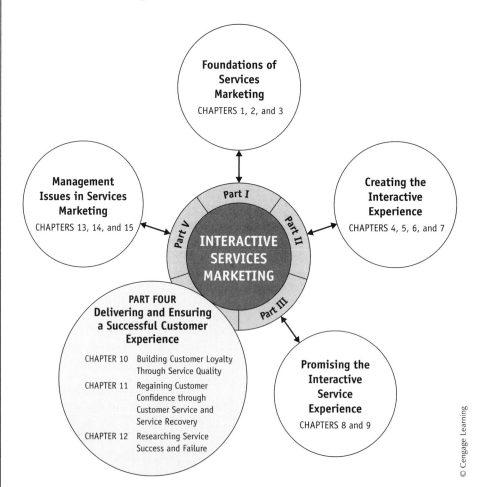

Foundations of Services Marketing
CHAPTERS 1, 2, and 3

Management Issues in Services Marketing
CHAPTERS 13, 14, and 15

Creating the Interactive Experience
CHAPTERS 4, 5, 6, and 7

Part I

Part V

Part II

INTERACTIVE SERVICES MARKETING

Part III

PART FOUR Delivering and Ensuring a Successful Customer Experience

CHAPTER 10 Building Customer Loyalty Through Service Quality

CHAPTER 11 Regaining Customer Confidence through Customer Service and Service Recovery

CHAPTER 12 Researching Service Success and Failure

Promising the Interactive Service Experience
CHAPTERS 8 and 9

"Shoppertainment": Creating and Delivering the Customer Experience

If you visit Jordan's Furniture **(http://www.jordans.com)**, you can enjoy the Mardi Gras multimedia show on its Bourbon Street; play a variety of carnival games, such as the Duck Tour Race game; attend the Flying Trapeze School; watch an IMAX movie; observe a dancing water and light show; or ride a 4-D Motion Odyssey Movie (MOM). You can only find these entertainment options at one of four Jordan's Furniture locations in the greater Boston area. A fifth location opened on December 21, 2011, in Warwick, Rhode Island. This new location features "SPLASH," a state-of-the-art show that combines the magic of laser, light, water, and music, and which President and CEO Tatelman claims is "nothing like anyone has ever seen before. Not even in Vegas." The store in Reading, Massachusetts, is home to Beantown, a replica of downtown Boston made up of nearly 25 million jellybeans. The Avon store features the Enchanted Village, which includes 59 mechanical figurines and 18 scenes, and was originally created in 1958 by a Bavarian toy maker. Of course, the establishments also offer their guests customary free coffee, cake, cookies, ice cream, and balloons.

Warren Buffet, famed investor and one of the richest man in the world, liked the stores so much that he bought them for his financial services company, Berkshire Hathaway, because, in his words: Jordan's Furniture "… is truly one of the most phenomenal and unique companies that I have ever seen. The company is a gem!"

Brothers Eliot and Barry Tatelman, whose family started the store about eighty years ago, are revered for treating their 1,200 employees like family. The employees, called the J-Team, handle about 5,000 visitors per day at each store location. Each location generates six times more inventory turnover per year and sales per square foot than the average furniture store.

The Tatelman brothers note that "the primary goal is making sure that every single customer who comes into the store has a great time" and that "excellent customer service is an obsession." Customers can schedule a free courtesy premeasure to ensure a proper space fit prior to purchase of any furniture. They receive thank-you notes from the sales personnel following a transaction and a postsale customer satisfaction phone call from the customer service desk. Every single piece of furniture is completely inspected and cleaned by the quality control team before delivery.

Jordan's calls the service it creates "shoppertainment." Hang tags answer questions for the customer and provide care instructions. Furniture retail experts have acclaimed the lighting and music in the store as most appropriate. Merchandise presentation is theatrical, with themed music, aromas, and such. Add to the entertainment excellent merchandise displays, exemplary customer service, a lowest-price guarantee, and a pressure-free sales effort on its shop floor, and you have a winning customer experience.

It's not surprising that Jordan's has won numerous awards in the furniture retailing business. Further, as strong supporters to a number of charitable organizations, Eliot and Barry have received national recognition and numerous awards for their generous spirit.

CHAPTER 10
Building Customer Loyalty Through Service Quality
What Is Service Quality?
How Customers Evaluate Service Quality
Why and When to Guarantee a Service
What Makes an Extraordinary Service Guarantee?
How to Design a Service Guarantee

CHAPTER 11
Regaining Customer Confidence Through Customer Service and Service Recovery
Customer Service
Customer Service as a Strategic Function
Developing a Customer Service Culture
The Need for Service Recovery
Steps to Service Recovery
Hidden Benefits of Service Recovery

CHAPTER 12
Researching Service Success and Failure
Why Is Researching Service Success and Failure Necessary?
Why Is Service Success So Difficult to Achieve?
Research Methods for Services
Creating a Service Quality Information System

Source: **http://www.jordans.com**; **http://www.bostoncentral.com** (accessed January 30, 2012).

CHAPTER 10

Building Customer Loyalty Through Service Quality

If you were shopping at Jordan's, what would you expect from the shopping experience? Is it likely that you would be loyal to the store after your first experience there? Would you be happy with the service as described in the vignette? What features of your experience and of the service offering would you evaluate? Would your assessment be based on your own past experiences at other retail stores? Generally, we gather information, form attitudes, or take actions based on what we already know. We react to every new happening based on what we have experienced previously. Consider your experiences at a retail store that you patronize and how you judge the quality of the service you receive there. What do you evaluate? What features do you compare regarding your experience across stores? Now try to transfer these features to other types of services. Does a common set of features transfer across all types of services? These issues are discussed in this chapter.

Services marketers recognize that they must meet customers' service quality expectations in order to retain their loyalty. How can services marketers assure their customers that the quality of the service is going to meet their expectations? As we have seen, the interactive nature of services makes it difficult to evaluate a service before it has been experienced. Hence, customers perceive high risk, which marketers attempt to reduce before the service experience occurs. Various techniques may be used to *guarantee* their experience. Consider how Jordan's assures customers of the quality of its furniture and why that is important. Is it effective? This chapter addresses several aspects related to service *guarantees*.

The chapter has five specific objectives:

- To examine the concept of customer loyalty with service providers
- To examine the concept of service quality
- To discuss how customers evaluate service quality
- To discuss the role of service guarantees in relation to quality
- To examine the design of effective service guarantees and their payoff

Customer loyalty is a key determinant of any organization's ability to sustain long-term profitability. Without the long-standing commitment and continued patronage of profitable customers, firms may have to depend too heavily on acquiring new customers. Customer relationship management (CRM) systems are intended to help organizations attract and retain profitable customers for the long term. The lifetime value of a customer can be quite significant if the benefits from that customer outweigh the costs that are required to service the customer. The benefits come in the form of the revenue the customer provides, as well as referrals and positive word-of-mouth communication he generates (John 2003). In the quest for customer loyalty, Reinartz and Kumar (2002) note that it is important to understand that the revenues from a loyal customer must exceed the costs to serve that customer.

Lemon, Rust, and Zeithaml (2001) propose "customer equity" as a term for the value of a customer, a phenomenon that is driven by value equity (the customer's objective assessment of the firm's offering), brand equity (the customer's subjective assessment of the firm's offering), and relationship equity (the customer's commitment to the firm's offering above and beyond her objective and subjective assessments). Developing customer equity is critical to the long-term success of an organization. What generates customer loyalty and equity?

Researchers exploring relationships between profitability, quality, and customer relations find that loyal customers bring increased profits because they can be cheaper to serve, are heavy users of the organization's goods and services, and are likely to refer new clients to the organization. The Strategic Planning Institute **(http://www.pimsonline.com)** in Cambridge, Massachusetts, found that market share, return on investment, and asset turnover are linked to perceived quality. The Profit Impact of Market Strategy (PIMS) data confirmed that firms offering superior service achieve above-average market share growth. Rust, Zahorik, and Keiningham (1995) developed the Return on Quality (ROQ) model demonstrating that quality improvement efforts can yield significant financial returns. Heskett and colleagues (1994) found a strong link between customer loyalty, employee loyalty, and investor loyalty. Calling it the "service profit chain," they found that as customer satisfaction drives customer loyalty, companies grow and become more profitable, leading to investor interest and capital. More capital provides more resources to improve infrastructure and hire the best people. Hiring the best people and providing them with the best resources ensures that the company is able to produce superior quality that leads to loyal customers. As discussed in Chapters 1 and 6, excellent internal marketing ensures improved employee performance. Table 10.1 shows the extent to which the profit potential of selected service industries is affected by a 5% increase in customer retention.

If customer loyalty is driven by customer satisfaction, and satisfaction is driven by perceptions of quality of the service provided by the organization, then the key to customer loyalty lies in creating and delivering superior quality and customer experience. Arguably, service firms are better situated than manufacturers to develop customer knowledge, because customer-firm interactions occur at the individual customer level (Brown 2000). Consequently, it is possible

TABLE 10.1   Impact of Loyalty on Profit Potential

Selected Service Industries	Increase in Profit Potential with a 5% Increase in Retention Rate
Bank branch deposits	85%
Credit card	75%
Insurance brokerage	50%
Industrial laundry	45%
Office building management	40%
Software	35%

Source: Frederick Reichheld and Earl Sasser (1990), "Zero Defections: Quality Comes to Services," *Harvard Business Review*, 68 (September–October), 105–111. Reprinted by permission.

for service firms to have an intimate knowledge of the consumption patterns of all its customers. Those that do and who are successful may reap the recognition that accompanies winning one of several awards related to quality. For example, the Malcolm Baldrige National Quality Award instituted in the United States in 1987 became a hallmark of excellence in quality, including several service sectors. Additionally, ISO 9000, a program developed in Europe, has enjoyed similar stature as the quality standard that many organizations throughout the world strive to achieve.

> **Customer delight** occurs when customer expectations are significantly exceeded.

To win loyal customers, you should seek to "delight customers" (Keiningham and Vavra 2001). **Customer delight** occurs when customer expectations are significantly exceeded. Because customers adjust their expectations based upon their experiences, customer delight is a moving target. For example, the first time you stay at a Doubletree hotel **(http://www.dou-bletree.com)** and receive free cookies when you check in might be a delightful experience. However, upon staying at a Doubletree for a second time, receiving cookies might merely be satisfying because now you expect them. This pattern implies that customer delight will always be an elusive phenomenon. Services organizations must constantly seek new ways to delight their customers.

WHAT IS SERVICE QUALITY?

> **Service quality** from the provider's perspective means the degree to which the service's features conform to the organization's specifications and requirements; from the customer's perspective it means how well the service meets or exceeds expectations.

Depending on whether we are a provider or a user, we have many different ways to define **service quality**. Service quality from the *provider's perspective* means the degree to which the service's features conform to the organization's specifications and requirements. Typically, this operations orientation focuses on productivity and internal efficiencies that reflect the maximum output of product for the minimum cost. From the *customer's perspective*, service quality means how well the service meets or exceeds expectations. A key distinction between the provider-based and customer-based definitions of quality is that the latter definition recognizes that for the same level of product performance, different customers will perceive different levels of quality. To understand the difference between the two perspectives, consider the following example. A hotel might decide that having ironing boards and irons available on request and delivered within fifteen minutes is a sign of excellent service. However, the customer who thinks that each room should contain its own iron and ironing board is likely to rate this hotel poorly on service. In determining its service quality standards, the hotel might have focused on keeping costs low by purchasing fewer irons and ironing boards. However, the customers may have determined that keeping a guest waiting for something the customer expects to have at hand undermines the hotel's service quality. Thus, service quality is more appropriately termed *perceived* service quality and defined as the level of service delivery that meets or exceeds *customer* expectations.

Quality creates a chain reaction with regard to loyalty and customer inclination to establish enduring relationships with service providers. Recognizing this interaction, let us examine how service quality affects the customer and the service organization. The greater the level of customer satisfaction, the stronger is the link between the customer and the provider. Satisfied customers are loyal and form strong relationships with service organizations. Service providers are then better positioned to provide high-quality service delivery to these loyal customers, thus strengthening the service delivery link with the customer even more. Figure 10.1 illustrates the chain of connections that link service customers and service provider by their actions and reactions.

Three links connect the customer and provider: the *service delivery link*, the *customer satisfaction link*, and the *customer–provider link*. The service delivery link represents the interactive nature of the service and is strengthened through satisfying service encounters. The customer satisfaction link represents the connection between the customer's level of satisfaction and degree of loyalty to the service provider. The customer–provider link represents the mutually rewarding relationship between the customer and the service provider, resulting in the

FIGURE 10.1 The Service Quality Cycle

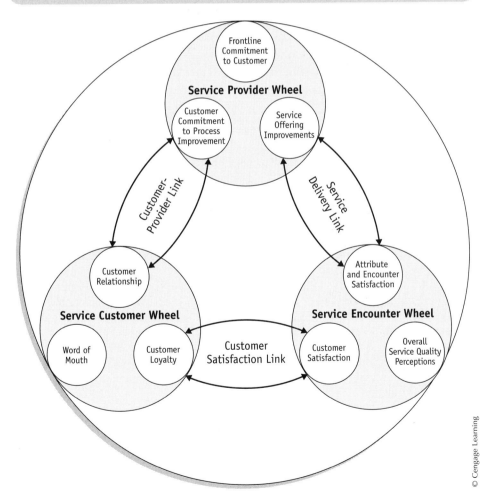

© Cengage Learning

customer's commitment to that service provider. These links connect activities that fall into three domains, or *wheels*, representing the domains of the customer, the provider, and the service encounter, respectively. The *service quality cycle* is driven by three wheels connected by three links. We use the term cycle to denote that service quality involves important links between the service organization and the customer in a recurring series of activities.

When customers repeatedly enjoy satisfactory service encounters, that is, when encounters meet or exceed their expectations for all of the service attributes, they perceive overall service quality as high and are likely to remain loyal to the service provider. At the Ritz-Carlton Hotel **(http://www.ritzcarlton .com),** whoever first sees a problem "owns it" until it is resolved. Workers are encouraged and trained in creative problem solving, which includes learning to anticipate and identify potential service breakdowns. This kind of customer-focused culture has made the Ritz-Carlton a two-time winner of the coveted Malcolm Baldrige Award for quality (see Spotlight 10.1).

Loyal customers provide positive word-of-mouth communications about the service organization, feel a sense of belonging, and commit to relationships with the service provider. As loyalty is further nurtured by ongoing satisfying encounters, the customer–provider relationship becomes mutually rewarding and customers feel even more committed to the service organization. It is in the customer's best interest to help the service provider improve its service offerings. With continual improvements, the service offering will more closely match customer needs. The interactive nature of services also fosters provider–customer familiarity,

---

════ SPOTLIGHT 10.1 ════

Ritz-Carlton Hotels: Two-Time Malcolm Baldrige National Quality Award Winner

 Ritz-Carlton has won the Malcolm Baldrige Award twice. This rare feat is the result of a disciplined approach to delivering quality with consistent and reliable services. At each Ritz-Carlton hotel, a quality leader serves as a resource and advocate when workers develop and implement their quality plans. The company president and other senior executives personally instruct new employees at new locations about Ritz-Carlton's "gold standards" during a two-day orientation. Each of its 38,000 employees at seventy-six hotels in twenty-five countries is a customer service department. Every employee has more than 100 hours of customer service training annually. To ensure quick resolutions to problems, workers are required to act at first notice, regardless of the type of problem or customer complaint. Whoever first sees a problem owns it until it is resolved. Daily quality reports derived from 720 work areas in Ritz-Carlton's service delivery system serve as an early warning system for identifying problems that can impede meeting quality and customer satisfaction goals.

Data such as percentage of check-ins with no queuing, time spent to achieve industry-best clean room appearance, and time to service an occupied guestroom are continually tracked. Each employee is trained on a cross-functional guest database called "Mystique," a company-wide tool created to meet and anticipate repeat customers' preferences and requirements. Nine-step quality improvement teams have designed the guestroom child safety program, POLO (Protect Our Little Ones) and a program for the most defect-free guestrooms in the industry called CARE (Clean and Repair Everything), among other such quality-enhancing initiatives. A front-desk project team at the Ritz-Carlton, Osaka, reduced check-in time by 50%. It is not at all a surprise that the Ritz-Carlton is the only hotel to ever receive the Baldrige award, which recognizes exceptional achievement in the practice of Total Quality Management.

Source: Ritz-Carlton (2011), **http://www.corporate .ritzcarlton.com** (accessed October 12).

which in turn enables the customer to receive a more personalized service. The cycle is complete when these process improvements lead to even better and more satisfying service encounters and overall customer satisfaction.

Consider the simple example of a neighborhood restaurant. Customers who frequent the restaurant are those for whom the establishment continually provides a satisfactory experience. These loyal customers have a personal stake in improving the restaurant's offerings to meet their needs. They spread positive word-of-mouth communications about the restaurant, their relationship with the restaurant is strong, and, because they know one another, they enjoy a mutual feeling of community. It is in the restaurant's best interests to improve its service offering to meet these customers' needs and expectations, such as providing new menu items in response to customer requests. Thus, both the restaurant and its customers derive a mutual and reciprocal benefit from strengthening their relationship. The same logic applies to large service organizations in which satisfactory service encounters similarly lead to continued customer satisfaction and loyalty accompanied by positive referrals. The strength of the customer–provider relationship fosters a mutual desire to continually improve the quality of service encounters and discourages customers from switching to other service providers. Service quality's critical influence on service organization success makes it important for us to understand how the customer evaluates it and what factors enhance perceived service quality.

HOW CUSTOMERS EVALUATE SERVICE QUALITY

Customers evaluate services differently from physical goods because services tend to be inherently low in *search* characteristics but high in *experience* and *credence* characteristics (see Figure 10.2). Search characteristics are attributes we can evaluate before purchase, as in the color or size of an automobile. Experience characteristics are attributes we can evaluate only during or after consumption, as in the pleasure associated with a visit to a theme park. Credence characteristics are attributes that are difficult to evaluate even after consumption, as in the soundness of a financial consultant's advice. Although the intangibility of services constrains customers in objectively evaluating their quality, customers do routinely assess the quality of their service experiences. How do they make this assessment, and what attributes do they evaluate?

Researchers have developed various conceptualizations of service quality to explain the complex nature of the phenomena. Grönroos (2000) suggests that service quality involves technical (i.e., outcome) and functional (i.e., process) dimensions that reflect both *what* is delivered and *how* it is delivered. In health care service, what is delivered is referred to as the *curing*, while how the service is delivered may be labeled the *caring* (John 1991).

The most widely used measure of service quality was developed through the combined efforts of Parasuraman, Zeithaml, and Berry (1985). Their research resulted in **SERVQUAL** (Parasuraman, Berry, and Zeithaml 1988), a

> **SERVQUAL** is a scale designed to measure customer perceptions of service quality along five key dimensions: tangibles, reliability, responsiveness, assurance, and empathy of the service provider.

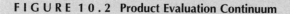

FIGURE 1 0 . 2 **Product Evaluation Continuum**

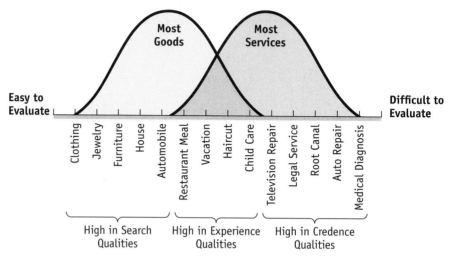

Source: Valarie A. Zeithaml and Mary Jo Bitner (2006), *Services Marketing: Integrating Customer Focus Across the Firm*, 4th ed., New York: McGraw-Hill, 52. Reprinted with the permission of the McGraw-Hill Companies

scale designed to measure customer perceptions of service quality along five key dimensions: reliability, assurance, tangibles, responsiveness, and empathy of the service provider. Table 10.2 illustrates how these aspects of the service are interpreted. Note that the first letter of the five dimensions in the order presented read "RATER," a useful acronym to remember the dimensions that customers use to "rate" the quality of service received.

Parasuraman (2004) proposed a definition for service quality provided by Web sites. He defines e-service quality as "the extent to which a website facilitates efficient and effective shopping, purchasing and delivery of products and services." E-customers assess the following dimensions of e-service: access, ease

TABLE 10.2   **SERVQUAL Measures of Consumer Perceptions of Service Quality**

Reliability	Ability to perform the promised service dependably and accurately
Assurance	Knowledge and courtesy of employees and their ability to convey trust and confidence
Tangibles	Physical facilities, equipment, and appearance of personnel
Empathy	Caring, individualized attention the firm provides its customers
Responsiveness	Willingness to help customers and to provide prompt service

Source: From A. Parasuraman, Leonard L. Berry, and Valarie A. Zeithaml (1988), "SERVQUAL: A Multiple-Item Scale for Measuring Consumer Perceptions of Service Quality," Journal of Retailing, 64 (Spring), 12–37. Reprinted by permission of New York University, Stern School of Business.

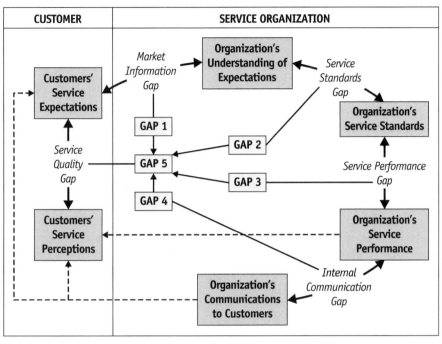

FIGURE 10.3 Conceptual Model of Service Quality—Gaps Model

of navigation, efficiency, customization/personalization, security/privacy, responsiveness, assurance/trust, price knowledge, site aesthetics, reliability, and flexibility.

A major contribution of Parasuraman, Zeithaml, and Berry (1985) is their conceptualization of service quality as the gap between customer expectations and perceptions of the service performance. According to their research, four major discrepancies in service systems contribute to this service quality gap. As diagrammed in Figure 10.3, these discrepancies reflect problems regarding the communication, design, and delivery of the service.

Gap 1—The Market Information Gap   This gap is the difference between what the customer expects and management's perception of what the customer expects. It occurs through errors in the way an organization obtains information regarding customers. Too often, managers believe they know what the customer wants without having actually asked the customer. For example, a restaurant manager who believes that his customers are happy as long as he offers good food may be surprised to find that a significant number of customers have defected to a competitor because they had to wait a long time to be served in his restaurant. The competitor's food may not be as good, but the service may be better and more efficient. In this case, the manager of the first restaurant may simply have failed to ascertain what customers really wanted in their dining experience.

Gap 2—The Service Standards Gap   This gap occurs when management fails to accurately translate its perceptions of customer expectations into the service design. Problems can stem from a lack of resources or from management's failure to take a customer-oriented approach to its organization's product development. For example, management might interpret customers' desire for courtesy as wanting employees to say "hello" and "come again." To the customer, courtesy might also require a genuine smile, a helpful manner, and a greeting that feels personal.

Gap 3—The Service Performance Gap   This gap is the difference between what the service organization is designed to deliver and the actual service provided to the customer. It arises when people or equipment produce failures in the delivery system. Sometimes the selection, training, and motivation of employees may be inadequate to carry out the service design. At other times, equipment failures may be responsible. For example, an airline may have designed its check-in process to accommodate an average of 100 passengers per hour during peak demand periods. However, if ticket agents aren't trained to handle contingencies such as flight delays or late passenger arrivals, the airline may fail to process the estimated 100 customers per hour, thereby contributing to an unhappy customer experience. See Spotlight 10.2 for another example of Gap 3.

Gap 4—The Internal Communications Gap   This gap is the difference between the service provided and the service portrayed in various forms of marketing communication, including advertising. More often than not, it occurs because the service organization promises what the system is simply incapable of delivering. As noted in Chapter 9, service organizations occasionally *overpromise and underdeliver.* Consider, for example, the airlines whose slogans proclaim,

---

SPOTLIGHT 10.2

Barcodes in Health Care Reduces Human Error in Medications

 You may have heard or read news stories like these. A physician ordered a 260-milligram medication called *Taxol*, but the pharmacist prepared 260-milligrams of *Taxotere* instead. A patient received an overdose of methotrexate, a 10-milligram daily dose, instead of the intended 10-milligram *weekly* dose. Another patient received 200 units of insulin rather than the prescribed 20 units. A patient hemorrhaged after receiving *another patient's prescription* for the blood anticoagulant warfarin. The patient died in all four cases.

The U.S. Food and Drug Administration (FDA) got serious about medication errors with a barcode labeling rule in April 2004 requiring all hospitals to use bar coding for patient medications by 2006. Medication errors are preventable events that may cause or lead to inappropriate medication use or patient harm while the medication is in the control of the health care professional, patient, or consumer. In 2006, the Institute of Medicine reported that approximately 7,000 deaths occur from hospital medication errors; it estimated the costs of preventable adverse drug events at approximately $3.5 billion. According to the American Hospital Association, four of the five common types of medication errors are incomplete patient information, unavailable drug information, miscommunication of drug orders, lack of appropriate labeling, and errors. Along with the bar code rule, computerized physician order entry and electronic medication-administration system are two additional information technology solutions to medication errors.

Sources: **http://www.fda.gov/Drugs/DrugSafety/MedicationErrors/default.htm**; and, **http://iom.edu/Reports/2006/Preventing-Medication-Errors-Quality-Chasm-Series.aspx** (accessed, January 30, 2012).

"We love to fly and it shows" or "Something special in the air." How often do passengers' actual experiences reflect these claims?

Gap 5—The Service Quality Gap This final gap is the difference between the service expected and that actually received, which may result in delight, satisfaction, dissatisfaction, or disgust. Each of the first four gaps contributes to this service quality gap. The role of customer expectations and perceptions of service delivery cannot be overemphasized.

Identifying customer expectations is not an easy task; customers have several standards or levels of expectations: what they desire, what they consider adequate, and what they consider an ideal service performance. For example, waiting a mere two minutes in line for a bank teller might be adequate, but not having to wait at all would be ideal! Customers possess a **zone of tolerance** (the range between desired service and adequate service) influenced by such factors as predicted service, service promises, word-of-mouth communications, past experiences, service alternatives, personal needs, and situational factors (Berry and Parasuraman 1991). It is in a service organization's best interest to understand customers' zones of tolerance and accommodate them by ensuring that service is always better than adequate and, hopefully, ideal. This practice will help eliminate Gap 5. See Spotlight 10.3 for an example of how accreditation and ratings by unbiased agencies can improve the customer experience.

> **Zone of intolerance** is the range between desired service and adequate service; it is influenced by such factors as predicted service, service promises, word-of-mouth communications, past experiences, service alternatives, personal needs, and situational factors.

═══ SPOTLIGHT 10.3 ═══

Quality Improvement by Rating Child Care Services

The gold standard for child care centers in the United States used by parents, educators, and facilities has been accreditation by the National Association for the Education of Young Children (NAEYC). There are ten standards for accreditation categorized under children, teachers, family and community partners, and program administration; each has its own set of criteria. In 2009, the NAEYC launched a review of these accreditation criteria with field input, expert review, and an analysis of program performance data to develop streamlined assessment measures. In addition to the NAEYC accreditation, individual states have rating systems evaluating facilities on criteria such as child–teacher ratios, teacher credentials, curriculum, class size, safety, and richness of environment. These criteria have been established by research on early childhood development. The U.S. Department of Health and Human Services has a National Child Care Information and Technical Assistance Center that oversees a quality rating and improvement system (QRIS), which it describes as a "systematic approach to assess, improve and communicate the level of quality in early and school-age care and education programs." QRIS awards quality ratings that meet a set of defined program standards. By participating in their state's QRIS, early and school-age care and education providers commit to continuous quality improvement. QRIS has five elements: (1) standards; (2) accountability measures; (3) program and practitioner outreach and support; (4) financial incentives; and (5) parent/consumer education efforts. Currently, twenty-five states have a statewide QRIS with all five elements.

Sources: **http://nccic.acf.hhs.gov/poptopics/qrs-impact-qualitycc.html** (accessed October 13, 2011); and, **http://www.naeyc.org/** (accessed October 13, 2011).

With all the complexity stemming from the intangibility of services, managers find it hard to maintain consistently high service quality. Conversely, customers cannot evaluate services in advance and therefore associate their purchase with a high degree of perceived risk. Marketers sometimes offer to guarantee service quality as a way to reassure customers regarding their choice.

WHY AND WHEN TO GUARANTEE A SERVICE

A **service guarantee** is a promise to compensate customers if the service delivery fails to meet established standards.

A guarantee can be a great tool to lower perceived risk if the price of service is high, the customer's ego is on the line, or if the negative consequences of service failure are great. A **service guarantee** is a promise to compensate customers if the service delivery fails to meet established standards. L.L. Bean's **(http://www.llbean.com)** legendary reputation for service can be traced to its 100% satisfaction guarantee. Its promise states: "Our products are guaranteed to give 100% satisfaction in every way. Return anything purchased from us at any time if it proves otherwise. We do not want you to have anything from L.L. Bean that is not completely satisfactory." The service guarantee of Radisson Hotels **(http://www.radisson.com)** is simple: "If you aren't satisfied with something, please let us know during your stay and we'll make it right or you won't pay. It's guaranteed."

Service guarantees provide several advantages for the service provider (Hart 1988). First, a service guarantee forces the company to focus on the customer. It signals that the service organization will let the customer decide whether the organization has done a good job. Second, a service guarantee sets standards for the employees and customers. Customer-contact personnel and others backstage in the service system know what is expected of them and what the customer is going to measure them against. Service guarantees minimize surprises on either side. Third, a service guarantee generates feedback. It invites customers to contact the company when the service fails. This feedback can be a valuable source of information that enables the service organization to identify and study problems to correct. Repeated failures in the same service aspect tell management to consider redesigning the service. Finally, service guarantees build loyalty and discourage switching behavior. Customers who are guaranteed quality service can rest assured that even if service failure occurs, the provider will make good.

In industries with poor service reputations or where business is drastically affected by negative word-of-mouth communications, service guarantees may entice customers to give an organization a chance. In addition, services that depend on frequent repeat purchases find service guarantees an effective way of giving the company one more opportunity to make amends for a mistake. Nevertheless, service organizations that enjoy a reputation for quality may find a service guarantee unnecessary.

WHAT MAKES AN EXTRAORDINARY SERVICE GUARANTEE?

Hart (1988) characterizes a good service guarantee as one that is unconditional, easy to understand and communicate, meaningful, simple (and painless) to invoke, and easy and quick to collect on. A service company should guarantee quality without setting conditions. The Sleep Well Guarantee offered by British Airways **(http://www.british-airways.com)** ensures its business class passengers will receive an automatic upgrade to first class when they next book Club World business-class flights if for some reason they don't sleep well.

A service guarantee should be both concise and precise. Complicated and confusing guarantees with myriad conditions footnoted in fine print simply do not work. Guarantees are meaningful only if they cover what is important to the customer and have a reasonable and significant payoff. A good guarantee is also easy to invoke and collect on. If the customer must go through a lot of effort to prove dissatisfaction and if the process of compensation is complicated, the guarantee will not work.

A service guarantee should be viewed as a vehicle to improve service quality Conversely, if an organization offers a service guarantee on quality it cannot deliver, that organization is setting itself up for failure! Extraordinary service guarantees improve the customer experience by improving service quality. In a synthesis of twenty years of research on service guarantees, Hogreve and Gremler (2009) noted that out of the 109 research papers they reviewed, 16 focused on the outcome of improvement in service operations, including employee motivation and learning, quality improvements, and service innovation.

In Australia, McColl and Mattsson (2011) found the following common mistakes in the design and implementation of service guarantees: inadequate market research, ambiguity in guarantee specifics, lack of organizational structure and CEO commitment, and an absence of performance evaluation.

HOW TO DESIGN A SERVICE GUARANTEE

Designing a service guarantee requires careful consideration of the organization's objectives, key customer concerns prior to purchase, and measures that would alleviate customers' perceived risk as well as displeasure if their expectations were not met. If the service is entirely new or involves offering a new service feature, customers will be unfamiliar with its benefits and are unlikely to have received word-of-mouth recommendations. In such cases, a service guarantee becomes an important communication device. A new restaurant or dry-cleaning service might use a service guarantee to attract customers, for example, because customers often are uncertain of a new service's quality before experiencing the service. In the case of the dry-cleaning service, they may fear damaged clothes, lost clothes, or delayed service. The organization must therefore determine what would be necessary to comfort and assure customers that they will be adequately compensated if dissatisfied with service delivery.

When deciding on a service guarantee, an organization must make three major decisions: the degree of explicitness, the scope of what is covered, and the conditions of coverage. Some organizations publish a specific and detailed promise and communicate it clearly to each customer. They might even use it in their advertising and at the time of sale. Meineke **(http://www.meineke.com),** the automobile muffler service company, became easily recognized when it stressed its guarantee in its advertising: "If you are not satisfied, you will have your money back!" Others may be less overt about their guarantee in their communications and instead attempt to handle customers on a case-by-case basis, adapting to any situation. What the guarantee covers is an important decision as well. For FedEx **(http://www.fedex.com),** a money-back guarantee hinges on delivery within 60 seconds of published or quoted time. Finally, organizations must specify the conditions that qualify the guarantee. For example, in what circumstances are customers eligible for the guarantee? Some retail stores specify return of merchandise within a certain number of days in the original package, accompanied by the original sales receipt, before the customer is entitled to receive a refund, an exchange, or a merchandise credit. These decisions must be made carefully so that the service guarantee appeals to customers and supports the organization's objectives.

Summary and Conclusion

Customer loyalty to a service provider is key to long-term profitability. Loyal and profitable customers become a worthy goal for any firm. Service quality is an imperative because it is linked to customer satisfaction and customer loyalty. Service quality is defined as the customer's evaluation of the service received compared with the service expected. It is a function of what the organization communicates, designs, and delivers to the customer. Service quality is generally measured along the five dimensions of reliability, assurance, tangibles, empathy, and responsiveness. Because services are not physical in nature, their quality is difficult for the customer to evaluate. By the same token, managers find it hard to ensure consistently high service quality.

Service guarantees are a powerful way to attract and retain customers. They lower the risk customers associate with the purchase of an intangible offering that cannot be evaluated until during or after its consumption. For the service provider, a guarantee forces the organization to focus on the customer and to set strict standards for both employees and customers. A service guarantee assures the service customer that the quality of the service experience will be excellent.

Exercises

1. Interview people dining at a restaurant about how they evaluate the quality of their dining experience. Then interview the restaurant manager. Use your observations of the restaurant and its advertising to illustrate the SERVQUAL gap model of service quality. What recommendations would you make to reduce the gaps and improve service quality?

2. Obtain a customer feedback card from a service establishment that you patronize. Review the contents of the survey and compare it with the SERVQUAL model. What is your assessment of management's view of customer expectations? How would you change the survey to reflect all the concerns of customers such as yourself?

3. Design a guarantee for a service organization and demonstrate how it meets Hart's guidelines for an extraordinary service guarantee. Indicate how the service manager can use the guarantee system for service design improvements.

4. Evaluate the effectiveness of a standard service guarantee by contrasting it with an extraordinary service guarantee.

Internet Exercise

Visit an online retailer who offers a service guarantee (this can be a brick-and-mortar store with e-commerce transactions as well):

1. Describe the offer in terms of its scope and conditions.
2. How does the service guarantee affect a customer's perceived risk?
3. How would you assess the effectiveness of the guarantee?

References

Berry, Leonard L. and A. Parasuraman (1991), *Marketing Services: Competing Through Quality*, New York: The Free Press.

Brown, Stephen W. (2000), "The Move to Solution Providers," *Marketing Management*, 9 (1), 10–11.

Grönroos, Christian (2007), *Service Management and Marketing: Customer Management in Service Competition*, 3rd ed., Chichester, England: John Wiley & Sons, Ltd.

Hart, Christopher (1988), "The Power of Unconditional Service Guarantees," *Harvard Business Review*, 66 (July–August), 54–62.

Heskett, James L., Thomas O. Jones, Gary W. Loveman, W. Earl Sasser Jr., and Leonard Schlesinger (1994), "Putting the Service-Profit Chain to Work," *Harvard Business Review* (March–April), 25–36.

Hogreve, Jens and Dwayne D. Gremler (2009), "Twenty Years of Service Guarantee Research: A Synthesis," *Journal of Service Research*, 11 (May), 322–343.

John, Joby (1991), "Improving Quality Through Patient-Provider Communication," *Journal of Health Care Marketing*, 11 (December), 51–60.

John, Joby (2003), *Fundamentals of Customer-Focused Management: Competing Through Service*, Westport, CT: Praeger Publishers.

Keiningham, Timothy and Terry Vavra (2001), *The Customer Delight Principle: Exceeding Customer Expectations for Bottom-Line Success*, New York: McGraw-Hill.

Lemon, Katherine N., Roland T. Rust, and Valarie A. Zeithaml (2001), "What Drives Customer Equity," *Marketing Management* (Spring), 20–25.

McColl, Rod and Jan Mattsson (2011), "Common Mistakes in Designing and Implementing Service Guarantees," *Journal of Services Marketing*, 25 (6), 451–461.

Parasuraman, A., Leonard L. Berry, and Valarie A. Zeithaml (1988), "SERVQUAL: A Multiple-Item Scale for Measuring Consumer Perceptions of Service Quality," *Journal of Retailing*, 64 (Spring), 12–37.

Parasuraman, A., Valarie A. Zeithaml, and Leonard L. Berry (1985), "A Conceptual Model of Service Quality and Its Implications for Future Research," *Journal of Marketing*, 49 (Fall), 41–50.

Reinartz, Werner and V. Kumar (2002), "The Mismanagement of Loyalty," *Harvard Business Review* (July), 5–12.

Rust, Roland T., Anthony J. Zahorik, and Timothy L. Keiningham (1995), "Return on Quality (ROQ): Making Service Quality Financially Accountable," *Journal of Marketing*, 59 (April), 58–70.

CHAPTER 11

Regaining Customer Confidence Through Customer Service and Service Recovery

Based on the Jordan's Furniture vignette, how would you expect to be treated at Jordan's if you had a service problem? Do you think the procedure for fixing your problem would be simple and straightforward? Do you believe that Jordan should establish a procedure for customers to identify incorrectly marked products or poor service delivery? Should Jordan's encourage customers to complain so that service failures can be rectified? What has your experience been at service organizations where you received poor service? Did you complain? If so, how did the service organization handle your situation, what was your reaction, and how did it affect your future behavior? Or did you simply tell your family and friends about the poor service without filing a complaint to the service organization? If you didn't complain, why not?

Marketers of both goods and services offer customer service, sometimes referred to as facilitating services (see Chapter 1). Organizations can win or lose customers based on how well they provide customer service. However, excellent customer service cannot compensate for a poor core product. Unfortunately, even well-designed systems for providing a service organization's core product sometimes fail. When they do, steps must be taken to win back customers who experience service failure. This chapter explores the issue of customer service and how service organizations can design service recovery procedures to accommodate inevitable service breakdowns. The chapter has six specific objectives:

- **To provide an overview of customer service**
- **To assess customer service as a strategic function**
- **To explore how to develop a customer service culture**
- **To discuss why organizations should plan for service recovery**
- **To present the steps to service recovery**
- **To explore the hidden benefits of service recovery**

CUSTOMER SERVICE

Facilitating services accompany most goods and services transactions. In many instances, organizations compete based on these facilitating services, especially in situations where the core product is easily matched and becomes a standard commodity. Organizations then begin to use their facilitating services that supplement the core to create a competitive advantage.

Customer service refers to all customer–provider interactions other than the core product offering that facilitate the organization's relationship with its customers. It includes the manner in which the core and supplementary elements are delivered, but it does not include the core product itself. For example, in a hairstyling service, the haircut does not qualify as customer service, but the manner in which the customer is treated before, during, and after the haircut does. If the customer makes special requests, customer service constitutes how the organization handles these. Appreciating and acknowledging the

Customer service refers to all customer–provider interactions other than proactive selling and the core product delivery offering that facilitate the organization's relationship with its customers.

customer's patronage or providing various types of follow-up support after the service has occurred are also forms of customer service. In the case of manufactured goods, all interactions with the customer other than the actual sales presentation count as customer service. It bears noting that customer service in any form can be good or bad. Some organizations do such a bad job of providing customer service that it could be more accurately called "disservice" (Grove et al. 2012).

CUSTOMER SERVICE AS A STRATEGIC FUNCTION

Most organizations see customer service as unavoidable. While it should be the responsibility of all employees, customer service is sometimes relegated to a few individuals within a specific organizational department, such as customer relations or customer affairs departments. Employees often consider customer services the most difficult department to work in because they associate it with handling angry customers who are difficult to appease. To make matters worse, the organization's costumer service policies are often of little help because of rigid rules and numerous standard operating procedures. Many customer service personnel feel constrained by company policy, which undermines their ability to handle complaints, facilitate product returns, offer refunds, allow exchange of merchandise and, in general, maintain customer goodwill. To serve customers properly, we believe that customer service should be viewed strategically as a way to make positive connections with the customer. The potential benefits of customer service to an organization cannot be achieved unless its status in the organization is elevated and it becomes proactive rather than reactive. Proactive customer service offers an organization the following benefits: an information resource, an input for service design improvements, and opportunities for enhanced customer relationships.

Customer Service as an Information Resource

All customer service interactions provide valuable sources of information about customer needs. When captured in a database, the information gleaned from customer service interactions can assist planning and marketing decision making to enhance segmentation and positioning decision effectiveness. Managers involved in any of the marketing mix decisions (the seven Ps) would benefit from incorporating information on customers' reactions into existing practices. Stew Leonard's **(http://www.stew-leonards.com),** a Danbury, Connecticut, gourmet grocery store, conveniently places customer complaint and suggestion boxes in various spots in the store and regularly incorporates customer comments into its marketing decisions. On a more general level, organizations such as Angie's List **(http://www.angieslist.com)** help customers searching for reputable service providers through its comprehensive collection of favorite service companies compiled by over half a million homeowners. (See Figure 11.1.)

FIGURE 11.1 Finding the Best Customer Service

Source: Angie's List (2012), **http://www.angieslist.com** (accessed September 17, 2012).

Customer Service as an Input for Service Design Improvements

Customer service workers can assist in the decision-making process for service improvements and help introduce new services. New ideas might emerge from customer comments heard by customer service workers. Is the organization failing to meet the needs of one market segment? Do the customer-to-customer interactions suggest an opportunity that the service organization might pursue?

Customer Service as an Opportunity to Enhance Customer Relationships

If the service organization fails to pay attention to special customer requests or does not heed customers who have reason to make suggestions for improvements, it risks losing those customers to a competitor. Responding to unique

---

SPOTLIGHT 11.1

Planning for Customer Service: Improvisation Training at Aer Arann

 One hallmark of excellent customer service is responding to customers' needs and wants in real time. The interactive nature of services demands rapid and creative response to unfolding circumstances on the part of service personnel. Recognizing this factor, an Irish regional airline, Aer Arann **(http://www.aerarann.com),** conducted a field experiment to discern whether cabin crew training that involved improvisation skills could enhance crew performance. Compared to their counterparts, cabin personnel that received nine hours of improvisation training guided by those skilled in teaching

improvisation in a school of drama felt more confident, more capable of adapting to situations, more spontaneous, and more effective overall. Further, those receiving improvisation training rated their training as enjoyable and satisfying. As one participant commented, the training "taught me new ways of dealing with an unusual situation." Aer Arann provides a good example of service theater in action.

Source: Daly, Aidan, Stephen J. Grove, Michael J. Dorsch, and Raymond P. Fisk (2009), "The Impact of Improvisation Training on Service Employees in a European Airline: A Case Study," *European Journal of Marketing*, 43 (3/4), 459–472.

---

circumstances during service delivery requires flexibility and creativity. Spotlight 11.1 discusses how one service organization has explored ways to foster a better customer experience. Further, customer complaints and suggestions are often a valuable resource that can enhance customer relationships. When systematically organized, selected information from the customer service database can help the organization make appropriate changes in the service offering to prevent customers from defecting to competitors. Information obtained from customer service interactions provides valuable insights regarding what customers desire. Long-distance telephone carrier Sprint **(http://www .sprint.com)** calls customers who terminate their service to find out what Sprint did wrong and inquires whether it can do anything to win them back.

DEVELOPING A CUSTOMER SERVICE CULTURE

By elevating the customer service function to a strategic level, the service organization signals the function's importance to all its employees. The information from dissatisfied customers is now viewed as a strategic organizational resource. As a former CEO of American Express **(http://www.americanexpress.com)** noted, "A dissatisfied customer is an opportunity." Both service and manufacturing organizations are realizing that customer service represents a major corporate asset. Customer service departments rely on substantial high-technology investments in customer interaction software that immediately links calls to a customer support center. The software enables the employee responding to incoming inquiries to access customer data necessary to assist the customer in a timely and personal fashion.

One significant function of customer service is enabling organizations to recover from failures that have generated customer dissatisfaction and complaints.

FIGURE 11.2 Service Recovery Effects on Customer Loyalty

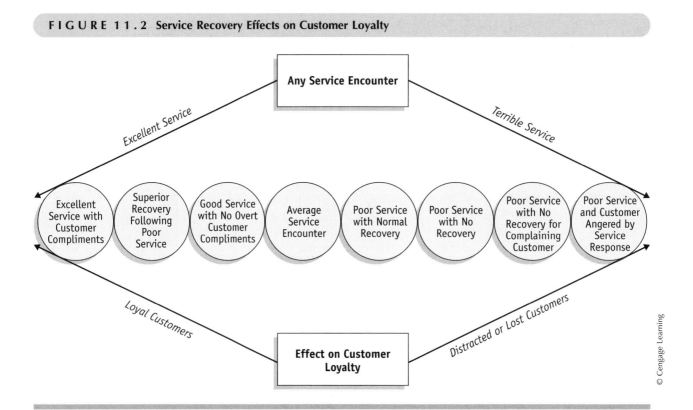

Every customer service encounter leads to one of several outcomes, depending on whether the encounter was a success or a failure and how the customer was subsequently treated if failure occurred. Figure 11.2 presents various possible outcomes of a service encounter and their effects on customer loyalty. In the best-case scenario, the service encounter is exceptional and the customer offers a compliment. From this interaction, organizations may learn what aspects of the service delivery motivated the customer to offer a compliment and file that information away for future use. Such customers are moving down the path to becoming loyal. They may, in fact, become service *ambassadors* who work hard to promote the organization (Kaufman 2005). At the other extreme are customers who have had a bad experience and complain, and are subsequently treated shabbily. They are likely to become even more angry and frustrated at the *double deviation* (Bitner, Booms, and Tetreault 1990, p. 80) from excellent service they have witnessed. If these customers have a choice, they may defect to competitors and are likely to share their experience with others via negative word-of-mouth communication. In a sense, they may become service *terrorists* who work hard to hurt the organization (Kaufman 2005). Between these two extremes lie plausible scenarios, each with a commensurate impact on the customer's disposition to continue or terminate the relationship with the service provider. Where the service delivery has been less than desirable, the service organization must respond and recover from the failure to at least minimize the damage and preempt customer defections.

THE NEED FOR SERVICE RECOVERY

The numerous steps involved in providing services create many opportunities to fail. Further, because services occur in real time, it is impossible to verify their quality at the factory door, unlike a manufactured good. Add to these circumstances the fact that services are interactive and often rely on human labor. People can be inconsistent, moody, detached, or incapable of sustaining a high level of performance over time, all of which can lead to a bad service experience. Other factors beyond an organization's control may affect service excellence as well: weather, equipment breakdown, supplier failure, and competitive forces. Enlightened service organizations accept these realities and devise contingency plans to manage failures when they occur. In other words, they anticipate the need for service recovery.

A good example of an organization that needs a service recovery effort is provided in Spotlight 11.2. The airline passenger's ordeal described in Spotlight is an extreme example of service failure and poor customer service. Unfortunately, the story is true. Although service failures don't always take on such horrific proportions, everyone reading this passage has probably had an experience similar to John's. The question is, what could or should the airline have done to rectify the situation?

Service recovery is the effort an organization expends to win back customer goodwill once it has been lost due to service failure. Some organizations make no attempt at service recovery whatsoever, while others make only a half-hearted attempt. Few institute a comprehensive policy designed to restore customer franchise to its fullest. Organizations often lack the knowledge or the inclination to initiate a program targeted at regaining customers' faith in them. Perhaps they believe they have an endless stream of customers to tap and see no reason to bother with dissatisfied customers. Or maybe they think the time and effort needed to recover customers are just not worthwhile. In either case, their reasoning is faulty.

> **Service recovery** is the effort an organization expends to win back customer goodwill once it has been lost due to service failure.

The High Cost of Lost Customers

Losing a customer is expensive. Consider first that a new customer must replace a lost customer and that the cost of constantly finding new customers is high. Varying estimates place the cost of replacing a lost customer at three to five times higher than retaining a loyal one, depending on the nature of the service. Acquiring new customers demands significant advertising and sales expenses. On the other hand, loyal customers generate significant revenues, spend more than first-time users of a service, and are often willing to pay a premium price. They require lower transaction and communication costs, and they do not require credit checks or other start-up costs. Loyal customers are also more familiar with using the service and thus do not require costly assistance. In addition, they frequently generate new patrons through positive word-of-mouth communication, whereas a customer who "jumps ship" may actively persuade their friends not to patronize the organization (Lovelock 1994; Hogan, Lemon, and Libai 2003).

SPOTLIGHT 11.2

An Airline Passenger's Nightmare

 John arrived at the Memphis airport one Friday afternoon to board a flight for Springfield, Missouri. He had carefully planned for all eventualities before departure: traffic to the airport, time needed for parking, check-in, and the predictably distant gate for the small airplane on which he would be flying. What he didn't expect and could not plan for were the following events.

John and the other fifteen passengers waiting for the small turboprop plane were told their departure would be postponed for twenty to thirty minutes while mechanical difficulties with the aircraft were corrected. No one wants to board an unsafe plane, so John and the others accepted the delay with little protest. Then matters began to deteriorate. The twenty to thirty minutes stretched into an hour, with no further word about the postponed departure time. Two other planes belonging to the airline landed and departed, each carrying only three or four passengers. Interesting! The gate agent could provide no information or assurances about when exactly the flight would be ready.

As another hour passed, passengers inquired whether they had time to make the hike of some distance to the nearest telephone or restroom. The agent said yes but warned them not to be gone too long. When the plane was ready, it would take off immediately. John and the others were now hungry, but no food was available nearby. The passengers could strike out for the main terminal, but the threat of a quick departure kept them shackled to the gate area. After three and a half hours with no concrete information about the flight status, passengers shed civility and began to aggressively search for answers. "What in damnation is going on?" "Will this stinking flight ever get off the ground?" "Why are all those other planes leaving with no one on board, while we've been sentenced to passenger hell?" "Who is in charge of this backwater operation?" The passengers became relentless in their verbal abuse of the gate agent, who represented the only potential source of resolution to their frustrating situation. It was really getting ugly.

Nearly five hours after the scheduled departure time, a representative from the airlines came to rescue the agent from her precarious situation. Armed with five-dollar vouchers for food anywhere in the airport, he successfully dispersed the angry pack; apparently, their hunger superseded their contempt, but only barely. Only one food server in the airport was still open, and it, too, was closing by the time the passengers arrived. To make matters worse, the airline's food voucher scarcely covered the cost of a hot dog at exorbitant airport prices.

When the herd of still-angry passengers returned to the gate, they were told that their flight would be leaving within the hour, as soon as a replacement aircraft had arrived from Little Rock. No one explained why it had taken so long for the airline to locate another aircraft.

When the plane arrived and duly took off, the weary passengers were too grateful to be airborne to recognize that the airline had not even extended an apology for the unconscionable delay. Finally, more than seven hours late, the aircraft touched down at its destination. Unfortunately, John's bags hadn't made the trip—but that's another story.

Another way to consider the costs of lost customers is to take a long-term view of their value. Instead of considering the customer's worth in terms of a single transaction, the organization should factor in all of the possible purchases over the lifetime of a customer's business. Carl Sewell, owner of Sewell Cadillac **(http://www.sewell.com)** in Dallas, Texas, estimates the lifetime value to his company of one satisfied Cadillac buyer at well over $500,000 (Sewell and Brown 2002). Consider the impact of losing a customer who makes even minor purchases. If, a businessperson regularly stops at a diner in the morning for a cup of coffee and a breakfast roll it might cost a total of $3.50. This is a small amount, until you realize that the customer makes that same purchase twice a week for fifty weeks each year (the other two weeks our businessperson is away on vacation). Because the businessperson might work in the area for ten years before moving, we can now see that the lifetime value ($3.50 × 2 × 50 × 10) of the customer rings out at $3,500! Such numbers underscore the long-term costs of losing a customer.

As noted in Chapter 10, reducing customer defections by as little as 5 percent can double an organization's profits (Reichheld 1996). Against this backdrop, it makes sense to win back a customer who has been dissatisfied with a service experience. It also highlights the folly of ignoring or making light of customer complaints. It is important to note that not all customers are equally attractive to a firm. Some customers spend less money, patronize less frequently, and may be more difficult to accommodate. Further, research has demonstrated that the value of a lost customer is different over the life cycle of a product, with the loss of one that is an early adopter costing the firm much more than the loss of a later adopter (Hogan, Lemon, and Libai 2003).

When Is Service Recovery Needed?

This book has emphasized how services involve a sequence of events that combine to create successful or unsuccessful customer experiences. Each point at which customers encounter the service organization may influence their perception of the service's excellence. It may be the organization's advertisements, the state of its parking lot, its receptionist's manner, the availability of advice, or any other aspect of the service delivery. A **moment of truth** (Carlzon 1987) is any contact point with a service organization that the customer uses to evaluate service delivery. Such moments are opportunities for the organization to succeed or fail in its effort to endear itself to the customer. When a service organization fails during a moment of truth, it may need to engage in service recovery efforts. Spotlight 11.3 describes the stories of service failure and recovery collected by Consumerist.com.

> A **moment of truth** is any contact point with a service organization that the customer uses to evaluate the service delivery.

SPOTLIGHT 11.3

The *Consumerist* Is "Where Shoppers Bite Back"

No matter how bad your service experiences have ever been, the *Consumerist* (**http://www.consumerist.com**) has probably already collected even worse examples. All of these bad examples were moments of truth for the customers telling their tales of woe. The *Consumerist* is an edited blog that collects customer experiences daily. Most of those stories are descriptions of neglect, mistreatment, or extreme disservice. The *Consumerist* is a subsidiary of the magazine *Consumer Reports* (**http://www.consumerreports.org**), which is published by the Consumers Union (**http://www.consumersunion.org**).

The experiences described are often amazing examples of bad service and the customer's subsequent efforts to get the service organization to fix the problem. Such publicity in the *Consumerist* has been known to help convince a service organization to finally do the right thing by a customer. Also, the *Consumerist* makes it possible for customers to tell each other how they finally got a service organization to do the right thing.

Source: **http://www.consumerist.com,** (accessed on September 18, 2012).

Several aspects of moments of truth contribute to whether such a recovery effort will be needed. First, complex services (i.e., services that involve many steps in the process of service assembly) entail more moments of truth than simple services and are therefore more likely to require service recovery. For example, more can go wrong with a hotel stay than with an ATM encounter. However, some complex services offer customers relatively few moments of truth to evaluate, because much of the service takes place backstage away from customer inspection and critical assessment.

Second, not all moments of truth carry the same significance for customer satisfaction. The important ones are critical because they enhance or detract from the customer's perception of excellence. For instance, in a hotel experience, mispronouncing the customer's name is unlikely to have the same impact as failure to hold a reserved room. Service organizations face the challenge of determining which moments of truth are most likely to influence customer satisfaction, because such moments are when service recovery plans are needed.

Third, any particular moment of truth may include several different opportunities for failure. Consider the simple act of delivering a plate of food to a restaurant patron and all of the ways a restaurant can trip over that particular step in the service delivery process. The wrong plate of food might be delivered, it might be cold, the waiter's thumb impression might be in the mashed potatoes, and so on. When an organization determines which moments of truth are most important, it then must consider what can go wrong at that particular contact point and prepare a system to recover from such failures.

Other Means of Identifying Recovery Needs

Service organizations have many ways to learn when service recovery efforts are needed. For instance, one method is to offer customers an opportunity to voice their dissatisfaction by providing customer response cards, telephone numbers, e-mail addresses, or Web sites (Brown 1997). Such means make it easy for an unhappy customer to express a complaint. For example, Holiday Inn (**http:// www.ichotelsgroup.com**) posts a phone number in its rooms for travelers to use if they wish to complain to headquarters rather than to the hotel property. Many organizations, such as the Scandinavian airline SAS (**http://www.scandinavian .net**), routinely provide the Web address of their central office to allow irked customers to communicate their complaints with ease. An organization should facilitate complaining behavior rather than letting a customer "walk, talk, and squawk" to share his disdain with other potential customers instead of the organization. Although these same channels might also be used by a service organization to harvest suggestions or compliments, it is their ability to gather information about a failed moment of truth and identify disgruntled customers that is particularly helpful. By monitoring the responses generated through these means, the organization can identify customers requiring recovery measures and discover other aspects of the service delivery system needing closer attention. Unfortunately, customer response cards and other feedback mechanisms do not allow for immediate recovery measures. Any response to a failed moment of truth using this system is likely to occur long after the failure occurred.

A better way to identify when service recovery is needed is through empowered frontstage personnel. Workers who have been given the responsibility and the authority to satisfy customers can be excellent buffers against poor service experiences. They can provide an immediate response to problems that emerge during service delivery. As active participants in the service process, frontline employees can observe problems, solicit information, and field customer complaints. If dissatisfaction is apparent, the empowered worker can instantly set in motion a process to recapture the customer's goodwill. This capability is one of the key benefits of an empowered workforce (Bowen and Lawler 1992). However, empowered workers must be able to detect dissatisfaction when it occurs as well as have the means to address it. To enjoy the recovery payoff derived from an empowered workforce, a service organization may need to rethink its hiring, training, and worker retention practices.

Another means of discovering opportunities for service recovery is through "management by walking around" (MBWA). Service managers who routinely make a practice of spending time "in the trenches" are more likely to detect incidences of customer ire that may require recovery efforts. Although this outcome may not have been its original intent, MBWA places a frontstage manager in a position to monitor service delivery and to respond to service failure firsthand. Like her empowered workers, the manager practicing MBWA can solicit information regarding service excellence, present herself as a visible contact point for customer complaints, and recognize when failure occurs. When service disappoints, she can take the necessary steps toward recovery. The interactive nature of services provides an opportunity for such actions.

STEPS TO SERVICE RECOVERY

We have established the importance of recovery for service organizations. The next question is "*How* can recovery be implemented successfully?" As noted earlier, a failed effort at service recovery may be as bad or worse than no effort at all. Hence, a service organization must have a systematic plan in place for winning back customers who have been disappointed by some facet of service delivery. One such plan, offered by Zemke and Schaaf (1989), entails a five-step procedure: apology, urgent reinstatement, empathy, symbolic atonement, and follow-up. Each step builds on the previous one.

Apology

The process of service recovery begins with an apology. When an organization becomes aware of customer dissatisfaction, someone should apologize. However, there is often no apology. To apologize is in a sense to admit failure, and such admissions are foreign to some organizations. Yet it is important for service organizations to recognize that they will sometimes fall short. The risk of failure is an inherent aspect of operating a service business, because services are highly variable. Once an organization accepts that failure sometimes occurs, it can instill in its employees the necessity of extending a genuine apology when a customer is disappointed. This simple act can go a long way in framing the customer's perception of his value to the organization and helps pave the path for subsequent steps to regain his goodwill.

Urgent Reinstatement

The second step is a natural extension of an apology, one that the dissatisfied customer will certainly expect. Customers want to know that something will be done to remove the source of their disappointment. Urgent means the action is taken quickly; reinstatement means making an effort to correct the problem. When a service organization carries out urgent reinstatement, it demonstrates to the customer that it takes the complaint seriously. Like the well-executed apology, this action sends a message that customer satisfaction is important to the organization. An organization slow to address customer dissatisfaction or failing to present evidence of some action risks the customer's perception that her concerns are unimportant. She will then join the ranks of other dissatisfied customers who, in the words of former baseball great Yogi Berra, "stay away in droves."

Empathy

Following an indication of urgent reinstatement, an expression of empathy usually is required for successful recovery. The service organization must convey to the angered customer that it understands the extent to which it failed to meet her needs. However, empathy means more than simply acknowledging failure, which is accomplished with the apology. Empathy means making the effort to comprehend why the customer is disappointed with the organization. If service workers can identify with the customer's role, they may grasp the disappointment she feels and successfully convey that understanding. The payoff of empathy is the customer's realization that the organization is in fact sensitive to her dilemma. That realization can defuse a lot of anger and help build a common ground of mutual respect. However, an insincere attempt at empathy can backfire. Feigned empathy appears patronizing, which only increases customer displeasure. It is therefore advisable for service organizations to develop workers' listening and empathy skills as part of their training.

Symbolic Atonement

Being empathetic is important, but it leaves the customer uncompensated. The next step in the recovery process is to make amends in some tangible way for the organization's failure, perhaps by offering a gift as a form of symbolic atonement. The gift may take the form of a coupon for a free dessert, a ticket for a future flight, a room upgrade on the next visit to the hotel, or some other means of making up for the customer's poor service experience. This step is called symbolic atonement because the gesture is designed not to provide a replacement service, but to communicate to the customer that the organization takes responsibility for his disappointment and is willing to pay a price for its failure. Again, caution should be exercised in the atonement effort. If the cost to the organization is too large, the gesture may negatively influence its bottom line. On the other hand, if the atonement is too meager, even its symbolic value is compromised. Hence, it is important for service organizations to determine customers' thresholds of acceptability.

Follow-Up

At some point, the organization must check whether its effort to win back the customer's goodwill was successful. By following up to see whether the gesture of symbolic atonement was well received, the organization can gauge how well it placated the customer. If it appears that the organization has fallen short of that goal, the recovery process will require additional measures. The follow-up can take many forms, depending on the service type and recovery situation. It could be a telephone call several hours after the atonement gesture, a letter or e-mail message a few days later, or a verbal inquiry at the end of the service experience. The key is to determine whether the organization's atonement effort was appreciated and whether the customer's low regard for the organization has been overcome. In addition, a follow-up gives an organization a chance to evaluate the recovery plan itself and identify where improvements are necessary.

In summary, an organization that takes these steps can expect to make great strides in overcoming customer dissatisfaction. However, it should be apparent that each case of customer disappointment may not require every step. Sometimes a customer is simply upset about one specific aspect of a company's service delivery (e.g., it took too long to be waited on, a lamp in a hotel room doesn't work). According to Zemke and Schaaf (1989), this type of circumstance results in *annoyance*, and service recovery may be achieved simply by successfully navigating the first two steps of the process. An apology and an indication of urgent reinstatement should suffice. At other times, the customer is exasperated by the organization's failure in a transaction (e.g., it did not deliver an important document on time, it mistakenly cut off his telephone service). This type of failure results in *victimization*, which is an occasion that demands all five of the recovery steps. It requires a greater effort at demonstrating the customer's importance to the organization, because he has been significantly affected by the organization's failure. The organization must attempt to demonstrate that it understands his dissatisfaction and is willing to sacrifice something to compensate for it. When the complete recovery process is implemented, the victimized customer is likely to recognize that his concerns are being taken seriously. At the heart of this matter is the realization that customers assess what the service provider could and should have done given the circumstances and, if it is not appropriate, they are likely to exhibit negative emotions such as anger and frustration (McColl-Kennedy and Sparks 2003).

HIDDEN BENEFITS OF SERVICE RECOVERY

In addition to the more obvious payoffs that flow from turning service failure into customer satisfaction, systematic service recovery programs benefit an organization in several ways. For one thing, the process can help improve the overall quality of service delivery as the service occurs (Tax and Brown 1998). This service quality improvement is possible if the customer provides feedback during the service experience or if the organization discerns dissatisfaction as the service unfolds. In other words, the dissatisfied customer provides information, which allows the organization to refine its service process. As discussed earlier, empowered workforces are capable of addressing the source of customer disappointment in real time, thereby obliterating its effect.

Keeping track of the sources of dissatisfaction that create a need for recovery can help the organization, too. Whether trouble spots are identified during the process of service delivery or discovered afterward, careful collection and storage of information regarding the incidents may produce a rich database of information on service quality. When the organization analyzes these data, patterns may emerge that specify particularly troublesome aspects of its service delivery system. Scrutiny of these aspects may reveal why failure is rampant at particular junctures and yield insights into how to correct the problem. Ultimately, assembling, analyzing, and correcting the causes behind the need for service recovery can result in a much stronger service delivery system. Such data can also indicate if an organization is successfully reducing customer defections through its recovery efforts (Reichheld 1996). The critical element here is to gather the information in a systematic way. Hence, organizations should consider developing feedback devices that allow workers to file simple, useful, and easily accessible reports of recovery efforts.

Service recovery can reduce the incidence of bungled moments of truth if the information regarding customers' dissatisfaction is put to good use. An organization must recognize that service failures sometimes occur and that they can also sow the seeds for future service success.

Summary and Conclusion

Customer service should be an important component of any service organization's plan for success. Service systems will occasionally fail. The question is what should be done when failure occurs. Although customers are likely to forgive failure, they may be less reasonable if no recovery is attempted. Enlightened organizations address failure directly and turn potential perceptions of poor quality into information that can help them better serve their customers. They put this information to use and in the meantime take steps to win dissatisfied customers back, using a systematic approach that communicates their importance to the organization. Having a service recovery plan in place sends a strong message to customers that the organization values their satisfaction, and it makes an equally powerful statement to the employees that the organization is serious about service quality.

Exercises

1. Find a customer comment card from a local service business. Examine it closely. Does it provide sufficient detail about the business to determine why a customer was pleased or unhappy with its service? How could it be improved?

2. Consider a recent occasion when you were dissatisfied with an organization's service. What did you do about it? If you complained to the organization, how did you go about registering your complaint, and how did the organization handle it? If you did not complain, why not?

3. Think of a service business that you patronize regularly. Calculate your lifetime value to that business. Why is this an important value for the business to consider?

Internet Exercise

EXPLORE

Visit the companion site for this text at **www .cengagebrain.com** to explore key concepts in the service industry. You will find tools to help you expand your services marketing knowledge, including ACE self-tests, Web links to companies and organizations featured in this chapter, and much more!

1. Search one of the many Web sites (Yelp!, TripAdvisor, Open Table, etc.) that contain customer reviews and ratings. Pick a particular service that has numerous comments.
2. Select and describe a service failure or recovery account from a customer on the Web site.
3. Did the service organization reply regarding the incident?
4. What impact could such negative publicity have on the organization?

References

Bitner, Mary Jo, Bernard M. Booms, and Mary S. Tetreault (1990), "The Service Encounter: Diagnosing Favorable and Unfavorable Incidents," *Journal of Marketing*, 54 (January), 71–84.

Bowen, David E. and Edward L. Lawler III (1992), "The Empowerment of Service Workers: What, Why, How, and When," *Sloan Management Review*, 33 (Spring), 31–39.

Brown, Stephen W. (1997), "Service Recovery Through IT," *Marketing Management*, 6 (Fall), 25–27.

Carlzon, Jan (1987), *Moments of Truth*, New York: Ballinger.

Grove, Stephen J., Raymond P. Fisk, Lloyd Harris, Emmanuel Ogbonna, Joby John, Les Carlson, and Jerry Goolsby (2012), "Disservice: A Framework of Sources and Solutions," in *Marketing Dynamism & Sustainability: Things Change, Things Stay the Same...*, Proceedings of the Annual Conference of the Academy of Marketing Science, 32, Jr. Leroy Robinson, ed. New Orleans, Louisiana, 169–172.

Hogan, John E., Katherine N. Lemon, and Barak Libai (2003), "What Is the True Value of a Lost Customer?" *Journal of Service Research*, 5 (3), 196–208.

Kaufman, Ron (2005), *Up Your Organization*, 3rd ed., Singapore: Ron Kaufman, Pte Ltd.

Lovelock, Christopher H. (1994), *Product Plus: How Product + Service = Competitive Advantage*, New York: McGraw-Hill.

McColl-Kennedy, Janet R. and Beverley A. Sparks (2003), "Application of Fairness Theory to Service Failures and Service Recovery," *Journal of Service Research*, 5 (3), 251–266.

Reichheld, Frederick H. (1996), "Learning from Customer Defections," *Harvard Business Review*, 74 (March–April), 56–69.

Sewell, Carl and Paul R. Brown (2002), *Customers for Life: How to Turn That One-Time Buyer into a Lifetime Customer*, 3rd ed., New York: Pocket Books.

Tax, Stephen S. and Stephen W. Brown (1998), "Recovering and Learning from Service Failure," *Sloan Management Review*, 40 (Fall), 75–88.

Zemke, Ron and Dick Schaaf (1989), *The Service Edge: 101 Companies That Profit from Customer Care*, New York: Plume.

Jordan's Furniture understands the importance of staying close to the customer. The store follows up every sale with a postsale customer satisfaction phone call from the customer service desk. Without such customer feedback, the store might not know when a customer was dissatisfied. Surveys are useful in measuring the customer's evaluation of the service experience *after* it happens. However, some research methods are available that can be employed *during* the service experience. This chapter discusses the importance of measuring customer experiences and examines measurement techniques appropriate for service organizations. The chapter has four specific objectives:

- To emphasize the importance of researching service success and failure
- To examine why service success is so difficult to achieve
- To discuss methods for researching services
- To explore creating a service quality information system

Leonard Berry (1995) writes that "great service companies measure service providers' performance and reward their excellence." Two significant points are implicit in this statement. First, an organization must measure its progress to know whether it is doing a good job. Second, rewarding excellent performance is a hallmark of excellent organizations. Measurement is the heart of quality improvement. Hertz **(http://www.hertz.com),** the car rental leader, compiles numerous statistical reports, which its management uses to measure and improve performance. These reports range from accident and safety rates to warranty claims and usage figures. Berry cites Mary Kay **(http://www.marykay.com)** as an organization that excels in its superior award system for its star performers. Mary Kay showers its star performers with a variety of awards, ranging from the company's famous pink Cadillacs to hard cash. These star performers also receive appreciation in the form of praise, respect, spirituality, and love. Similarly, Southwest Airlines **(http://www.southwest.com)** holds an annual awards banquet to recognize its employees for making it an industry leader for on-time performance, baggage handling, and fewest complaints per number of passengers flown. To determine who should receive rewards, organizations first need to ascertain their successes and failures. Organizations that measure their performance regularly benefit in many ways.

WHY IS RESEARCHING SERVICE SUCCESS AND FAILURE NECESSARY?

Service performance measurement seeks to understand customers' and employees' points of view to determine what an organization is doing right or wrong. Customers assess their service experiences according to whether their expectations were met. When a service organization satisfies a customer, it experiences success. When it dissatisfies a customer, the organization experiences failure. Service successes are service performances that meet or exceed customer expectations. Organizations should study successful performances to find out what they must replicate to ensure future excellence. Conversely, when performances fall short of customer standards and failures occur, service performances must be modified or improved.

When service organizations know why they have succeeded or failed with their customers, they can use the information to reward excellent performance, set priorities among process improvement options, and preempt customer switching behavior. Later, this chapter discusses how information gathered through customer research can enhance managerial decision making. Measurement efforts also have a direct impact on service providers and customers. The service organization that measures its performance can set implicit service standards or communicate acceptable levels of performance to let employees know what is expected of them. Without service standards, both frontstage and backstage workers lack specific goals and may believe that their roles make no meaningful contribution. Service organizations that regularly measure their performance by surveying customers signal that they care about the workers and the quality of the service they provide. In addition, they convey the message that they value customer loyalty.

Service organizations should seek feedback on their performance whenever possible and appropriate. In a restaurant, the attentive waiter asks patrons during their meal, "Is everything okay?" Retailers such as car dealerships or furniture stores may contact recent customers to inquire about their service experience. Similarly, credit card companies may telephone cardholders who transfer their balances to another credit card company to determine how they could have kept them from doing so. The effort of listening to their customers provides service organizations with valuable information.

The interactive nature of most service performances allows many opportunities to solicit customer opinions. In cases of extreme dissatisfaction or satisfaction, customers are often vocal in letting the organization and its employees know their feelings. However, only unusual cases inspire customers to complain or praise. Most experiences fall in between these extremes, and the vast majority of customer evaluations go unseen and unheard.

WHY IS SERVICE SUCCESS SO DIFFICULT TO ACHIEVE?

As we have seen, services are dynamic and experiential in nature. Services exist only when they are rendered, which makes it difficult to predict and anticipate all the variables likely to affect performance quality. For example, airplanes may be late for reasons beyond the airline's control. Weather, at the origin, at the destination, or en route can delay the flight. In fact, weather at other locations can affect the timeliness of connecting flights and create havoc for the traffic patterns at several other airports. Equipment failures, security checks for unidentified baggage, passengers needing physical assistance, or medical emergencies all can delay flights. Each circumstance is difficult to predict in advance.

The same forces that contribute to unpredictable service quality complicate investigating services through traditional research methodologies. As noted earlier in the chapter, surveys obtain information after the fact and cannot capture the experiential nature of services. Fortunately, alternative methods can be used to evaluate the service performance. Each method has strengths and weaknesses. It is best to measure performance using a combination of methods, thereby offsetting the limitations of any single approach. The next section discusses several appropriate research methods for investigating services experiences.

RESEARCH METHODS FOR SERVICES

Many service organizations use survey and focus group research methodologies. Less frequently, experimental methods are used to test new service products. Observational techniques and the Critical Incident Technique help evaluate processes and assess behaviors like those found in service performances. Levy and Kellstadt (2012) propose "integraphy," a mix of qualitative methods, to capture the richness of detail and complexity in studying consumer situations that would be most appropriate in the case of services. Table 12.1 provides an overview of these and other service research methods and shows how managers use the information gathered from each method.

Observational Techniques

Observational techniques allow the researcher to gain a firsthand and thorough picture of service phenomena, depending upon the specific technique selected. When choosing from the various observational methods of investigation available, Grove and Fisk (1992) suggest three key dimensions to examine:

- What is the mode (human or mechanical) of observation?

- When (during or after the service performance) are data collected?

- How open (concealed or revealed) are observations?

If humans observe the service experience, observers might be service contact personnel, managers, service customers, or independent observers. Human observers use judgment and add value to the data they are collecting. On the other hand, subjective biases may undermine the accuracy of their observations. It is difficult for human observers to be objective, even when they are trained and work hard at being unbiased. In contrast, observations made by mechanical devices such as video cameras or computers provide a permanent body of data for decision makers. Further, the data gathered by mechanical means are held in automated form, which assists in tracking a particular service performance, a specific service location, or a service provider. In using any observational technique, service researchers must respect and protect the customer's privacy. Spotlight 12.1 demonstrates the incredible vulnerability of individual privacy on the Internet.

Whether by a human or a machine, data can be collected through direct (i.e., in real time) or indirect (i.e., after the fact) observation. Sometimes service organizations employ mystery shoppers to observe a service performance as

TABLE 12.1   Research Methods

Methods	Description	Examples of Uses
Observational Techniques	Service delivery observations can be made by humans or machines, can be direct or indirect, and can be revealed or concealed.	Data from observations can be used to check whether the service is being provided as planned.
Mystery Shopping	Mystery shoppers observe the service performance in terms of employee behaviors, service delivery, and physical evidence of the service.	Mystery shopper reports provide useful information on frontstage employee performances for use in training and evaluation.
Employee Reports	Employee reports provide feedback on the service process and the service delivery environment.	Employee reports can be used to guide service improvements, to learn from service failures, and to suggest service recovery procedures.
Surveys	Surveys of customer needs, expectations, and service experiences are obtained through questionnaires conducted by mail, over the telephone, or in person.	Customer surveys can assess market behavior, service quality, and customer satisfaction. The results can be used to determine service improvement priorities.
Focus Groups	Small groups of customers or employees are gathered to solicit insight on service issues with the help of a moderator.	Focus group reports can test new service concepts and service improvement proposals and can obtain feedback from customers or employees on specific service issues.
Experimental Field-Testing	Specific service features are tested in controlled environments to examine effects on customers or employees.	Experiments can test new service offerings, service delivery options, or improvements in existing services.
Critical Incident Technique	Customers are asked to describe significant events during service experiences that led to satisfactory or unsatisfactory outcomes.	The Critical Incident Technique can help examine service failure scenarios and determine the effectiveness of service recovery efforts.
Moment of Truth Impact Analysis	A moment of truth is analyzed for customer expectations and the actual experience that may have detracted or enhanced the customer experience.	The impact analysis of moments of truth can uncover those points in the service script or blueprint that have negative and positive effects on customer experience.

SPOTLIGHT 12.1

The Internet and Your Privacy

 Every time you use a search engine, your keyboard actions are being recorded and the data manipulated to provide you with results you are looking for. Such search data can reveal personal information, such as your hobbies and interests, and possibly your political and religious beliefs and medical and financial information. "Cookies" are used to track the pages you have viewed on your Web browser. Misuse of cookies forced Google to pay a $22.5 million fine for evading privacy settings on Apple's Safari Web browser.

Then there are the data leaks, resulting from both inadvertent and sloppy security as well as malicious hackers. Over the years, Yahoo!, AOL, and Google have suffered security breaches on their databases. On July 2012, almost half a million usernames and passwords were exposed. According to CNNMoney, here are the top three security breaches (from a list of nine):

- Sony PlayStation Network—Hackers accessed 77 million accounts, including 22 million unencrypted credit card numbers and personal information.
- Epsilon, the world's largest permission-based email marketing company—60 million customer e-mails from over 100 clients were revealed.
- RSA Security, the security division of storage company EMC—Hackers accessed 40 million authentication tokens used by employees to access corporate and government networks.

As we write this revision, the jury is still out on whether a group of hackers known as Anonymous accessed 12 million iPhone and iPad IDs from a FBI computer in the United States, as it has claimed.

Source: **http://money.cnn.com/galleries/2012/technology/1206/gallery.9-worst-security-breaches.fortune/index.html,** Accessed: October 1, 2012.

it unfolds. American Airlines, for example, uses a program of secret fliers to assess how passengers experience its services. The advantage is that this method can assess the actual service performance firsthand, as opposed to reconstructing it from proxy data that measure the consequences of the service performance after the fact. Examples of indirect observation include *trace analysis* (e.g., studying the physical environment after a service has occurred to ascertain aspects of its delivery) and *receipt analysis* (e.g., reviewing data provided on billing statements to uncover information about service customers). *Mortality rates* are an example of an indirect measure of quality in medical care. Direct observation provides a more comprehensive type of information than indirect observation; however, it can be expensive, time-consuming, and impractical.

Observational data collection can also be obtrusive or unobtrusive. Those being observed may or may not know it. Although undisclosed observation might create ethical concerns, it removes the possibility of subjects staging behavior. Obtrusive observation alerts the observed parties to be on their best behavior. Hence, the service researcher who reveals his or her identity may not see the service as it normally occurs.

As we saw in the previous chapter, many organizations rely on "management by walking around" (MBWA) to collect information about their service delivery systems. In such an approach, the employees know the manager, which might cause them to act differently. Still, the service manager who practices MBWA may discern a wealth of information that might go undetected if she were to rely on survey methods or other forms of input regarding the service operation. For those who can conceal their identity to customers, MBWA might generate even more provocative discoveries concerning the service delivery system.

These human/mechanical, direct/indirect, or revealed/concealed observations can be combined in many different ways. Ultimately, the researcher's interest determines the specific method that is chosen. Concealed, direct human observation is often the method of choice, because it produces a deep, close-up view of the service as it happens.

Mystery Shopping

One way to obtain direct, undisclosed human observations is to use mystery shoppers. **Mystery shopping** is an unobtrusive method of gathering data in which people pose as bona fide shoppers to observe and collect information about an organization's service performance. These mystery shoppers conduct systematic and comprehensive observations of their service experience when they either visit a service establishment or receive an organization's service at a distance.

> **Mystery shopping** is an unobtrusive method of gathering data in which people pose as bona fide shoppers to observe and collect information about an organization's service performance.

Mystery shoppers complete questionnaires and submit them to organizations for review. The questionnaires may be simple or elaborate, depending on the amount of information desired. Ultimately, these reports identify service problems that require corrective actions. Numerous service organizations use mystery shoppers to evaluate frontline employee performance, the physical environment, and the entire service process. See Spotlight 12.2 for an example of mystery shopping in health care.

SPOTLIGHT 12.2

Health Care Taps "Mystery Shoppers": To Improve Service, Hospitals and Doctors Hire Spies to Pose as Patients and Report Back

 Mystery shopping is better known in industries like retailing and hospitality, but the health care industry is also turning to mystery shopping. Growing health care competition has led hospitals and medical facilities to look for ways to improve the patient experience. "Health-care facilities that use mystery shoppers say the reports have led to a number of changes in the patient experience, including improved estimates of wait times, better explanations of medical procedures, extended hours for hospital administration workers, escorts for patients who have gotten lost, and even less-stressful programming on the television in the waiting room."

Many hospitals and doctor's offices tell their staff that mystery patients will visit. They might be told the visit will occur anytime between a week and an entire year. Most employees adapt to this practice, but some feel spied upon. The mystery patients may reveal themselves at the end of the visit, but many

times the staff never find out the mystery patient's identity.

To initiate the health care experience, mystery patients might call with a question, visit a doctor's office or emergency room for a checkup, or even fake symptoms. Typically, the mystery patient pretends to be an uninsured patient so that the health care facility pays any fees. To record the details of the experience without blowing their cover, mystery patients might hide tape recorders in their clothes or in a bag or take notes in an appointment book or while they're in the bathroom. "Medical mystery shopping can raise some thorny issues—among them the fear that mystery patients will take up time and resources needed by truly sick patients." To minimize this risk, mystery patients are told to visit emergency rooms only during less-busy hours.

Source: Shirley S. Wang (2006), "Health Care Taps 'Mystery Shoppers': To Improve Service, Hospitals and Doctors Hire Spies to Pose as Patients and Report Back," Wall Street Journal (August 8), D1.

Employee Reports

The employee report is an important method of collecting information regarding an organization's service performance. Employee reports are useful when a service organization desires comprehensive feedback either from its frontline employees or from those who labor backstage. These personnel have firsthand information regarding the service delivery system, and, in the case of frontline employees, interactions with customers. Employee reports can provide insights unavailable from customer surveys because employees know more about the process, the backstage support, and other aspects of the business not visible to the customer. This method may include biases, but it is a useful complement to other methods of monitoring service performance. After all, service workers have a unique and enlightened view of the service performance, which neither customers nor managers possess.

Survey Methods

Traditional research methods such as surveys and interviews can also assess the service performance. Surveys typically record large numbers of respondents for statistical testing of data. Organizations conduct surveys that ask customers to evaluate a service transaction or assess their customer's total relationship with the organization. Such surveys can be distributed to every customer following a service consumption experience or to a list of customers at regular intervals. Comment cards such as those passed out at restaurants or found on hotel room nightstands are examples of transactional surveys. See Figure 12.1 for an example of a comment card from the U.S. Social Security Agency. More general surveys may either be handled internally or contracted to outside professional market research agencies. Bizrate **(http://bizrate.com)**, primarily a comparison shopping Web site, also provides a survey feedback service for retailers. Spotlight 12.3 shows Bizrate Insights as an example of a research service for online retailing services.

Focus Groups

Focus group interviews can provide important qualitative feedback. Just as they do for packaged goods marketing, focus groups include eight to twelve customers led by a moderator and probe specific aspects of a service in depth. Focus groups also can generate useful ideas for new services and service improvements or simply explore a service's strengths and weaknesses. Focus groups prove especially useful for concept testing of new services or service features or for testing a creative concept for an advertising campaign.

Experimental Field-Testing

Service organizations can choose to examine new service concepts and features through experimental field-testing. This method allows service organizations to evaluate new service concepts on a small scale before committing the extensive financial resources needed to introduce them across the board. Feedback from the experiment can be used to determine the efficacy of the service concept and modify it until the appropriate design is achieved.

SPOTLIGHT 12.3

The Bizrate Smiley Scale

Bizrate **(www.bizrate.com)**, a leading resource for shopping and retailers, began as a business school assignment by Farhad Mohit. Mohit wanted to give customers a way to assess the quality of different online stores and thus launched the first online customer feedback and ratings platform. Bizrate is now owned and operated by Shopzilla, Inc. **(www.shopzilla.com)**. Bizrateinsights is a Bizrate service that provides 6,000 retailers worldwide with customer feedback and analysis to help their clients build customer loyalty.

Customers evaluate the online store on sixteen quality ratings, eight of which are about the "checkout." The survey appears as an invitation on the receipt page. Retailers, the clients of Bizrate, receive a Smiley Report Card if there are at least twenty reviews in a three-month period. The report card uses a rating scale designed as follows:

 Outstanding

Good

Satisfactory

Poor

The **BizRate Smiley Scale** is a simple and intuitive way to visualize a lot of rigorous research about a store's capabilities, so you, the consumer, can at a glance tell the good from the not-so-good when comparison shopping.

Bizrate provides a suite of services to its retail customers with its Customer Feedback and Ratings platform. Retailers receive services such as Vital Mail, customer feedback data for the previous two weeks; BizAdvisor, benchmarked customer feedback data; Quick-Response, open comments by customers; Vital Signs, on-demand aggregated data for past thirty days; and Comments, categorized customer comments.

Source: **http://bizrateinsights.com/** (accessed August 16, 2012).

Marriott **(http://www.marriott.com)** developed the concept of its Courtyard hotels to attract business travelers. To test it, the company configured a truck with the room design and features planned for the new hotel chain and sent it to various businesses to solicit opinions from potential hotel guests. Other service organizations have used similar field-testing methods. McDonald's **(http://www.mcdonalds.com)** field-tests new menu items. Citibank **(http://www.citibank.com)** evaluates new designs for its ATMs. The Olive Garden restaurant chain **(http://www.olivegarden.com)** also uses experimental field tests to study new franchise locations.

The Critical Incident Technique

The **Critical Incident Technique** is a research method especially useful to study the service experiences of customers and frontline employees. You might recall from Chapter 11 that a critical incident is an observable event during a service encounter that contributes in a significant way toward a satisfactory or unsatisfactory service experience. The research method based on the analysis of critical incidents has been

> The **Critical Incident Technique** is a research method used to identify and explain memorable and significant aspects of service experiences.

adapted to study service experiences of customers and employees across a variety of service types, including banks, restaurants, tourist attractions, and airlines (Gremler 2004). In these cases, the organization reviews critical incidents by asking subjects to report such occasions and provide details of their circumstances. Their responses are recorded and painstakingly reviewed to identify patterns and details that denote superior or inferior service delivery. The method

FIGURE 12.1 **Example of an Electronic Survey**

OUR COMMITMENT TO YOU

When you conduct business with us:

- We will provide service through knowledgeable employees who will treat you with courtesy, dignity and respect every time you do business with us.

- We will provide you with our best estimate of the time needed to complete your request and fully explain any delays.

- We will clearly explain our decisions so you can understand why and how we made them and what to do if you disagree.

- We will make sure our offices are safe and pleasant and our services are accessible.

- When you make an appointment, we will service you within 10 minutes of the scheduled time.

- When you call our 800 number, you will get through to it within 5 minutes of your first try.

- If you request a new or replacement Social Security card from one of our offices, we will mail it to you within 5 working days of receiving all the information we need. If you have an urgent need for the Social Security number, we will tell you the number within 1 working day.

PRIVACY ACT

The Social Security Administration is authorized to collect the information on this comment card under Section 702 of Title VII of the Social Security Act. Your response to these questions is strictly voluntary. The information you provide will be used to help us improve the service that we give you.

Paperwork Reduction Act Statement – This information collection meets the requirements of 44 U.S. C. § 3507, as amended by section 2 of the Paperwork Reduction Act of 1995. You do not need to answer these questions unless we display a valid Office of Management control number. We estimate that it will take you about 5 minutes to read instructions, gather the facts, and answer the questions. **SEND OR BRING THE COMPLETED FORM TO YOUR LOCAL SOCIAL SECURITY OFFICE. The office is listed under U.S. Government agencies in your telephone directory or you may call Social Security at 1-800-772-1213 (TTY 1-800-325-0778).** *You may send comments on our time estimate above to SSA, 6401 Security Blvd., Baltimore, MD 21235-6401. Send only comments relating to our time estimate to this address, not the completed form.*

PLEASE FILL OUT AND MAIL

FIGURE 12.1 Continued

Social Security Administration   Form Approved CMB No. 0060-0528

HOW ARE WE DOING?

DATE	TIME

DID YOU VISIT FOR:

◯ A Social Security Card	◯ An Appeal
◯ Retirement or Survivors Benefits	◯ A Personal Earnings Statement
◯ Disability Benefits	◯ Report a Change for Your Records
◯ SSI Benefits	◯ Other (specify) _____

Did you have an appointment?	How long did you wait to be served?
◯ Yes If yes, appt. time _____	◯ 30 minutes or less
◯ No	◯ More than 30 minutes

Blacken the circle which corresponds closest to your feelings.

HOW SATISFIED WERE YOU WITH:

	Very Satisfied				Very Dissatisfied	
The overall service you received?	①	②	③	④	⑤	⑥
Our appointment system?	①	②	③	④	⑤	⑥
The time you waited to be served?	①	②	③	④	⑤	⑥
The comfort of the waiting area?	①	②	③	④	⑤	⑥
The privacy in the office?	①	②	③	④	⑤	⑥
The courtesy of the staff?	①	②	③	④	⑤	⑥
The knowledge of the staff?	①	②	③	④	⑤	⑥
The helpfulness of the staff?	①	②	③	④	⑤	⑥
The accuracy of our information?	①	②	③	④	⑤	⑥
The clarity of our information?	①	②	③	④	⑤	⑥

COMMENTS/SUGGESTIONS TO IMPROVE OUR SERVICE

_____

_____

_____

_____

_____

Name (Optional)	Telephone Number (Optional)
	(Area Code)

Address (Optional)

Form SSA-117-PC (01-2010)

Source: http://www.ssa.gov/online/ssa-117pc.pdf

provides researchers with rich and emotion-filled perspectives about service phenomena and can be used to generate insights unavailable through more traditional survey methods.

Moment of Truth Impact Analysis

We have already seen that critical incidents resemble the concept of "moments of truth." It is possible to study moments of truth closely to discern information leading to or undermining successful service delivery. Moment of Truth Impact Analysis (Zemke and Schaaf 1989) involves a combination of three distinct measurements. First, it measures the customer's expectations of the service organization at the contact point in question (e.g., when making a reservation with a hotel).

TABLE 12.2   Moment of Truth Impact Analysis: A Customer Contacts the Telephone Repair Answering Center

Experience Enhancers	Standard Expectations	Experience Detractors
• The operator had a melodious, well-modulated voice. • The operator communicated a sense of urgency. • The operator understood my problem or situation and knew just what to do. • The operator apologized sincerely. • The operator asked me about medical emergencies or other special situations that may warrant extra attention. • The operator made a comment that let me know she was aware of my area (i.e., sounded like a neighbor). • The operator offered to have work done at my convenience. • The operator told me how I could prevent the problem in the future.	• I will only have to call one number. • I will call a local number. • I will be treated fairly. • The operator will speak clearly. • The phone will not be busy. • The operator will answer within a reasonable period. • The operator will be a real person. • The operator will speak pleasantly. • The operator will listen to my problems in a manner that lets me know he understands my problem. • The operator will seem competent, helpful, and understanding. • The operator will promise me a solution with a reasonable deadline. • The operator will explain exactly what will happen next.	• I couldn't understand the operator's words. • I had to call more than once to get through. • I had to listen to a recording that made me feel unwelcome. • While I was on hold, I heard silence, which made me wonder if I had been disconnected. • The operator sounded like he was following stock or routine questions. • I felt the operator rushed me and didn't really listen. • I got Mirandized: "Are you aware that there may be a charge for this service …?" • I couldn't walk into an office and talk with someone personally. • The operator sounded bored.

Source: Ron Zemke and Dick Schaaf (1989), *The Service* Edge. New York: Plume, 36. From *The Service Edge* by Ron Zemke and Dick Schaaf. © 1989 by Ron Zemke and Dick Schaaf. Used by permission of Plume, an imprint of Penguin Putnam, Inc.

════ SPOTLIGHT 12.4 ════

Survey Fatigue

"We appreciate your decision to read this story. Would you take a short survey about your satisfaction with your reading experience? Could you review this article on a Web site? Rate it for other readers?" This is a request from the provider of the article on survey fatigue!

Almost every time you purchase something, you are asked to fill out a survey about your experience with the service provider. From doctor's offices and law firms to everyday retail purchases, customers are inundated with surveys asking for feedback. What do you do when you get such surveys? Do you fill them out? Are you sincere in your responses? Do you wonder if anyone ever reads your completed survey and whether someone is going to do something about your comments?

The Pew Research Center knows a thing or two about public opinion polls. Its survey director (who is also the president of the American Association for Public Opinion Research) says that response rates are shrinking. Pew's response rates have fallen from about 36% in 1997 to 11% in 2011. The Associated Press, which conducts regular opinion surveys, has also seen similar trends in response rates. Customers say they are tired of providing feedback.

Sources: **http://lifeinc.today.msnbc.msn.com/_news/2012/06/20/12300983-survey-fatigue-do-companies-care-what-you-think?lite**, (Accessed on October 1, 2012).; **http://www.usatoday.com/money/story/2012-01-07/consumer-feedback-fatigue/52432412/1**, (Accessed on October 1, 2012).

Second, it identifies what the customer has experienced in the past that detracted from his perception of service excellence at that specific point. Third, it assesses what the customer has experienced at that contact point in the past that enhanced his perceptions of the service organization. Table 12.2 depicts the type of information that might be gleaned through this method of analysis. In a sense, moment of truth impact analysis provides a map of key service experience aspects from the customer's point of view and indicates what an organization can do to create a memorable and positive service experience. In addition, merely conducting the analysis may help an organization to discover or reaffirm the notion that service excellence is a matter of customers' perceptions. An organization that *thinks* it is doing a good job of navigating a moment of truth will sometimes discover that the customer *perceives* the situation quite differently. Hence, if used properly, moment of truth impact analysis can detect specific trouble spots that require attention and ultimately enable an organization to fashion a better service experience for its customers.

Many of the research methods discussed require contacting the customer to review his or her experience. As you can see in Spotlight 12.4, in this Internet age, customers are experiencing survey fatigue with the proliferation of feedback requests. Indeed, we used the video call service Skype **(http://www.skype.com)** as we worked on this edition from three different locations. After each and every call, Skype asked us to rate the overall quality of the video call, because our "feedback will help make Skype better."

CREATING A SERVICE QUALITY INFORMATION SYSTEM

Research on service successes and failures is a necessary first step toward service profitability. According to Berry and Parasuraman (1997), a comprehensive *service quality information system* (SQIS) will encourage and enable the organization to

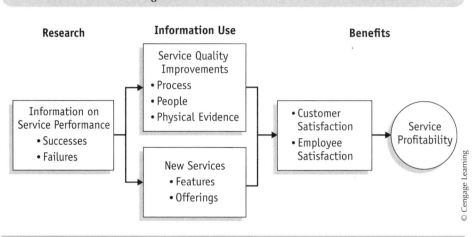

FIGURE 12.2 Managerial Benefits of Service Performance Measurement

incorporate the customer's voice into decision making. Such a system allows the organization to assess the impact of service quality initiatives and investments and offers performance-based data to reward service excellence and correct poor service. Figure 12.2 demonstrates how research into service performance can increase profitability for a service organization. By processing the information they obtain from studying service successes and failures, managers determine the appropriate priorities in service improvements and new service development. These priorities can be based on the customer's voice. Such focused efforts should, therefore, lead to greater customer and employee satisfaction through improved service quality. As noted in previous chapters, satisfied employees and customers lead to increased customer retention and reduced customer switching, which in turn contribute to increased profitability.

Berry and Parasuraman (1997) said that the SQIS should always include four service quality research methods: transactional surveys; customer complaints, comment, and inquiry capture; total market surveys; and employee surveys. These four methods tap three critical groups: customers, employees, and competition. Berry and Parasuraman's guidelines for an SQIS are:

- Measure service expectations.

- Emphasize information quality.

- Capture customers' words.

- Link service performance to business results.

- Reach every employee.

What to Measure

Organizations that engage in systematic measurement of their service performance must first choose what aspects of the service delivery system they need to study and then decide what questions to ask (if using the survey research method) or what to observe (if using observational techniques). Measurement should occur on a regular basis, and the information produced should be stored and available for review.

An organization might use a service blueprint as a guide to structure questions, make direct observations, and ensure that all essential aspects of the service experience are covered. For example, when a bank offers services through its Web site, the bank might find it useful to trace the various steps the customer will likely go through to use any of its many Web-based services. The blueprint directs the researcher to the specific steps that make up the services. Another approach might be to construct questions based on the items in the SERVQUAL scale discussed in Chapter 10. In all cases, it is beneficial to pose open-ended questions that enable the respondents to provide the feedback *they* deem important rather than restricting them to providing input only on topics that the service organization considers critical. If the study focuses on customers' view of the service experience, researchers might elicit demographic and service usage information to determine which types of customers are saying what about the service. For example, research might reveal that elderly customers are critical of the service environment's physical layout, prompting the service organization to address the special challenges that the elderly may face regarding parking, use of space, or signage.

What to Do with the Information

Even an organization that systematically measures its service performance will not benefit from these efforts unless it puts the information to good use. Measurement is only a means to an end. The ultimate goal is to improve service performance, and the information derived from the measurement must therefore help direct and focus the organization toward achieving this end. Specifically, the information might help uncover problem areas in the process of service delivery, the physical setting, and employee behaviors. Measurement results might also be used to evaluate how well the standards set for any aspect of the service performance have been met. Such data can determine who should be rewarded, what needs to change, and so on. Further, the information should indicate which activities or service aspects should receive the highest priority.

If the research focuses on assessing employees' performance, the service organization must emphasize fairness, use multiple measures and inputs, keep the measurement process simple, and measure both group and individual performance of backstage and frontstage personnel. Also, regardless of rank, everyone in the organization needs to be measured (Berry 1995).

The information gleaned from the service measurement can also help implement marketing decisions regarding positioning, segmentation, and the services marketing mix. Take the case of a financial institution: if the data derive from the organization's clients, any resulting feedback can be used in decisions related to hiring, training, and evaluating brokers and other client-service personnel. It might also help monitor and improve aspects of the service setting, such as the physical layout of the customer service area or the design and layout of the organization's Web site (including all the Web pages) for online clients. Research that generates feedback from the financial institution's frontline workers might then be used to evaluate processes and procedures established for client interactions. The focus might be on how clients obtain information on investments, place orders for various investment products, or submit complaints or requests.

Summary and Conclusion

Studying successes and failures is essential for any service business committed to providing excellent customer experiences. Accurate measurement of customers' responses to service delivery provides a wealth of information that can help improve the overall service. A variety of methods might be used to gather important information. The experiential nature of services allows an organization to gather customer or worker feedback through observational methods. Information gleaned from these and more traditional research activities can improve decision making and implementation of service improvements, new service offerings, and training and evaluation of frontline personnel.

Exercises

1. Design an observation report form for a mystery shopper's visit to a service organization such as a restaurant or a retail store. Explain what can be done with the information obtained from the visit.
2. Obtain and critique a customer survey from a service establishment. Compare question contents with the service quality dimensions specified in the SERVQUAL model (described in Chapter 10).
3. Consider the instructor evaluation survey you complete at your school. Does it cover all relevant aspects of your educational experience? What would you add or delete from the questionnaire, and why?
4. Design a customer feedback card for a service of your choice and explain the rationale behind the questions you include.
5. Conduct a moment of truth impact analysis for a recent service encounter you have had. Based on this analysis, provide some recommendations for service improvements.

Internet Exercise

 Find a customer satisfaction survey on a service organization's Web site and answer the following:

1. Comment on the structure of the survey—its number of screens, the number of questions, how long you take to fill out the survey, the response format for the questions.
2. Critique the survey content. How well does it align with the service quality model presented in Chapter 10?
3. Assess the utility of the information you can gather from the survey.

EXPLORE

Visit the companion site for this text at **www .cengagebrain.com** to explore key concepts in the service industry. You will find tools to help you expand your services marketing knowledge, including ACE self-tests, Web links to companies and organizations featured in this chapter, and much more!

References

Berry, Leonard L. (1995), *On Great Service: A Framework for Action*, New York: Free Press.

Berry, Leonard L. and A. Parasuraman (1997), "Listening to the Customer—The Concept of a Service-Quality Information System," *Sloan Management Review*, 38 (Spring), 65–76.

Gremler, Dwayne D. (2004), "The Critical Incident Technique in Service Research," *Journal of Service Research*, 7 (August), 65–89.

Grove, Stephen J. and Raymond P. Fisk (1992), "Observational Data Collection Methods for Services Marketing: An Overview," *Journal of* the *Academy of Marketing Science*, 20 (Summer), 217–224.

Levy, Sidney J. and Charles H. Kellstadt (2012), "Integraphy: A Multi-Method Approach to Situational Analysis," *Journal of Business Research*, 65 (7), 1073–1077.

Wang, Shirley S. (2006), "Health Care Taps 'Mystery Shoppers': To Improve Service, Hospitals and Doctors Hire Spies to Pose as Patients and Report Back," *Wall Street Journal* (August 8), D1.

Zemke, Ron and Dick Schaaf (1989), *The Service Edge: 101 Companies That Profit from Customer Care*, New York: Plume.

Management Issues in Services Marketing

The following three chapters explore the management issues involved in marketing a service. Chapter 13 discusses marketing strategies for services, including positioning and segmentation. In addition, this chapter examines strategic challenges for services and describes service strategies for competitive advantage. Chapter 14 explores the challenges of coping with the fluctuating demand for services, considers why services demand is such a problem, and discusses strategies for balancing service capacity and demand. Chapter 15 explores the globalization of service organizations, paying particular attention to the various challenges associated with global services marketing.

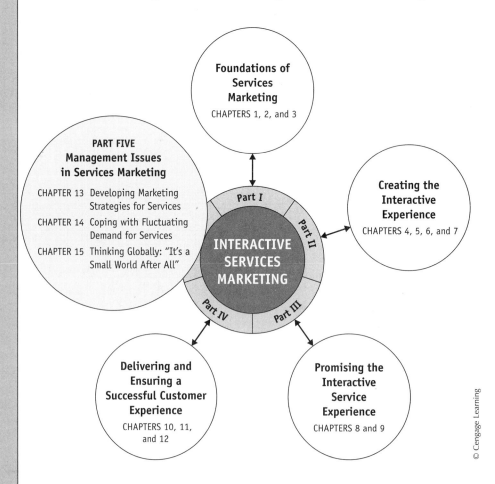

Foundations of
Services
Marketing

CHAPTERS 1, 2, and 3

PART FIVE
Management Issues
in Services Marketing

CHAPTER 13 Developing Marketing
Strategies for Services

CHAPTER 14 Coping with Fluctuating
Demand for Services

CHAPTER 15 Thinking Globally: "It's a
Small World After All"

Part I

Part II

INTERACTIVE
SERVICES
MARKETING

Part IV

Part III

Creating the
Interactive
Experience

CHAPTERS 4, 5, 6, and 7

Delivering and
Ensuring a
Successful Customer
Experience

CHAPTERS 10, 11,
and 12

Promising the
Interactive
Service
Experience

CHAPTERS 8 and 9

© Cengage Learning

IBM Wants You to Live on a "Smarter Planet"

Forbes **(www.forbes.com)** publishes the Global 2000, an annual ranking of the world's biggest companies that takes into account sales, profits, assets, and market value. Its 2011 list ranked IBM at number thirty-two and labeled it as a "computer services" organization. In 2011, IBM recorded U.S. $107 billions in revenue and operated in over 170 countries. IBM expects to bring in about 50% of its revenue from software and 30% of geographic revenues from what it calls growth markets by 2015. IBM is a global services organization.

In 2011, IBM opened 100 new branch offices in non-BRIC (Brazil, Russia, India, and China) locations. Their hubs of expertise around the world are all in the services domain: the Institute for Electronic Government and the Energy and Utilities Solution Lab in China; Natural Resource Solution Centers in Perth and Rio de Janeiro; banking centers in Singapore and Sao Paolo; and a Latin American microfinancing center in Lima.

IBM plans to grow in areas such as business analytics, the cloud, and all things digital to get us to be a "smarter planet" by infusing digital intelligence and changing the way people, organizations, and entire industries approach what they do. On a smarter planet, IBM says, it will change the paradigm from "react" to "anticipate." IBM is working with 2,000 cities worldwide as part of its "Smarter Planet" business started in 2008. In Dublin, IBM set up the Smarter Cities Technology Centre, for research collaboration with the city's local authorities. In Rio, IBM has designed the Intelligent Operations Center, a computerized command center to pull data from dozens of city agencies, weather stations, and web sites. With predictive analytics, these agencies can anticipate and preempt crimes and disasters, as well as better manage traffic, water usage, power utilization, waste management, and other such city services that have to match the peaks and valleys in fluctuating demand for these services. Brazil wants to be well prepared for the World Cup Soccer in 2014 and the Olympics in 2016.

Eduardo Paes, mayor of Rio de Janeiro, a sprawling, complicated, beautiful city of 6.3 million inhabitants, professes four commandments for Rio: a city of the future must be environmentally friendly; must deal with mobility and integration of its people; must be socially integrated; and must use technology to be present. Paes says that "At the end of the day, when we talk about cities, we talk about a gathering of people. And we cannot see that as a problem."

CHAPTER 13
Developing Marketing Strategies for Services
Overview of Marketing Strategy in Service Organizations
Scanning the Environment
Planning the Services Marketing Strategy
Positioning and Service Segmentation
Marketing Mix Strategy
Strategic Challenges for Services
Service Strategies for Competitive Advantage
Dramatize Your Performance

CHAPTER 14
Coping with Fluctuating Demand for Services
Why Is Services Demand a Problem?
The Nature of Service Demand
Chasing Demand with Service Capacity
Smoothing Demand to Fill Service Capacity
Maximum Versus Optimum Capacity

CHAPTER 15
Thinking Globally: "It's a Small World After All"
Services and Culture
Global Trade in Services
Entry Strategies for Global Service Markets
Standardization Versus Adaptation of Global Services
Multilingual Service Systems
Technology and Global Services

Source: **http://www.forbes.com/sites /scottdecarlo/2012/04/18/the-worlds -biggest-companies/; http://www.ibm .com/annualreport/2011/ghv/; http:// www.ted.com/talks/lang/en/eduardo _paes_the_4_commandments_of _cities.html.**

CHAPTER 13

Developing Marketing Strategies for Services

As the opening vignette shows, IBM **(http://www.ibm.com)** has pursued a global "Smarter Planet" strategy, which positions the company as a provider of important business services everywhere on our planet. This strategy allows IBM to customize its message and business services for each country while maintaining Smarter Planet as the strategic umbrella.

This chapter examines various dimensions of the marketing strategy common to all marketed products, but it focuses on the special challenges of designing a marketing strategy for a service organization. The chapter has six specific objectives:

- **To provide an overview of marketing strategy in service organizations**
- **To describe the process of scanning the service environment and examine how the external environment affects the service sector**
- **To explain the process of planning a service's marketing strategy**
- **To examine the tasks of positioning and segmentation for the service organization**
- **To present the unique strategic challenges facing service organizations**
- **To convey the importance of service strategies for competitive advantage**

OVERVIEW OF MARKETING STRATEGY IN SERVICE ORGANIZATIONS

A **customer-oriented marketing strategy** allows service organizations to retain existing customers and acquire new ones in both good and bad economic times. The fundamental characteristics of services require different marketing strategies from those applied to physical goods. Because marketing activities are intimately linked with human resource management and operations functions in service organizations, a successful marketing strategy is extremely more important for service organizations. A service marketing strategy must not only consider the operational goals of efficiency and productivity, but it must also consider the human resource issues of hiring, training, and motivating the work force.

A **marketing strategy** can be defined as the process of adjusting *controllable* marketing factors to cope with or exploit *uncontrollable* environmental forces. *Controllable* marketing factors hinge on the service offering. *Uncontrollable* environmental factors affect the service organization and the marketplace. Although an organization may sometimes influence these uncontrollable forces through various activities (e.g., lobbying to change the legal environment), such influence is rare. Usually, an organization

Marketing strategy is the process of adjusting controllable marketing factors to cope with or exploit uncontrollable environmental forces.

must cope with and adapt to conditions in the external environment. A successful marketing strategy matches service offerings to market needs. In other words, it adapts organizational resources to environmental conditions. This approach requires that service organizations carefully scan the environment, plan and implement the strategy, and assess the outcomes of the strategy.

External trends from uncontrollable forces carry great significance for service organizations. Rising discretionary income from improving *economic and competitive* conditions in various parts of the world has encouraged more customers to buy services rather than perform them themselves. Deregulation (the result of changes in the *ethical and legal* environment) has radically altered the nature of retail banking, airline service, and various professional services in the United States. Changes in *social, cultural, and demographic* conditions have led to the dual-income family and provide opportunities for a variety of service industries such as child care, dry-cleaning services, and home delivery services. Finally, changes in *technology* alter the way people live and work in both major and minor ways. For example, the Internet allows individuals to find information about airfares and purchase their tickets directly from the airline, which has significantly reduced the number of bookings at travel agencies. The key for services marketers is to search for opportunities and threats arising from uncontrollable forces.

The primary controllable factors for service organizations are the *seven Ps* (the *four Ps* of the traditional marketing mix—product, price, promotion, and place and the additional *three Ps* of the services marketing mix—participants, physical evidence, and process of service assembly), as outlined in Chapter 2. Although the uncontrollable forces are the same as those facing marketers of physical goods (e.g., economic and competitive forces), services marketers face added challenges. Unlike manufacturers, which compete with other firms based on the brands they offer, service organizations must sometimes compete with the customer as well as with other service organizations. After all, customers can choose to perform many services themselves. Homeowners, for instance, may elect to take care of their yards rather than hire a landscaping service to do it for them. The choice of performing a service yourself versus paying a service provider affects restaurants, fitness centers, hairstylists, tax preparation businesses, appliance repair shops, automobile repair garages, housecleaning services, laundries, and transportation companies. Some bold individuals may even opt to educate themselves rather than attend a university or attempt to change their own watch batteries rather than visit a jeweler.

Hamel and Prahalad (1994) argue that truly innovative organizations must learn to compete with a clear vision of the future. Such organizations are adept at finding unmet and unarticulated customer needs and filling them. In short, they are good at reaching the future first. Figure 13.1 illustrates four strategic choices available to any service organization. Complacency might lead an organization to choose to stay within the boundaries of *today's business.* The hazards of such a strategy are that competitive pressures would slowly, but surely erode the organization's position. Service organizations can seek *unserved opportunities* by identifying new customers that the organization might serve through what is called a market expansion strategy. An example would be the expansion of Starbucks **(http://www.starbucks.com)** coffee from the United States to other countries. Alternatively, a service organization might seek *unarticulated opportunities* by looking for new needs their customers might have, using a product expansion strategy.

FIGURE 13.1 Competing for the Future

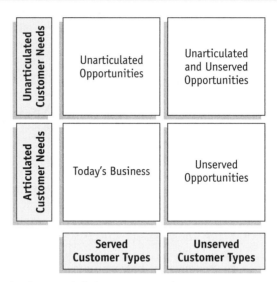

Source: Gary Hamel and C. K. Prahalad (1994), "Seeing the Future First," *Fortune* (September 5), 64–68. Reprinted by permission of Harvard Business School Press. From *Competing for the Future* by C. K. Prahalad and Gary Hamel. Boston, MA 1996. Copyright © 1996 by the Harvard Business School Publishing Corporation. All rights reserved.

An example of this strategy would be the addition of downloadable television programs to the iTunes Web site **(http://www.apple.com/itunes/).** The most difficult strategy is to pursue *unarticulated and unserved opportunities.* This strategy requires simultaneously pursuing new customers with new service products and doubles the degree of strategic risk. New entrepreneurial service organizations are pursuing such a strategy. When larger and older service organizations pursue this strategy, it is considered a diversification strategy. An example of this strategy of pursuing unarticulated needs and unserved markets would be the decision by McDonald's **(http://www.mcdonalds.com)** to offer the Chicken Maharaja Mac when it entered India in 1996, out of respect for the Hindu religion. Because many Indians are vegetarians, the organization also offered a vegetable burger.

SCANNING THE ENVIRONMENT

Environmental scanning is the process of carefully monitoring external environments for changes that pose threats or opportunities to the service organization.

Before a service organization can develop a winning marketing strategy, it needs a clear understanding of the conditions it faces. **Environmental scanning** is the process of carefully monitoring external environments for changes that pose *threats* or *opportunities* to the service organization (see Figure 13.2). A wide range of external environmental or uncontrollable factors may affect the service organization. In addition, internal environmental or controllable factors that create the service experience require careful monitoring. Once it knows the threats and opportunities posed by external environments,

FIGURE 13.2 Environmental Scanning

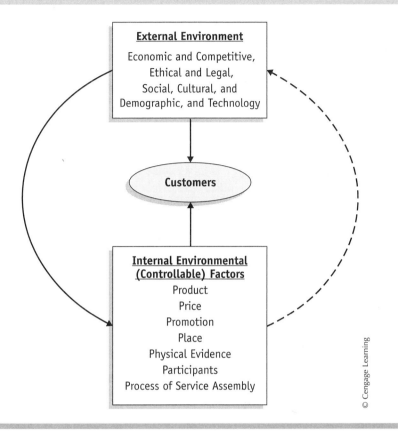

the service organization can adjust its controllable factors to minimize threats and maximize opportunities.

Successful environmental scanning is a continuous process. Today's business environments change so quickly that service organizations must be constantly vigilant. It is fortunate that modern information technology enables service organizations to gather a wealth of environmental information.

The most interesting aspect of environmental scanning is that the difference between a threat and an opportunity is a matter of perspective. Take, for example, America's Great Depression of the 1930s, which was widely seen as a threat to businesses of all kinds. Nonetheless, some businesses were successfully developed during this bleak period, such as the first A&P grocery store **(http://www .aptea.com).** By offering better prices and selections to its customers in a self-service environment, A&P became the precursor of modern supermarkets and megastores. Hence, even in the most difficult economic conditions, creative entrepreneurs can find opportunities.

Strategic adjustments to environmental conditions take three forms: *reactive, proactive,* and *hyperactive* (see Figure 13.3). A **reactive strategy** is a slow response to environmental changes and sometimes occurs only when an organization

Reactive strategy is a slow response to environmental changes.

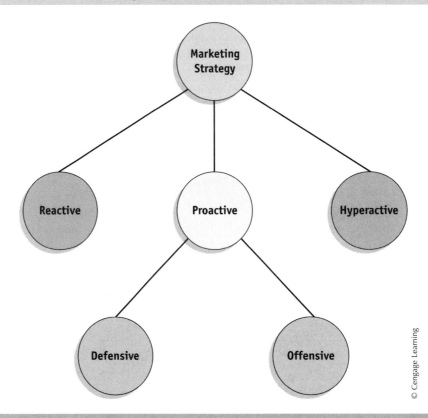

FIGURE 13.3 Strategic Adjustments to Environmental Conditions

© Cengage Learning

Proactive strategy is a rapid response to environmental changes.

Hyperactive strategy is a hasty response to environmental changes.

Defensive strategy is a rapid responses used to protect the organization from environmental threats.

Offensive strategy is a rapid response employed to capture opportunities.

is forced to act. By contrast, a **proactive strategy** is a rapid response to environmental changes. A **hyperactive strategy** is a hasty response to environmental changes. Alert service organizations seek to avoid reactive strategies by carefully monitoring their environments and quickly responding to changes as they are scanned, but without veering into a hyperactive strategy.

Unfortunately, many service organization strategies are merely reactive. For example, Sears **(http://www.sears.com)** was once the world's largest retailer. Sears was often criticized for responding too slowly to the many changes in its retailing environment, including the steady growth and market encroachment of Walmart **(http://www.walmart.com).** In the 1990s, Sears finally made significant changes in its operations. It was too late. Walmart is the largest retailer today.

Proactive strategies can take two forms: *defensive* and *offensive.* A **defensive strategy** is a rapid response to protect the organization from environmental *threats,* whereas an **offensive strategy** is a rapid response that captures *opportunities.*

Defensive strategies require quick action to prevent damage to the organization from an environmental threat. When Microsoft **(http://www.microsoft.com)** realized that its software products and services were poorly positioned for the Internet, Bill Gates launched a defensive strategy that became known as "Embrace and Extend." In a short time, Microsoft repositioned all of its offerings to be more compatible with the Internet.

A great way to understand how offensive strategies can capture opportunities is to think of ways to invent future services. Fred Smith, founder of FedEx **(http://www.fedex.com),** saw changes in the business environment that inspired him to invent the overnight package delivery industry. Ted Turner, the founder of CNN **(http://www.cnn.com),** saw changes in the pace of news technology as an opportunity to create the first twenty-four-hour television news channel. Robert Earl, founder of the Hard Rock Cafe **(http://www.hardrock.com),** saw the global popularity of rock music as an opportunity to create a theme-based restaurant with worldwide appeal.

Hyperactive strategies occur whenever service organizations rush prematurely into new markets or new products without proper planning. The explosive growth of the Internet in its early days yielded many examples of these strategies. For example, Furniture.com **(http://www.furniture.com)** was launched in 1998 as a freestanding online furniture store, but closed in 2000. Furniture.com was purchased in 2001 by a group of former employees with a better strategic plan. The new company works in partnership with leading furniture retailers to provide quick delivery and local service.

Every service organization is affected by dynamic external environments: economic and competitive; ethical and legal; social, cultural, and demographic; and technology environments.

Economic and Competitive Environment

The rapid growth of the service economy is a major source of economic progress in most countries. Service industries sometimes face greater ease of entry than do manufacturing industries. Whereas manufacturing plants require a significant investment in capital goods, many services can start up with modest capital investments. Probably the most challenging economic and competitive force is the globalization of service markets. More and more service organizations have found it attractive to operate in other countries. Today, for example, we have global banks, restaurants, hotels, hospitals, retailers, and engineering firms. Communications technology has contributed greatly to the globalization of markets. Indeed, few service industries have no global competitors. In addition, global service organizations face increased pressures to be more concerned about the ecological impact of their economic decisions (see Spotlight 13.1).

Ethical and Legal Environment

Ethics concern personal and professional codes of values. Codes of values determine the purpose and course of our personal lives and the lives of organizations. Marketing practices are often subjected to severe ethical criticism. Nonetheless, ethics seldom receive enough attention in marketing circles.

SPOTLIGHT 13.1

Green Marketing Issues in the Service Sector

 When environmental consciousness and green marketing issues are discussed, the focus is usually upon manufacturers that produce automobiles, canned goods, disposable diapers, mobile homes, and other manufactured products. It is easy to understand that production of physical goods requires scarce raw materials, processes, and outputs that may be ecologically harmful. The intangibility and perishability that characterize most services may seem to render service products as little threat to the environment. However, despite the intangibility of the core service, many services rely on physical components to deliver their benefits. To illustrate, airline transportation requires a jet plane and numerous other physical elements, lawn maintenance relies on various tools and chemicals, and physician services may necessitate a wide variety of tangible components, from tongue depressors to high-tech medical equipment. Further, though they are invisible by nature, service processes often require resources that may generate waste. For example, in transporting travelers from one place to another, an airline, train, bus, taxicab, or other transportation service consumes significant quantities of energy and expels various energy by-products as pollutants. In short, services often involve the support of a wide spectrum of physical components and reliance on natural resources. Given the sheer size of the service economy, ecological considerations regarding the tangible aspects of service products have a major impact upon the environment.

Numerous well-known service organizations have produced examples of environmental activities.

For instance, Universal Studios Florida regularly recycles almost all of the paper products it uses. Harrah's hotels have cut energy consumption by nearly 30% through measures that include, most significantly, a request that long-term guests consider not changing their sheets on a daily basis. Similarly, the Essex House Hotel in New York has eliminated throwaway wire hangers by utilizing reusable baskets to return guests' laundry. Retail giant Walmart has made a concerted effort to reduce consumption of natural resources by pressuring its suppliers to become green oriented. Among other examples are AT&T's effort to reduce various toxic pollutants by changing the chemicals and processes used to color its equipment, and the Royal Bank of Canada's program to save paper in its 1,600 branches by converting almost exclusively to electronic data processing.

Attention to the ecological soundness of service processes could also play a major role in preserving the environment. Consider the effect if a hotel chain such as Hyatt or Marriott adopted an energy conservation policy that involved setting thermostats in the back office and public areas at a mere two-degree difference. Such a difference is unlikely to be noticed by most patrons and workers, yet could result in a significant reduction in energy consumption. Obviously, if the entire hospitality industry adopted such a measure, the effects might be tremendous.

Source: Adapted from Grove, Stephen J., Raymond P. Fisk, Gregory M. Pickett, and Norman Kangun (1996), "Going Green in the Service Sector: Social Responsibility Issues, Implications, and Implementation," *European Journal of Marketing*, 30 (5), 56–66. Reprinted by permission of MCB University Press.

Many services rely on the fact that the public trusts them to do the "right thing." When a hospital removes the wrong foot, a bank mismanages its funds, a jet crashes into a mountainside, or a levee failure floods a large city, the news media carry front-page stories. Although such examples may not appear to be ethical failures, they are often rooted in ethical mistakes.

The legal environment of service businesses varies greatly across service industries and countries. Many service industries are heavily regulated, often to a greater degree than are their manufacturing counterparts. For example, the banking, airline, telecommunications, and health care industries are subject to complex regulatory environments in many countries. Global services organizations face complicated multicountry regulatory environments. For instance, the air express industry is dependent on bilateral negotiations between governments to approve new air routes and reduced regulations. Nonetheless, the prevailing global trend appears to be toward deregulation of service industries. Public sector companies in European countries are finding it hard to compete in a free market without government subsidies. Efforts since the 1980s to remove government involvement in airlines, telecommunications, banking, and utilities has left the United States with one of the most deregulated service environments in the world.

Before leaving the topic of legal issues, we should note that although government activities are the primary force in this environment, government is also a service. The most basic service provided by any government is the protection of its citizens. Hurricane Katrina showed the world a horrific example of government failure to protect its citizens. All over the world, government services are coming under greater and greater public scrutiny. In country after country, citizens are asking their government to be more responsive, more efficient, and more accountable.

The ethical and legal failings of numerous service organizations have been the subject of intensive media coverage. Enron, WorldCom, Global Crossing, and several other major service organizations were bankrupted amid allegations of illegal and unethical conduct on the part of key executives. In addition, the scandal seriously damaged the reputations of such venerable institutions as Arthur Andersen and Merrill Lynch.

Social, Cultural, and Demographic Environment

Service industries, particularly professional services, have often been slow to respond to changing customer tastes and preferences. Sweeping social and cultural changes around the world have made it difficult for service organizations to anticipate and cope with changing customer tastes. Regardless, service organizations must diligently strive to stay abreast of social, cultural, and demographic changes. Changes in lifestyles create new service industries. Dual-income families need daycare workers and nanny services. The sedentary lives of today's white-collar workers, combined with increased health concerns, have spawned a slew of fitness clubs.

Social changes include alterations in family structure and lifestyles, as well as the growth of subcultures. Cultural changes include changing work ethics and the growth of the "consumer" culture. Demographic changes are reflected in fluctuating birthrates, age distributions, gender distributions, and population trends. Such changes exert powerful influences on societies and service organizations. For example, in the United States, the disproportionate size of the baby boom generation has distorted the demand for services at every stage of their life cycle (schools, music, restaurants, retirement services, etc.).

Technology Environment

Technology is arguably the strongest force shaping the external environment of services. Advances in information technology, medical technology, and transportation technology have caused significant and sweeping changes in service industries As describe in Chapter 3, information technology has played an especially large role in transforming business and markets.

The fast pace of technological change in advanced economies increases demand for new services and more technologically sophisticated services. Technology also improves the quality of services such as medical care or communications. Technology allows people to save time and increase their standard of living, resulting in higher demand for entertainment and recreational services, including tourism, movies, hotels and restaurants, and sporting activities. In addition, technology provides mechanisms for human interactions that have changed the whole nature of service delivery. In particular, service organizations can now reach and interact with the entire world from one location via information technology.

PLANNING THE SERVICES MARKETING STRATEGY

To understand the process of developing a service organization's marketing strategy, imagine yourself in the shoes of a services marketing manager who must plan the launch of a new service offering. The manager must take a systematic approach to analyzing the situation facing the organization. Usually, that approach involves a sequence of steps that includes planning, designing, implementing, and controlling a strategy to achieve desired goals. In reality, these steps are no different from those facing organizations that must develop a strategy regarding a manufactured good. What is different is the set of considerations that the service organization should address at each step. Spotlight 13.2 provides an example of computer games being used to help city planners develop a better strategy.

Planning the Strategy

This step involves determining the service's objectives and the manner in which they will be accomplished. Planning begins with identifying opportunities and threats by continuous environmental scanning. Besides continually monitoring the external environment, astute service organizations gather data from

---

SPOTLIGHT 13.2

Strategy Gaming for Cities: IBM's CityOne

As part of the IBM Smarter Planet initiative, IBM created several games that they call serious games for business professionals. CityOne was launched in 2010 as a strategy simulator for city planners. CityOne is a sim-style game that guides players through a series of missions. Players are given the opportunity to optimize banking, retail, energy, and water solutions. The players can make decisions to improve the city by attaining revenue and profit goals for companies, increasing customers' and citizens' satisfaction, and making the environment greener. These goals are often described in business as the *triple bottom line*—economic, social, and environmental success.

As part of the game, players also learn about business process management and collaborative technologies that can make all of the organizations in a city system more agile. The game includes more than 100 real-world scenarios. You can learn more about the game by Googling the phrase "CityOne game." You can even find a brief YouTube video at **http://www.youtube.com/watch?v=TmfOugQrDFk.**

Sources: IBM (2012), **http://www-01.ibm.com/software/solutions/soa/innov8/cityone/; http://www-01.ibm.com/software/solutions/soa/newsletter/aug10/cityone.html** (accessed September 19, 2012).

a wide assortment of sources regarding numerous aspects of their enterprise. Regularly collected customer surveys, employee feedback, transactional data, complaint audits, competitive analysis, and other such categories of information provide insights that guide managers in detecting threats or opportunities. For example, trends in the social and cultural environment or information derived from analyzing customer surveys may indicate an increase in people's willingness to accept self-service checkout as an option. Armed with this information, a service manager may set a goal of altering the process of service delivery to include a self-service alternative.

Designing the Strategy

For an organization to design a strategy that will realize its objectives, it must carefully specify the central marketing problem or opportunity it faces. This step is closely linked to the planning step. Problem statements should be phrased in terms of the action needed, identify the services marketing tools needed, and focus on customers. Recognizing the difference between symptoms and problems is critical. Access to continually updated data provides managers with the knowledge to make those distinctions. Such information may help determine whether a service breakdown in the frontstage is merely a symptom of an operations problem backstage or a human resources problem involving customer contact personnel.

If the problem or opportunity is correctly specified, it is easier to derive alternatives and solutions. As an aspect of designing the strategy, this process requires creativity and imagination. In some situations, the alternatives will be relatively obvious, whereas in others, considerable insight and deliberation will be needed to develop them. A wise marketing strategist carefully considers all reasonable alternatives to ensure that the one selected is consistent with good marketing practice. As suggested in Chapter 2, most service offerings share some characteristics with other services. Hence, it makes sense for service managers to study the successful marketing techniques of other services when searching for insights and solutions to a problem. This practice is known as *benchmarking*. In some cases, hospitals might benefit from benchmarking hotels, lawyers from studying podiatrists, and educators from scrutinizing ministers. Any possible alternatives that are identified should be detailed and analyzed to determine whether they can be fully implemented. Further, criteria for assessing and comparing each alternative should be established.

Once an alternative is chosen, it is important to state explicitly how the recommended course of action is expected to solve the central marketing problem. In addition, it is imperative to consider the human resources and operations requirements of any recommendation. For instance, a decision to implement a self-service option to service delivery will affect the operational design of the service setting and the number and type of employees required to assemble the service offering.

Implementing the Strategy

Implementation is the hardest step in developing a marketing strategy for any service organization. A plan must be formulated that specifies a logical sequence of implementation steps and a detailed timetable for carrying them out. In addition, an itemized budget is necessary that includes the specific short- and long-term costs of implementation. It is best to have contingency plans to cover deviations from the projected implementation. A key part of implementing the service's marketing strategy is checking expenditures for variations from the budget. Implementing a marketing strategy allows little room for error because most services are produced and consumed in real time. Service organizations that lose control of their time and their money during implementation are doomed to fail.

Controlling the Strategy

Controlling the strategy refers to carefully assessing the strategy's success. If problems threaten success, corrective tactics may be needed to overcome the problems. For example, it might be necessary to hire more employees, use newer equipment, or add another step in the service process. Only by closely monitoring the strategy will the services marketer know whether these new tactics are effective. Indeed, the organization must also assess whether the over-all strategy (as planned, designed, and implemented) succeeded. Multiple mea-sures of marketing strategy outcomes are desirable. Usually, these measures include evaluation of service profitability and quality (see Chapters 8 and 10, respectively).

The steps of planning, designing, implementing, and controlling constitute the typical process of developing a marketing strategy for any product. The next section presents the additional elements that a marketing strategy for a service offering should encompass. The process requires two fundamental decisions: how the service will be positioned and what service segments should be targeted. Once these decisions are made, the organization considers strategic options regarding the marketing mix. Each strategic decision requires an imple-mentation plan for contingencies and a control plan for deviations or contingencies.

P O S I T I O N I N G   A N D   S E R V I C E   S E G M E N T A T I O N

> **Positioning** is how marketers attempt to create favorable customer perceptions of their product in relation to all other products.

Positioning is how marketers attempt to create favorable customer perceptions of their product in relation to all other products. A position has been described as a *share of mind* (Ries and Trout 2000). Consider the relative positions of these two tourist attractions: Disney World **(http://www .disney.com)** and SeaWorld **(http://www.seaworld.com).** Each has a distinctive share of mind developed over many years of marketing efforts. Share of mind strongly influences such customer behaviors as word-of-mouth communication, repeat purchasing, and brand loyalty. Choosing a brand name is one of the first steps in positioning a service. The challenge for the services marketer is to plan a branding strategy that estab-lishes a position for an intangible product. Because a service is a process, it is difficult to demonstrate the product before consumption and even harder to prove to customers its differentiating features. One way the service marketer differentiates a service is by using visuals of the tangibles or physical evidence. Most services use advertisements, brochures, or videos to describe the service and show their facilities.

Not every individual or organization is an appropriate customer for every service offering. Therefore, effective marketing requires selecting the best customer by a process called **market segmentation,** that is, the division of a heterogeneous market into homogeneous segments. Understanding market segments is critical to the success of a marketing strategy, because the selected segments become target markets for the organization's positioning efforts. Spotlight 13.3 discusses some of the key challenges in marketing hotel services to women as a market segment. Today, mass markets are splintering into a mosaic of smaller segments. Marketing success increasingly requires niche marketing instead of mass marketing. Numerous computer tools now help services marketers serve their market segments. Many companies have adopted computerized databases to track customer preferences more effectively. In addition, it is possible to create computer maps of market segments. Because services marketers interact with every customer in some way, they have many opportunities to accumulate a rich database on each customer. Monitoring these databases facilitates making appropriate changes in the marketing strategy for the positioning, targeting, and the services marketing mix.

> **Market segmentation** is the division of a heterogeneous market into homogeneous segments.

SPOTLIGHT 13.3

Serving the Needs of Women Travelers

 Business travelers can be segmented by gender into male travelers and female travelers. Of course, men and women have different needs, but hotels were once primarily serving the needs of male business travelers. Today, the number of women business travelers is approximately half of business travelers. Unfortunately for women, far too few hotels have carefully rethought their service offerings for the needs of businesswomen. Women often complain about not being valued as travelers by hotels.

For example, women value safety in a hotel much more than men. Covered and well-lit parking lots are desirable. Better hotel door locks are, too. Women also prefer amenities such as room service, spas, and fitness centers more than men do. Nicer room amenities like better bathrooms and stylish furnishings matter more to women than men, too.

Fortunately, there are signs of improvements. In Copenhagen, Denmark, the Bella Sky Hotel made its seventeenth floor a woman-only floor with bathrooms, furnishings and amenities selected after extensive research with women. Many other hotels are trying out entire floors reserved for women or exclusive rooms redesigned for women. Even more hotels are making sure their rooms have ironing boards, expanded room service menus, shower caps, nail files, and many other features popular with women business travelers.

Sources: Gargiulo, Susan (2012), "Women-Only Hotel Floors Tap Boom in Female Business Travel" CNN.com, March 20, **http://edition.cnn.com/2012/03/07/business/women-hotels-business-travelers/** (accessed September 19, 2012); Simpson, Elizabeth (2011, August 16), "Report: Focus on Women Travelers Is Growing," physorg.com, **http://phys.org/news/2011-08-focus-women.html#jCp** (accessed September 19, 2012).

MARKETING MIX STRATEGY

To position a service to reach a target market requires adjusting the services marketing mix to customer needs. Marketers must decide what service personnel, facilities and equipment, and process design they need to create and deliver the service as well as how it will be priced and promoted. Each decision confronts the services marketer with a unique set of challenges and opportunities linked to the fundamental differences between services and goods.

The *services marketing approach* an organization chooses should reflect its desired positioning and market segment. The approach also manifests itself in the core product and supplementary services the organization offers. The services marketing approach also determines the resources needed to create and deliver the service. For example, a hotel positioned as a no-frills lodging facility for the budget-minded traveler might conceive its core service product as low-cost lodging with very few supplementary services. A premium hotel for traveling executives, on the other hand, might include an expensive restaurant, facilities for client meetings, a business center, and a host of other supplementary services, such as valet parking, Internet access, and video conferencing.

TABLE 13.1 Special Strategic Implications for Services

	Participants	Physical Evidence	Process
Intangibility	Frontline service personnel are part of the product. Customers can influence each others' service experiences in shared services.	Customer has no physical product to evaluate before consumption. Any means of reducing customers' perceived risk must be used.	Product is a performance. The process is created and produced by personnel, facilities, and equipment.
Simultaneity	Customers are co-producers and interact with the service provider. Service providers must be recruited, trained, and have their roles carefully scripted so that customer participation is managed effectively.	Customers evaluate the physical evidence in the process and outcome. All costumes and props are evaluated. Product outcome should be documented for customer evaluation.	Consumption and production are simultaneous, and product is produced in real time. Performance must be planned with techniques such as blueprinting and dramatization.
Perishability	Customer demand and service providers' supply must match. Peaks and valleys in demand fluctuation must be smoothed.	Capacity to produce is lost when staff, physical facilities, and equipment are idle. Consider outsourcing, subcontracting during high demand, or renting and leasing equipment and facilities during low demand.	Product cannot be inventoried. Services can be bundled and priced attractively to maintain consistent level of demand for maximum profitability.
Heterogeneity	The product varies from customer to customer and from provider to provider. Backstage and frontstage employees should be motivated and compensated based on customer satisfaction.	Physical evidence must be tailored to segment(s). Physical facilities and equipment can be divided and separated to accommodate different segments.	Process can be customized or standardized, and varying levels of customer participation in different steps of the process (self-service) can be considered.

Before creating and delivering the core and supplemental service product, an organization also must consider its *services operations approach.* For example, a hotel must make decisions in advance regarding location, facility design, number of rooms, and staffing levels. Processes for reservations, room service, and check-in must also be designed. These decisions affect and are affected by the services marketing approach; and both influence the organization's pricing and promotional strategies. For instance, a hotel's room rates and advertising campaigns are strongly influenced by services marketing and operation decisions. Here, it must be noted that many service organizations struggle to synchronize services operations approach and services marketing approaches. Also, the strategic choices a service organization makes regarding the services marketing mix support the positioning and segmentation strategies.

Each marketing mix decision for services incorporates issues that distinguish services from other products and cause complex strategic choices. The three additional Ps discussed in Chapter 2 (participants, physical evidence, and process) present additional challenges and opportunities because of the differences between services and physical goods. As Table 13.1 shows, the intangibility, inseparability, perishability, and heterogeneity of many services present marketers with formidable challenges as they make strategic decisions regarding those three additional Ps. They can, however, also provide opportunities to create and build strategic advantage.

STRATEGIC CHALLENGES FOR SERVICES

Overall, seven basic strategy-related challenges affect most service industries: leadership, employees, customers' performance, demand, setting, and service quality. All of these issues arise because consuming a service means consuming an experience, not consuming a thing. Each of these challenges for services is briefly described here.

Leadership

Leadership is perhaps one of the greatest challenges in service organizations. Services organizations are fundamentally dependent on the performance of people: both employees and customers. As mentioned in Chapter 1, external marketing makes promises to customers, and internal marketing enables employees to be ready and able to keep promises. Groysberg and Slind (2012) argue that leadership is a conversation that requires intimacy, interactivity, inclusion, and intentionality with employees and customers. The strongest service organizations are those where the top management has established a core set of service values and carefully cultivated and protected those values through conversations with employees and customers.

Employees

In most service organizations, a large proportion of employees interact with customers. Customers extrapolate their perceptions of the service personnel they meet to the entire organization. A gruff waiter, a haughty salesclerk, or a sloppy room service waiter can seriously undermine patrons' loyalty to a restaurant, department store, or hotel. This reality makes the tasks of recruiting, training, compensating, and motivating employees even more essential for a service organization than they might be in a manufacturing operation. It has been argued that human intellect is the core resource of service organizations (Quinn 1992). At the Ritz-Carlton hotel **(http://www.ritzcarlton.com),** the human resource function is considered an essential business process.

> The **upside-down organization** inverts the typical organizational chart by putting frontline personnel at the top, middle management in the middle, and the CEO at the bottom.

Recognizing that customer-contact workers are the most important element in building customer satisfaction with the service provider, the concept of the **upside-down organization** inverts the typical organizational chart by putting frontline personnel at the top, middle management in the middle, and the CEO at the bottom. This structure places greater emphasis on recruiting and selecting persons who can fulfill the organization's vision of excellence. Hence, the haphazard hiring practices that are common in much of the service sector today should be replaced with more systematic approaches. Finding the right service employees is too important to leave to chance. Organizations need to compete for the best recruits by developing employee benefits and practices that are more attractive than those common today. Higher entry-level salaries, more pleasant working conditions, and greater opportunities for personal and occupational development make strong recruitment tools. The costs associated with such efforts will be significant, yet not unreasonable, because the demands placed on tomorrow's service workers will be greater.

Customers

In marketing, it is axiomatic that all businesses should be concerned about their customers. Because most service organizations have much more direct contact with their customers than manufacturers do, they must be especially sensitive to customer needs. For instance, FedEx began offering tracking information when it found that many customers wanted to know where their time-sensitive package was at any given time. In addition, because customers often are physically inside the service system, the organization must be concerned with the effects customers have on each other. This can require efforts to manage customer-to-customer interactions. As an example, when customers must stand in line to wait for a service, each individual's behavior influences the rest of the people in line. Many movie theaters urge patrons to be considerate of each other by keeping the area around their seats clean and being quiet during the movie.

Another important strategic issue is creatively encouraging customers to co-produce services. Such approaches are particularly prevalent on the Internet. Facebook **(http://www.facebook.com)** and Wikipedia **(www.wikipedia .com)** are a success because of the collaborative efforts of their customers. In addition, Web sites like Amazon.com **(http://amazon.com)** and iTunes make it possible for their customers to make recommendations on virtually any search page. Such collaborative service strategies have the potential for building strong customer loyalty.

Performance

Service organizations must perform their services in real time. The interactive dynamics of these performances make it essential for an organization to plan its performances carefully using techniques such as blueprinting, scripting, and dramatization. In particular, the theatrical approach (Grove, Fisk, and John 1999) offers a holistic framework for understanding the service performance. A bank customer might see only the teller, but the ability of the teller to serve the customer depends on an infrastructure that includes backroom operations support and frontstage activity.

Demand

The challenges of managing fluctuating demand greatly increase the complexity of services marketing and are discussed in more detail in Chapter 14. The inability to inventory most service supply is a major obstacle for services. Organizations must develop flexible systems to match their service supply to demand in real time. Such systems often require adjustments to demand through part-time staffing, flexible scheduling, promotional specials, demarketing (i.e., efforts to reduce demand), and demand-based pricing systems. Automated delivery mechanisms such as ATMs are another way of managing demand. While the physical goods marketer is most concerned with building demand, the services marketer attempts to build demand at specific times, often having to shift demand from peak demand periods to off-peak demand periods.

Setting

The service setting poses a strategic challenge because it is often the only tangible representation of the service organization's quality. Hence, service organizations are learning to use their setting as a marketing tool. In services where the customer must enter the service organization, many opportunities arise to take advantage of the setting as a marketing tool. For example, Hard Rock Cafe's success is heavily influenced by its elaborate rock-and-roll decorations. Similarly, Planet Hollywood (**http://www.planethollywood.com**) restaurants use original movie and celebrity memorabilia to authenticate the Hollywood feel of their settings. In addition, any waiting time in the setting must be pleasant or at least alleviate boredom by providing magazines, music, and other pleasant distractions. IKEA (**http://www.ikea.com**), the home furnishings store, has a children's play area. Frugal Fannie's (**http://www.frugalfannies.com**), a Boston-area discounted women's designer label clothing store, has a television area where men can watch sports while the women shop in the store.

Service Quality

A large body of services literature has developed regarding the challenge of delivering service quality (see Chapter 10). Service organizations often have limited ability to standardize their service quality, especially if humans deliver the service. To grasp the complexity of the task, consider three levels of variation. For example, hair salon quality varies by hairstylist, by customer, and over time.

Hence, numerous techniques have been developed to measure and improve service quality. Some service organizations seek strategies that will delight or excite their customers, not merely satisfy them. To accomplish this goal, service organizations must first enumerate all service experiences and identify the critical variables in each experience so that key vulnerabilities can be isolated and overcome. The organization must then leverage its people and physical evidence in such a way as to provide a service that exceeds the customer's greatest expectations. Sometimes, this goal may be neither practical nor desirable, especially if the investment required to accomplish it renders it unprofitable in the long run.

One thing is certain: service organizations only grow by retaining profitable customers and attracting new customers. Services marketers must provide consistent service quality, but they also must formulate innovative strategies to sustain existing competitive advantage and create new competitive advantage.

SERVICE STRATEGIES FOR COMPETITIVE ADVANTAGE

Innovation is an essential element of successful service strategies and is at the heart of earlier comments on inventing the future.[1] Here are five highly recommended innovation strategies for competitive advantage and examples of such strategies in practice.

Surpass Your Competition

Edward de Bono (1992) coined the term *sur/petition* to describe his concept of surpassing the typical kinds of competition by surpassing competitors. Sur/petition offers a variety of ideas for creating innovative value monopolies that serve customers more effectively.

Southwest Airlines **(http://southwest.com)** makes an excellent example of sur/petition. When Southwest Airlines first formed, the organization decided to compete against the bus industry, not other airlines. With that simple decision, Southwest created a highly efficient, low-cost system that surpassed what other airlines were offering. In the aftermath of the tragedy of September 11, 2001, Southwest Airlines was virtually the only airline that canceled no air routes, and shortly afterward began adding new routes.

Dramatize Your Performance

As Shakespeare said, "All the world is a stage...." The most effective service organizations learn to stage their performances. This production requires managing their frontstage and backstage areas, their actors (employees), and their audience (customers). Teams of several service workers deliver most service experiences. Such teams must cooperate—through careful casting, developing

---

[1]This section is based upon a presentation made by Raymond Fisk to the PDVSA Services Leadership Conference in Caracas, Venezuela, September 2002.

parts/routines for each cast member, and careful rehearsal—to create a single impression to which the audience responds.

The Disney organization has managed its theme parks as theatrical productions from the beginning. Disney's roots in cartoon entertainment made approaching theme park management in theatrical terms a natural. Disney calls its theme park employees *cast members* and its customers *guests*. The frontstage of a Disney theme park is always immaculately clean. Elaborate backstage activities occur in every park to make sure that guests are not distracted by cast members that are out of costume or by noisy garbage trucks.

Build Relationships

Customer relationship management (CRM) has become a hot business buzzword. An even better approach is customer-managed relationships (CMR) (Shaw and Ivens 2004). In this approach, we let customers manage their relationship with service organizations. This means that we need their permission to build a relationship. Strong customer relationships can lead to customer loyalty. Loyal customers spend more as relationships develop, cost less to serve, recommend new customers, and are more willing to pay regular prices instead of shopping for discounts.

Harley-Davidson **(http://www.harley-davidson.com)** has developed an amazing relationship with its motorcycle riders. In 1983, Harley-Davidson started a factory-sponsored motorcycle club called the Harley Owners Group (or HOG). HOG now has more than 600,000 members and 1,200 chapters worldwide. HOG produces magazines, rallies and events, a fly-and-ride rental program, roadside assistance, financial assistance, and motorcycle shipping. Being a Harley rider is much more than a lifestyle choice—it is virtually a subculture.

Harness Technology

Modern communication and transportation technologies allow service organizations to operate in multiple countries but maintain close contact with employees and customers. Harnessing technology to become the customer's and employee's servant includes real-time customization and personalization of the customer experience. Ideally, the services technology should seem invisible to the customer.

FedEx has been a consistent leader in the use of communication and transportation technology. Their package tracking system communicates where a package is at all times to employees, customers, and package recipients. The organization maintains a sophisticated transportation system including large fleets of planes and trucks to deliver its packages overnight.

Jazz Your Delivery

Jazz music, as originated in New Orleans, is characterized by its distinctive collective improvisation. Jazz improvisation is "spontaneous musical composition." Like great jazz musicians, great service organizations are great improvisers. Teaching service employees improvisational techniques can strengthen their ability to serve customers. The jazz approach can encourage employees to develop emotional commitment to their work. Also, the jazz approach can help us enliven the customer experience and delight our customers (John, Grove, and Fisk 2007).

The Nordstrom (**http://www.nordstrom.com**) department store provides legendary service. Nordstrom began as a shoe store that gave exemplary service. In order to cater to customer needs, Nordstrom created fashion departments that fit individuals' lifestyles, instead of more traditional departments. To make this approach work, Nordstrom hires outstanding staff and empowers them with the discretion to spontaneously solve customer problems. Nordstrom employees are known for their ability to improvise as they meet patrons' needs.

Summary and Conclusion

A marketing strategy is essential to the success of any service organization. Alert service organizations continually scan the environment for threats and opportunities. A services marketing strategy must be carefully planned and designed before it is launched. Implementation and control of services marketing strategies requires careful monitoring and evaluation. Services positioning and market segmentation are essential to establish a position in the customer's mind and a niche in the marketplace. Service organizations must employ creative marketing strategies to overcome the many challenges they face. Innovative services marketing strategies are a powerful means of achieving sustainable competitive advantages.

In any year, many service organizations fail and many new ones start. Service organizations do not fail because the environment changed but because the organization failed to anticipate and adapt to those changes. The innovative service organization thrives on change and the creative strategies necessary to make change happen.

Exercises

1. Summarize the marketing strategy of your college or university or some other service provider that you patronize.

   a. What threats and opportunities are part of the environmental scanning for the service provider?

   b. How does the service provider plan and design its strategies?

   c. How does the service provider implement and control its strategies?

   d. How does the service provider cope with issues of service performance, demand, employees, setting, customers, and service quality?

2. Identify a service organization that recently failed in your community. What strategic mistakes might have caused the business to fail?

3. Identify a successful service organization in your community. What creative strategy accounts for its continued success?

4. Scan the environment in your community and use your observations to predict some changes in the environment. Select a service industry affected by these changes and make specific recommendations regarding how an organization in that industry might adapt or redesign its strategy.

5. Find and discuss an example of a service organization that a) repositioned itself in response to uncontrollable environmental factors and b) targeted a new segment or segments in the marketplace.

Internet Exercise

EXPLORE

Visit the companion site for this text at **www .cengagebrain.com** to explore key concepts in the service industry. You will find tools to help you expand your services marketing knowledge, including ACE self-tests, Web links to companies and organizations featured in this chapter, and much more!

Use the Internet to research the strategy of a major service organization. Many organizations reveal many details of their marketing strategies on their Web sites. See if you can find the following details:

1. Mission statement
2. Target market
3. Marketing mix strategy
   a. Product strategy
   b. Pricing strategy
   c. Promotion strategy
   d. Place strategy
   e. Physical evidence strategy
   f. Participants strategy
   g. Process strategy

References

de Bono, Edward (1992), *Sur/petition: Creating Value Monopolies When Everyone Else Is Merely Competing*, New York: HarperCollins.

Grove, Stephen J., Raymond P. Fisk, and Joby John (1999), "Services as Theater: Guidelines and Implications," in *Handbook of Services Marketing and Management*, Teresa Swartz and Dawn Iacobucci, eds., Beverly Hills, CA: Sage, 21–36.

Groysberg, Boris and Michael Slind (2012), "Leadership Is a Conversation," *Harvard Business Review*, 90 (June), 76–84.

Hamel, Gary and C. K. Prahalad (1994), *Competing for the Future*, Boston: Harvard Business School Press.

John, Joby, Stephen J. Grove, and Raymond P. Fisk (2007), "Improvisation in Service Perfomances: Lessons from Jazz," *Managing Service Quality*, 16 (3), 247–268.

Quinn, James Brian (1992), *Intelligent Enterprise: A Knowledge and Service Based Paradigm for Industry*, New York: Free Press.

Ries, Al and Jack Trout (2000), *Positioning: The Battle for Your Mind, The 20th Anniversary Edition*, New York: Warner Books.

Shaw, Colin and John Ivens (2004), *Building Great Customer Experiences: Revised Edition*, New York: Palgrave Macmillan.

CHAPTER 14

Coping with Fluctuating Demand for Services

As we saw in the IBM vignette, the composition, volume, timing, and location of demand may vary greatly across various services, which make anticipating and adapting to demand an arduous task. Consider the case of metropolitan areas and the spectrum of public services that city governments provide to their citizens such as police protection, public works, emergency medical services, and traffic control. Personnel, facilities, and equipment must be available to respond to citizens' needs in a timely fashion. If demand for a public service were predictable, responding would not be too great of a task. Unfortunately, that is often not the case, which is why an initiative such as IBM's "smarter planet" is so attractive. The information it organizes and provides can go a long way to helping cities balance their public services' capacity with dynamic changes in the demand that may occur, ultimately resulting in more efficient and effective utilization of their resources. This chapter covers the issue of managing demand fluctuations, a challenge common to nearly all services. The chapter has five specific objectives:

- **To show why demand management is a significant problem for services marketing**
- **To explain the nature of service demand**
- **To explore chasing demand with service capacity**
- **To examine smoothing demand to fill service capacity**
- **To discuss the distinction between maximum and optimum capacity**

Early in 2012, with nary a peep of protest that sometimes greets the occasion, a Hooters (**http://www.hooters.com**) restaurant opened its doors for business in Rohnert Park, California, for the first time. Known more for its scantily clad waitresses than for its excellent food, the Hooters Restaurant chain includes more than 430 establishments and stretches across forty-six states, as well as twenty-seven countries worldwide. Hooters employs 25,000 folks, 17,000 of whom are female, with a nice portion of that group at the managerial level (Hooters.com 2012). As is often the case, the restaurant's opening was eagerly awaited by throngs of mostly male diners. For many, the restaurant could not open soon enough! When the day finally came, a line of anxious customers wrapped around the building as an overflow crowd of diners eagerly awaited their chance to eat, drink, and "see Mary." Business greatly exceeded expectations during the first week of operation (Solomon 2012) and continued briskly until the novelty wore off. Over time, the flood of customers predictably dwindled to a much smaller stream of diners. Hooters still enjoys steady customer traffic during peak hours, but at some times of the day and days of the week it longs for the rush of diners it enjoyed during its first few days of operation. The Rohnert Park Hooters now faces the same fluctuating customer demand that confronts most restaurants.

Airlines, telecommunications companies, restaurants, hotels, delivery services, and even e-services are plagued by the same phenomenon. Quite often, when a new service enterprise first opens for business, it experiences tremendous customer interest. Many factors may contribute to the excitement, such as the public's desire to try something new or a successful promotional campaign to launch the enterprise. However, newness fades, and soon the organization must contend with potentially radical swings in customer demand. During some periods, the organization's business may be dismal. Customers may be scarce, and empty seats or vacant rooms may abound. During other periods, the organization may serve a constant flow of customers who keep the cash registers ringing. During still other stretches of time, the organization may face an ironic and frustrating situation. It may have so many customers that it cannot serve them all effectively, and without enough space or service personnel to handle the demand, it must turn many disappointed or disgruntled customers away.

WHY IS SERVICES DEMAND A PROBLEM?

At the heart of the services demand problem are two circumstances that face nearly all service organizations: demand cycles and the perishability of services. In the first case, services must often cope with ebbs and flows of demand that may be deeply ensconced in the behavioral patterns of the customer. These patterns often create a "feast or famine" situation for services. For example, restaurants must deal with culturally defined times of the day when dining is appropriate. Hotels and airlines must contend with the Monday-through-Friday work schedule of the business traveler. Vacation destinations that cater to families must accept the impact of climatic conditions and children's school calendars. Demand for each of these services is likely to be strong during some periods and probably quite weak at others. Fluctuating demand is sometimes linked to conditions that are difficult to change.

The second circumstance contributing to the problem, the perishability of services, arises because services usually exist only while they are performed. Hence, if an organization's capacity to provide a service goes unused when customer demand is low, the ability to generate service revenue during that time frame is lost forever. Further, the empty hotel room or the vacant airline seat cannot be stockpiled for later use when customer demand is greater than the service organization's capacity can accommodate. Practitioners have identified this aspect of services marketing as one of its most troublesome challenges. Consider how much easier the job of services marketers would be if they could store their unused service capacity and have it available whenever a service shortage occurs!

What can service managers do to address the uneven demand facing service organizations? To answer that question, we need a clear picture of the nature of service demand.

THE NATURE OF SERVICE DEMAND*

Many critical issues must be examined to understand service demand. Services need to determine whether the peaks and valleys of their customer demand follow a predictable cycle or are the result of random fluctuations. *Random fluctuation* occurs without warning and is hard to accommodate. For example, severe weather conditions may keep fans away from a college football game that would normally

Much of the information presented here is based on the observations of Lovelock and Wirtz (2011).

be a sellout or create a catastrophe that overflows a hospital's emergency room. Service organizations have great difficulty dealing with such unpredictable demand situations.

Fortunately, service organizations often encounter more manageable *predictable fluctuations* of demand. Predictable fluctuation occurs when customer demand follows a pattern that repeats itself over time. The key for service organizations is to recognize and understand the pattern so that they can then adjust to the fluctuating demand. Careful study of customer patronage may identify varying levels of demand for an organization's service offering across hours, days, weeks, months, seasons, or years. For example, by charting customer traffic, a movie theater may discover that the *daily* demand for its service peaks in the early evening hours and diminishes for its late-night showing. It may also learn that *weekly* demand increases steadily from Monday to Thursday, with a significant leap Friday and Saturday before a marked drop-off on Sunday. Similarly, an investment broker may discern that *monthly* demand for investment services peaks at about the first and the fifteenth of the month. A ski resort in the northern hemisphere will surely discover a *seasonal* demand cycle that peaks between late November and mid-March. Some cycles of demand are obvious, while others are not. Further, as suggested by the example of the movie theater, analysis of a service organization's demand cycle may reveal dynamics that vary across time. Overall, the determination of a service's demand pattern may provide valuable information that enables an organization to plan for and successfully adapt to variations in demand. Recognizing the demand cycles may also help customers adapt their behavior accordingly. Consider the types of accommodations both businesses and customers must make to deal with the demand cycle dynamics related in Spotlight 14.1.

SPOTLIGHT 14.1

Italians' Love for August Vacations Poses Challenges to Visitors

Need to do business or desire a vacation in Italy in August? Good luck. August has always been the main vacation month for most of Europe, with life—and business—in Portugal, Spain, France, and Greece all grinding to a halt as shops close and almost everyone heads to the seaside or mountains. But nowhere is the trend more pronounced than in Italy, where swaths of the population move and dramatically change the country's demographics. Productivity for the entire country falls by nearly 50% as Italians flee major cities for vacations spots. Most midsize and large corporations keep only skeleton crews, and many small firms close for the month. It is reported that the volume on the national stock exchange plummets by a third. Simply put, the pace of business and life slows greatly, posing some potential challenges for travelers to Italy in August. While some bargains may be had for visitors to the cities vacated by Italian vacationers, prices are likely to be higher than usual at Italian tourist destinations. If your destination is an inland city, you may find many shops are not open. A word to the wise: forget about "hitting the highway"—even the largest, A1—on any Saturday in August. It is the peak day for the mass exodus of Italians to vacation spots, and the roads are jammed. By the way, if it's June and you're hoping for a well-placed hotel room for August at a trendy Italian island resort or along the country's coastline, you better hurry. There are likely to be just a handful of rooms left because Italians plan ahead for that all-important August vacation.

Source: **http://www.dreamofitaly.com/public/The -Lowdown-on-Traveling-to-Italy-in-August-Free-Italy -Travel-Advice.cfm** (accessed September 14, 2012).

Once an organization uncovers its demand patterns, it should look for explanations for those patterns. This task is particularly important for an organization that attempts to shift customer demand. Sometimes, it may be nearly impossible to shift customer demand because of factors beyond the customers' and the organization's control. The five-day workweek that causes fluctuations in hotel and airline demand is a good example. Business travelers in the United States normally have little choice but to conduct business from Monday through Friday between 8:00 A.M. and 5:00 P.M. During the week, therefore, hotel rooms in major cities and seats on early morning and evening flights to and from these cities are usually in great demand. Services catering to such travelers can do little to change their demand cycle. Efforts to divert some businesspersons' hotel patronage to the weekend and air travel to midday to take advantage of unused capacity are not feasible. Instead, hotels, airlines, and other organizations serving business travelers must find other ways to adjust to their periods of low demand, such as attracting a totally different type of customer to occupy those empty seats and rooms.

A service's demand cycle may be more flexible in other cases. For instance, the demand cycle for restaurant services is strongly associated with customary dining times for each meal. These times are well established in any culture, but they are merely a social convention that many individuals are free to ignore or work around. Hence, restaurants may have a greater opportunity than many other services to develop successful strategies that shift customer demand to periods that might otherwise be marked by low patronage. Many service organizations have successfully convinced a significant portion of their clientele to purchase earlier or later than normal by offering special rates during otherwise slow periods. Figure 14.1 depicts just such an offer for a local eatery in Austin, Texas.

Almost all services have distinct patterns of demand that can be traced to specific causes. To illustrate the process of identifying the demand cycle and its sources, we have discussed rather simple situations. In reality, service demand cycles are often much more complicated, because any given service organization is likely to target multiple customer segments, each with its own patronage pattern and underlying causes. Consider, for example, the case of the car rental agency. The demand for its services may be grouped into two major customer segments: business travelers and leisure travelers. Each customer segment requires a rental car at different times for different reasons. The business traveler's pattern of demand is likely to resemble that discussed earlier for hotel and airline services. The leisure traveler's demand cycle may depend on factors such as school calendars, work schedules, or social convention. To form an accurate picture of the overall demand, a car rental agency must chart the patronage patterns of the two segments together. Such a chart reveals periods of high and low demand more precisely than a demand estimate based on one segment alone. It also provides a clearer picture of the fluctuating demand that a particular service organization faces. Table 14.1 depicts various demand cycles service organizations face and their underlying causes.

> **FIGURE 14.1** **Kerbey lane**

Kerbey Lane Café

CHASING DEMAND WITH SERVICE CAPACITY

The problem of fluctuating demand has so far been presented as one of too many or too few customers. However, another side to this dilemma is the issue of service capacity. After all, excessive demand can result from insufficient capacity, just as insufficient demand can result from excess capacity. According to this reasoning, the overbooked airline flight is clearly the result of too few seats on the airplane. The hairstyling salon with a full waiting room may reflect understaffing, too few workstations, or both. Conversely, too many empty beds at the hospital may be the result of either surplus capacity or low demand from patients.

TABLE 14.1 The Nature of Service Demand

Demand Cycle	Reasons for Demand Cycle Fluctuation	Service Examples
Hours of day	Work schedules	Parking garages Restaurants
Days of week	Work schedules "Play" schedules	Movie theaters Hospital emergency rooms
Weeks or days of month	Pay periods Established schedules	Banks Spectator sport venues
Months or seasons of the year	Government regulations School calendars Predictable weather patterns	Income tax preparation Beach or ski resorts
Holidays or special events	Cultural norms Government regulations	Telephone services Retailing services

© Cengage Learning

Most service organizations are *capacity-constrained services.* Their productive capacity limits the number of customers they can accommodate and the quality of the service they provide. **Service capacity** has three aspects: (1) the **physical facility** in which the service is performed or rendered (e.g., hotels, airplanes, apartment complexes, and dentists' offices) or that supports the service process (e.g., parking lots, waiting areas, delivery space); (2) the **personnel** whose labor and skill level create the service (e.g., hairstylists, wait staff, teachers, and delivery persons); and (3) the **equipment** that enables the service to occur (e.g., computer hardware and software, stoves and dishwashers, X-ray machines and stethoscopes, movie projectors and screens). An organization can provide service only up to the respective capacities of its physical facility, service personnel, and equipment. The cruise ship can hold only so many passengers, the lawyer can advise only so many clients, the Web site can only handle so much traffic, and the movie theater can show only so many movies at one time.

> **Service capacity** has three aspects: (1) the **physical facility** in which the service is performed or rendered; (2) the **personnel** whose labor and skill level create the service; and (3) the **equipment** that enables the service to occur.

The key for any service organization is to have enough capacity to accommodate customers when demand is high, yet not so much that it goes to waste when demand is low. In other words, successful service organizations strike a balance between capacity and demand. One way to achieve this kind of balance is to *chase demand* with capacity by temporarily stretching or shrinking the organization's productive capacity—facilities, personnel and equipment—to meet fluctuating demand. For example, during periods of peak demand, a restaurant may schedule more waitstaff and kitchen help to process food orders more quickly. Similarly, a subway train may add additional cars to accommodate peak-hour passenger traffic. In contrast, during slow periods, a hotel may close a floor of rooms and a retailer may schedule employee vacations. Other means exist for adjusting capacity to chase demand. For instance, service organizations can hire part-timers, lease additional facilities or equipment, invest in cross-trained personnel to stretch capacity, and rent out or schedule necessary maintenance

══════ **SPOTLIGHT 14.2** ══════

The Peachtree Road Race: Atlanta Puts Its Best Foot Forward

 Each Fourth of July as part of the Independence Day festivities, a throng of runners from across the country and the globe descend upon Atlanta to participate in the Peachtree Road Race. Billed as the world's largest 10K run, the event is currently capped at 55,000 participants, who wind their way down Peachtree Street in Atlanta from the Buckhead area of Atlanta to the city's Piedmont Park. Clearly, a great deal of preparation is needed to stage such an occurrence; the planning process is virtually never-ending. Consider the number of people, amount and type of equipment, and the availability of various facilities that are needed. A staff of workers is augmented by 3,500 volunteers who direct participants, manage traffic, control spectators, set up and disassemble barriers, hand out T-shirts at the finish line, and provide medical support among other tasks. Musicians are scheduled to provide entertainment at various locations along the route, including the finish line. Tables and workers who dole out the 500,000 cups of water to ensure the runners' comfort are strategically placed as well. Hundreds of barriers are positioned at potential trouble spots for crowd control (of the estimated 200,000 spectators along the route) and to funnel runners effectively. Gaining access and control of a major roadway that winds through the heart of Atlanta from the fashionable Buckhead area to Piedmont Park for several hours on the morning of the Fourth of July, finding and scheduling facilities for ancillary activities, such as an annual runners' expo and other pre- and postrace events, and ensuring that the hospitality and mass transit support to accommodate the masses is available are also a big part of the planning activity. In sum, all three forms of capacity—facilities, personnel, and equipment—are used to chase the demand the annual Peachtree Road Race creates.

Source: The Peachtree Road Race Magazine (2012), July 4, Atlanta, GA: Atlanta Track Club.

for unused equipment or facilities to shrink capacity. Using more than one means of capacity adjustment is common. However, to chase demand successfully, an organization must first acquire an accurate picture of its demand cycle. Spotlight 14.2 provides a brief examination of the incredible amount of planning that is needed to have enough capacity to handle the thousands of runners at the yearly Atlanta Peachtree Road Race in Georgia.

In some circumstances, chasing demand by stretching capacity may be impractical. Take the case of the car rental industry. Each year during the Christmas holiday season, rental companies typically face the frustrating situation of having so many customers that some must be turned away. Holiday travel makes the two-week period beginning before Christmas and ending after New Year's Day the busiest time of the year for car rental agencies in the United States, with customer demand for cars far exceeding the available inventory of many agencies. The ramifications of random events such as the aftermath of September 11, 2001, of course, may create an interruption of this and other predictable patterns of demand for any service organization or industry. Normally, however, the auto rental industry can expect to revisit the situation that occurs every year—customer demand far exceeding its supply of autos. The issue is that rental agencies can do little to boost their supply of cars for a short period of high demand such as occurs during the Christmas holidays. As one industry spokesperson observes, "You don't build a church for Easter Sunday." Purchasing additional automobiles to accommodate the demand during the holiday season would create a greater problem of excess capacity during slower periods of the year. It is important to remember that stretching capacity involves a temporary adjustment that does not result in a permanent, long-term increase in capacity resources.

SMOOTHING DEMAND TO FILL SERVICE CAPACITY

Beyond chasing demand with capacity, another broad approach to balancing service capacity and demand is to try to influence or change the nature of customer demand itself. Many service organizations pursue such a strategy to reconcile conditions of excess or insufficient capacity. Remember, demand that falls short of capacity renders that capacity a wasted resource, while demand that exceeds capacity results in customers having to wait or—worse yet—flee to the competition. See Table 14.2 for a summary of demand strategies.

Smoothing demand means shifting patronage to times when a service's productive capacity is underused and deflecting or discouraging patronage when it is oversubscribed. Many marketers focus on increasing demand for services, while the concept of decreasing or deflecting demand is foreign to most. Nevertheless, both are means by which an organization may achieve more effective and efficient capacity utilization. Let's look at each in turn.

> **Smoothing demand** means shifting patronage to times when a service's productive capacity is underused and deflecting or discouraging patronage when it is oversubscribed.

An organization can employ any of the elements of the traditional marketing mix to *increase demand* for its service at times when patronage is low and capacity is underutilized. For instance, an organization may drop its *prices* to entice customers to use its service during normally slow times. To maximize capacity utilization, airlines offer special fares, hotels charge less for rooms, and telephone companies provide reduced rates at times when demand is likely to be weak. Vacationers to the Caribbean can find resorts' summer rates significantly lower than winter rates. Service organizations may also alter the nature of their *product* to increase demand. For example, to fill their rooms in the summer months, many ski resorts convert their establishments by adding outdoor swimming pools, horseback riding, hiking trails, tennis courts, and other warm-weather attractions. Spotlight 14.3 provides another example of how a service

TABLE 14.2	**Demand Strategies**
Strategies	**Tactics**
Chase Demand	Facilities
	Personnel
	Equipment
Smooth Demand	Price
	Product
	Promotion
	Place/distribution
Inventory Demand	Formal queuing
	Reservation systems
Do Nothing	

© Cengage Learning

━━━━━ **SPOTLIGHT 14.3** ━━━━━

Funeral Homes Become Lively

 At various locations throughout the United States, funeral homes are attracting a totally different clientele than is typically the case. Taking advantage of their sometimes vast and elegantly decorated servicescapes that are sometimes underutilized, some funeral homes are marketing themselves as sites for weddings, holiday parties, proms, and various other occasions. Their manicured lawns, marble floors, chandeliers and flowing fountains, coupled with their greater availability and typically lower cost than more traditional venues for special events, make the funeral home an attractive alternative that in some cases can lead to dozens of bookings a month. Clearly, changing the nature of their service product from a somber setting to a lively one has the potential to build business and capitalize on unused capacity.

Source: Hayes, Melanie D. (2011), "Funeral Homes Discover New Life," **http://www.usatoday.com/news /offbeat/2011-01-19-weddingsandfunerals19_ST_N.htm** (accessed September 14, 2012).

establishment can attempt to increase demand by altering its product offering. In addition, a service's problem of excess capacity might be addressed through *place or distribution* modifications. Consider the veterinarian who devises a work schedule that includes house calls to fill potentially slow hours or days of the week with client demand that might normally be missed. Finally, service organizations can employ forms of *promotion* to increase customer demand. A physician may fill an appointment book through advertising that reminds members of the public to schedule a yearly checkup. Similarly, fast-food restaurants regularly use sales promotions such as coupons, merchandise tie-ins with movies, sweepstakes, and contests to increase their customer demand.

Just as a successful effort to increase customer demand for a service often involves a combination of astute price, product, place, or promotion decisions, a service organization might similarly rely on any or all of these marketing mix elements to *decrease demand* during periods that exceed the organization's capacity. Often, the organization's goal here is actually to deflect or shift some of this demand to slower periods. Such *demarketing* efforts might involve *promotions* that encourage patrons to use the service at other times. An example is U.S. Postal Service (**http://www.usps .com**) advertising that aims to persuade customers to mail their Christmas packages early. *Prices* set higher to take advantage of customer demand may serve a similar purpose. Consider the probable decision a leisure traveler will make when choosing between a hotel room rate of $199 a night during the week and $109 for the same room on the weekend! *Product* and *place or distribution* decisions may also address the problem of excess demand. For instance, many restaurants convert to a buffet-style service or restrict their dining selections during periods of great demand such as Christmas or New Year's Eve. Although such maneuvers may increase the efficiency of dealing with large numbers of diners, they may also persuade those who want a wider set of dining choices to visit at another time. Likewise, service organizations may choose to restrict their hours of operation, even during periods of great customer demand, with the belief that such a strategy will divert some potential patronage to slower periods.

Excess demand may be addressed with other means besides increasing capacity or demarketing. It is not surprising that many organizations would rather accommodate the customers who want to use their service at a particular time than risk losing their business by attempting to deflect their patronage to another period. After all, to coin a phrase, "a customer in the store is worth two in the street." Nevertheless, what can an organization do if it wants to (or must) forgo increasing capacity to meet demand or shifting demand to another time? One answer is to *inventory demand* by having strategies in place to deal with excess demand when it occurs.

Establishing a *reservation system* is one way to inventory demand. Many service organizations use reservation systems to deal with potential problems resulting from having to serve too many customers at once. Airlines, automobile repair shops, hotels, cruise ships, physicians, and restaurants use reservations to manage their demand effectively. A reservation system allows the service organization to identify and organize its customer demand before it actually occurs to efficiently utilize its capacity. Such a system also benefits customers by assuring them that they will receive the service they want at a specified time. Today, computerized reservation systems allow service organizations to monitor and schedule demand for large numbers of customers.

Another means to inventory demand is through a *formal queuing system* (see Figure 14.2). Traditionally, many organizations have relied on a "first come, first served" system to queue customers. Other organizations, recognizing that not all patrons are equally desirable, have developed different approaches to accommodate the most desirable patrons first. For example, trendy nightclubs allow entrance to people among a waiting crowd based on their perceived fit with the establishment's customer mix. In addition, many restaurants, retailers, and other service organizations will often serve their regular, higher spending, or more desired customers first, as well as those who require special attention. Consider the boarding process for the typical commercial airline flight or the admission process at a hospital's emergency room. Different circumstances dictate some in the queue are served before others. Whatever the rationale behind the queuing method, the organization that devises a formal system ensures that some patrons must wait. Therefore, many service organizations using this approach also develop ways of placating waiting customers (e.g., by providing free beverages) or occupying their time (e.g., by entertaining them). It is also a good idea to provide some justification for the wait. After all, as Table 14.3 (see page 222) suggests, "fair waits are shorter."

F I G U R E   1 4 . 2   Formal Queuing: The Managed Wait

Source: Anderson Independent-Mail (1999) (December 27), C3. FRANK & ERNEST: © Thaves/Dist. By Newspaper Enterprise Association, Inc.

TABLE 14.3   Principles of Waiting
1. Empty minutes are long minutes.
2. In-process minutes are shorter.
3. Unknown waits are longer.
4. Waits for valued outcomes seem shorter.
5. Fair waits are shorter.
6. Overpromising stretches reasonable waits.
7. Observable time-saving actions make waits seem shorter.

Source: From Haynes, Paula J., "Hating to Wait: Managing the Final Service Encounter," *Journal of Services Marketing*, 4 (4), 20–26. © 1990 by MCB University Press. Reprinted by permission.

Another way in which organizations can balance service capacity and customer demand is to *do nothing*. As unlikely as it seems, this strategy can be a conscious one, and it often works. By resisting the temptation to chase, smooth, or control demand, the organization is allowing other forces to work out the problem of fluctuating patronage patterns. Discouraged customers learn from their own experience the periods in which they are least likely to receive satisfactory service from an organization, and they revise their patronage patterns accordingly. Guests realize that, barring a miracle, being seated in a popular restaurant at 8:00 P.M. on a Friday or Saturday evening without a reservation made days or weeks in advance is impossible. Instead, they dine earlier or later, or they may even choose another night of the week to visit the establishment. Similarly, bank customers may discover that lines are shorter and service is better if they visit their branch during the mid-morning or mid-afternoon hours. By refraining from any actions, an organization may actually divert some excess customer demand to times when its capacity to serve is less strained. It should be obvious, however, that the do-nothing strategy cannot divert the demand to a specific or desired time. It may also result in lost customers who simply seek services elsewhere. Nevertheless, the overcrowded and less enjoyable conditions found during the organization's peak demand periods may cause some customers to use the service during alternative times and thus diminish some of the excess capacity. In short, sometimes doing nothing makes sense.

MAXIMUM VERSUS OPTIMUM CAPACITY

Whether through random events or through the actions of an organization, occasions when demand exceeds maximum capacity occur regularly. According to conventional wisdom, *maximum capacity* is *optimum capacity*. As suggested previously, a service's maximum capacity is dictated by the size of the organization's facilities, the number and skill level of its personnel, and the nature of its equipment. When capacity is pushed to the limit, service quality often deteriorates. **Optimum capacity** refers to the number of customers the organization can handle effectively under ideal conditions.

Optimum capacity refers to the number of customers who can be effectively handled under ideal conditions.

When optimum capacity is exceeded, facilities feel overcrowded, personnel become harried and careless, and equipment is overtaxed. Consider the example of the hotel where every room is full. The likely effects include slower elevators, slower response time to front-desk inquiries or room-service requests, overburdening of the physical plant, and increased staff irritability. In some instances, these circumstances can light the fuse of customer rage discussed in Chapter 7.

In a sense, each additional customer served beyond an organization's optimum capacity diminishes the service experience for all customers and the organization's ability to offer excellence. Hence, creating demand beyond optimum capacity is questionable, while chasing demand by stretching capacity past its normal maximum level is foolish. In some cases, however, maximum capacity and optimum capacity are the same. For instance, if every seat is filled at a sporting event, the maximum capacity may result in negative experiences (e.g., long lines and crowded conditions), but the excitement created by a full house might overcome them.

Beyond the negative consequences already discussed when maximum capacity is exceeded, other issues bear noting. For instance, demand exceeding maximum capacity can result in customers having to wait to enter the service delivery system or have the service performed. Waiting is an unpleasant experience for most people and is often considered a waste of their time. It's also costly. It's been estimated that time spent waiting for the cable repair, retail home delivery, or phone repair person costs customers in the United States nearly forty billion dollars annually and results in nearly 60% of all Americans suffering fist-pounding frustration (Perman 2011). However, organizations must recognize that demand cycles make waiting a common occurrence, so they must find ways to make the customers' waiting experience more tolerable. Table 14.3 presents some principles of waiting that proactive service organizations might consider. For instance, recognizing that "empty minutes are long minutes" and knowing where patrons are likely to be waiting, retailers, airports, and amusement parks have installed screens that broadcast various forms of entertainment to help fill the time. Also, knowing that customers are likely to perceive a longer wait when they are uncertain as to how long the wait will be (i.e., "unknown waits are longer"), many service organizations work diligently to keep customers informed as to how long it will be before they can expect to be served. These types of efforts that reflect the principles of waiting can make a wait seem shorter and help to keep customer morale on an even keel. The ability to address customers' perception of waiting time may pay big dividends by improving the customers' experience once they enter the service delivery system, as well as the nature of the customer–service provider interaction.

Often in the effort to fill capacity and maximize revenue, organizations create too much demand by systematically overbooking, anticipating that some customers will cancel or be no-shows. Even though the practice may make sense from a revenue-generating perspective, some costs need to be considered. Customers who are denied service as a result of such practices are likely to reduce their transaction and spending activity with the guilty organization in the future. Some evidence indicates that the likelihood is even more pronounced for higher status customers (e.g., "gold" level frequent flyers) who are victimized by overbooking (Wangenheim and Bayon 2006).

Excess customer demand can result in significant lost revenue when customers are turned away, though the wasted resources associated with insufficient demand can be even greater. Addressing the dilemma of demand fluctuation requires care. Increasing demand may have undesirable financial consequences. For instance, the costs associated with setting low prices or offering special sales promotions to increase patronage may outstrip the income produced by the additional customers such actions generate. A freight company may fill every truck if it lowers its prices enough, offers the right inducements, or engages in enough advertising. Yet, in doing so, the organization may spend more money than it receives in return. A high occupancy rate, a full load and other measures of maximum capacity utilization do not always equal profit maximization. Hence, it is wise to carefully assess the likely returns in relation to the costs of any decision to increase demand. Ideally, to strike a balance between capacity and demand, the astute service organization will attempt to chase demand while also smoothing it.

Summary and Conclusion

Fluctuating customer demand is a significant problem for most service organizations. Service organizations must understand the nature of their demand patterns and consider all relevant factors before they attempt to manage demand fluctuations and their effects. The organization's goal should be to balance demand and capacity so that it functions as close to optimum capacity as possible. Optimum capacity is usually less than maximum capacity. Even though maximum capacity utilization may increase revenues, it involves some potentially significant costs. Crowded conditions and less attentive service may mar customers' experiences; personnel may become overworked and unhappy; and even the equipment may be overtaxed. As a result, customers may fail to return, personnel may opt for less challenging work environments, and equipment may break down more rapidly. To ensure service excellence for customers and personnel, a successful organization will identify and pursue a demand level that fills its service's capacity to the optimal level.

Excess demand on a service's capacity can be distressing, but insufficient demand can be devastating. Organizations facing excess demand must work hard to maintain standards of excellence and so continue to satisfy any number of customers. Shortchanging service quality because demand is too high is simply poor business. However, organizations may need to work even harder to attract customers to patronize a service establishment at times that are unpopular or inconvenient. A good starting point is to focus on providing excellent service at all times. If an organization can accomplish this feat, problems of insufficient demand and excess capacity are likely to greatly decrease. The marketing mix is a set of tools that can help manage demand. Capacity management measures and marketing mix techniques can be effectively combined to balance demand and capacity. Finally, any service organization must evaluate how effectively it manages its demand fluctuations. The costs of the capacity and demand management measures must be compared with the incremental profits generated.

Exercises

1. Identify a service type, other than those listed in Table 14.1, to illustrate the following:

   a. How services demand can vary over time

   b. Each of the reasons for fluctuation in services demand

2. Billy Ardd recently opened an upscale pool parlor in his mid-sized hometown of Cuestick, Kansas. Like many service operations, Billy's establishment, "Stripes and Solids," faces uneven customer demand. Using Table 14.2 and material from the chapter as a guide, offer Billy some suggestions for solving his problem by (1) chasing demand and (2) smoothing demand.

3. Consider a recent visit to a service organization that required you to wait a long time before being served, and the principles of waiting presented in Table 14.3.

   a. How long did you wait?

   b. How did you feel during the wait, and why?

   c. How did the wait make you feel about the organization?

   d. What do you think could have been done to make the wait more pleasant?

   e. Did the organization do anything to alleviate the tedium of your wait?

Internet Exercise

EXPLORE

Visit the companion site for this text at **www.cengagebrain.com** to explore key concepts in the service industry. You will find tools to help you expand your services marketing knowledge, including ACE self-tests, Web links to companies and organizations featured in this chapter, and much more!

Identify three Internet service businesses. They can be organizations that retail over the Internet or provide information over the Internet, or any other type of entity that uses the Internet to communicate with its customers or clients. Make sure that the organizations you select invite the customer to enter questions or requests through the Web site. Request information as to (1) their busiest times of the day, the week, the month, and the year and (2) what drives the traffic to their site at those times. Consider what might be done to change those patterns.

References

Haynes, Paula J. (1990), "Hating to Wait: Managing the Final Service Encounter," *Journal of Services Marketing*, 4 (4), 20–26.

Hooters.com (2012), **http://www.hooters.com/About.aspx** (accessed September 13, 2012).

Lovelock, Christopher H. and Jochen Wirtz (2011), *Services Marketing; People, Technology, Strategy*, 7th ed., Englewood Cliffs, NJ: Prentice Hall.

Perman, Cindy (2011), "How Much Is Waiting for the Cable Guy Costing You?", **http://www.usatoday**

.com/money/industries/story/2011-11-05/cnbc-cable-costs-toa-technologies/51073006/1 (accessed September 14, 2012).

Solomon, Ricky (2012, February 6), "Locals Flock to Hooters Grand Opening," http://www.sonomastatestar.com/features/locals-flock-to-hooters-grand-opening (accessed September 13, 2012).

The Peachtree Road Race Magazine (2012, July 4). Atlanta, GA: Atlanta Track Club.

Wangenheim, Florian V. and Tomas Bayon (2006), "Effects of Capacity-Driven Service Experiences on Customer Usage Levels: Why Revenue Management Systems Are Due for Change," Marketing Science Institute: Report No. 06-103.

IBM **(http://www.ibm.com)** is a truly multinational organization. It has operations in 170 countries and almost half a million employees worldwide. The United Nations currently has 193 member states, which means that IBM operates in 88% of the countries of the world. By the turn of the century, IBM had changed from a computer company to a computer *services* company, with only 35% of its revenues coming from hardware. In 2011, IBM had only 16% of revenues in hardware. IBM is a global services organization. Therefore, it is only natural for an organization such as IBM to use its expertise and experience in "all things digital" to envision a leadership role in the "Smarter Planet" concept, as you saw in the IBM vignette.

This chapter examines ways in which service organizations can globalize their services. The chapter has six specific objectives:

- ■ **To explore the relationship of services and culture**
- ■ **To examine the phenomena of global trade in services**
- ■ **To consider strategies for entering global service markets**
- ■ **To contrast standardization and adaptation strategies for global services**
- ■ **To communicate the imperative of adapting to a multilingual global marketplace**
- ■ **To briefly examine technology and global services**

João (the Portuguese equivalent of the English name *John*) is a Portuguese college student at Universidade do Porto. He buys his gasoline at the Shell Oil **(http://www.shell.com)** service station on the way to school. He pays for it with his Visa **(http://www.visa.com)** credit card. In his marketing class, the professor is part of an exchange program with the United States. João and several classmates like to at lunch at a local Pizza Hut restaurant **(http://www.pizzahut.com)**. When he gets home, he checks the world news on CNN International **(http://www.cnn.com)** via satellite. He meets several classmates at a Brazilian restaurant in the nearby shopping center for dinner. Later, he and his friends go to a local club for some late-night dancing to a Jamaican reggae band. Like so many members of his generation, João takes for granted the global origins of the various services he consumes.

Few services trends have more significance than the rapid transition to global markets. The Dutch East India Company established in 1602 and considered the first truly multinational corporation was a trading company: a services organization. Historically, manufacturing firms have been quicker than service organizations to pursue global markets. However, in the late twentieth century, many service organizations began to export their services. International markets continue to offer growth opportunities for many service organizations. Given the rising tide of global services trade, João's perspective seems quite understandable. Indeed, as seen in Spotlight 15.1, the speed with which the Arab Spring uprisings spread across North Africa and the Middle East is a testament to the porosity of boundaries between nations facilitated by modern transportation and communications.

===== **SPOTLIGHT 15.1** =====

The Arab Spring Changes Government Services in the Middle East

 The wave of uprisings in Tunisia, Egypt, Libya, and Yemen were phenomenal, given that these countries were under decades of authoritarian rule. It began in Tunisia on December 18, 2010, and on January 14, 2011, the Tunisian government was overthrown. On January 25, 2011, Egyptians took to the streets. In two weeks, the Egyptian government was overthrown, and in the summer of 2012, Hosni Mubarak, who had been the president of Egypt for thirty years, was sentenced to life in prison for ordering the killing of protestors. Almost a thousand Egyptians died in the protests. Next came Libya; its uprising began in February, and on August 23, 2011, its government was overthrown. Muammar Gaddafi, president of Libya for over forty years, was killed by rebel forces. By some estimates, almost 30,000 people died in Libya over the seven months of revolt. In Yemen, the government was overthrown on February 27, 2012, after one year and one month of revolts. After his twenty-two-year rule, Yemeni President Saleh was granted immunity by Yemeni legislators.

The civil war continues in Syria; it is estimated that almost 30,000 people have died there. Lesser-known civil uprisings have occurred and continue to occur in Bahrain, Algeria, Jordan, Morocco, Mali, and other nations. How far this movement will spread is yet to unfold. What is certain is that these profound events are reshaping the region's social, economic, and political terrain.

The power of social media in these uprisings cannot be undervalued. It allowed the world to stay informed of the activities and the progress made by the rebels. Images and messages were distributed via various forums on the Internet. This ten-minute video on YouTube (**http://www.youtube.com /watch?v=IMyiLklQQRk**) is a compilation of fantastic images from January 25, 2011. The world is a smaller place in many ways today, thanks to transportation and communication technology.

Source: **http://www.huffingtonpost.com/raymond -schillinger/arab-spring-social-media_b_970165.html** (accessed September 18, 2012).

SERVICES AND CULTURE

Services marketers face interesting challenges and opportunities in international markets. The way frontline service personnel execute and deliver services reveals a host of differences, from language and customs to values and behavior. Organizations must be prepared to adapt to and otherwise accommodate differences between foreign and home markets. Aside from differences in the economic, competitive, legal, and technological landscapes, cultural issues form a major category of cross-national differences. *Culture* is the set of shared values and beliefs in a society. Researchers have categorized cultures along various dimensions. Each dimension brings interesting and managerially useful perspectives when applied to the services field. Edward Hall (1959) classified cultures into high- and low-context cultures, based on the way people communicate with each other. High-context cultures typically place a greater reliance on contextual and nonverbal cues in personal interactions, while low-context cultures place a greater emphasis on verbal cues. Hence, in communication across cultures, individuals from low-context cultures such as the United States would favor directness and more structure, while individuals from high-context cultures such as Japan might see this approach as abrupt, demanding, or intrusive. In related research, management consultant and scholar Hofstede (2001) studied the behavior of managers and workers in different countries and classified cultures along four dimensions: power distance (acceptance of inequality of power among individuals), individualism (primacy of self-interest versus group-interest), uncertainty avoidance (ability to cope with uncertain situations), and masculinity (societal roles defined biologically). Similarly, studies by ethnographic sociologists Kluckhohn and Strodtbeck (1960) categorized cultures based on their orientation along five dimensions: the individual's orientation toward God, nature, activities, time, and others. The following examines four of these dimensions as they apply to services. (See John 1996 for an application in the health care context.)

Cultural Orientation Toward Nature

What is the relationship of people with their environment? Do they seek to control it, or do they consider it impossible or inappropriate to control? Cultures differ in the extent to which individuals expect uncertainties to be controlled at the service encounter and in the attribution of lack of control to the service provider or nature. Broadly speaking, Western cultures such as the United States and Canada are less accepting of service encounter failures and more likely to expect the service provider to take responsibility for service failures.

Cultural Orientation Toward Activities

What is the modality of human activity? In other words, do individuals focus on the activity or on the results of the activity? Do individuals place greater emphasis on the experience of "being" or on "doing"? Cultures can differ based on whether individuals focus on the process or the outcome of service delivery. Eastern cultures such as found in South Asia are more likely to emphasize the service experience as opposed to the outcome of a service delivery.

Cultural Orientation Toward Time

How does society approach the phenomenon of time? What is the temporal focus of human life? Do people focus on the past, present, or future? Is time relative or absolute? Cultures differ in how individuals perceive the duration and the immediacy of the service encounter. For example, Western cultures such as Germany are more rigid and precise about time compared to Eastern cultures where the concept of time varies. Service delivery times in Eastern cultures such as Saudi Arabia may expand or contract depending on such criteria as social status or familiarity between provider and customer. In Western cultures, time is more absolute and punctuality is an important requirement in service delivery. Thus, reservation systems in managing service demand are easier to implement in Western cultures.

Cultural Orientation Toward Others

How do people view relationships with others? Is individual welfare relatively more or less important than group welfare? Group-oriented cultures place less importance on self and more importance on social hierarchy and primary reference groups such as family and friends. When customers of higher status in such cultures are served ahead of their turn in a service queue, others in the queue are unlikely to see this as an injustice. Many Western cultures such as the United States take a strongly egalitarian approach to waiting and would reject any attempt to violate the "first come, first served" rule.

GLOBAL TRADE IN SERVICES

Services replaced manufacturing and agriculture as the driving force of the world economy long ago. In the industrialized world, services now represent more than half of gross domestic product (GDP) in most countries. Sharp increases in trade volume and foreign investment in services in recent years demonstrate a strong global presence across many service industries, especially health care, entertainment, and tourism. Global trade in banking, insurance, shipping, aviation, and communications plays a vital role in supporting trade in manufactured goods, too. Indeed, most trade in manufacturing could not occur without these and other critical facilitating services. The central bank of the European Union struggles with the sovereign debt of its weaker members and its single currency suffers turbulence in its valuation (see Spotlight 15.2).

SPOTLIGHT 15.2

Globalism and Financial Services

The global recession of 2008–2010 continues to change the landscape of global finance. The Great Recession began in December 2007, according to the National Bureau of Economic Research (NBER), a private nonprofit, nonpartisan research organization founded in 1920 to promote a greater understanding of how the economy works. The Business Dating Committee of NBER determined that the recession hit bottom in June 2009, and that the recession had lasted 18 months in the United States. Typically, a recession is a period of reduced economic or business activity. What is remarkable about this recession is not just that it was the longest since World War II, and the worst financial crises since the Great Depression of the 1930s, but that it was global in nature. Massive financial events—such as bank failures and troubled mortgage guarantors Freddie Mac and Fannie Mae in the United States and serious sovereign

debt problems in Greece, Ireland, Italy, Portugal, and Spain—forced central banks around the world to cut key interest rates, purchase troubled assets, inject massive amounts of liquidity in the marketplace, and take other unprecedented fiscal measures. The rating of countries by agencies such as Moody's, Standard and Poor's, and Fitch came under scrutiny and were the subject of reform. Indeed, the efficiency of financial markets was brought into question. UNCTAD concluded that globalization of trade and finance called for global cooperation and global regulation and answers to the question of how to revive and extend multilateralism in a globalizing world. Globalism is firmly in place. We live in an interconnected world, where individual nations living in isolation is a thing of the past.

Sources: **http://www.nber.org/cycles/sept2010.html #navDiv=6**; **http://www.ft.com/indepth/global-financial -crisis**; **http://unctad.org/en/Docs/gds20091_en.pdf**.

Several factors complicate measuring the service sector's global significance. First, as organizations grow in size, they frequently incorporate services previously supplied by independent firms (such as advertising, legal, and marketing services). This tendency leads organizations to overstate their manufacturing outputs and understate their service activity outputs.

Second, when a customer travels to a service provider's country to be served, the transaction is classified as foreign trade. Consider the case of students, patients, and tourists from foreign countries. The impact of revenues from foreign customers in such situations is rarely, if ever, fully reported in trade figures, primarily because the expenditures are difficult to capture.

Third, as more and more women enter the work force, many services previously performed in the household are now performed by professionals (e.g., daycare and laundry services). To further complicate international service comparisons, the economic impact of women in the labor force varies tremendously by country. As a result, the proportion of women working, the range of careers available to them, and the average salaries paid all differ widely.

Fourth, organizations often combine their services data with nonservices data, making it nearly impossible to obtain exact figures for each area's relative contribution to the overall economy. And consensus is rare on exactly what constitutes a service. Unfortunately, the categorization of services according to financial concepts such as balance of payments is open to wide interpretation. It is sometimes easier to define services by what they are not rather than what they are. Such a method is crude, and allows trade in services to slip through the cracks of the typical accounting system.

Regardless of these difficulties in measuring the global impact of services, the world's economy is almost certainly becoming a service economy. China, for instance, discovered that more than 40% of its economy was a service economy when it changed the way it measured GDP, which had been previously constructed to measure factory output rather than service output (*Economist* 2006).

One of the more intriguing aspects of a service economy is that exporting services is more complex than exporting physical goods. Essentially, we have only one way to export physical goods. We must ship them to the foreign market. However, the interactive nature of services compels those exporting them to consider different strategies. We export services in three primary ways: outbound service export, inbound service export, and teleservice export.

Outbound Service Export: Send the Service Provider to the Foreign Market

An **outbound service export strategy** involves sending the service provider to other countries. This approach has prevailed for fast-food restaurants and similar services. It is difficult to find a city anywhere in the world that does not already have a McDonald's **(http://www.mcdonalds.com),** Kentucky Fried Chicken **(http://www.kfc.com),** or Pizza Hut.

> An **outbound service export strategy** involves sending the service provider to other countries.

McDonald's, for instance, operates thousands of stores worldwide. Similarly, many professional services and health care services use this export strategy. For example, architects provide their services in the world market by traveling to other countries to design new buildings. Although not all of the architect's work might be done in the local country, a significant part of his service entails meeting with the client and supervising the construction site abroad.

Inbound Service Export: Bring the Foreign Customer to the Service Provider

An **inbound service export strategy** involves bringing foreign customers to the service provider's country

An **inbound service export strategy** involves bringing foreign customers to the service provider's country. This category includes tourism, health care, and educational services sold to those from other countries. For example, to receive a special or preferred medical treatment, many patients travel to health care providers in distant parts of the world. In addition, consider the record numbers of college students who leave their home country each year to study abroad. The United States, the United Kingdom, and Australia are the three most popular host countries for foreign students. As discussed earlier, this form of service delivery contributes to the underestimation of global trade in services.

Teleservice Export: Deliver the Service to Foreign Markets Electronically

A **teleservice export strategy** involves exporting services by delivering them electronically.

A **teleservice export strategy** involves exporting services by delivering them electronically. This export strategy serves telecommunications, financial, management consulting, and computer software design services. It is also used in facilitating services such as customer service hotline support for manufactured goods. Further, the explosion of technological innovations in the telecommunications industry has made services such as long-distance education and telemedicine possible. The real-time nature of services (i.e., their simultaneous production and consumption) requires interaction between service provider and customer and often makes teleservices exporting a desirable strategy. An organization need not allocate significant additional resources to gain electronic access to geographically distant markets. Telecommunications has rendered distance irrelevant for many services, especially those directed at people's minds and intangible assets.

Offshoring—a special case of outsourcing—is a form of teleservice export for the outsource firms. Just about any business function or process can be outsourced. Organizations outsource information technology and operations, including administration, customer service, finance, human resources, sales, and marketing. See Spotlight 15.3 for examples of offshoring from the United States to India. Organizations benefit from reduced operating costs, free up internal resources to focus on strategically important issues, and most importantly, gain access to world-class capabilities not otherwise locally available within the organization.

=== **SPOTLIGHT 15.3** ===

Offshoring Services in India

In 2011, the global offshoring revenues stood at $464 million. The most often outsourced services are logistics, sourcing, and distribution services; information technology (IT) services; and business process outsourcing (BPO), such as call centers, financial transaction processing, and human resources management. India is the leading country for offshore outsourcing. Firms in the United States employ engineers, marketers, analysts, and other jobs created in India and other countries. Indeed, the copy and permissions editorial services for this book were handled in an operation in Chennai, India. Almost two-thirds of India's offshoring services market comes from the United States; the rest comes from Europe. In 2009, the IT and BPO offshoring industry in India employed about 2.2 million people. India was the most favored country for offshoring in a survey of CFOs, followed by Indonesia and China. India's trade in services is growing much faster than trade in goods. Services were at 35% of total trade, making India the twelfth largest services exporter in the world at 2.7% of the world total in 2008–2009.

Sources: **http://www.plunkettresearch.com/outsourcing -offshoring-bpo-market-research/industry-statistics; http://www.sourcingline.com/outsourcing-location/india; http://www.rbi.org.in/scripts/bs_viewcontent.aspx ?Id=2249.**

ENTRY STRATEGIES FOR GLOBAL SERVICE MARKETS

A service organization may employ several strategies to enter global markets, but whichever strategy it adopts, it will seek to maximize opportunities while minimizing risks. Three of the most popular strategies for entering global service markets are foreign direct investment, licensing and franchising, and joint ventures.

Foreign Direct Investment

Foreign direct investment means that the service organization chooses to invest its resources directly in another country. Because sending service providers to the country is a major form of exporting services, the incidence of foreign direct investment is rather high. For example, Service Corporation International **(http:// www.sci-corp.com)**, the largest U.S. funeral home operator, expanded into Argentina, Australia, Canada, Chile, France, and the United Kingdom by purchasing funeral home operators in those countries. Retailers such as Laura Ashley **(http://www.lauraashley.com)**, the Body Shop **(http://www.thebodyshop-usa.com)**, and Benetton **(http://www.benetton.com)** have also fueled part of their growth with foreign direct investment.

Franchising

Franchising services is an increasingly popular strategy. Fast-food entrepreneurs such as McDonald's and Burger King **(http://www.bk.com)** pioneered franchising to expand their service operations around the world. Franchise systems have been particularly popular in retail industries as a means of globalizing. Franchising has been quite successful in the hotel industry, too. Wyndham Worldwide **(http://www.wyndhamworldwide.com)** owns the Days Inn **(http:// www.daysinn.com)**, Howard Johnson **(http://www.hojo.com)**, Ramada **(http:// www.ramada.com)**, and Super 8 **(http://www.super8.com)** brands.

Joint Ventures

Joint ventures are a common strategy that allows the service organization to contract with a local organization and thereby share the risks and rewards of the venture. For example, the global tours of Russian circus artists and U.S. rock artists are often handled by joint ventures. In addition, joint ventures are popular in the retail industry in cases where knowledge of the local market is essential. For example, leading U.S. retailer Walmart **(http://www.walmart.com)** arranged a joint venture with Bharti Enterprises **(http://www.bharti.com)** to open Walmart stores in India.

STANDARDIZATION VERSUS ADAPTATION OF GLOBAL SERVICES

Standardization means providing the same service in the same manner around the world.

Adaptation means tailoring service offerings to accommodate conditions in each local market.

Service organizations that conduct business globally must choose between strategies of standardization or adaptation. **Standardization** means providing the same service in the same manner around the world. In contrast, **adaptation** means tailoring service offerings to accommodate conditions in each local market. When determining strategies for a foreign market, a service organization must consider standardization and adaptation possibilities for every aspect of the service offering, including the design of the frontstage and backstage elements. Any of the frameworks discussed in Chapter 2 (services marketing mix, servuction, or service theater models) can serve as a guide.

Using the "services as theater" framework, Table 15.1 shows the types of issues a service organization must consider when choosing between standardization and adaptation. In such an exercise, the organization first considers *audience* issues, that is, whether the current service offering to targeted segments in the domestic markets would be just as appropriate in foreign markets. An organization might ask, "How do these customers differ from those we currently serve in our domestic markets?" For example, in some Western markets, a hotel might include elaborate facilities (restaurants, bars, meeting rooms, business services) well suited to business travelers who conduct most of their business in the hotel. However, in some Asian countries, business is usually conducted in the host's offices. Hotels in Asia can forgo these elaborate facilities unless a significant amount of international business is conducted in that location.

Second, the service organization reviews policies and practices regarding its *actors*. Personnel policies regarding selecting, hiring, training, and motivating

TABLE 15.1   Taking the Show Abroad—Standardization or Adaptation?

Services Theater Decisions	Examples of questions to determine the standardization or adaptation of services in other countries
Audience	Do we target the same types of customers? How do the customers differ? How should the core and supplementary products be adapted for the targeted segments in the foreign market? Do the customers interact differently among themselves than they do with the service providers (actors) in the foreign market?
Actors	Do we use the same types of personnel? What is the nature of the labor and management pool? How should we adapt training? What kinds of compensation and evaluation mechanisms would be appropriate in the particular foreign environment?
Setting	How should the setting be (re)designed, and what adaptations are necessary? Should we evaluate any cultural symbols in physical evidence such as signage, costumes, and props?
Performance	How should the process be (re)designed, and how should the acts and the scripts be adapted? Is the required technology infrastructure available? Are other options for delivering the performance available? Do the structure, content, and process of our service delivery fit the cultural, economic, legal, and industry norms?

© Cengage Learning

employees affect the customer–provider interaction and should be reviewed. For example, working in a hotel might carry a stigma in some cultures, making it difficult for a hotel chain in those locations to attract labor with the same skills as it employs in its domestic market. As a result, the hotel might have to adapt its personnel policies.

The third aspect to consider is the *setting*. A hotel might require a different design if cultural symbols suggest that different color schemes would better suit the physical facility. Every detail, from dining room napkins and carpets to furniture fabric, wall paint, and the corporate logo, should be reviewed. For example, red is considered an attractive color in China, green is a popular color in the Middle East, and orange or saffron is a sacred color in most parts of India. The signage may also require alterations. Hotels may choose to label the bathroom facility as a restroom, men's/women's room, WC, toilet, or bathroom, depending on the accepted practice. In South Asia, it is customary to eat with your fingers even when cutlery is provided. A Western restaurant opening there would have to conform to the custom of providing a wash area in the back of the dining room or finger bowls (bowls of water with a lemon slice) on the table for diners to wash their fingers after the meal.

Finally, the *performance* might require some rethinking. Actors' scripts may need adaptation to the foreign markets. For a hotel, the appropriate norms of greeting and receiving customers might vary by country: folded hands with palms together in India; a slight bow from the waist in the Far East. In most Eastern cultures, many activities may need to incorporate a religious ritual. From the first to the last step in the service blueprint, all actions and words are subject to rescripting and adaptation in global markets.

Standardization

A standardization strategy implies that aspects of the service offered in all markets are provided in the same manner. In general, the standardization of physical goods makes it easier to market them with a similar approach worldwide (Johansson 2005). The Coca-Cola Company (http://www.coca-cola.com) is often used as the classic example of a global brand. Many aspects of Coca-Cola's marketing efforts for its centerpiece product are similar in the nearly 200 countries around the world where the product is available. As already noted, standardization of services is more difficult because of their interactive nature. Most aspects of the frontstage, where the customer-provider interaction takes place, require careful review. Even though the backstage area of a service is generally conducive to a uniform design (e.g., computerization of hotel reservations, quality control of food preparation, or international air traffic control systems), the interactive and real-time nature of the service performance in the frontstage makes its standardization an arduous and probably undesirable undertaking.

Most of the economies of scale a company hopes to achieve by marketing a service globally are the result of standardization efforts (see Spotlight 15.4). When a service organization standardizes its backstage operations, it also improves its quality control. In many instances, backstage activities can be standardized with less accommodation of local circumstances than is typical in frontstage activities. Further, when standardized equipment and systematic procedures are used backstage, they generate predictability and control. Ultimately, uniform backstage operations create benefits for all customers and markets involved. For instance, the standardization of international air traffic control systems reduces the risks of flying for passengers everywhere. In this case, standardization includes the use of English by pilots and air traffic controllers to protect against mishaps that might accompany variable modes of communication. Although standardization can be beneficial, an organization should take care not to sacrifice the needs of its local customers simply for the sake of efficiency.

Adaptation

As the Burger King Spotlight example demonstrates, global service organizations may need to adjust their frontstage interactions with customers to reflect local market circumstances. Adaptation of a service requires attention to various

---

SPOTLIGHT 15.4

Burger King Worldwide

 Burger King (BK) (http://www.bk.com) found globalization relatively easy. The popular fast-food eatery operates more than 12,300 outlets in more than seventy-six countries around the world, serving more than 11 million guests daily from Hong Kong to the streets of Santiago, Chile, to rustic Pendleton, South Carolina.

In its global effort, Burger King standardized many aspects of its overall effort, such as layout design,

research and development, and some of its promotional activity. Yet, like many global organizations, BK leaves some room to accommodate local tastes and preferences. Whether it's offering a spicy chicken drumstick sandwich in Taiwan, a breakfast tamale in El Salvador or tapas and seasonal wraps in Spain, the fast-food restaurant tries to satisfy diverse dining preferences wherever it operates.

Source: **http://investor.bk.com/phoenix.zhtml?c=87140 &p=irol-IRHome** (accessed September 19, 2012).

aspects, large and small, pertaining to any local environment (Johansson 2005). The large issues include adjustment to obvious differences in local language, customer preferences, and business practices. The small details include adapting to subtle and seemingly minor cultural variations, such as different math notation symbols and different business hours. For example, the transition from the twentieth century to the twenty-first century challenged the notation systems for dates, starting with the year 2000 and continuing until 2032. In the United States, dates are abbreviated as month/day/year, as in 7/28/08. In most of the world, however, dates are abbreviated as day/month/year, with the same date being written as 28/07/08. To complicate the issue further, in some parts of the world, the order of abbreviation is year/month/day, which would be 08/07/28. Although such abbreviations caused confusion, until the end of 1999, they could usually be deciphered. However, the abbreviation of the years 2000 to 2032 increases confusion. A date written as 04/06/08 is of uncertain day, month, or year. Service organizations operating in multiple countries should be extra careful to adapt their convention and notation to the local culture.

Training service employees to be adaptable is also a major concern. Many services in economically developed nations such as the United States, Sweden, Japan, and Australia rely heavily upon highly skilled service personnel for their delivery. Health care, hairstyling, air transportation, education, automobile repair, retailing, and a wide range of other services are labor-intensive operations. Hence, skilled personnel are a critical element in the service quality of such services. Once hired, service personnel should undergo comprehensive training for adaptability. Both the technical and social skills discussed in earlier chapters should be emphasized so that service workers can carry out the important interpersonal aspect of their jobs as effectively as possible. Careful attention to identifying customer needs, developing a wide repertoire of potential responses to those needs, and cultivating a genuine desire to satisfy the customer should be the key concerns in training frontline service workers.

MULTILINGUAL SERVICE SYSTEMS

Related to the various considerations in the standardization versus adaptation decision are the challenges of working in a *multilingual* world. Multilingual service systems are increasingly crucial in meeting the varied needs of global customers, especially when a service system simultaneously serves customers who speak various languages. One of the authors visited the Vienna offices of the Ogilvy & Mather advertising agency **(http://www.ogilvy.com)** and observed an excellent model of multilingual service. Internally, all Ogilvy & Mather employees write and speak English. Externally, they always speak the native language of the customer. Hence, the Vienna office holds staff meetings in English but conducts visits to clients in German. In short, for any multilingual service system, the greatest concern should be accommodating the needs of the service system and the needs of the customer.

Service organizations can call on numerous methods to deliver services multilingually, such as developing appropriate signage, introducing automated systems, creating written communications, and hiring and training a multilingual staff that can handle the diverse language differences throughout the global market. A recent visit to the Hotel Miraparque **(http://www.miraparque.com)** in Lisbon, Portugal, revealed several aspects of effective multilingual systems. Signage was in Portuguese and English. The front-desk staff switched effortlessly

---

TABLE 15.2   Seven Key Questions of a Language Audit

- Is a unilingual approach alienating new prospects for your service?

- What signage, written communication, and electronic displays of information are currently available in other languages (and in which languages)?

- How good is the quality of each item of information in a foreign language?

- Are your English-language materials easy for nonnative English speakers to understand?

- If you use symbols in signage or written materials, are they widely recognized and understood around the world?

- In what languages are personnel who answer incoming telephone calls to your organization able to respond?

- Do you know what language skills each employee in your organization possesses?

Source: Lovelock, Christopher H. (1994), *Product Plus*, New York: McGraw-Hill, 310–312. Reprinted with the permission of the McGraw-Hill Companies.

---

from Portuguese to English to German to French as different guests arrived. Guest information in the room was printed in several languages. In the morning, the hotel provided an automated, multilingual wake-up call. As another example, non-English-speaking visitors to Edinburgh Castle, Scotland, can rent a tape player to give them a guided tour of the castle in their native language.

Several language considerations should be addressed by organizations serving global markets. These language issues are aptly summarized by Lovelock (1994) and presented in Table 15.2. The questions posed in the *language audit* presented in the table direct the global service organization to some potential trouble spots when dealing with a culturally diverse customer mix. Any service organization pursuing a global strategy should ask these same questions, substituting its native language for English as the base comparison. Finally, we should note that the adoption of English as the business language of the world does not mean that other languages will disappear (Naisbitt 1994). English may become everyone's second language, but native tongues will continue to prosper precisely because they bind those who speak them together. If anything, electronic communications technology makes it easier for those working far from home in a different country to continue using and practicing their native language via telephone, e-mail, and Web messaging.

TECHNOLOGY AND GLOBAL SERVICES

Technology is rapidly becoming an essential means of expanding the global reach of services. In particular, communications and transportation technology allow a service organization to operate in multiple countries while maintaining close contact with employees and customers. Technology has created more possibilities in all three service delivery options discussed earlier: sending the service provider to the foreign customer, bringing the foreign customer to the service provider, or delivering the service electronically. Technology is perhaps the single most influential force behind the globalization of markets. This book, especially Chapter 3, offers many examples of how technology allows service organizations to perform business functions in cross-national contexts that would otherwise have been

SPOTLIGHT 15.5

The Olympics: The Most International Service

Ever heard of Sochi? Situated in Russia on the Black Sea, with a population of just 400,000, Sochi will host the 2014 Winter Olympics. In 2018, Pyeongchang, South Korea, will host the XXIII Olympic Winter Games, having beaten out Munich, Germany, and Annecy, France, in the choice for host location. The International Olympics Committee (IOC) is the supreme decider of Olympic venues. As you can imagine, the selections are always fiercely contested. The XXXI Summer Olympics in 2016 will be held in Rio de Janeiro, Brazil.

The Summer and Winter Olympic games are held every four years. They alternate every two years between summer and winter games and are arguably the biggest and most complex events in the world. Over the two-week period in the London 2012 summer Olympics, for example, there were an average of 180,000 spectators each day and a total of 8.8 million tickets sold. About 10,500 athletes competed in 302 medal events. Over 21,000 accredited media communicated with 4 billion people. Among the folks who made this happen were 2,961 technical officials and 5,770 team officials, a workforce of 200,000 people, including 6,000 staff, 70000 volunteers, and 100,000 contractors. Try this on for size: about 1 million pieces of equipment—including 356 pairs of boxing gloves, 510 adjustable hurdles, 600 basketballs, and 2,700 footballs—were sourced for the games. About 14 million meals were served at the games, including 45,000 per day at the Olympic Village, where the athletes lived for the two weeks it lasted.

Former UK gold-medal distance runner Sebastian Coe was the chief organizer of the London games. Talk about pressure! How would you like his job? While the Olympics was the main event, there were other major accompanying events, such as a sixty-day festival of sport and culture across the UK and the Paralympic sports for the physically handicapped immediately following the summer games.

The ancient Olympic Games began in 776 B.C. They continued for nearly twelve centuries, until they were banned by Greek emperor Theodosius. The modern era for the Olympics began in 1894. Just as France is known for wine, Italy for fashion, and India for curried food, in the Olympics, Japan is known for Judo, India for field hockey, China for table tennis, Kenya for long distance running, and Jamaica for bobsledding. You may also recognize some 2012 Olympic icons: U.S. swimmer Michael Phelps and Jamaican track star Usain Bolt.

The IOC was created in 1894. The first Olympic Games of the modern era opened in Athens in April 1896, and the Olympic movement has not stopped growing ever since. Indeed, there are a total of 29,132 medalists in the modern era. The goal of the Olympic movement is "to contribute to building a peaceful and better world by educating youth through sport practised in accordance with Olympism and its values." The Olympics is probably the most international of all services.

Source: **http://www.olympic.org/** (accessed September 19, 2012).

---

impossible. Consider the example of the world traveler who withdraws funds in local currency from any bank's ATM anywhere in the world. This seemingly simple action is possible only because the traveler's local bank communicates electronically with banks in other countries via the NYCE, Cirrus, or other electronic funds transfer network. Now consider the business traveler who uses the Internet services of AT&T (**http://www.att.com**) to communicate with headquarters or home via e-mail from anywhere in the world where AT&T operates.

Summary and Conclusion

Few services trends are as significant as the globalization of the service economy. Spotlight 15.5 describes the Olympics, the most global of international services. Global expansion requires that service organizations familiarize themselves with the many cultural differences that might affect their global operations. Although we know that technological innovations have led to great increases in global services trade, measuring global services is difficult. Organizations export services in three ways: (1) sending the service provider to the foreign market; (2) bringing the foreign customer to the service provider; and (3) delivering the service to foreign markets electronically. The service organization can then choose to either globalize or localize the service offering. This decision involves systematically reviewing the various aspects of the service interaction framework. The organization must consider all environmental factors in the foreign market in deciding whether to standardize or adapt the services marketing strategy. The power of technology offers several options in global markets. Multilingual service systems must be created to meet the needs of service customers. Service organizations can use several strategies to enter global services markets, among them foreign direct investment, franchising, and joint ventures.

Exercises

1. Take an inventory of services you've bought in the past week.
    a. How many of those services were provided by local service organizations?
    b. How many of those services were provided by global service organizations?
2. Visit or e-mail a global service organization that operates in your city and ask to interview one of its managers. Discover the following:
    a. To what extent are the company's operations *standardized* everywhere in the world?
    b. To what extent have the company's operations *adapted* to their local market?
3. Search for a great local service organization in your community that might have the potential to export its services to other countries.
    a. What methods could it use to export its service?
    b. What strategy would you recommend?

Internet Exercise

Pick a large multinational service organization that operates in your city or area and visit its Web site:

1. In how many countries does this service organization operate?
2. What portion of its business is domestic versus foreign?
3. How many different language versions does the Web site offer?
4. What evidence can you find of service adaptation and standardization?

EXPLORE

Visit the companion site for this text at **www.cengagebrain.com** to explore key concepts in the service industry. You will find tools to help you expand your services marketing knowledge, including ACE self-tests, Web links to companies and organizations featured in this chapter, and much more!

References

Economist (2006, January 14), "Are You Being Served?," 61.

Hall, Edward T. (1959), *The Silent Language*, New York: Doubleday.

Hofstede, Geert (2001), *Culture's Consequences: Comparing Values, Behaviors, Institutions, and Organizations across Nations*, 2nd ed., Newbury Park, CA: Sage Publications.

Johansson, Johnny K. (2005), *Global Marketing: Foreign Entry, Local Marketing, and Global Management*, 4th ed., Chicago: McGraw-Hill/Irwin.

John, Joby (1996), "A Dramaturgical View of the Health Care Service Encounter: Cultural Value-Based Impression Management Guidelines for Medical Professional behavior," *European Journal of Marketing*, 30 (9), 60–74.

Kluckhohn, F. and F. Strodtbeck (1960), *Variations in Value Orientations, Evanston*, IL: Row, Peterson.

Lovelock, Christopher H. (1994), *Product Plus*, New York: McGraw-Hill.

Naisbitt, John (1994), *Global Paradox: The Bigger the World Economy, the More Powerful Its Smaller Players*, New York: Morrow.

Careers in Services

This appendix is designed to help you evaluate possible career choices in services and plan your career search process.

CAREER CHOICES IN SERVICES

College graduates can pursue marketing careers in a wide range of service industries. Organizational growth and marketing employment trends have been quite strong in virtually all service industries. Although several service industries have been slower to adopt marketing practices, most now actively engage in marketing and hire marketing personnel. Following are comments on careers in various service industries:

Health Care Services

Marketing positions are available in several types of health care organizations. Hospitals, clinics, nursing homes, and physician groups employ marketing personnel to market their services. Marketing in this service industry is rapidly becoming more sophisticated.

Financial Services

Marketing positions in financial services exist for banks, insurance companies, and brokerages. Despite significant consolidation and restructuring in this service industry, financial institutions are finding it essential to hire talented marketing personnel to survive the fierce competition in this service industry.

Professional Services

Marketers for professional service organizations work for accounting, legal, real estate, advertising, architectural, engineering, construction, and consulting firms, among others. Marketing positions are new to many of these services, but opportunities are increasing rapidly.

Knowledge Services

Marketing employees in educational services may work for a daycare center, tutoring organization, public or private elementary or high school, vocational school, college, university, or employee training firm. Marketing positions in research services may exist for a wide array of research firms, information services, or libraries. Greater competition in these service industries has fueled an increased reliance on marketing for both private and public services, although to a greater extent in the private sector.

Travel and Hospitality Services

Marketers in the leisure service industry work for hotels, resorts, restaurants, airlines, and travel agencies. This industry has seen significant growth, which has in turn led to substantial increases in marketing jobs.

Entertainment Services

Entertainment services entail a wide spectrum of opportunities for employment. Among these are sport organizations, such as automobile racing, basketball, baseball, soccer, and hockey. Employment growth in sports marketing has been strong. Entertainment services also encompass the arts, such as ballet, opera, music, theater, and museums. Despite the nonprofit status of many of these organizations, they often hire marketing personnel. Other entertainment services include special events, amusement parks, circuses, and festivals. Larger entertainment service organizations offer various marketing positions.

Information Services

Information services offer marketing positions in radio, television, cable, telephone, satellite, computer networking, and Internet companies. All of these information services, especially those that are Web-based, continue to grow significantly. Marketers in these service industries must possess sophisticated technology skills.

Supply Services

Marketing positions in channel, physical distribution, and rental and leasing services are in growing demand. Channel services include retailing, wholesaling, franchising, and agents. These services, especially retailing and franchising, have a long history of relying on marketing professionals. Physical distribution services include shipping and transportation. The rapid globalization of world trade has increased the demand for marketing personnel. Rental and leasing companies range from small organizations to large international chains. Many of the larger firms in this industry employ marketing managers.

Personal and Maintenance Services

Marketing opportunities for college graduates are more limited in personal and maintenance services because many of the organizations in this service industry are relatively small. Personal services include employment, hairstyling, fitness, morticians, and housecleaning. Repair and maintenance services include automobile maintenance, computer repair, plumbing, and lawn care. Only the largest of these organizations—for example, a chain of hairstyling salons or fitness clinics—would be likely to hire a marketing manager.

Governmental, Quasi-Governmental, and Nonprofit Services

Marketing is relatively new to these service industries. Marketing positions may exist in most of these types of organizations, but the job titles may not be labeled marketing. Governmental services include national, state, local, utility, and police departments. Quasi-governmental services include social marketing, political marketing, and postal services. Nonprofit services include religions, charities, museums, and clubs. Nonprofit service organizations have rapidly become more sophisticated in their marketing practices, which has led to employment growth in this area.

THE CAREER SEARCH PROCESS

To conduct a successful career search, you should follow a series of steps (see Table A.1). Planning your career search process begins with the introspective phase of deciding your personal objectives and preferences and determining your skills profile. First, review the questions, considerations, and issues involved in each step listed in Table A.1. This information will enable you to create a list of potential employers. Note the versatility and effectiveness of the theater framework in this exercise. As a potential recruit for a services marketing position, you are actually marketing a service offering—the skills and knowledge you have acquired from your education and experience and your personality characteristics. You will be marketing yourself as a services actor with particular skills

TABLE A.1   Theater Framework to Help Career Search

Services as Theater	Career Search Equivalents
Actor—Yourself	Your objectives and skills: • Career track—what is your overall career growth objective? • Industry choices—in what types of industries are you interested in working? • Functional areas—in what kinds of marketing or organizational functions and processes are you most interested? • Geographic areas—in which regions of the country or areas of the world are you interested in living?
Audience—Your Potential Service Employer's Clients	Potential employer/client needs: • Growth sectors—which sectors of the economy do you see as having growth potential? • Growth regions—in which regions of the country or areas of the world are these sectors most prevalent? • Skills gaps—what kinds of skills are most in demand by organizations seeking to better serve their own customers? • Trends in employment—what are current trends in the types of positions and job descriptions?
Performance—Your Role with the Service Employer	Specific contributions: • Competence areas—what functional skills, education, experience, and other qualifications do you have that are most relevant for your potential employers? • Growth potential—what potential do you have to grow with the organization? • Personal traits—what personal characteristics complement your areas of competence that are relevant to the kinds of roles you are looking to fill?
Setting—The Work Environment	Work location and environment: • Geographic flexibility—can the target employer locate you in your preferred geographic area? • Corporate culture—what will your colleagues be like, and does the nature and climate of the workplace suit your work style? • Cost of living and lifestyle—are the cost of living and the lifestyle commensurate with your personal preferences?

that make you a desirable performer in an organization's service production. The audience is the target market—in this case, the potential employer and its clients. You are looking for a setting that best meets your personal objectives and preferences. The search is, therefore, an attempt to obtain invitations to audition for a role in the services theater, either frontstage or backstage.

You proceed with your career search effort by analyzing the organization's need for people with skills such as yours. This *needs assessment* is the most logical starting point when it comes to marketing any product. To do this analysis, you must understand the issues in the employment market, in terms of both present and future trends. Just as these trends shape opportunities in the career marketplace, they inevitably also influence our personal lives. Individuals develop their life goals, consciously or unconsciously, by virtue of what they have learned through their education and experiences. Serious self-examination should reveal your own *personal goals and objectives.* You should now perform a *skills assessment,* that is, identify the specific skills you possess that will help you to achieve your personal objectives. Examine and organize aspects of your qualifications—education, work-related experience, and personal characteristics—and the contributions that you can make using these qualifications.

The next step is to conduct a *needs–skills evaluation* by matching your skills with the needs of the employment market. This exercise reveals how you might position your unique skills set for the specific requirements of the career marketplace; this is your *positioning strategy.* Once you have completed the evaluation, specify the types of career positions and types of industries you want to target—your target *employers.* This specification helps identify the organizations that match the profile of the types of industries that you deem desirable and that are likely to have suitable positions. Finally, you will design a plan—a *promotion campaign*—to deliver the specific message detailing your needs–skills concept to the appropriate individuals in the organizations you decided to target.

Trends in the Services Career Marketplace

As you have seen throughout the text, technological advancement ranks as one of the most significant phenomena of the latter part of the past century. Technology—specifically, the convergent technologies of computing and communicating—is responsible for the trend toward the digitization and the globalization of business activities. The information age has created a need for organizations to hire people knowledgeable about information technology. These skills are a necessary prerequisite for employment in some industries. Review the career opportunity pages of newspapers or the Web, talk with knowledgeable people, and use whatever sources you can locate to assess career trends involving types of industries, occupations, and opportunities you are targeting.

Needs Assessment

As the workplace changes, many opportunities are emerging in the form of new positions, new forms of organizations, and new types of industries. These opportunities require special skills and knowledge to meet the challenges they present. For example, more and more organizations are beginning to institute enterprise resource planning software, an integrated information system that connects all of the various information systems within an organization. Such organizations need employees who possess strong technology skills in addition to business education. Similarly, the trend toward globalization is reflected in the fact that more businesses participating in foreign markets are placing a premium on workers' foreign language skills.

Your Personal Objectives

Just as you assess the career marketplace to discover employers' needs, as a prospective employee, you must recognize and acknowledge your personal objectives. Identifying your objectives is a logical first step to designing your career plans. The objectives you determine can serve as a guide as you plan a career track over several years. You may wish to be an entrepreneur, or you may want to work in a particular type of service industry. Perhaps nonprofit organizations interest you, or maybe you wish to work in a specific geographic area. You may want to avoid certain types of service occupations because of the lifestyle they engender. Other career areas may be attractive, but only under certain conditions. For example, a career that involves computer software may be appealing but only if you can help customers determine their software requirements and design the computer programs that provide solutions to their needs. Sometimes a hobby may drive your personal objectives. For instance, you may have a flair for designing Web pages that you now want to embrace as a key aspect of your professional position.

Skills Assessment

Achieving your personal objectives requires putting your skills to use. It is important to recognize and articulate your specific skills. Review the chapters in the text and select the types of managerial functions that you believe will be your strengths. What is the sum of your qualifications? Examine your aptitude based on your performance in academic work as well as the practical experience you may have developed in the workplace. For example, if you have worked as a customer service representative, your customer interaction skills count as a qualification that can easily be added to your formal university education. If your abilities are in great demand, or if your skills are better than those of other candidates, your prospects for employment in the service sector could be excellent.

Competitive Positioning

Your task is to identify your competitive advantage over others also in the employment marketplace. To do this, you must establish the special features of your skill set in relation to the various opportunities that present themselves in the career marketplace. First, match the results of the general needs assessment you conducted with those of your particular skill assessment. Now select the points of differentiation that potential employers are likely to find meaningful and relevant. Simply being different is not adequate; what matters is making your differentiation attractive to an employer. For example, an employer who has a global market presence is likely to select an applicant who has multiple language skills or has perhaps lived in other countries.

Target Employers

Specify the types of industries, organizations, and positions where your particular competitive positioning (needs–skills concept) will likely be most successful. Where will your contributions stand out from those of other candidates with similar skills sets. Consider career marketplace trends and select organizations either in a growth area or with strong performances and good prospects. Consider your personal objectives and preferences against such organizational issues as corporate culture, reputed treatment of employees, worker retention, and other issues important to you. For example, if you are interested in working in the financial services sector, you might weigh the dress code and formality of the environment against employee perks, opportunities for advancement, and job security.

A variety of Internet Web sites list job openings. Some of them are employment search firms. Among the most useful sites are **http://www.careerbuilder.com**, **http://www.idealist.org/info/jobs, http://www.nationjob.com, http://www.marketingjobs .com,** and **http://www.jobsite.com**

Promoting Yourself

Construct a promotional message that best represents your competitive positioning and the features of your skill set. The specific message—as stated in your cover letter and represented in your résumé (or "biodata," as it is called in some parts of the world)—should reflect how your skill set fits the needs of the potential employer. It must quickly make clear to the reader how you might be able to contribute to the goals of the target employer. Next, determine the best means of reaching the decision makers at these organizations who select and hire individuals to fill their positions. How can you ensure that your message will reach them? You have a variety of options, including posting your résumé on the Internet (e.g., **http://www.monster.com**) or sending your résumé to specific individuals in organizations via e-mail and/or regular mail. You might even try targeted telephoning to prospective employers. Using a combination of methods allows you to benefit from the advantages of each in delivering your message on target.

Follow-Up

Even after your career search secures a position, you will need to continually keep abreast of trends in the industry and the changing needs of employers. The label "career search," as opposed to "job search," implies that finding a job is not the end of the search process but just one step in your career development. Therefore, keeping track of opportunities is a necessary activity for long-term career growth. Scan the needs of the employment marketplace. Continue to review and consider changes in your personal objectives. Update your portfolio of personal skills, and strive to be the best at what you do. Take advantage of professional development opportunities. Be true and loyal to your employer as long as you can contribute to the organization's goals and as long as your employer can contribute to your growth and the accomplishment of your personal objectives. As your personal objectives change and your employer can no longer meet your needs, anticipate having to alter your career path. Update your résumé regularly. In sum, assess the trends and needs of the employment marketplace constantly, review and keep your own objectives and skills current, and maintain a dynamic view of your career at all times.

One of the most effective means of professional development is joining and participating in professional marketing associations. The American Marketing Association (AMA) (**http://www.marketingpower.com**) is the oldest marketing association in the world. The AMA publishes many of the most respected marketing publications and sponsors numerous conferences. If you live in a major North American metropolitan area, your city may have an AMA professional chapter. In addition to the AMA, numerous specialized marketing associations focus on nearly every aspect of marketing (advertising, direct marketing, sales, etc.) or industry (health care marketing, professional services marketing, tourism marketing, etc.). Also, various local marketing associations are active in cities and countries around the world. All of these afford you an opportunity for continuous learning and/or personal contacts with potential employers. They may be a good place for you to test the career search process discussed here.

Here are the Web sites for several professional associations that may be useful in your career search process:

American Health Care Association (**http://www.ahcancal.org**)

Association for Financial Professionals (**http://www.afponline.org**)

The American Finance Association (**http://www.afajof.org**)

American Financial Services Association (**http://www.afsaonline.org**)

American Accounting Association (**http://aaahq.org**)

National Association of Realtors® (**http://www.realtor.org**)

The Advertising Association (**http://www.adassoc.org.uk**)

Architectural Association School of Architecture (**http://www.aaschool.ac.uk**)

American Engineering Association (AEA) (**http://www.aea.org**)

The Associated General Contractors (AGC) of America (**http://www.agc.org**)

National Educational Association (**http://www.nea.org**)

Marketing Research Association (**http://www.marketingresearch.org**)

The Management Association (**http://www.mranet.org**)

American Educational Research Association (**http://www.aera.net**)

Market Research Society (**http://www.mrs.org.uk**)

U.S. Travel Association (**http://www.ustravel.org**)

Travel and Tourism Research Association (**http://www.ttra.com**)

United States Specialty Sports Association (**http://www.usssa.com**)

College Art Association (**http://www.collegeart.org**)

National Art Education Association (**http://www.naea-reston.org**)

PLASA: Worldwide Standards for the Entertainment Industries (**http://www.plasa.org**)

Telecommunications Service in Rural America (**http://www.fcc.gov/cgb/rural**)

United States Telecom Association (**http://www.ustelecom.org**)

National Cable & Telecommunications Association (**http://www.ncta.com**)

CTIA: The Wireless Association **(http://www.ctia.org)**

Truck Renting and Leasing Association **(http://www.trala.org)**

American Rental Association **(http://www.ararental.org)**

Equipment Leasing and Finance Association **(http://www.elfaonline.org)**

Aerobics and Fitness Association of America **(http://www.afaa.com)**

The National Funeral Directors & Morticians Association, Inc.
(http://www.nfdma.com)

Plumbing-Heating-Cooling Contractors Association (PHCC)
(http://www.phccweb.org)

Automotive Service Association **(http://www.asashop.org)**

Nonprofit Services Center **(http://www.nonprofitservices.org)**

GLOSSARY

Adaptation—means tailoring service offerings to accommodate conditions in each local market.

Approach environment—An **approach environment** is a setting in which the customer feels comfortable and wants to spend time.

Avoidance environment—is a setting that the customer finds undesirable and uninviting.

Boundary spanners—are the frontstage employees who link an organization with its customers; they represent the service in the customers' eyes.

Complexity—The greater the **complexity** of the service, the greater the number of steps in its service blueprint.

Critical Incident Technique—The **Critical Incident Technique** is a research method used to identify and explain memorable and significant aspects of service experiences.

Customer compatibility management—is the practice of selecting the appropriate customer mix to encourage satisfying customer-to-customer relationships when customers interact, yet have different backgrounds or different reasons for using the service.

Customer delight—occurs when customer expectations are significantly exceeded.

Customer mix—The **customer mix** refers to the array of people of differing ages, genders, socio-economic backgrounds, knowledge or experience, ethnicity, and so on, who patronize a service organization.

Customer rage—is the expression of mild to extreme anger about some aspect of the service experience.

Customer service—refers to all customer–provider interactions other than proactive selling and the core product delivery offering that facilitate the organization's relationship with its customers.

Defensive strategy—is a rapid responses used to protect the organization from environmental threats.

Discretionary effort—is the difference between the maximum effort one can bring to a task and the minimum effort needed simply to get by.

Divergence—The greater the **divergence** of the service, the greater the amount of flexibility or variability involved in any particular step in the service blueprint.

Empowerment—is the management practice of sharing information, rewards, knowledge, and power with frontline service employees so that they can better respond to customers' needs and expectations.

Environmental scanning—is the process of carefully monitoring external environments for changes that pose threats or opportunities to the service organization.

e-servicescape setting—An **e-servicescape setting** is any Web site on the Internet. E-servicescape settings are subject to the same concepts that apply to managing the tangible evidence of a conventional service environment.

Hyperactive strategy—is a hasty response to environmental changes.

Inbound service export strategy—An **inbound service export strategy** involves bringing foreign customers to the service provider's country.

Inseparability—For most services, the production and consumption of the service occur simultaneously.

Intangibility—Most services cannot be seen, touched, held, or put on a shelf.

Interactive imagery—uses pictorial representations, verbal associations, and letter accentuations that combine an organization's name and its service to establish a strong link between service name and performance in customer minds.

Internal marketing—is the policy of treating employees as internal customers of the service organization, responding to employees' needs or wants, and promoting the organization and its policies to the employee.

Market segmentation—is the division of a heterogeneous market into homogeneous segments.

Marketing strategy—is the process of adjusting controllable marketing factors to cope with or exploit uncontrollable environmental forces.

Moment of truth—A **moment of truth** is any contact point with a service organization that the customer uses to evaluate the service delivery.

Mystery shopping—is an unobtrusive method of gathering data in which people pose as bona fide shoppers to observe and collect information about an organization's service performance.

Offensive strategy—is a rapid response employed to capture opportunities.

Optimum capacity—refers to the number of customers who can be effectively handled under ideal conditions.

Outbound service export strategy—An **outbound service export strategy** involves sending the service provider to other countries.

Perishability—Most services cannot be produced and stored before consumption. They exist only at the time of their production.

Positioning—is how marketers attempt to create favorable customer perceptions of their product in relation to all other products.

Price bundling—links several service offerings or features into one attractive price to give different customer segments a packaged service offering.

Proactive strategy—is a rapid response to environmental changes.

Profit-oriented—objectives stress generating high returns on the service's investments in resources and labor.

Promotional mix—The **promotional mix** consists of advertising, sales promotions, personal selling, publicity, and public relations.

Reactive strategy—is a slow response to environmental changes.

Rental/Access—Services provide temporary possession or access instead of ownership.

Service—Service is "a deed, a performance, an effort."

Service blueprint—A **service blueprint** is a graphic representation of the essential components of the service performance, both frontstage and backstage.

Service capacity—has three aspects: (1) the **physical facility** in which the service is performed or rendered; (2) the **personnel** whose labor and skill level create the service; and (3) the **equipment** that enables the service to occur.

Service encounter—is the period of time during which the customer directly interacts with some aspect of the service organization, often in a marketer-controlled environment.

Service guarantee—A **service guarantee** is a promise to compensate customers if the service delivery fails to meet established standards.

Service quality—from the provider's perspective means the degree to which the service's features conform to the organization's specifications and requirements; from the customer's perspective it means how well the service meets or exceeds expectations.

Service recovery—is the effort an organization expends to win back customer goodwill once it has been lost due to service failure.

Service script—A **service script** is a chronologically ordered representation of the steps that make up the service performance from the customer's point of view.

Service setting—A **service setting**, sometimes called a **servicescape**, includes all aspects of the physical environment in which the service provider and customer interact.

Services marketing mix—adds three new Ps— participants, physical evidence, and process of service assembly—to the four Ps of the traditional marketing mix.

Services theater framework—involves the same theatrical elements as a stage production: actors, audience, setting, frontstage, backstage, and a performance.

Servicescape—See **service setting.**

Servqual—is a scale designed to measure customer perceptions of service quality along five key dimensions: tangibles, reliability, responsiveness, assurance, and empathy of the service provider.

Smoothing demand—means shifting patronage to times when a service's productive capacity is underused and deflecting or discouraging patronage when it is oversubscribed.

Social skills—are the manner in which service employees interact with customers and fellow workers.

Standardization—means providing the same service in the same manner around the world.

Tangibilizing the service—means making the service more concrete, thus enabling customers to understand it better.

Technical skills—are the proficiency with which service employees perform the tasks associated with their position.

Teleservice export strategy—A **teleservice export strategy** involves exporting services by delivering them electronically.

Upside-down organization—The **upside-down organization** inverts the typical organizational chart by putting frontline personnel at the top, middle management in the middle, and the CEO at the bottom.

Value—is an assessment of the benefits of a service versus the costs associated with it.

Variability—It is hard for a service organization to standardize the quality of its service performance.

Vividness strategy—A **vividness strategy** is an advertising approach that uses concrete language, tangible objects, and dramatization techniques to tangibilize the intangible.

Volume-oriented—objectives stress processing large numbers of customers or their possessions.

Zone of intolerance—is the range between desired service and adequate service; it is influenced by such factors as predicted service, service promises, word-of-mouth communications, past experiences, service alternatives, personal needs, and situational factors.

NAME INDEX

Armstrong, Louis, 80

Berra, Yogi, 48
Berry, Len, 90
Berry, Leonard, 174
Bolt, Usain, 239
Buffet, Warren, 145

Coe, Sebastian, 239

de Bono, Edward, 208
Disney, Walt, 64

Earl, Robert, 197

Gates, Bill, 197

Hall, Edward, 228

Lovelock, Christopher H., 50–52

Paes, Eduardo, 191
Patrício, Lia, 61
Pei, I. M., 48
Phelps, Michael, 239

Sewell, Carl, 89, 166
Shostack, Lynn, 8
Smith, Fred, 197
Stanislavsky, Konstantin, 87

Tatelman, Barry, 145
Tatelman, Eliot, 145
Theodosius, 239
Turner, Ted, 197

ORGANIZATION INDEX

Aer Arann, 163
Air rage, 105
AirTran, 141
Amazon.com, 35, 61, 74, 206
American Airlines, 40, 178
American Express, 163
American Marketing Association (AMA), 249
America's Disney World, 64
Ancestry.com, 61
Angie's List, 161, 162f
A&P, 195
Apple Computer, Inc., 6, 20
Approach environment, 69
Arthur Andersen, 199
AT&T, 140, 198, 239
Avoidance environment, 69

Barnes & Noble, 51, 61
Bella Sky Hotel, 203
Benetton, 233
Benihana, 73
Bharti Enterprises, 234
Bizrate, 180
Boots and Coots, 7
Body Shop, 233
British Airways, 133, 157
Broadmoor Hotel, 111, 126
Burberry, 128
Burger King, 53, 138, 233, 236
Business Dating Committee (NBER), 230

Carnival Line, 68
Chicken Maharaja Mac, 194
Chick-Fil-A, 139
Citibank, 136, 181
Club Med, 69
CNN, 197
CNN International, 227
Coca-Cola Company, 236

Days Inn, 234
Delta Air Lines, 69, 135
Denny's, 87
Deutsche Bahn, 27
Disneyland Paris, 89
Disney World, 64, 202, 209

Domino's Pizza, 137
Doubletree Hotel, 153
Dutch East India Company, 227

eBay, 35, 61
Energy and Utilities Solution Lab, 191
Enron, 199
Essex House Hotel, 198

Facebook, 127, 206
Fannie Mae, 230
FedEx, 40, 61, 84, 140, 158, 197
Fitch, 230
Flickr, 124
Flyaway Farms and Kennels, 92
Forbes, 191
Fotolog, 124
Freddie Mac, 230
Frugal Fannie's, 207
Fuddruckers, 67
Furniture.com, 197

Global Crossing, 199
Google Inc., 35, 141, 178

Hard Rock Cafe, 66–67, 197, 207
Harley-Davidson, 209
Harley-Davidson Café, 67
Harley Owners Group (HOG), 209
Hertz, 174
Holiday Inn, 111, 168
Hollywood, 207
Home Depot, 51, 79
Hooters Restaurant, 212
Hotel Miraparque, 237
Howard Johnson, 234
Hyatt, 198
Hyatt Hotels, 24

IBM, 191–192, 200, 212, 227
IKEA, 207
Institute for Electronic Government, 191
Intelligent Operations Center, 191
International Olympics Committee (IOC), 239

Jiffy Lube, 28, 137
Jolly Trolly, 77
Jordan's Furniture, 145–146, 174

Kentucky Fried Chicken, 231

Lands' End, 61
La Quinta, 74
Laura Ashley, 233
L.L.Bean, 22, 61, 156
London Underground, 68
Louvre Museum, 47–49, 64, 77, 95

Malcolm Baldrige National Quality Award, 57, 150
Marriott Hotels, 24, 74, 123, 181, 198
Mary Kay, 174
McDonald's, 53, 66, 88, 138, 181, 194, 231, 233
Meals on Wheels, 137
Meineke, 158
Merrill Lynch, 134, 199
Microsoft, 197
Minimundus, 67
Minus 5 Ice Bar, 128
Moody's, 230
Motel, 111
MySpace, 38, 141
Mystery shopping, 82

National Association for the Education of Young Children, 155
National Bureau of Economic Research (NBER), 230
Natural Resource Solution Centers, 191
NCAA, 141
New Orleans Police Department, 97
Nordstrom, 25, 79, 81, 84, 210
Novotel, 66

Ogilvy & Mather, 237
Olive Garden, 127, 181
OneGreatFamily.com, 61

Pizza Hut, 141, 227, 231
Planet Hollywood, 67, 207
Priceline.com, 133
Prudential Insurance, 134

Radisson Hotels, 156
Ramada, 234

Red Adair, 7
Ritz-Carlton Hotels, 51, 57, 79, 80, 83, 84, 127, 140, 150, 206
Romano's Macaroni Grill, 87
Royal Bank of Canada, 198

SAS. *See* Scandinavian airline (SAS)
Scandinavian airline (SAS), 83, 127, 168
Schiphol Airport, 68
Sears, 196
SeaWorld, 202
Service Corporation International, 233
Sewell Cadillac, 89, 166
Shell Oil, 227
Sheraton Hotels, 66
Shutterfly, 124
Singapore Airlines, 88
Smarter Cities Technology Centre, 191

Smugmug, 124
Snapfish, 124
Southwest Airlines, 80, 81, 96, 135, 174, 208
Sprint, 163
Standard and Poor's, 230
Stew Leonard's, 161
Strategic Planning Institute, 152
Super 8, 234

Travelers Insurance, 134
Travelocity, 40
Twitter, 127

UNCTAD, 230
United Nations, 227
United Parcel Service (UPS), 133
Universal Studios Florida, 198
US Airways, 142

U.S. Department of Health and Human Services, 155
U.S. Postal Service, 12, 50, 220

Veterinary Pet Insurance, 12
Visa, 227
Visit Ancestry.com, 61

Walmart, 196, 198, 234
Walt Disney Company, 64, 89, 130
Weather Channel, 34
Wembley Stadium, 104
Wendy's, 138
Westin Hotels, 70
Wikipedia, 206
WorldCom, 199
Wyndham Worldwide, 234

Yahoo!, 141
YouTube, 127, 141

SUBJECT INDEX

Page numbers followed by "*f*" refer to figure; and those followed by "*t*" indicate table.

Activities, cultural orientation toward, 229
Actors, 28, 31, 234, 235*t*
Adaptation, of global services, 234, 236–237
Advance fare, 114
Advertising, 130
    to employee, 135
    objectives, 132
    the service, 132–137
    services, guidelines for, 133–135
AIDA (attention, interest, desire, and action), 132
Air rage, 105
Allocated overhead cost, 118
Amsterdam Airport Schiphol, 68*f*
Apology, 169
Approach environment, 69
    vs. avoidance environment, 69
Arab Spring, 228
Assessment
    needs, 246–247
    skills, 247
Atmospherics, 65
Audience, 28, 31, 234, 235*t*
Augmented product, 53
Automated delivery mechanisms, 207
Automated idiocy, 43
Auto rental industry, 218
Avoidance environment, 69
    vs. approach environment, 69

Backstage, 26, 28, 32
    vs. frontstage decisions, 73–74
Benchmarking, 201
Benihana, 103
Blueprint, service, 59–61, 60*f*
Boundary spanners, 79
Brand equity, 147
Breakeven analysis, 120
Breakeven point, 120
Business analytics, 191
Business process outsourcing (BPO), 233
Business-to-business services, 14
Business travelers, 203, 213, 215

Call centers, 233
Capacity, maximum *vs.* optimum, 222–224
Capacity-constrained services, 217
Career choices
    in entertainment services, 244
    in financial services, 243
    in governmental, quasi-governmental, and nonprofit services, 244
    in health care services, 243
    in information services, 244
    in knowledge services, 243
    in personal and maintenance services, 244
    in professional services, 243
    in services, 243–244
    in supply services, 244
    in travel and hospitality services, 243
Career search process, 245–250, 245*t*
Channel services, 244
Chase demand, 217–218, 219*t*
Christmas, 218, 220
CityOne (sim-style game), 200
Civil uprisings, social media and, 228
Communication
    integrated marketing communications (IMC), 126–127
    marketing communications and services, 128–129
    word-of-mouth, 133–134, 146
Communications technology, 197, 200
Competition, surpass your, 208
Competition-based approach of pricing, 117
Competitive advantage, service strategies for, 208
Competitive environment, 197
Competitive positioning, 247
Complexity, 60
Concrete language, 136
Consumer services, 8, 12
Contribution margin, 119
Convenience services, 50
Cost-based approach of pricing, 116
Cost–benefit analysis, 117
Costuming service employees, 88–90
Courtyard hotels, 181

Critical incident technique, 176, 181–184
Cross-train personnel, 81–82
Cultural conditions, 193
Cultural environment, 199
Cultural orientation, 229–230
    toward activities, 229
    toward nature, 229
    toward time, 229
Culture
    defined, 228
    dimensions of, 229
    group-oriented, 229
    high-context, 228
    low-context, 228
    services and, 228–230
Customer-based approach of pricing, 116
Customer compatibility management, 103–105, 104*f*
Customer delight, 148
Customer education, 103
Customer equity, 146
Customer interfaces
    steps for improving, 44
    technological weak links in, 42–44
Customer loyalty, 146, 147
    impact on profit potential, 147*t*
    service recovery effects on, 164*f*
Customer-managed relationships (CMR), 209
Customer mix, 101
Customer-oriented marketing strategy, 192
Customer-provider link, 149
Customer rage, 105
    managing, 105–107
Customer relationship management (CRM), 146, 209
Customer relationships, customer service as an opportunity to enhance, 162–163
Customers, 206
    curating information of, 41–42
    empowering, 40
    high cost of lost, 165–167
    perspective, 148
    satisfaction, 147
    selecting and training, 100–105

Customer satisfaction link, 149
Customer scripts, 103
Customer segmentation, with price
     bundling, 121
Customer service, 160–161
     as an information resource, 161
     as an input for service design
          improvements, 162–163
     as an opportunity to enhance
          customer relationships,
          162–163
     developing a culture, 163–164
     as strategic function, 161–163
Customer-to-customer interactions,
     97–98
Customer-to-employee interactions,
     99–100
Customer training
     guidelines, 100–102
     tools, 102–103
Customization, 54–57
Cyberspace, 47, 65

Defensive strategies, 196–197, 196f
Delivery, jazz your, 209–210
Demand, 207
     chasing with service capacity,
          216–218
     inventory, 221
     predictable fluctuations of, 214
     smoothing to fill service capacity,
          219–222
     strategies, 219t
Demand-based pricing systems, 207
Demand cycle, seasonal, 214
Demand/price elasticity, 118
Demographic conditions, 193
Demographic environment, 199
Digital intelligence, 191
Direct costs, 118
Discretionary effort, 90, 90f
Disservice, 161
Divergence, 60
Double-barreled training, 81
Double deviation, 164
Dramatization techniques, 136
Dress codes, employees, 89
Dual-income families, 193, 199
Duration, of service setting, 66

Early-bird prices, 114
Economic conditions, 193
Economic environment, 197
Elasticity of demand/price, 118

Electronic mail (e-mail), 37
Electronic surveys, 182–183f
Emotions
     emotional side of services, 61–62
Empathy, 170
Employees, 205–206
     addressing poor performance, 83
     advertising to, 135
     dress codes, 89
     empowering through technology,
          39–40
     equally importance of all service
          employees, 79–80
     importance of service employee,
          78–79
     reports, 174, 180
Empowerment, 84–86
     benefits of, 84–85
     costs of, 85–86
Entertainment services, 244
     career choices in, 244
Entrepreneurial service organizations,
     194
Environment
     ethical and legal, 197–199
     scanning, 194–200
     social, cultural and demographic,
          199
     technology, 199–200
Environmental conditions, strategic
     adjustments to, 195–196, 196f
Environmental consciousness, 198
Environmental scanning, 194–200,
     195f
Equipment, 217–218
E-service quality, 152
E-servicescape setting, service setting
     as an, 74–75
Ethical environment, 197–199
European Union, 230
Expected product, 53
Expedia, 43
Experimental field testing, 177, 180–181

Fan rage, 105
Fast-food entrepreneurs, 233
Financial services, 243
     career choices in, 243
Financial transaction processing, 233
Fixed costs, 118
Focus groups, 177, 180
Follow-up, 171
Foreign direct investment, 233
Formal queuing system, 221, 221f

Four Ps of traditional marketing mix,
     193
Franchising, 233–234
Frontstage, 25, 28, 31
     vs. backstage decisions, 73–74
Funeral homes, 220

Gaps model of service quality,
     153–156, 153f
Global 2000 (Forbes' list), 191
Globalism, 230
Global service markets, 233–234
     entry strategies for, 233–234
     foreign direct investment and, 233
     franchising and, 233–234
     joint ventures and, 234
Global services
     standardization vs. adaptation,
          234–235, 235t
     technology and, 238–239
Global services organizations, 198
Goals, advertising, 132
Great Depression of 1930s, 195, 230
Great Recession, 230
Green marketing, 198
Gross domestic product (GDP), 230
Group-oriented cultures, 229

Hammer, law of, 43
Health care services, 243
     career choices in, 243
Heterogeneity, 204t, 205
High-context cultures, 228
Hi-tech vs. hi-touch, 43–44
Home away from home, service
     setting as workers', 69–70
Hurricane Katrina, 199
Hyperactive strategy, 195–197, 196f
     defined, 196

IBM Smarter Planet initiative, 200
IMC. See Integrated marketing
     communications (IMC)
Inbound service exports, 232
Inbound service export strategy, 232
Indirect costs, 118
Individualism, 229
Industrial (manufacturing), 35
Information
     curating customer, 41–42
     customer service as resource, 161
     information age and, 35–37
     services, 35
     technology, 36–37

Information services, 244
    career choices in, 244
Information technology, 195,
    199–200
Informing, 130
Inseparability, 10–11
Intangibility, 9–10, 198, 204t, 205
Intangible dominant services, 7
    vs. tangible dominant physical
        goods, 8, 8f
Integrated marketing
    communications (IMC), 126–127
Intelligent agents, 40
Interactive imagery strategy, 137
Internal communications gap, 154
Internal marketing, 92
International Olympics Committee
    (IOC), 239
Internet
    promoting services on, 141–142
    service performances and, 61
Inventory demand, 221
ISO 9000, 148

Jazz music, 209
Jazz musicians, 209
Joint ventures, 234

Knowledge services, 243
    career choices in, 243

Labor cost, 85
Language audit, 238
Last inch, 44
Law of the hammer, 43
Legal environment, 197–199
Letter accentuation, 137
Lovelock's classification, 14, 15t
Lovelock's service petals, 50–52, 51f
Low-context cultures, 228

Malcolm Baldrige National Quality
    Award, 148
Management by walking around
    (MBWA), 169, 178
Market expansion strategy, 193–194
Market information gap, 153
Marketing communications, services
    and, 128–129
Marketing employment trends, 243
Marketing factors, controllable, 192
Marketing mix strategy, 204–205, 204t
    services marketing approach, 204
    services operations approach, 205

Marketing strategy
    customer-oriented, 192
    defined, 192
    overview of, 192–194
Marketing tool, service setting as an,
    70–74
Market segmentation, 203
Maximum capacity, 222–224
    vs. optimum capacity, 222–224
MBWA. *See* Management by walking
    around (MBWA)
Mixed price bundling, 121
Moment of truth, 167
    impact analysis, 177, 184–185, 184t
Mona Lisa, 47
Mortality rates, 178
Multilingual service systems,
    237–238
Multinational organizations, 227
Mystery shopping, 82, 177, 179

Nature, cultural orientation toward, 229
Needs assessment, 246–247
Needs–skills evaluation, 246
Net profit, 119
Networking, 39
Nonprofit service organizations, 244

Observational data collection, 178
Observational techniques, 176–179
Offensive strategies, 196–197, 196f
Offshoring, 232–233
    in India, 233
Olympics, 191
Operational tool, service setting as an,
    66
Opportunities
    unarticulated, 193–194, 194f
    unserved, 193–194, 194f
Optimizing service experience
    quality, 105, 105f
Optimum capacity, 222–224
    defined, 222–223
    vs. maximum capacity, 222–224
Organizational growth, 243
Orientation tool, service setting as an,
    67
Outbound service export strategy,
    231–232

Parking rage, 105
Participants, 25, 128
Peachtree Road Race, 218
Performance, 28, 31, 207, 235, 235t

addressing poor employee, 83
    dramatize, 208–210
Perishability, 10, 198, 204t, 205
Personal and maintenance services,
    244
    career choices in, 244
Personal objectives, 247
Personal selling, 131
    services and, 139–140
Personnel, 217
Petals, 50–51
Physical evidence, 24–25, 25f, 128
Physical facility, 217
Physical goods, tangible dominant, 6
Physical goods marketing , services
    marketing differ from, 7
Pictorial representations, 137
PIMS. *See* Profit Impact of Market
    Strategy (PIMS)
Place, 128
Positioning, 202–203, 247
    competitive, 247
    defined, 202
    service segmentation and,
        202–203
Postalspace, 65
Potential product, 53
Predictable fluctuations, 214
Price, 128
Price bundling, 120–123
    customer Segmentation with, 121
    defined, 120
    mixed price bundling, 121
    pure price bundling, 121
Price/demand elasticity, 118
Pricing
    additional considerations,
        123–124
    competition-based approach of,
        117
    cost-based approach of, 116
    customer-based approach of, 116
    early-bird prices, 114
    objectives and approaches,
        116–117
    service offerings, 112
    service price and value, 117–118
    three C's of, 117
Primary reference groups, 230
Proactive strategy, 195–196, 196f
    defensive strategy, 196–197
    defined, 196
    forms of, 196
    offensive strategy, 196–197

Process of service assembly, 25, 134
Product, 128
  and place or distribution, 220
Product evaluation continuum, 152*f*
Professional services, 243
  career choices in, 243
Profit Impact of Market Strategy
  (PIMS), 147
Profit-oriented, 116
Promotion, 128
Promotional mix, 130–132
Promotion campaigns, 246
Props, 31
Provider's perspective, service quality
  from, 148
Publicity
  public relations and, 137
  services and, 140–141
Public relations, and publicity, 132
Pure price bundling, 121

Random fluctuation, 213
RATER, 152
Reactive strategy, 195–196, 196*f*
  defined, 195
Receipt analysis, 178
Recovery needs, other means of
  identifying, 168–169
Relationship between service price
  and value, 117–118
Relationship equity, 147
Relationships, building, 209
Rental/Access, 12
Rental and leasing companies, 244
Research methods for services,
  176–185, 177*t*
Reservation system, 221
Return on Quality (ROQ) model, 147
Rewards, 82–83
Roles, 31
ROQ model. *See* Return on Quality
  (ROQ) model

Sale promotions, 131
  services and, 137–139
Satisfaction link, 149
Scanning the environment, 194–200
Seasonal demand cycle, 214
Segmentation, market, 203
September 11, 2001 terrorist attacks,
  218
Service ambassadors, 164
Service blueprint, 59–61, 60*f*
Service capacity, 216–218

aspects of, 217
  chasing demand with, 216–218
  smoothing demand to fill, 219–222
Service costs, calculating, 118–120,
  119*f*
Service customers, 20
  behavior and, 95–97
Service delivery link, 149
Service design improvements,
  customer service as an input for,
  162–163
Service economy, 6, 6*f*
Service effectiveness, 54
Service efficiency, 55
Service employees
  behavior and, 78–86
  costuming of, 88–90
  empowering, 84–86
  ensuring excellence, 81–83
  importance of, 78–79
  maximizing productivity, 90–92
Service encounter, 20
Service experience
  comparing frameworks,
    27–30, 29*t*
  components of, 21–22
  framing, 22–28
Service exports
  inbound, 232
  outbound, 231–232
  teleservice export, 232
Service factory, 65
Service framework, 21
Service guarantee, 156
  extraordinary, 157
  how to design, 157–158
Service identifier, service setting as,
  66–67
Service identifier, service setting as,
  48–49
Service improvisation, need for, 87
Service organizations
  overview of marketing strategy in,
    192–194
  predictable fluctuations of demand
    and, 214
  primary controllable factors for,
    193
  reservation systems, use of, 221
Service performance, 49–50
  blueprinting, 59–61, 60*f*
  customizing, 54–57
  differentiating, 52–54
  internet and, 61

measurement of, 186–187, 186*f*
  scripting, 57–58, 58*f*
  supplementing the basic, 50–52
Service performance gap, 154
Service price
  relationship between value and,
    117–118
  why do they vary, 113–114
Service process, 21
Service quality, 148, 207–208
  gap model of, 153*f*
  how customers evaluate,
    151–156
  perceived, 148
  from provider's perspective, 148
Service quality cycle, 149*f*, 150
Service quality gap, 155
Service quality information system
  (SQIS), creating, 185–187
Service recovery, 165
  effects on customer loyalty, 164*f*
  hidden benefits of, 181
  need for, 165–169
  steps to, 169–171
  when is it needed, 167
Service robots, 39
Services
  advertising, 132–137
  business-to-business, 14
  career choices in, 243–244
  characteristics, 9–12
  complexity of, 60
  consumer, 8, 12
  convenience, 50
  culture and, 228–230
  definition of, 6–7
  divergence of, 60
  emotional side of, 61–62, 88
  global impact, measurement of,
    231
  global trade in, 230–233
  guidelines for advertising,
    133–135
  intangibility, 9–10
  intangible dominant, 8
  integrated marketing
    communications and, 126–127
  marketing communications and,
    128–129
  perishable, 10
  personal selling and, 139–140
  pricing considerations for,
    123–124
  process of service assembly, 129

Services (*continued*)
  produced and consumed
    simultaneously, 8
  promoting on the Internet, 141–142
  publicity and, 140–141
  researching success and failure,
    174–175
  research methods for, 176–185
  sales promotions and, 137–139
  shopping, 50
  specialty, 50
  strategic challenges for, 205–208
  strategic implications for, 204*t*
  supplementary, 9
  tangibilizing the, 128
  variable, 9
  why and when to guarantee, 156
  yield management in, 116
Servicescape. *See* Service setting
Services career marketplace, trends in,
    246
Service script, 57–58, 58*f*
Services customers, classifications
    based, 13–14
Services demand, 213
  nature of, 213–215, 217*t*
  problem, 213
Service segmentation, positioning
    and, 202–203
Service setting, 21, 48–49, 65
  appeal of, 69
  cyberspace as, 74–75
  designing the, 64–75
  duration of, 66
  experimenting, 74
  key considerations in designing,
    66–70
  as marketing tool, 70–74
  as operational tool, 67–68
  as orientation tool, 67–68
  as service identifier, 66–67
  as workers' home away from home,
    69–70
Services marketing
  approach, 204
  mix, 22–25
  physical goods marketing differ
    from, 8–9
  pyramid, 36, 36*f*
  triangle, 14–16, 16*f*
Services marketing strategy,
    200–202
  controlling, 202
  designing, 201

  implementing, 201–202
  planning, 200–201
Services operations approach, 205
Service standards gap, 154
Services technology, coping with
    negative impacts of, 42
Services theater, 26–28, 27*f*
  framework, 26–28
  raising the curtain on, 30–31
Service strategies for competitive
    advantage, 208
Service success, difficult to achieve,
    175–176
Service systems, multilingual,
    237–238
Service worker profile, 91, 91*f*
Service workers, 21
SERVPERF, 98
SERVQUAL, 98, 151, 152*t*
Servuction framework, 25–28, 26*f*
Setting, 25, 31, 207, 235, 235*t*
Shared costs, 119
Shared fixed costs, 118
Shared variable costs, 118
Share of mind, 202
Shopping services, 50
Simultaneity, 204*t*
Skills assessment, 247
"Smarter Planet" strategy, 191–192
Smoothing demand, 219–222
Social conditions, 193
Social environment, 199
Social hierarchy, 230
Social skills, 80–81
  See also Technical skills
Specialty services, 50
Standardization, of global services,
    234, 236
Standby fares, 114
Strategic challenges for services,
    205–208
  customers, 206
  demand, 207
  employees, 205–206
  leadership, 205
  performance, 207
  service quality, 207–208
  service setting, 207
Strategic function, customer service
    as, 161–163
Suggestive selling, 140
Summer Olympics, 239
Supplementary services, 9
Supply services, 244

  career choices in, 244
Survey methods, 180
Surveys, 177
  electronic survey, 182–183*f*
Symbolic atonement, 170

Tangibilizing the service, 128
Tangible dominant physical
    goods, 8
  vs. intangible dominant services,
    8, 8*f*
Tangible evidence, managing,
    71–72
Tangible objects, 136
Target employers, 248
Technical skills, 80–81
  See also Social skills
Technology
  in core service, 36
  devices, 39
  empowering employees through,
    39–40
  environment, 199–200
  harness, 209
  information, 35–37
  lock, 43
  as supplementary service support
    tool, 39–40
  using to manage customer
    interfaces, 42–44
Technology, global services and,
    238–239
Telecommunications industry, 232
Teleservice export, 232
Teleservice export strategy, 232
Telespace, 65
Three Cs of pricing, 117
Three Ps of services marketing mix,
    193
Three stage of communications
    interactivity, 37–38, 37*f*
Three stages of economic activity,
    37–38
Time, cultural orientation toward,
    229
Time sink, 44
Trace analysis, 178
Travel and hospitality services, 243
  career choices in, 243

Unarticulated opportunities, 193,
    194*f*
Uncertainty avoidance, 229
UNCTAD, 230

Unserved opportunities, 193–194,
　194*f*
Upside-down organization, 206
Urgent reinstatement, 170

Value, 117
　relationship between service price
　　and, 117–118
Value equity, 146
Variability, 11

Variable costs, 118
Verbal associations, 137
Vividness strategy, 136
Volume-oriented, 116

Waiting, principles of, 222*t*
Walk-up fares, 114
Web rage, 105
Web site, 74
Winter Olympics, 239

Word-of-mouth communication,
　133–134, 146
World Cup Soccer, 191
World War II, 230
World Wide Web, 38

Yield management in
　services, 116

Zone of tolerance, 155